THE SHO[illegible]
PROSE READER

W9-CRA-462

MVFOL

THE SHORT PROSE READER

EIGHTH EDITION

Gilbert H. Muller
The City University of New York
LaGuardia

Harvey S. Wiener
Adelphi University

The McGraw-Hill Companies, Inc.
New York St. Louis San Francisco Auckland Bogotá
Caracas Lisbon London Madrid Mexico City
Milan Montreal New Delhi San Juan Singapore
Sydney Tokyo Toronto

This book was set in Times Roman by The Clarinda Company.
The editors were Tim Julet, Laura Lynch, and Larry Goldberg;
the production supervisor was Annette Mayeski.
The cover was designed by Joan O'Conner;
cover illustration by Betsy Everitt.
R. R. Donnelley & Sons Company was printer and binder.

THE SHORT PROSE READER

Copyright © 1997, 1994, 1991, 1989, 1987, 1985, 1982, 1979 by The McGraw-Hill Companies, Inc. All rights reserved. Printed in the United States of America. Except as permitted under the United States Copyright Act of 1976, no part of this publication may be reproduced or distributed in any form or by any means, or stored in a data base or retrieval system, without the prior written permission of the publisher.

Acknowledgments appear on pages 467–471, and on this page by reference.

This book is printed on acid-free paper.

1 2 3 4 5 6 7 8 9 0 DOC DOC 9 0 9 8 7 6

ISBN 0-07-044016-6

Library of Congress Cataloging-in-Publication Data

The short prose reader / [compiled by] Gilbert H. Muller, Harvey S. Wiener.—8th ed.
p. cm.
Includes bibliographical references and index.
ISBN 0-07-044016-6
1. College readers. 2. English language—Rhetoric. I. Muller, Gilbert H., (date). II. Wiener, Harvey S.
PE1417.S446 1997
808′.0427—dc20 96-24813

ABOUT THE AUTHORS

Gilbert H. Muller, who received a Ph.D. in English and American literature from Stanford University, is currently professor of English and Special Assistant to the President at LaGuardia Community College of the City University of New York. He has also taught at Stanford, Vassar, and several universities overseas. Dr. Muller is the author of the award-winning study *Nightmares and Visions: Flannery O'Connor and the Catholic Grotesque, Chester Himes,* and other critical texts. His essays and reviews have appeared in *The New York Times, The New Republic, The Nation, The Sewanee Review, The Georgia Review,* and elsewhere. He is also a noted author and editor of textbooks in English and composition, including *The McGraw-Hill Reader* and, with John Williams, *The McGraw-Hill Introduction to Literature.* Among Dr. Muller's awards are National Endowment for the Humanities Fellowships, a Fulbright Fellowship, and a Mellon Fellowship.

Harvey S. Wiener is Vice Provost for Academic Affairs at Adelphi University. Previously University Dean for Academic Affairs, the City University of New York, he was founding president of the Council of Writing Program Administrators. Dr. Wiener is the author of many books on reading and writing for college students and their teachers, including *The Writing Room* (Oxford, 1981). He is coauthor of *The McGraw-Hill College Handbook,* a reference grammar and rhetoric text. Dr. Wiener has chaired the Teaching of Writing Division of the Modern Language Association (1987). He has taught writing at every level of education from elementary school to graduate school. A Phi Beta Kappa graduate of Brooklyn College, he holds a Ph.D. in Renaissance literature. Dr. Wiener has won grants from the National Endowment for the Humanities, the Fund for the Improvement of Post-secondary Education, and the Exxon Education Foundation.

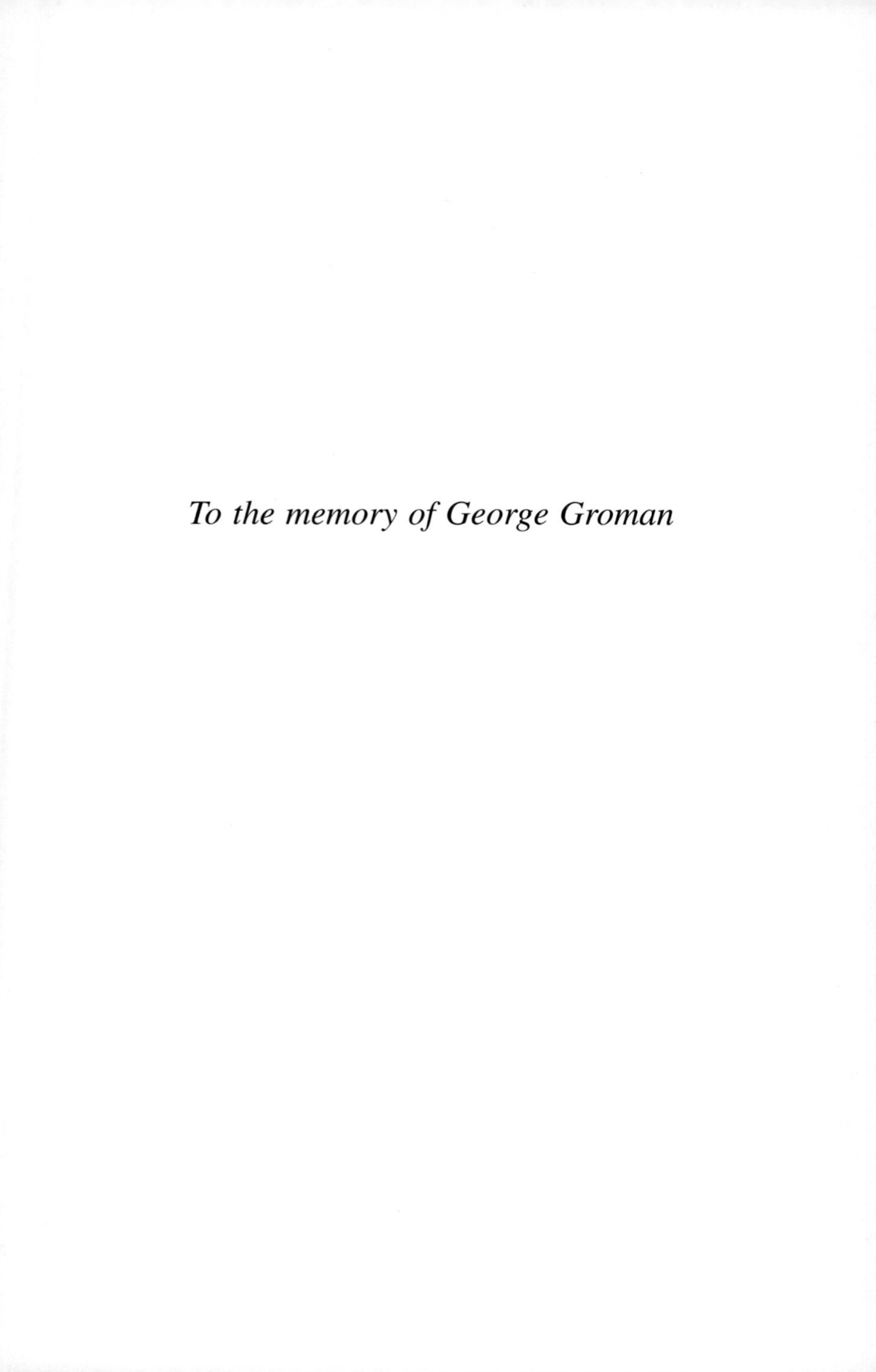

To the memory of George Groman

CONTENTS

CHAPTER 2

CHAPTER 3

CHAPTER 4

CHAPTER 5

CHAPTER 8

CHAPTER 11

CHAPTER 12

THEMATIC CONTENTS

Childhood and Family

Social Problems and Issues

Men and Women Today

The Minority Experience

City and Country

Sports, Travel, and Leisure

Psychology and Behavior

Science, Technology, and Medicine

Language and Thought

Humor and Satire

PREFACE

The eighth edition of *The Short Prose Reader* maintains the best features of the earlier editions: lively reading selections supported by helpful apparatus to integrate reading and writing in college composition and reading courses. Each of the twelve chapters presents an essential pattern of writing. The student progresses from basic description and narrative through the more rigorous forms of analysis and argument by means of diverse and lively prose models suited for discussion, analysis, and imitation.

Maintaining the organization of previous editions, this new version of *The Short Prose Reader* features many new reading selections by women, minority authors, and writers with immigrant backgrounds. Students will find engaging essays on issues of gender, race, and class by such women as Gloria Naylor, Alice Walker, Yolanda Cruz, Amy Tan, Anna Quindlen, and Maxine Hong Kingston. Ellen Tashie Frisina recalls the perils and inspirations of immigrant ancestry. Michele Ingrassia explores women's views of their own bodies. Also new are essays by Nicholas Weinstock and Andrew R. Rooney exploring the nature of manhood, as well as investigations of our changing culture, such as Janice Castro's view of a hybrid language called "Spanglish" and Carol B. Knight's piece on guns and neighbors. Kurt Vonnegut, Jr., the renowned futuristic writer, explains how to write with style.

We balance these new readings with some favorites from the earlier editions of *The Short Prose Reader.* Akira Kurosawa returns with his vivid recollections of early memory in "Babyhood" and Langston Hughes's "Salvation," Malcolm X's "Prison Studies," Jonathon Kozol's "Are The Homeless Crazy?" and Judy Brady's "I Want a Wife" continue to offer timely and controversial subjects for reading and writing.

The organization of *The Short Prose Reader* is one of its major strengths. Chapter 1, "On Writing," is followed by a chapter offering four unique views on the craft of reading by well-known writers. Each of the following nine chapters contains four short essays that illustrate clearly a specific pattern or technique—description, narration, illustration, comparison and contrast, definition, classification, process analysis, causal analysis, or argumentation. Students learn to build upon earlier techniques and patterns as they progress through the book. The last chapter, consisting of twelve essays, offers students the opportunity to read and discuss short prose pieces that reflect the various rhetorical strategies.

This is a readable text, and one that has ample representation by many different types of writers. Moreover, the essays, which range typically between 300 and 1,200 words, achieve their goals succinctly and clearly and are easy to read and to understand. The essays will alert students both to the types of college writing expected of them and to the length of an essay required frequently by teachers. The detailed questions that follow each essay can be used in reading as well as writing classes, since they ask the student to analyze both the content and the form of the prose selections.

Finally, the exercises we have included for each piece are comprehensive and integrated—designed to develop and reinforce the key skills required in college writing.

We have added a new activity before each essay. Called "Prereading: Thinking about the Essay in Advance," this activity helps students think and talk about the topic before learning what the writer says about it. Studies show that such prior discussion arouses interest and holds the reader's attention. Each selection includes two vocabulary exercises. "Words to Watch" alerts students to words they will read in context, and "Building Vocabulary" uses other effective methods (prefix/suffix, context clues, synonym/antonym, abstract/concrete) of teaching vocabulary.

To emphasize critical thinking as the main reason for questioning and discussion, we have grouped our conversational prods and probes under the heading "Thinking Critically about the Essay." A section called "Understanding the Writer's Ideas" reinforces reading comprehension. Sections entitled "Understanding the Writer's Techniques" and ""'Exploring the Writer's

Ideas" provide excellent bases for class discussion and independent reading and analysis.

A new section called "Prewriting" helps students record informal thoughts for writing in advance of producing an essay. A key exercise for each essay involves a dynamic approach to writing projects. Guided writing activities—a novel feature of *The Short Prose Reader*—tie the writing project to the reading selections. Instead of simply being told to write an essay on a certain topic, students through "Guided Writing" will be able to move from step to step in the process of composition. A new activity called "Thinking and Writing Collaboratively" encourages students to work together in groups on essays and ideas for writing. At the end of each chapter we provide a "Summing Up" section, a means for students to focus their attention on linking comparative issues in the chapter's essays and on more writing topics.

Students and teachers alike can use *The Short Prose Reader* flexibly and effectively. An alternate table of contents suggests thematic groupings of readings. The text is simple yet sophisticated, inviting students to engage in a multiplicity of cultural and traditional topics through essays and exercises that are easy to follow but never condescending. Weighing the needs and expectations of today's college freshmen, we have designed a rhetoric reader that can serve as the major text for the composition course.

We wish to thank our colleagues across the country for their support and are especially grateful to those who read the manuscript for this and previous editions: Judith Branzburg, Pasadena City College; Patricia P. Buckler, Purdue University North Central; Dan Gallagher, Laredo Junior College; Joyce Jenkins, Fort Valley State College; William L. Knox, Northern Michigan University; Valden Madsen, Brooklyn College; Inez Martinez, Kingsborough Community College; Mark Picus, Houston Community College; Richard Rios, San Joaquin Delta College; Billie Theriot, Southeastern Louisiana State University; Barbara P. Thompson, Columbus State Community College; and Barbara Truesdell, Purdue University.

Gilbert H. Muller
Harvey S. Wiener

THE SHORT PROSE READER

CHAPTER 1

On Writing

WHAT IS WRITING?

Writing helps us to record and communicate ideas. It is the definitive and essential part of daily human experience. Whether we write a shopping list or a great novel, we use a tool without which we would find ourselves isolated. Without writing we cut ourselves off from vital processes like the expression of political opinions, the description of medical emergencies, the examination of our feelings in diaries and letters.

Writing crosses many cultures. Whether we consider historic cave drawings or the transmission of fax messages during the Chinese rebellion in Tienamen Square, we find evidence of the human instinct to communicate ideas to other people.

In the past, writing brought about change. African-American slaves were frequently forbidden to learn to read or write, but some managed to find ways to gain literacy anyway. Their narratives of slave life helped fire the abolition movement. Women in the nineteenth century used writing to advance the cause of suffrage, winning votes with passionate speeches and articles in newspapers. Immigrants struggled to learn English in order to find a better life in the New World.

Writing celebrates human achievement. In religion, in love, in wartime and in peace, in astronomy and medicine and archaeology, in the arts and humanities, writing reminds us of our shared human identity. From the Song of Solomon in the Bible to the words of Martin Luther King, Jr.'s "I Have a Dream," from the Declaration of Independence to song lyrics by Bruce Springsteen or Elton John, writing helps us to come to terms with who we are and what we want.

What is writing, exactly? For most of us, writing is so familiar that the question seems silly. We all know what writing is. Yet when we try to write ourselves, we may find that asking and answering the question is vital.

Writing is both a product and a process. Writing is, of course, *what* we write: a letter, a law brief, a term paper, an inaugural address. Since it is a product, we must think of writing as having a public as well as a private purpose. While some writing, like shopping lists or a diary, may be meant only for our own eyes, most writing is intended for an audience. In learning what writing is we need to think about who the audience is, and what the purpose of the writing is.

Writing is also a process; it is *how* we write. In learning to write well, we examine the process of transferring ideas from head to hand. We realize that the actual, mechanical practice of writing out ideas helps us to think more carefully, to plan and arrange ideas, to analyze our vague thoughts into solid words on a page.

HOW DO WE WRITE?

The process of writing is not absolute; there is no one sure way to learn to write well. However, there are some common elements in this process that will help anyone getting started as a writer.

Warming Up: Prewriting

Like an athlete, the writer benefits from warm-up exercises. Usually called prewriting, these steps help a writer prepare gradually and thoughtfully for the event of writing a long essay. Writers stretch their intellectual muscles by thinking about a topic before they write about it. They talk to friends and colleagues. They visit a library and flip through reference books, newspapers, magazines, and books. Sometimes, they make notes and lists as a way of putting pen to paper for the first time. Some writers brainstorm: they use free association to jot down ideas as thoroughly as possible in an unedited form. Others use "timed writing": they write nonstop whatever comes to mind in a set time period—fifteen or twenty minutes, say. Freewriting like this loosens up ideas without the worry of correctness in language too early in the writing process. After these preliminary warm-ups, many writers try to group or classify ideas by making a rough outline or drawing boxes or making lists to try to bring some plan or order to their rough ideas.

Once the writer has a rough topic area outlined, he or she may return to the audience and purpose for the essay. Who will read the essay? How will the writer aim the essay sharply at the audience by selecting the best material from the rough notes? How will the writer choose the most appropriate language for the intended audience? What is the purpose of the essay? How can the writer help make writing the essay easier by carving out a clear intent? Often the purpose or intent becomes clearer as the writer continues to think and write. Choosing the audience and purpose carefully makes the writer's as well as the reader's task easier.

First Draft

Prewriting leads to the first draft. Drafts are usually meant for the writer's eyes only; they are messy with rethinking, rewriting, and revision. Drafts help the writer figure out what to write by giving him or her a place to think on paper before having to make a public presentation of the writing. Everyone develops his or her own style of draft writing, but many writers find that double-spacing, leaving wide margins, and writing on only one side of the paper are steps that make rewriting easier. If you can write on a word processor, you'll find you can easily revise and produce several drafts without discarding earlier versions of the essay.

In a first draft, a writer begins to shape paragraphs, to plan where to put each piece of the essay for maximum effect. Sometimes, a first draft doesn't have an introduction. The introduction can be written after the writer has finished the draft and has a better sense of what the essay is about. The audience will see only the final draft, after all, and will never know when the writer wrote the introduction.

Having finished the first draft, the writer tries to become the audience. How will the essay sound to someone else? Does it make sense? Are the ideas and expression clear? Is there a main point? Do all the ideas in the essay relate to this main point? Is there a coherent plan to the essay? Do ideas follow logically one from the next? Would someone unfamiliar with the topic be able to follow the ideas? Should more information be added? What should be left out?

In attempting to answer these questions, writers often try to find a friendly reader to look over the draft and give advice. Whatever else they may look for at this stage, they do not pay too much attention to spelling or grammar. A helpful reader will enable the writer to see the essay as the audience will see it, and suggest ways to reorganize and clarify ideas.

Additional Drafts

After getting responses from a reader, the writer begins the second draft. And the third. And maybe the fourth. No one can predict how many drafts are necessary for a final essay, but very few writers get by with fewer than two or three drafts. Revision usually involves working first on the clear expression of ideas and later on revision for spelling, grammatical correctness, and good sentence structure.

Final Draft

The final draft is intended for public, rather than private, reading. It must be the writer's best effort. Most editors and teachers require final drafts to be double-spaced, neatly written or typed with wide margins, and clearly identified with the writer's name, the date, and information to locate the writer (such as class code or home address).

This brief overview sketches in some of the important steps in the writing process. But you don't want to lose the idea that writing is a process both of inspiration and of craft. Many writers have tried to explain how the two connect in their own particular efforts to create. The novelist and short story writer Katherine Anne Porter, for example, tells how inspiration becomes communication in her writing: "Now and again thousands of memories converge, harmonize, and arrange themselves around a central idea in a coherent form, and I write. . . ." Jean Cocteau, the playwright, asserts the need to shape inspiration into language for a page of writing: "To write, to conquer ink and paper, accumulate letters and paragraphs, divide them with periods and commas, is a different matter from carrying around the dream of a play or a book." The point made by Porter and Cocteau is that writing emerges from both creativity and skill, instruction and technique, talent and effort. As we said, writing is a process *and* craft.

The four writers in this chapter represent a variety of approaches to both the inspiration and the craft of writing. Kurt Vonnegut, Jr., for instance, sees style as the defining essence of good writing, while William Saroyan combines personal reminiscence with theories of art. Amy Tan finds her writer's voice when she realizes that her mother is the ideal audience. Like William Zinsser pleading for the preciseness that comes only with simplicity, Tan advises us to aim for direct and simple language instead of academic jargon or pretentious style.

The four writers represented here also introduce expository techniques discussed in subsequent chapters. Careful examination of their sources of inspiration *and* their revelations about the nuts and bolts of how to get the writing done prepares the way for later chapters and writing assignments.

Finally, though films and floppy discs may seem to replace the printed page, the basic medium of communication is still words. Whether we scratch them onto stone tablets, draw them on parchment with turkey feathers, or charge them onto computer storage boards, we still use words. Without writing, we risk the loss of our political freedom and our personal history. With words, we pass ideas and values on from one generation to the next. The words of Henry Miller will always ring true: "Writing, like life itself, is a voyage of discovery."

How to Write with Style

Kurt Vonnegut, Jr.

Kurt Vonnegut, born in 1922, is one of America's most imaginative writers. He is best known for his biting political satire in such novels as *Slaughterhouse-Five* and *Breakfast of Champions.* He has also published nearly a hundred short stories. In this selection he offers young writers some secrets of his success.

PREREADING: THINKING ABOUT THE ESSAY IN ADVANCE

What are your thoughts about "writing with style"? What does the phrase mean? What qualities of writing do you admire? What qualities of writing do you not admire?

Words to Watch

piquant (par. 10) pleasantly disturbing
galvanized (par. 10) to coat
locutions (par. 11) speaking style
higgledy-piggledy (par. 15) in disorder or confusion
egalitarian (par. 20) equal rights for all citizens
aristocrat (par. 20) member of the nobility

1 Newspaper reporters and technical writers are trained to reveal almost nothing about themselves in their writings. This makes them freaks in the world of writers, since almost all of the other ink-stained wretches in that world reveal a lot about themselves to readers. We call these revelations, accidental and intentional, elements of literary style.

2 These revelations are fascinating to us as readers. They tell us what sort of person it is with whom we are spending time. Does the writer sound ignorant or informed, crazy or sane, stupid or bright, crooked or honest, humorless or playful—? And on and on.

When you yourself put words on paper, remember that the most damning revelation you can make about yourself is that you do not know what is interesting and what is not. Don't you yourself like or dislike writers mainly for what they choose to show you or make you think about? Did you ever admire an empty-headed writer for his or her mastery of the language? No. 3

So your own winning literary style must begin with interesting ideas in your head. Find a subject you care about and which you in your heart feel others should care about. It is this genuine caring, and not your games with language, which will be the most compelling and seductive element in your style. 4

I am not urging you to write a novel, by the way—although I would not be sorry if you wrote one, provided you genuinely cared about something. A petition to the mayor about a pothole in front of your house or a love letter to the girl next door will do. 5

Do not ramble, though. 6

As for your use of language: Remember that two great masters of our language, William Shakespeare and James Joyce, wrote sentences which were almost childlike when their subjects were most profound. "To be or not to be?" asks Shakespeare's Hamlet. The longest word is three letters long. Joyce, when he was frisky, could put together a sentence as intricate and glittering as a necklace for Cleopatra, but my favorite sentence in his short story "Eveline" is this one: "She was tired." At that point in the story, no other words could break the heart of a reader as those words do. 7

Simplicity of language is not only reputable, but perhaps even sacred. The Bible opens with a sentence well within the writing skills of a lively fourteen-year-old: "In the beginning God created the heavens and the earth." 8

It may be that you, too, are capable of making necklaces for Cleopatra, so to speak. But your eloquence should be the servant of the ideas in your head. Your rule might be this: If a sentence no matter how excellent, does not illuminate my subject in some new and useful way, scratch it out. Here is the same rule paraphrased to apply to storytelling, to fiction: Never include a sentence which does not either remark on character or advance the action. 9

The writing style which is most natural for you is bound to echo speech you heard when a child. English was the novelist 10

Joseph Conrad's third language, and much that seems piquant in his use of English was no doubt colored by his first language, which was Polish. And lucky indeed is the writer who has grown up in Ireland, for the English spoken there is so amusing and musical. I myself grew up in Indianapolis, Indiana, where common speech sounds like a band saw cutting galvanized tin, and employs a vocabulary as unornamental as a monkey wrench.

11 In some of the more remote hollows of Appalachia, children still grow up hearing songs and locutions of Elizabethan times. Yes, and many Americans grow up hearing a language other than English, or an English dialect a majority of Americans cannot understand.

12 All these varieties of speech are beautiful, just as the varieties of butterflies are beautiful. No matter what your first language, you should treasure it all your life. If it happens not to be standard English, and if it shows itself when you write standard English, the result is usually delightful, like a very pretty girl with one eye that is green and one that is blue.

13 If myself find that I trust my own writing most, and others seem to trust it most, too, when I sound most like a person from Indianapolis, which is what I am. What alternatives do I have? The one most vehemently recommended by teachers has no doubt been pressed on you, as well: that I write like cultivated Englishmen of a century or more ago.

14 I used to be exasperated by such teachers, but am no more. I understand now that all those antique essays and stories with which I was to compare my own work were not magnificent for their datedness or foreignness, but for saying precisely what their authors meant them to say. My teachers wished me to write accurately, always selecting the most effective words, and relating the words to one another unambiguously, rigidly, like parts of a machine. The teachers did not want to turn me into an Englishman after all. They hoped that I would become understandable—and therefore understood.

15 And there went my dream of doing with words what Pablo Picasso did with paint or what any number of jazz idols did with music. If I broke all the rules of punctuation, had words mean whatever I wanted them to mean, and strung them together higgledy-piggledy, I would simply not be understood. So you, too,

had better avoid Picasso-style or jazz-style writing, if you have something worth saying and wish to be understood.

If it were only teachers who insisted that modern writers stay close to literary styles of the past, we might reasonably ignore them. But readers insist on the very same thing. They want our pages to look very much like pages they have seen before. 16

Why? It is because they themselves have a tough job to do, and they need all the help they can get from us. They have to identify thousands of little marks on paper, and make sense of them immediately. They have to *read,* an art so difficult that most people do not really master it even after having studied it all through grade school and high school—for twelve long years. 17

So this discussion, like all discussions of literary styles, must finally acknowledge that our stylistic options as writers are neither numerous nor glamorous, since our readers are bound to be such imperfect artists. Our audience requires us to be sympathetic and patient teachers, ever willing to simplify and clarify—whereas we would rather soar high above the crowd, singing like nightingales. 18

That is the bad news. The good news is that we Americans are governed under a unique Constitution, which allows us to write whatever we please without fear of punishment. So the most meaningful aspect of our styles, which is what we choose to write about, is unlimited. 19

Also: We are members of an egalitarian society, so there is no reason for us to write, in case we are not classically educated aristocrats, as though we were classically educated aristocrats. 20

For a discussion of literary style in a narrower sense, in a more technical sense, I commend to your attention *The Elements of Style* by William Strunk, Jr., and E. B. White (Macmillan, 1979). It contains such rules as this: "A participial phrase at the beginning of a sentence must refer to the grammatical subject," and so on. E. B. White is, of course, one of the most admirable literary stylists this country has so far produced. 21

You should realize, too, that no one would care how well or badly Mr. White expressed himself, if he did not have perfectly enchanting things to say. 22

BUILDING VOCABULARY

Use *context clues* (see Glossary) to determine the meanings of the words below. Use a dictionary to check your definitions.

a. intentional (par. 1)
b. compelling (par. 4)
c. intricate (par. 7)
d. reputable (par. 8)
e. eloquence (par. 9)
f. illuminate (par. 9)
g. exasperated (par. 14)

THINKING CRITICALLY ABOUT THE ESSAY

Understanding the Writer's Ideas

1. What is the difference between newspaper reporters and technical writers and the "ink-stained wretches," as Vonnegut puts it?
2. According to the writer, what is the best way to begin a "winning literary style" (par. 4)?
3. Why does Vonnegut believe that simple writing is best, and how does he try to prove his point?
4. What is the writer's attitude toward standard language versus the language "you heard when a child" (par. 10)?
5. For Vonnegut, writers should avoid "jazz-style" writing. Why?
6. How does the writer come to the conclusion that reading is "an art so difficult that most people do not really master it" (par. 17)?
7. Why does Vonnegut say it is good news that writers in America are "governed under a unique Constitution" (par. 19)?
8. What is the benefit of being a writer in an "egalitarian society" as opposed to an "aristocratic" one, according to Vonnegut (par. 20)?

Understanding the Writer's Techniques

1. What is the thesis of this essay? Who is Vonnegut's audience here? How can you tell?

2. Why does Vonnegut begin his essay with references to newspaper reporters and technical writers if he does not mention them in the rest of text?
3. Why is the *transition* (see Glossary) at the beginning of paragraph 3 effective, given the title of this essay?
4. Vonnegut suggests that writers use sentences that are almost "childlike." How can you tell that he follows his own advice?
5. What purpose does using direct quotes from William Shakespeare and James Joyce serve?
6. What is the effect of Vonnegut's switching to the first person in paragraph 13, pointing to the Indianapolis speech in his own writing?
7. How does the question "Why?" (par. 17) serve as a clear shift in the idea development of the essay?
8. The word "Also" in paragraph 20 is followed by a colon to signal a transition. Check a grammar handbook. Is this the way transitions should be punctuated?
9. Why does Vonnegut recommend the book *The Elements of Style?* Hasn't he already instructed us in these matters himself?
10. Explain how and why Vonnegut's last paragraph returns the reader to the essay's main idea in paragraph 3.

Exploring the Writer's Ideas

1. Vonnegut believes that since newspaper reporters and technical writers reveal almost nothing about themselves they are less fascinating to us. Based on your experiences as a reader, do you agree? Why or why not?
2. If you care deeply about a subject, Vonnegut claims this will make your writing more interesting to others. Has this been true in your experiences as a writer? Explain.
3. Vonnegut makes the case (par. 12) that using nonstandard English can make a writer's work "beautiful." Do you agree with him? Why or why not?
4. Vonnegut says you should use the speech you heard as a child (par. 10) to achieve a successful writing style. Then he says that if he broke all the rules of language, he "would simply not be understood" (par. 15). Is Vonnegut contradicting himself? What if a person's childhood language is not understandable outside his or her community?

5. Vonnegut reminds us that we live in an "egalitarian" society. What implications does this have for the development of your writing style?
6. Given a choice, which writers would you rather read—those that reveal "nothing about themselves" or those whose "revelations are fascinating"? Explain your preferences.

IDEAS FOR WRITING

Prewriting

Make a list of the steps you take in the process of doing something you have excelled in (for example, gardening, cooking, playing sports, making friends, and so on).

Guided Writing

Write an essay called "How to __________ with Style." Fill in the blank with something you do well, such as skiing, painting a room, and so on. Instruct the reader on how and why he or she should also do this activity and what you mean by doing it with style.

1. Begin by defining the most important quality you think someone needs to be successful at this activity.
2. In the next two or three paragraphs, elaborate on how and why this quality will help ensure a person's success in this activity.
3. Describe another quality needed to be a success at this activity. Give two or three paragraphs of supporting detail to show how others have been successful at this activity because they too have had the quality you just described. Here you should make clear what doing the activity "with style" means.
4. Tell if there is any reason why this activity can or cannot be done by most people. Is a special quality needed? Is this something a child can do? Why or why not?
5. Give personal testimony of how and why being a success at this activity is simple or complicated for you. What personal traits have you relied on to be a success at this activity?

6. Warn readers about the most common mistakes made by those who do not succeed at this activity, and suggest how to avoid such mistakes.
7. End with why you think this activity might (or might not) be well suited for people living in a society where they have the constitutional right to live freely. (Consider recommending a book that might assist the reader with this activity.)

Thinking and Writing Collaboratively

Write a short letter using the words of love you would share with someone close to you. Then write out a dictionary definition of "love." Form groups of three students each and share your letters and definitions with the members of the group, asking them: Which words would most appeal to you? Why? Note the responses and write an essay on how to write a love letter.

More Writing Projects

1. In your journal, write a short entry in language that you heard as a child. Try to capture the sounds and traits that will amuse and delight readers.
2. Write two paragraphs that contrast your language use. In paragraph one, describe with examples the kind of language you use with your friends and family. In paragraph two, describe with examples the kind of language you use with your professors or strangers.
3. Write an essay on something you care strongly about, using the language you feel best reveals something personal about yourself, as Vonnegut suggests.

Why I Write

William Saroyan

William Saroyan (1908–1981) won the 1939 Pulitzer Prize for his play *Time of Your Life.* His novel *The Human Comedy* (1942) is both an ironic and an optimistic look at the human condition. In this essay, Saroyan writes of how tragedy, memory, and art have combined to bring meaning to his life.

PREREADING: THINKING ABOUT THE ESSAY IN ADVANCE

Why does a writer write? What various reasons can you think of for someone to want to spend his or her life as a writer?

Words to Watch

isolated (par. 2) set apart
vineyards (par. 4) fields for growing wine grapes
sorrow (par. 5) sadness
impelled (par. 6) driven to do something
impulse (par. 7) sudden inclination prompting action
gradual (par. 10) by degrees; little by little

1 It is a quarter of a century, almost, since my first book was published, but as I began to write when I was nine, I have been writing for forty years: that is to say, I have lived in a special way for forty years—the way that takes hold of a man who is determined to understand the meaning of his own life, and to be prepared to write about it.

2 But I think it goes even farther back than forty years. I think I began to live in my own special way when I became aware that I had memory. That happened before I was three. I also had a memory that went back to a time before I was *two,* but it was an isolated one. At that age I wasn't given to remembering

everything, or rather I hadn't yet noticed that it had come to pass that I remembered.

In the past were some of the best things I had, several of 3
them gone: my father, for instance, who had died before I was three.

My first memory, the one that went back to a time when I 4
was not yet two, was of my father getting up onto a wagon, sitting beside my mother, and making a sound that told the horse to go. My two sisters and my brother and I sat in the back of the wagon as it moved slowly down a dusty road between vineyards on a hot afternoon in the summertime. I remembered sensing sorrow and feeling *with*—with mine, my people—a father, a mother, two sisters, a brother, our horse, our wagon, our pots and pans and books. The rest is lost in the sleep that soon carried me away. The next thing I knew my father was gone, which I didn't understand.

I was fascinated by having memory, and troubled by the 5
sorrow of it. I refused to accept the theory that things end, including people, including my father. I refused to believe that my father was dead. (In the sense that every man *is* his father, I wasn't much mistaken.)

All the same, I felt impelled from the time I knew I had 6
memory to do something about the past, about endings, about human death.

My first impulse was simple. I wanted to cause the impos- 7
sible to happen, because if I was able to do that, I knew I would be able to cause *anything* to happen. Thus, death would not be death, if anybody wanted it not to be.

I found two large empty cans. One I filled with water. The 8
empty can I placed two feet from the full can. I asked myself to cause the water in the full can to pass into the empty can, by itself, because I wanted it to.

The experiment failed. I had begun with the maximum, I had 9
failed, and so I began to consider what might be the next best.

For a long time there didn't appear to be *any* next best at 10
all. It was a matter of all or nothing, or at any rate the equivalent of nothing: continuous *gradual* loss, and finally total loss, or death.

What could a man do about this? Wait? That didn't seem to 11
be enough.

12 Why should I be troubled by memory at all if all memory told me was that things change, fail, decline, end, and die? I didn't want good things to do that, and I didn't think they should. How could I seize a good thing when I saw it and halt its decline and death? As far as people were concerned, there just didn't seem to be *any* way.

13 And so I came to accept the theory that as far as I knew, as far as *anybody* knew, as far as there appeared to be any order to the action of things at all, the end of the order was invariably and inevitably decline, disappearance, and death.

14 And yet the world was full of people all the time. And the earth, the sea, and the sky were full of all manner of other living things: plants, animals, fish, birds.

15 Thus, something *did* stay, something *was* constant, or appeared to be. It was the *kind* that stayed. *One* of a kind couldn't stay, and couldn't apparently be made to. I myself was one of a kind, and everybody I knew and loved was one of a kind, and so what about us? What could I do about our impermanence?

16 How could I halt this action? How had other men halted it?

17 I learned that they never had halted it. They had only pretended to.

18 They had done this by means of art, or the putting of limits upon the limitless, and thereby holding something fast and making it seem constant, indestructible, unstoppable, unkillable, deathless.

19 A great painter painted his wife, his son, his daughter, and himself, and then one by one they all moved along and died. But the painting remained. A sculptor did the same thing with stone, a composer with musical sounds, and a writer with words.

20 Therefore, as the next best thing, art in one form or another would have to be the way of my life, but which form of art?

21 Before I was eight I didn't think it could possibly be writing, for the simple reason that I couldn't read, let alone write, and everybody else I knew could do both. At last, though, I got the hang of reading and writing, and I felt (if I didn't think), "This is for me."

22 It had taken me so long to learn to write that I considered being able to write the greatest thing that could happen to anybody.

23 If I wrote something, it *was* written, it was itself, and it might continue to be itself forever, or for what passes as forever.

Thus, I could halt the action of things, after all, and at the 24
same time be prepared to learn new things, to achieve new forms of halting, or art.

That is roughly how and why I became a writer. 25

In short, I began to write in order to get even on death. 26

I have continued to write for many reasons. 27

A long time ago I said I write because it is the only way I 28
am willing to survive.

Mainly, though, I write because I want to. 29

BUILDING VOCABULARY

1. The words below from the essay contain *prefixes* and *suffixes* (see Glossary) that can help you determine the meanings of the words themselves. For each word define the prefix or suffix in italics and then define the word.
   a. *de*cline (par. 12)
   b. *in*vari*ably* (par. 13)
   c. *in*evit*ably* (par. 13)
   d. *dis*appear*ance* (par. 13)
   e. *im*perman*ence* (par. 15)
   f. limit*less* (par. 18)
   g. *in*destruct*ible* (par. 18)
   h. *un*stopp*able* (par. 18)
   i. *un*kill*able* (par. 18)
   j. death*less* (par. 18)
2. Write the *antonyms* (opposite meanings) for any five of the words in the exercise above. Then, use each antonym in an original sentence.

THINKING CRITICALLY ABOUT THE ESSAY

Understanding the Writer's Ideas

1. How old is Saroyan at the time of writing this essay? How do you know?
2. In your own words, describe the "special way" in which the writer has lived. When did this "special way" of living begin for Saroyan?

3. From what age does Saroyan remember his first memory? Summarize the memory in your own words. What is the importance of memory for this writer?
4. In what sort of environment did Saroyan live as a child?
5. How was the writer affected by his father's death? Explain the meaning of the parenthetical sentence: "(In the sense that every man *is* his father, I wasn't much mistaken)" (par. 5).
6. In paragraph 7, Saroyan writes, "I wanted to cause the impossible to happen." Why? How did this desire relate to his father's death? How did he go about trying to cause the impossible? Did he succeed?
7. What *definition* does the writer offer of "art"? Why did he choose art as a way of life? What relationship did this choice have to memory? To his father's death? How did he come to choose writing among all the arts?
8. The title may be read in two ways: (a) why Saroyan *started* to write, and (b) why he *continues* to write. Which seems predominant? Why? Cite the author's own reasons for both (a) and (b).

Understanding the Writer's Techniques

1. Is there a *thesis statement* (see Glossary) in this essay? Explain. Describe Saroyan's purpose for writing this essay. Who is his intended audience? Explain.
2. *Tone* (see Glossary) refers to the writer's attitude or stance toward his or her subject and is expressed in the word choices, rhythms, and overall "voice" of a piece of writing. How would you describe the tone of this essay? Point to three places in the essay that are particularly expressive of the tone.
3. What was your emotional response to reading the first paragraph of this essay? Explain what it was about Saroyan's writing that made you feel that way.
4. What idea is repeated in paragraphs 1 and 2? Why? For what effect?
5. A *process analysis* (see Chapter 9) tells the reader step by step how to do something. Trace the steps whereby Saroyan dealt with his father's death.
6. Paragraph 18 (just one sentence long) contains at least five words built from prefix, root, suffix combinations. What is

the cumulative effect of all these words? Why do you think Saroyan has used them here?

7. Throughout this essay, Saroyan makes liberal use of italics. For what reason does he use them? Which uses are most effective? Are there any which you feel are unnecessary? Why?
8. This essay is composed of a series of relatively short paragraphs, some only one or two sentences long. What is the effect of this type of writing? Do you feel any choppiness or incompleteness? Why or why not?
9. Throughout the essay, the author asks a number of questions, especially in paragraphs 15 and 16. What is his purpose in asking these questions? To whom does he address them? What effect do they create?
10. Do you think the title is meant as a question or as a statement? Explain your answer in the context of the essay.

Exploring the Writer's Ideas

1. What is your earliest memory? How old were you? What lasting effect has the memory had on you?
2. Compare the environment in which Saroyan lived with your own childhood surroundings.
3. Was the writer's reaction to his father's death typical? How does it compare with the way you have managed the loss of a loved one?
4. Have any of the arts given you the sort of consolation or life direction that they provided for Saroyan? For example, at a time of stress or sadness, has anything in music, literature, or the visual arts ever changed your mood? Do you practice any art form, either professionally or as a hobby? If so, explain why you do it and how it makes you feel.

IDEAS FOR WRITING

Prewriting

Think about an activity that you now do regularly and brainstorm on paper about why you do it. What reasons motivate you? Are you conscious of the reasons? Are they important to you?

Guided Writing

Write an essay entitled "Why I ________." Fill in the blank with an activity that is very important to you, that you believe will remain so throughout your life, and that reflects your creative talents. For example, you might want to write about "Why I Paint," "Why I Play the Piano," or "Why I Cook"—or, if you prefer, "Why I Write."

1. Begin with a statement of why and for how long this activity has been important to you.
2. Dig deeply into your memory to relate an early memory that is tied to your choice to pursue this activity.
3. Tell about a particular incident or person that especially affected your choice of this activity.
4. Relate the process whereby you chose this "special way of living."
5. Throughout your essay use questions to help your reader understand your thought processes as you developed this way of life.
6. Write in a simple, direct way, using mainly very short paragraphs.
7. Try to maintain an emotionally charged, serious tone.
8. End your essay with a series of quick, direct statements, the last of which should relate positively to your future in this activity.

Thinking and Writing Collaboratively

Form groups of three students each and consider draft versions of the essays you wrote in Guided Writing. Did each student follow the guidelines numbered 1–8? Which guidelines should be addressed more fully in the essay? Why? What suggestions can you make for improving the focus, content, or style of the essay?

More Writing Projects

1. Start a journal for the term. In your first entry, record some of your earliest memories of various creative acts—for instance, writing out letters of the alphabet, toying with a musical

instrument, playing with crayons and paint, and so forth. Try to capture the original sensations.

2. Summarize the main ideas presented by Saroyan in a paragraph of no more than 100 words. Then write another paragraph condensing the summary to 50 words.
3. Write a brief essay on what Saroyan calls the "fascination" and "sorrow" of memory.

Mother Tongue

Amy Tan

Amy Tan is a novelist and essayist who was born in California only two and a half years after her parents emigrated to the United States. Her first novel, *The Joy Luck Club* (1989), was extremely popular, and was followed by *The Kitchen God's Wife* (1991) and *The Hundred Secret Senses* (1995). Speaking and writing in standard English is essential, Tan argues, but the diversity of cultures in America requires that we acknowledge the different "Englishes" spoken by immigrants. As you read her essay, think about your own experience in learning English, and how you respond to the other Englishes you may have heard spoken by your family or neighbors. Consider why Tan chooses to write in standard English.

PREREADING: THINKING ABOUT THE ESSAY IN ADVANCE

What varieties of English do you speak? In other words, do you speak different kinds of English in different situations and to different individuals or groups of people? Why or why not?

Words to Watch

intersection (par. 3) crossroad
wrought (par. 3) made; worked
belies (par. 7) misrepresents; disguises
wince (par. 8) cringe; shrink
empirical (par. 9) relying on observation
guise (par. 10) outward appearance
benign (par. 14) not harmful
insular (par. 15) like an island; isolated

1 I am not a scholar of English or literature. I cannot give you much more than personal opinions on the English language and its variations in this country or others.

I am a writer. And by that definition, I am someone who has always loved language. I am fascinated by language in daily life. I spend a great deal of my time thinking about the power of language—the way it can evoke an emotion, a visual image, a complex idea, or a simple truth. Language is the tool of my trade. And I use them all—all the Englishes I grew up with. 2

Recently, I was made keenly aware of the different Englishes I do use. I was giving a talk to a large group of people, the same talk I had already given to half a dozen other groups. The nature of the talk was about my writing, my life, and my book, *The Joy Luck Club.* The talk was going along well enough, until I remembered one major difference that made the whole talk sound wrong. My mother was in the room. And it was perhaps the first time she had heard me give a lengthy speech, using the kind of English I have never used with her. I was saying things like, "The intersection of memory upon imagination" and "There is an aspect of my fiction that relates to thus-and-thus"—a speech filled with carefully wrought grammatical phrases, burdened, it suddenly seemed to me, with nominalized forms, past perfect tenses, conditional phrases, all the forms of standard English that I had learned in school and through books, the forms of English I did not use at home with my mother. 3

Just last week, I was walking down the street with my mother, and I again found myself conscious of the English I was using, the English I do use with her. We were talking about the price of new and used furniture and I heard myself saying this: "Not waste money that way." My husband was with us as well, and he didn't notice any switch in my English. And then I realized why. It's because over the twenty years we've been together I've often used that same kind of English with him, and sometimes he even uses it with me. It has become our language of intimacy, a different sort of English that relates to family talk, the language I grew up with. 4

So you'll have some idea of what this family talk I heard sounds like, I'll quote what my mother said during a recent conversation which I videotaped and then transcribed. During this conversation, my mother was talking about a political gangster in Shanghai who had the same last name as her family's, Du, and how the gangster in his early years wanted to be adopted by her family, which was rich by comparison. Later, the gangster 5 became more powerful, far richer than my mother's family, and one day showed up at my mother's wedding to pay his respects. Here's what she said in part:

6 "Du Yusong having business like fruit stand. Like off the street kind. He is Du like Du Zong—but not Tsung-ming Island people. The local people call putong, the river east side, he belong to that side local people. That man want to ask Du Zong father take him in like become own family. Du Zong father wasn't look down on him, but didn't take seriously, until that man big like become a mafia. Now important person, very hard to inviting him. Chinese way, came only to show respect, don't stay for dinner. Respect for making big celebration, he shows up. Mean gives lots of respect. Chinese custom. Chinese social life that way. If too important won't have to stay too long. He come to my wedding. I didn't see. I heard it. I gone to boy's side, they have YMCA dinner. Chinese age I was nineteen."

7 You should know that my mother's expressive command of English belies how much she actually understands. She reads the *Forbes* report, listens to *Wall Street Week,* converses daily with her stockbroker, reads all of Shirley MacLaine's books with ease—all kinds of things I can't begin to understand. Yet some of my friends tell me they understand 50 percent of what my mother says. Some say they understand 80 to 90 percent. Some say they understand none of it, as if she were speaking pure Chinese. But to me, my mother's English is perfectly clear, perfectly natural. It's my mother tongue. Her language, as I hear it, is vivid, direct, full of observation and imagery. That was the language that helped shape the way I saw things, expressed things, made sense of the world.

8 Lately, I've been giving more thought to the kind of English my mother speaks. Like others, I have described it to people as "broken" or "fractured" English. But I wince when I say that. It has always bothered me that I can think of no way to describe it other than "broken," as if it were damaged and needed to be fixed, as if it lacked a certain wholeness and soundness. I've heard other terms used, "limited English," for example. But they seem just as bad, as if everything is limited, including people's perceptions of the limited English speaker.

9 I know this for a fact, because when I was growing up, my mother's "limited" English limited *my* perception of her. I was

ashamed of her English. I believed that her English reflected the quality of what she had to say. That is, because she expressed them imperfectly her thoughts were imperfect. And I had plenty of empirical evidence to support me: the fact that people in department stores, at banks, and at restaurants did not take her seriously, did not give her good service, pretended not to understand here, or even acted as if they did not hear her.

10 My mother has long realized the limitations of her English as well. When I was fifteen, she used to have me call people on the phone to pretend I was she. In this guise, I was forced to ask for information or even to complain and yell at people who had been rude to her. One time it was a call to her stockbroker in New York. She had cashed out her small portfolio and it just so happened we were going to go to New York the next week, our very first trip outside California. I had to get on the phone and say in an adolescent voice that was not very convincing, "This is Mrs. Tan."

11 And my mother was standing in the back whispering loudly, "Why he don't send me check, already two weeks late. So mad he lie to me, losing me money."

12 And then I said in perfect English, "Yes, I'm getting rather concerned. You had agreed to send the check two weeks ago, but it hasn't arrived."

13 Then she began to talk more loudly. "What he want, I come to New York tell him front of his boss, you cheating me?" And I was trying to calm her down, make her be quiet, while telling the stockbroker, "I can't tolerate any more excuses. If I don't receive the check immediately, I am going to have to speak to your manager when I'm in New York next week." And sure enough, the following week there we were in front of this astonished stockbroker, and I was sitting there red-faced and quiet, and my mother, the real Mrs. Tan, was shouting at his boss in her impeccable broken English.

14 We used a similar routine just five days ago, for a situation that was far less humorous. My mother had gone to the hospital for an appointment, to find out about a benign brain tumor a CAT scan had revealed a month ago. She said she had spoken very good English, her best English, no mistakes. Still, she said, the hospital did not apologize when they said they had lost the CAT scan and she had come for nothing. She said they did not seem to

have any sympathy when she told them she was anxious to know the exact diagnosis, since her husband and son had both died of brain tumors. She said they would not give her any more information until the next time and she would have to make another appointment for that. So she said she would not leave until the doctor called her daughter. She wouldn't budge. And when the doctor finally called her daughter, me, who spoke in perfect English—lo and behold—we had assurances the CAT scan would be found, promises that a conference call on Monday would be held, and apologies for any suffering my mother had gone through for a most regrettable mistake.

15 I think my mother's English almost had an effect on limiting my possibilities in life as well. Sociologists and linguists probably will tell you that a person's developing language skills are more influenced by peers. But I do think that the language spoken in the family, especially in immigrant families which are more insular, plays a large role in shaping the language of the child. And I believe that it affected my results on achievement tests, IQ tests, and the SAT. While my English skills were never judged as poor, compared to math, English could not be considered my strong suit. In grade school I did moderately well, getting perhaps B's, sometimes B-pluses, in English and scoring perhaps in the sixtieth or seventieth percentile on achievement tests. But those scores were not good enough to override the opinion that my true abilities lay in math and science, because in those areas I achieved A's and scored in the ninetieth percentile or higher.

16 This was understandable. Math is precise; there is only one correct answer. Whereas, for me at least, the answers on English tests were always a judgment call, a matter of opinion and personal experience. Those tests were constructed around items like fill-in-the-blank sentence completion, such as, "Even though Tom was __________, Mary thought he was __________." And the correct answer always seemed to be the most bland combinations of thoughts, for example, "Even though Tom was shy, Mary thought he was charming," with the grammatical structure "even though" limiting the correct answer to some sort of semantic opposites, so you wouldn't get answers like, "Even though Tom was foolish, Mary thought he was ridiculous." Well, according to my mother, there were very few limitations as to what Tom could

have been and what Mary might have thought of him. So I never did well on tests like that.

The same was true with word analogies, pairs of words in which you were supposed to find some sort of logical, semantic relationship—for example, "*Sunset* is to *nightfall* as __________ is to __________." And here you would be presented with a list of four possible pairs, one of which showed the same kind of relationship: *red* is to *stoplight, bus* is to *arrival, chills* is to *fever, yawn* is to *boring.* Well, I could never think that way. I knew what the tests were asking, but I could not block out of my mind the images already created by the first pair, "*sunset* is to *nightfall*"—and I would see a burst of colors against a darkening sky, the moon rising, the lowering of a curtain of stars. And all the other pairs of words—red, bus, stoplight, boring—just threw up a mass of confusing images, making it impossible for me to sort out something as logical as saying: "A sunset precedes nightfall" is the same as "a chill precedes a fever." The only way I would have gotten that answer right would have been to imagine an associative situation, for example, my being disobedient and staying out past sunset, catching a chill at night, which turns into feverish pneumonia as punishment, which indeed did happen to me. 17

I have been thinking about all this lately, about my mother's English, about achievement tests. Because lately I've been asked, as a writer, why there are not more Asian Americans represented in American literature. Why are there few Asian Americans enrolled in creative writing programs? Why do so many Chinese students go into engineering? Well, these are broad sociological questions I can't begin to answer. But I have noticed in surveys—in fact, just last week—that Asian students, as a whole, always do significantly better on math achievement tests than in English. And this makes me think that there are other Asian-American students whose English spoken in the home might also be described as "broken" or "limited." And perhaps they also have teachers who are steering them away from writing and into math and science, which is what happened to me. 18

Fortunately, I happen to be rebellious in nature and enjoy the challenge of disproving assumptions made about me. I became an English major my first year in college, after being 19 enrolled as pre-med. I started writing nonfiction as a freelancer the week after I was told by my former boss that writing was my worst skill and I should hone my talents toward account management.

20 But it wasn't until 1985 that I finally began to write fiction. And at first I wrote using what I thought to be wittily crafted sentences, sentences that would finally prove I had mastery over the English language. Here's an example from the first draft of a story that later made its way into *The Joy Luck Club,* but without this line: "That was my mental quandary in its nascent state." A terrible line, which I can barely pronounce.

21 Fortunately, for reasons I won't get into today, I later decided I should envision a reader for the stories I would write. And the reader I decided upon was my mother, because these were stories about mothers. So with this reader in mind—and in fact she did read my early drafts—I began to write stories using all the Englishes I grew up with: the English I spoke to my mother, which for lack of a better term might be described as "simple"; the English she used with me, which for lack of a better term might be described as "broken"; my translation of her Chinese, which could certainly be described as "watered down"; and what I imagined to be her translation of her Chinese if she could speak in perfect English, her internal language, and for that I sought to preserve the essence, but neither an English nor a Chinese structure. I wanted to capture what language ability tests can never reveal: her intent, her passion, her imagery, the rhythms of her speech and the nature of her thoughts.

22 Apart from what any critic had to say about my writing, I knew I had succeeded where it counted when my mother finished reading my book and gave me her verdict: "So easy to read."

BUILDING VOCABULARY

Tan uses technical words to distinguish standard English from the English her mother speaks. Investigate the meanings of the following terms, and find examples to illustrate them for your classmates.

a. scholar (par. 1)
b. nominalized forms (par. 3)
c. transcribed (par. 5)
d. imagery (par. 7)
e. linguists (par. 15)
f. semantic opposites (par. 16)
g. word analogies (par. 17)
h. freelancer (par. 19)
i. quandary (par. 20)
j. nascent (par. 20)

THINKING CRITICALLY ABOUT THE ESSAY

Understanding the Writer's Ideas

1. Why does Tan start her essay by identifying who she is *not?* What does she see as the difference between a scholar and a writer?
2. What does Tan mean when she says, "Language is the tool of my trade"? What are the four ways she says language can work?
3. Tan speaks of "all the Englishes I grew up with" in paragraph 2, and later of the "different Englishes" she uses. Why does her mother's presence in the lecture room help her recall these Englishes? Why does she give us examples of what was "wrong" with her talk in paragraph 3?
4. In paragraph 4, Tan recognizes that she herself shifts from one English to another. Which English is "our language of intimacy"? Why?
5. Tan describes how she recorded her mother's words. Why does she give us her technique in paragraph 5 before presenting her mother's exact words in paragraph 6?
6. What do we know about Tan's mother when we learn she reads the *Forbes* report and various books? Why is it important for Tan to understand the way her mother sees the world? What connection does Tan make between the way we use language and the way we see the world?

7. In paragraph 8, Tan tries to find a suitable label for her mother's language. Why is she unwilling to use a description like "broken" or "limited" English? What does her mother's English sound like to you?
8. In what ways did outsiders (like bankers and waiters) make judgments on Tan's mother because of her language? Were the judgments deliberate or unconscious on their part?
9. How does Tan use humor as she contrasts the two Englishes in the telephone conversations she records? How does the tone change when Tan shifts to the hospital scene? Why do the authorities provide different service and different information when the daughter speaks than they do when the mother speaks?
10. How does Tan connect her math test scores with her mother's language? Why does she think she never did well on language tests? Why does she think the tests do not measure a student's language use very well? Why does Tan ultimately become an English major (par. 19)?
11. In paragraph 20, why does Tan show us the sentence: "That was my mental quandary in its nascent state"? How does it compare with the other sentences in her essay? What is wrong with this "terrible" sentence? What does it mean?
12. In her two final paragraphs, Tan returns to her mother. Why does selecting her mother as her reader help Tan learn to become a better writer? What are the elements of good writing her mother recognizes, even if she herself cannot write standard English?

Understanding the Writer's Techniques

1. What is the thesis statement in Tan's essay? Where does it appear?
2. Throughout her essay, Tan uses *dialogue,* the written reproduction of speech or conversation. Why does she do this? What is the effect of dialogue? Which sentences of dialogue do you find especially effective, and why?
3. In paragraph 3, Tan writes fairly long sentences until she writes, "My mother was in the room." Why is this sentence shorter? What is the effect of the short sentence on the reader?

4. *Narration* (see Chapter 4) is the telling of a story or series of events. *Anecdotes* are very short narrations, usually of an amusing or autobiographical nature. Point out uses of narration and anecdote in Tan's essay.
5. How does identifying her mother as her intended audience help Tan make her own language more effective? Does Tan suggest that all writing should be "simple"? Is her writing always "simple"? Why does her mother find it "easy" to read?
6. Why does Tan put quotation marks around "broken" and "limited"? What other words can describe this different English?

Exploring the Writer's Ideas

1. Why is an awareness of different kinds of English necessary for a writer? Why are writers so interested in "different Englishes"? Should all Americans speak and write the same English?
2. What is the role of parents in setting language standards for their children? How did your parents or other relatives influence your language use?
3. Reread Tan's essay, and look more carefully at her *point of view* (see Glossary) about other Englishes. How do we know what her point of view is? Does she state it directly or indirectly? Where?
4. Listen to someone who speaks a "different" English. Try to record a full paragraph of the speech, as Tan does in paragraph 6. Use a tape recorder and (or) a video camera so that you can replay the speech several times. Explain what the difficulties were in capturing the sound of the speech exactly. Write a "translation" of the paragraph into standard English.
5. Tan explores the special relation between mothers and daughters. How would you describe the author's relation with her mother?

IDEAS FOR WRITING

Prewriting

Free-associate on a sheet of paper about the language you use in daily communication, its delights, difficulties, problems, confusions, humor—in short, anything that comes to mind about the language you use in your daily life.

Guided Writing

Write a narrative essay using first-person point of view in which you contrast your language with the language of someone who speaks differently from you.

1. Begin by making some notes on your own language and by deciding whom you will choose as your other subject. It should be someone you can spend time with so that you can record his or her speech.
2. Following Tan's model, create a narrative to frame your subject's language. Tell who you are and why you speak the way you do. Introduce the other speaker, and tell why his or her speech is different.
3. Use dialogue to provide examples of both Englishes.
4. Analyze how listeners other than yourself respond to both types of speech. What are the social implications of speech differences?
5. Show how listening to the other speaker and to yourself has helped you shape your own language and write your essay. What can you learn about good writing from this project?
6. Be sure the essay has a clear thesis in the introduction. Add a strong conclusion that returns to the idea of the thesis.

Thinking and Writing Collaboratively

Exchange a draft version of your Guided Writing essay with another writer in the class. As you read each other's work, think about the suggestions you might make to help the writer produce the next draft. Is the thesis clear? Is the introduction focused? Is the conclusion linked to the thesis idea? Is the dialogue realistic?

More Writing Projects

1. In your journal, record examples of new words you have heard recently. Divide the list into columns according to whether the words are standard English or a different English.

How many different Englishes can you find in your community and in college?

2. Reread question 1 in Exploring the Writer's Ideas, and write a one-paragraph response to it.
3. Tan's experience as a daughter of recent immigrants has clearly shaped her life in fundamental ways. She writes about the "shame" she once felt for her mother's speech. Write about a personal experience in which you were once embarrassed by someone close to you who was "different." Tell how you would feel about the same encounter if it happened today.

Simplicity

William Zinsser

In this chapter from *On Writing Well,* William Zinsser begins with a fairly pessimistic analysis of the clutter that pervades and degrades American writing, and he offers many examples to prove his point. Zinsser deals with almost all major aspects of the writing process—thinking, composing, awareness of the reader, self-discipline, rewriting, and editing—and concludes that simplicity is the key to them all.

PREREADING: THINKING ABOUT THE ESSAY IN ADVANCE

Do you find writing difficult or easy? Why? What is there about the act of writing that annoys, frustrates, or satisfies you?

Words to Watch

decipher (par. 2) to make out the meaning of something obscure
adulterants (par. 3) added substances which make something impure or inferior
mollify (par. 4) to appease; to soothe
spell (par. 4) a short period of time
assailed (par. 8) attacked with words or physical violence
spruce (par. 8) neat or smart in appearance
tenacious (par. 10) stubborn; persistent
rune (par. 10) character in an ancient alphabet
bearded (par. 12) approached or confronted boldly

1 Clutter is the disease of American writing. We are a society strangling in unnecessary words, circular constructions, pompous frills and meaningless jargon.

2 Who can understand the viscous language of everyday American commerce: the memo, the corporation report, the business letter, the notice from the bank explaining its latest "simpli-

fied" statement? What member of an insurance or medical plan can decipher the brochure explaining his costs and benefits? What father or mother can put together a child's toy from the instructions on the box? Our national tendency is to inflate and thereby sound important. The airline pilot who announces that he is presently anticipating experiencing considerable precipitation wouldn't think of saying it may rain. The sentence is too simple—there must be something wrong with it.

But the secret of good writing is to strip every sentence to 3
its cleanest components. Every word that serves no function, every long word that could be a short word, every adverb that carries the same meaning that's already in the verb, every passive construction that leaves the reader unsure of who is doing what—these are the thousand and one adulterants that weaken the strength of a sentence. And they usually occur in proportion to education and rank.

During the 1960s the president of my university wrote a let- 4
ter to mollify the alumni after a spell of campus unrest. "You are probably aware," he began, "that we have been experiencing very considerable potentially explosive expressions of dissatisfaction on issues only partially related." He meant the students had been hassling them about different things. I was far more upset by the president's English than by the students' potentially explosive expressions of dissatisfaction. I would have preferred the presidential approach taken by Franklin D. Roosevelt when he tried to convert into English his own government's memos, such as this blackout order of 1942:

> Such preparations shall be made as will completely obscure all Federal buildings and non-Federal buildings occupied by the Federal government during an air raid for any period of time from visibility by reason of internal or external illumination.

"Tell them," Roosevelt said, "that in buildings where they 5
have to keep the work going to put something across the windows."

Simplify, simplify. Thoreau said it, as we are so often 6
reminded, and no American writer more consistently practiced what he preached. Open *Walden* to any page and you will find a man saying in a plain and orderly way what is on his mind:

> I went to the woods because I wished to live deliberately, to front only the essential facts of life, and see if I could not learn what it had to teach, and not, when I came to die, discover that I had not lived.

7 How can the rest of us achieve such enviable freedom from clutter? The answer is to clear our heads of clutter. Clear thinking becomes clear writing; one can't exist without the other. It's impossible for a muddy thinker to write good English. You may get away with it for a paragraph or two, but soon the reader will be lost, and there's no sin so grave, for the reader will not easily be lured back.

8 Who is this elusive creature, the reader? The reader is someone with an attention span of about 30 seconds—a person assailed by other forces competing for attention. At one time these forces weren't so numerous: newspapers, radio, spouse, home, children. Today they also include a "home entertainment center" (TV, VCR, tapes, CDs), pets, a fitness program, a yard and all the gadgets that have been bought to keep it spruce, and that most potent of competitors, sleep. The person snoozing in a chair with a magazine or a book is a person who was being given too much unnecessary trouble by the writer.

9 It won't do to say that the reader is too dumb or too lazy to keep pace with the train of thought. If the reader is lost, it's usually because the writer hasn't been careful enough. The carelessness can take any number of forms. Perhaps a sentence is so excessively cluttered that the reader, hacking through the verbiage, simply doesn't know what it means. Perhaps a sentence has been so shoddily constructed that the reader could read it in several ways. Perhaps the writer has switched pronouns in mid-sentence, or has switched tenses, so the reader loses track of who is talking or when the action took place. Perhaps Sentence B is not a logical sequel to Sentence A—the writer, in whose head the connection is clear, hasn't bothered to provide the missing link. Perhaps the writer has used an important word incorrectly by not taking the trouble to look it up. The writer may think "sanguine" and "sanguinary" mean the same thing, but the difference is a bloody big one. The reader can only infer (speaking of big differences) what the writer is trying to imply.

10 Faced with such obstacles, readers are at first tenacious. They blame themselves—they obviously missed something, and

they go back over the mystifying sentence, or over the whole paragraph, piecing it out like an ancient rune, making guesses and moving on. But they won't do this for long. The writer is making them work too hard, and they will look for one who is better at the craft.

Writers must therefore constantly ask: What am I trying to say? Surprisingly often they don't know. Then they must look at what they have written and ask: Have I said it? Is it clear to someone encountering the subject for the first time? If it's not, some fuzz has worked its way into the machinery. The clear writer is someone clearheaded enough to see this stuff for what it is: fuzz. 11

I don't mean that some people are born clearheaded and are therefore natural writers, whereas others are naturally fuzzy and will never write well. Thinking clearly is a conscious act that writers must force upon themselves, as if they were working on any other project that requires logic: adding up a laundry list or doing an algebra problem. Good writing doesn't come naturally, though most people obviously think it does. Professional writers are constantly being bearded by strangers who say they'd like to "try a little writing sometime"—meaning when they retire from their real profession, which is difficult, like insurance or real estate. Or they say, "I could write a book about that." I doubt it. 12

Writing is hard work. A clear sentence is no accident. Very few sentences come out right the first time, or even the third time. Remember this in moments of despair. If you find that writing is hard, it's because it *is* hard. It's one of the hardest things people do. 13

[Below are] two pages of the final manuscript of this chapter from the First Edition of *On Writing Well.* Although they look like a first draft, they had already been rewritten and retyped—like almost every other page—four or five times. With each rewrite I try to make what I have written tighter, stronger and more precise, eliminating every element that is not doing useful work. Then I go over it once more, reading it aloud, and am always amazed at how much clutter can still be cut. (In a later edition of this book I eliminated the sexist pronoun "he" to denote "the writer" and "the reader.")

is too dumb or too lazy to keep pace with the ~~writer's~~ train of thought. My sympathies are ~~entirely~~ with him. ~~He's not so dumb.~~ If the reader is lost, it is generally because the writer ~~of the article~~ has not been careful enough to keep him on the ~~proper~~ path.

This carelessness can take any number of ~~different~~ forms. Perhaps a sentence is so excessively ~~long and~~ cluttered that the reader, hacking his way through ~~all~~ the verbiage, simply doesn't know what it ~~the writer~~ means. Perhaps a sentence has been so shoddily constructed that the reader could read it in any of several ~~two or three different~~ ways. ~~He thinks he knows what the writer is trying to say, but he's not sure.~~ Perhaps the writer has switched pronouns in mid-sentence, or ~~perhaps he~~ has switched tenses, so the reader loses track of who is talking ~~to whom,~~ or ~~exactly~~ when the action took place. Perhaps Sentence B is not a logical sequel to Sentence A -- the writer, in whose head the connection is ~~perfectly~~ clear, has not bothered to provide ~~given enough thought to providing~~ the missing link. Perhaps the writer has used an important word incorrectly by not taking the trouble to look it up. ~~and make sure.~~ He may think that "sanguine" and "sanguinary" mean the same thing, but ~~I can assure you that~~ the difference is a bloody big one. ~~to the reader.~~ The reader ~~He~~ can only ~~try to~~ infer ~~what~~ (speaking of big differences) what the writer is trying to imply.

Faced with these ~~such a variety of~~ obstacles, the reader is at first a remarkably tenacious bird. He ~~tends to~~ blames himself. He obviously missed something, ~~he thinks,~~ and he goes back over the mystifying sentence, or over the whole paragraph, piecing it out like an ancient rune, making guesses and moving on. But he won't do this for long. ~~He will soon run out of patience.~~ The writer is making him work too hard, ~~— harder than he should have to work —~~ and the reader will look for ~~a writer~~ one who is better at his craft.

The writer must therefore constantly ask himself: What am I trying to say? ~~in this sentence?~~ Surprisingly often, he doesn't know. ~~And~~ Then he must look at what he has ~~just~~ written and ask: Have I said it? Is it clear to someone ~~who is coming upon~~ encountering the subject for the first time? If it's not, ~~clear.~~ it is because some fuzz has worked its way into the machinery. The clear writer is a person ~~who is~~ clear-headed enough to see this stuff for what it is: fuzz.

I don't mean ~~to suggest~~ that some people are born clear-headed and are therefore natural writers, whereas ~~other people~~ others are naturally fuzzy and will ~~therefore~~ never write well. Thinking clearly is ~~an entirely~~ a conscious act that the writer must ~~keep forcing~~ force upon himself, just as if he were ~~starting out~~ embarking on any other ~~kind of~~ project that ~~calls for~~ requires logic: adding up a laundry list or doing an algebra problem. ~~or playing chess.~~ Good writing doeesn't ~~just~~ come naturally, though most people obviously think ~~it's as easy as walking.~~ it does. The professional

BUILDING VOCABULARY

1. Zinsser uses a number of words and expressions drawn from areas other than writing; he uses them to make interesting combinations or comparisons in such expressions as *elusive creature* (par. 8) and *hacking through the verbiage* (par. 9). Find other such expressions in this essay. Write simple explanations for the two above and the others that you find.
2. List words or phrases in this essay that pertain to writing—the process, the results, the faults, the successes. Explain any with which you were unfamiliar.

THINKING CRITICALLY ABOUT THE ESSAY

Understanding the Writer's Ideas

1. State simply Zinsser's meaning in the opening paragraph. What faults of "bad writing" does he mention in this paragraph?
2. To what is Zinsser objecting in paragraph 2?
3. What, according to the author, is the "secret of good writing" (par. 3)? Explain this "secret" in a few simple words of your own. What does Zinsser say detracts from good writing? Why does Zinsser write that these writing faults "usually occur, in proportion to education and rank"?
4. What was the "message" in the letter from the university president to the alumni (par. 4)? Why does the writer object to it? Was it more objectionable in form or in content?
5. Who was Thoreau? What is *Walden?* Why are references to the two especially appropriate to Zinsser's essay?
6. What, according to Zinsser, is the relation between clear thinking and good writing? Can you have one without the other? What is meant by a "muddy thinker" (par. 7)? Why is it "impossible for a muddy thinker to write good English"?
7. Why does the author think most people fall asleep while reading? What is his attitude toward such people?
8. Look up and explain the "big differences" between the words *sanguine* and *sanguinary; infer* and *imply.* What is the writer's point in calling attention to these differences?
9. In paragraph 11, Zinsser calls attention to a writer's necessary awareness of the composing process. What elements of the *process* of writing does the author include in that paragraph? In that discussion, Zinsser speaks of *fuzz* in writing. What does he mean by the word as it relates to the writing process? To what does Zinsser compare the writer's thinking process? Why does he use such simple comparisons?
10. Explain the meaning of the last sentence. What does it indicate about the writer's attitude toward his work?

Understanding the Writer's Techniques

1. What is the writer's thesis? Is it stated or implied?
2. Explain the use of the words *disease* and *strangling* in paragraph 1. Why does Zinsser use these words in an essay about writing?
3. For what purpose does Zinsser use a series of questions in paragraph 2?
4. Throughout this essay, the writer makes extensive use of examples to support general opinions and attitudes. What attitude or opinion is he supporting in paragraphs 2, 4, 5, 6, and 9? How does he use examples in each of those paragraphs?
5. Analyze the specific structure and organization of paragraph 3:
   a. What general ideas about writing does he propose?
   b. Where does he place that idea in the paragraph?
   c. What examples does he offer to support his general idea?
   d. With what new idea does he conclude the paragraph? How is it related to the beginning idea?
6. Why does Zinsser reproduce exactly portions of the writings of a past president of a major university, President Franklin D. Roosevelt, and Henry David Thoreau? How do these sections make Zinsser's writing clearer, more understandable, or more important?
7. What is the effect on the reader of the words "Simplify, simplify," which begin paragraph 6? Why does the writer use them at that particular point in the essay? What do they indicate about his attitude toward his subject? Explain.
8. Why does the author begin so many sentences in paragraph 9 with the word "Perhaps"? How does that technique help to *unify* (see Glossary) the paragraph?
9. For what reasons does the writer include the two pages of "rough" manuscript as a part of the finished essay? What is he trying to show the reader in this way? How does seeing these pages help you to understand better what he is writing about in the completed essay?
10. Overall, how would you describe the writer's attitude toward the process and craft of writing? What would you say is his overall attitude toward the future of American writing? Is he generally optimistic or pessimistic? On what does his atti-

tude depend? Refer to specifics in the essay to support your answer.

11. Do you think Zinsser expected other writers, or budding writers, to be the main readers of this essay? Why or why not? If so, with what main ideas do you think he would like them to come away from the essay? Do you think readers who were not somehow involved in the writing process would benefit equally from this essay? Why?

Exploring the Writer's Ideas

1. Do you think that Zinsser is ever guilty in this essay of the very "sins" against writing about which he is upset? Could he have simplified any of his points? Select one of Zinsser's paragraphs in the finished essay and explain how you might rewrite it more simply.
2. In the reading that you do most often, have you noticed overly cluttered writing? Or, do you feel that the writing is at its clearest level of presentation and understanding for its audience? Bring to class some examples of this writing, and be prepared to discuss it. In general, what do you consider the relation between the simplicity or complexity of a piece of writing and its intended readership?
3. In the note to the two rough manuscript pages included with this essay, the writer implies that the process of rewriting and simplifying may be endless. How do you know when to stop trying to rewrite an essay, story, or poem? Do you ever really feel satisfied that you've reached the end of the rewriting process?
4. Choose one of the rough manuscript paragraphs, and compare it with the finished essay. Which do you feel is better? Why? Is there anything Zinsser deleted from the rough copy that you feel he should have retained? Why?
5. Comment on the writer's assertion that "Thinking clearly is a conscious act that writers must force upon themselves" (par. 12). How does this opinion compare with the opinions of the three other writers in this chapter?
6. Reread Kurt Vonnegut, Jr.'s essay "How to Write with Style" (pages 6–9). What similarities and differences do you note in Zinsser's and Vonnegut's approaches to writing and language?

IDEAS FOR WRITING

Prewriting

For the most part, teachers have called upon you to put your thoughts in writing from your elementary school days onward. Make a list of your writing "problems"—the elements of writing or the elements of your personality that create problems for you whenever you try to produce something on paper.

Guided Writing

In a 500- to 750-word essay, write about what you feel are some of the problems that you face as a writer.

1. In the first paragraph, identify the problems that you plan to discuss.
2. In the course of your essay, relate your problems more generally to society at large.
3. Identify what, in your opinion, is the "secret" of good writing. Give specific examples of what measures to take to achieve that secret process and thereby to eliminate some of your problems.
4. Try to include one or two accurate reproductions of your writing to illustrate your composing techniques.
5. Point out what you believe were the major causes of your difficulties as a writer.
6. Toward the end of your essay, explain the type of writer that you would like to be in order to succeed in college.

Thinking and Writing Collaboratively

Form groups of two and exchange drafts of your Guided Writing essay. Do for your partner's draft what Zinsser did for his own: edit it in an effort to make it "stronger and more precise, eliminating every element that is not doing useful work." Return the papers and discuss whether or not your partner made useful recommendations for cutting clutter.

More Writing Projects

1. Over the next few days, listen to the same news reporter or talk-show host on television or radio. Record in your journal at least ten examples that indicate the use of "unnecessary words, circular constructions, pompous frills, and meaningless jargon." Or compile such a list from an article in a newspaper or magazine you read regularly. Then write an essay presenting and commenting on these examples.
2. Respond in a paragraph to Zinsser's observation, "Good writing doesn't come naturally."
3. In preparation for a writing assignment, collect with other class members various samples of junk mail and business correspondence that confirm Zinsser's statement that these tend to be poorly written. Write an essay describing your findings. Be certain to provide specific examples from the documents you have assembled.

SUMMING UP: CHAPTER 1

1. It sounds simple enough. Many writers, famous and unknown, have tried it at one time or another. Now, it's your turn. Write an essay simply titled "On Writing." Develop the essay in any way you please: you may deal with abstract or concrete ideas, philosophical or practical issues, emotional or intellectual processes, and so forth. Just use this essay to focus your own thoughts and to give your reader a clear idea of what writing means to you.
2. William Zinsser ("Simplicity") tells writers to simplify their writing. Select any writer from this section, and write an essay about whether you think the writer achieved (or did not achieve) simplicity. How did the writer achieve it? Where in the selection would you have preferred even more simplicity? Make specific references to the text.
3. Think about the message implicit in Amy Tan's essay on using her mother as an ideal audience. Find your own ideal listener. Then write a letter to that person in which you discuss your reactions to becoming a writer. Include observations you think your listener or reader will enjoy, such as your everyday life as a student, daydreams, descriptions of teachers, or cafeteria food, or of interesting people you have met.
4. Write a letter from Kurt Vonnegut, Jr., to Amy Tan on how style affects good writing. Draw on what you understand of Vonnegut's philosophy of writing from his essay "How to Write with Style," and what Amy Tan says in "Mother Tongue."
5. The writers in this chapter all give some sense of *why* they write. For the most part, their reasons are very personal. For example, Kurt Vonnegut, Jr., writes about trusting his writing when he sounds "most like a person from Indianapolis," while William Saroyan simply states, "I write because I want to." However, many writers (including many represented in this book) feel that writing entails a certain social responsibility. For example, when Albert Camus received the 1957 Nobel Prize for Literature, he was cited for "illuminating the problems of the human conscience of our time." And, in his acceptance speech, he stated, "[T]he writer's function is not without arduous duties. By definition, he cannot serve today

those who make history; he must serve those who are subject to it."

What do you feel are writers' responsibilities to themselves and to others? Do you agree with Camus? Do you prefer writing that deals primarily with an individual's experience or with more general social issues?

Write an essay concerning the social responsibilities of writers. As you consider the issue, refer to points made by writers in this section.

CHAPTER 2

On Reading

WHAT IS READING?

"Reading had changed the course of my life forever," writes Malcolm X in one of the essays in this chapter. For many of us, the acquisition of reading skills may not have been quite as dramatic as it was for the author of "Prison Studies," but if we are to understand the value of literacy in today's society, Malcolm X's analysis of the power of the written word is vital. Reading allows us actively to engage the minds of many writers who have much to tell us and to hear a variety of viewpoints not always available on the cable channels, VCRs, and video forms that vie for our attention. Learning to read well means interacting with what you read. Such reading opens new universes, challenges your opinions, enhances your understanding of yourself and others and of your past, present, and future. Knowledge of books is the mark of a literate person.

But how do we learn this complex skill? Ellen Tashie Frisina's essay on teaching her grandmother to read may remind you of your own early experiences with printed words. Or, if you are a parent, you may be reading stories to your own children to help them learn to read. The joy of early reading experiences should remind us, though, that there are many levels of reading. As we become more mature readers, we read not just as we once did, for the story and its magical pleasures, but for information. We learn not to be passive readers but active ones.

That early love of stories, and the self-esteem that came with mastery of a once impossible task, is, however, only the first step in understanding the power of reading. "Prison Studies " and Robert MacNeil's "Wordstruck" extend our understanding of what reading is beyond the personal into the cultural sphere. Both writers explore not only the power of reading to excite and inspire them, but also the ways in which language connects to social identity. Malcolm X uses reading, and later writing, to challenge existing assumptions and find a place as an alert and engaged member of society. He argues that his reading outside of school made him better educated than most formally educated citizens in America. MacNeil believes that words heard early in life establish in us an interactive "mini-thesaurus . . . steeped in emotional colour and personal associations."

Reading gives us access to many printed stories and documents, old and new. By selecting and reading these records, we can see beyond the highly edited sound bites and trendy images that tempt us from the television screen. With a book, we can read what we want when we want to read it. We can reread difficult passages to be sure we understand them. We have time to question the author's idea, a luxury that high-speed visual media usually deny us. We have time to absorb and analyze ideas not only from contemporary life but also from ancient cultures and distant places. The diverse materials in libraries allow us to select what we read rather than be channeled into one TV director's point of view.

Reading, then, lets us share ideas. Reading can teach us practical skills that we need for survival in our complex world, such as how to repair a computer or how to become a biology teacher or a certified public accountant. Good reading can inspire us, educate us, or entertain us. It can enrich our fantasy lives. Reading critically also helps us analyze how society operates, how power is distributed, how we can improve our local community or the global environment. As Eudora Welty writes, reading can lead to a lifelong love affair with books and stories. The beauty of the written word and the stirrings of imagination and vision that the printed page can produce are all part of what reading is.

HOW DO WE READ?

To become a good reader, we need to think about what we read just as we think about what and how we write.

• What is the writer's primary purpose? Who is the intended audience?

We should first examine what we are about to read to determine what it is: Is it a romance? a history book? a religious tract? Who wrote it? Why was it written? When was it written? How do the answers to these questions shape our attitude toward the material? As readers of novels, for instance, we soon learn that a gothic romance with a cover featuring a heroine snatched from a fiery castle belongs to a particular genre, or type, of literature. As potential readers, we might prepare ourselves to be skeptical about the happy ending we know awaits us, but at the same time we are prepared for a romantic tale. In contrast, if we face a hard-covered glossy textbook entitled *Economics,* we prepare ourselves to read with far more concentration. We might enjoy the love story, but if we skip whole chapters it may not matter much. If, however, we skip chapters of the textbook, we may find ourselves confused. The first book *entertains* us, while the second *informs.* Only if we understand the *purpose* of a reading assignment are we ready to begin reading.

• What is the precise issue or problem that the writer treats?

Reading is often a process of analyzing and synthesizing. We read an entire chapter, and then we go back and look for the key points. We try to summarize the main idea. We look for subtopics that support the main idea. We identify the writer's *exact* topic. A writer's general topic might be the Battle of Gettysburg, for instance, but if she is writing about the women at Gettysburg, then her precise topic is narrower. What is she saying, we next ask, about these women?

• Who is the writer? For whom is he or she writing?

Clues to a writer's identity can often help us establish whether the material we are reading is reliable. Would we read a slave owner's account of life in slave quarters the same way we would read a slave's diary, for instance? If a Sioux writes about the effects of a treaty on Native-American family life, we might read the essay with a different eye than if the writer were General Custer. The *audience* is also important. If we are reading a handbook on immigration policies in the United States, we might read it differently if we knew it was written for officials at Ellis Island in 1990 than we would if it were written for Chinese men arriving to work on the railroads in the nineteenth century.

• What information, conclusions, and recommendations does the writer present?

The reader may find that note taking is helpful in improving understanding of a text. Creating an outline of materials after reading can help identify the writer's aims.

• How does the writer substantiate, or "prove," his or her case?

The reader must learn the difference between a writer who merely *asserts* an idea and one who effectively *substantiates* an idea. The writer who only asserts that the Holocaust never happened will be read differently from the writer who substantiates his or her claims that the Holocaust did exist with photographs of Germany in the 1940s, interviews with concentration camp survivors, military records of medical experiments, and eyewitness accounts of gas chambers.

• Is the total message successful, objective, valid, or persuasive?

Once you have answered all of the above questions, you are ready to *assess* the work you have read. As you make your evaluation, find specific evidence in the text to back up your position.

These steps will help you engage in an active conversation, or dialogue, with the writer, sharing ideas and debating issues. At the same time, becoming a better reader will help you become a better writer. Eudora Welty and Malcolm X became readers as part of their apprenticeship to becoming world-renowned writers. For Ellen Tashie Frisina, reading remains, as it does for most of us, a personal achievement. For Welty, words came to her "as though fed . . . out of a silver spoon." Malcolm X tells us how reading was so powerful for him that it allowed him to break down prison walls. Robert MacNeil, a well-known television news anchor, talks of his love affair with books as a child in Nova Scotia. Frisina reminds us that literacy is not a birthright, but a skill that can be painstakingly learned, and taught, at any age.

Moon on a Silver Spoon

Eudora Welty

Eudora Welty, born in 1909, is among America's foremost writers, often focusing on the ways of life in rural Mississippi. Her novel *The Optimist's Daughter* won the 1972 Pulitzer Prize, and her *Collected Stories* (1980) has been widely acclaimed. In this selection from her autobiography, *One Writer's Beginnings* (1984), Welty uses delightful descriptions and narrations of her childhood to tell how she developed her love for reading.

PREREADING: THINKING ABOUT THE ESSAY IN ADVANCE

What attitudes did your family have toward reading when you were a child? Did books surround you? Which books did your parents or other relatives read to you or suggest that you read? How did you feel about books as a child growing up?

Words to Watch

sap (par. 4) drain away
gratitude (par. 10) thankfulness
essential (par. 10) absolutely necessary
keystone (par. 10) something on which associated things depend for support
wizardry (par. 11) magic
acute (par. 13) very specific or serious
elders (par. 13) older people
ailment (par. 14) illness
insatiability (par. 16) inability to be satisfied
lingers (par. 18) stays with

On a visit to my grandmother's in West Virginia, I stood inside the house where my mother had been born and where she grew up. 1

2 "Here's where I first began to read my Dickens," Mother said, pointing. "Under that very bed. Hiding my candle. To keep them from knowing I was up all night."

3 "But where did it all *come* from?" I asked her at last. "All that Dickens?"

4 "Why, Papa gave me that set of Dickens for agreeing to let them cut off my hair," she said. "In those days, they thought very long, thick hair like mine would sap a child's strength. I said *No!* I wanted my hair left the very way it was. They offered me gold earrings first. I said *No!* I'd rather keep my hair. Then Papa said, 'What about books? I'll have them send a whole set of Charles Dickens to you, right up the river from Baltimore, in a barrel.' I agreed."

5 My mother had brought that set of Dickens to our house in Jackson, Miss.; those books had been through fire and water before I was born, she told me, and there they were, lined up—as I later realized, waiting for *me.*

6 I learned from the age of two or three that any room in our house, at any time of day, was there to read in, or to be read to. My mother read to me. She'd read to me in the big bedroom in the mornings, when we were in her rocker together, which ticked in rhythm as we rocked, as though we had a cricket accompanying the story. She'd read to me in the dining room on winter afternoons in front of the coal fire, with our cuckoo clock ending the story with "Cuckoo," and at night when I'd got in my own bed. I must have given her no peace.

7 It had been startling and disappointing to me to find out that storybooks had been written by *people,* that books were not natural wonders, coming up of themselves like grass. Yet regardless of where they came from, I cannot remember a time when I was not in love with them—with the books themselves, cover and binding and the paper they were printed on, with their smell and their weight and with their possession in my arms, captured and carried off to myself.

8 Neither of my parents had come from homes that could afford to buy many books, but though it must have been something of a strain on his salary, my father was all the while carefully selecting and ordering away for what he and Mother thought we children should grow up with.

Besides the bookcase in the living room, which was always called the library, there were the encyclopedia tables and dictionary stand under windows in our dining room. There was a full set of Mark Twain and a short set of Ring Lardner in our bookcase, and those were the volumes that in time united us as parents and children. 9

I live in gratitude to my parents for initiating me—and as early as I begged for it, without keeping me waiting—into knowledge of the word, into reading and spelling, by way of the alphabet. They taught it to me at home in time for me to begin to read before starting school. I believe the alphabet is no longer considered an essential piece of equipment for traveling through life. In my day it was the keystone to knowledge. You learned the alphabet as you learned "Now I lay me" and the Lord's Prayer, and your father's and mother's name and address and telephone number, all in case you were lost. 10

My love for the alphabet, which endures, grew out of reciting it, but before that, out of seeing the letters on the page. In my own storybooks, before I could read them for myself, I fell in love with various winding, enchanted-looking initials at the heads of fairy tales. In "Once upon a time," an "O" had a rabbit running it as a treadmill, his feet upon flowers. When the day came, years later, for me to see the Book of Kells, Gospels from the ninth century, all the wizardry of letter, initial and word swept over me, a thousand times over, and the illustration, the gold, seemed a part of the word's beauty and holiness that had been there from the start. 11

In my sensory education I include my physical awareness of the word. Of a certain word, that is; the connection it has with what it stands for. Around age six, perhaps, I was standing by myself in our front yard waiting for supper, just at that hour in a late summer day when the sun is already below the horizon and the risen full moon in the visible sky stops being chalky and begins to take on light. There comes the moment, and I saw it then, when the moon goes from flat to round. For the first time it met my eyes as a globe. The word "moon" came into my mouth as though fed to me out of a silver spoon. Held in my mouth the moon became a word. It had the roundness of a Concord grape that Grandpa took off his vine and gave me to suck out of its skin and swallow whole, in Ohio. 12

13 Long before I wrote stories, I listened for stories. Listening *for* them is something more acute than listening *to* them. I suppose it's an early form of participation in what goes on. Listening children know stories are *there.* When their elders sit and begin, children are just waiting and hoping for one to come out, like a mouse from its hole.

14 When I was six or seven, I was taken out of school and put to bed for several months for an ailment the doctor described as "fast-beating heart." I never dreamed I could learn away from the schoolroom, and that bits of enlightenment far-reaching in my life went on as ever in their own good time.

15 An opulence of storybooks covered my bed. As I read away, I was Rapunzel, or the Goose Girl, or the princess in one of the *Thousand and One Nights* who mounted the roof of her palace every night and of her own radiance faithfully lighted the whole city just by reposing there.

16 My mother was very sharing of this feeling of insatiability. Now, I think of her as reading so much of the time while doing something else. In my mind's eye *The Origin of Species* is lying on the shelf in the pantry under a light dusting of flour—my mother was a bread maker; she'd pick it up, sit by the kitchen window and find her place, with one eye on the oven.

17 I'm grateful, too, that from my mother's example, I found the base for worship—that I found a love of sitting and reading the Bible for myself and looking up things in it.

18 How many of us, the Southern writers-to-be of my generation, were blessed in one way or another if not blessed alike, in not having gone deprived of the King James Version of the Bible. Its cadence entered into our ears and our memories for good. The evidence, or the ghost of it, lingers in all our books.

19 "In the beginning was the Word."

BUILDING VOCABULARY

1. Identify the following references to authors, books, and stories from Welty's essay:
   a. Charles Dickens
   b. Mark Twain

c. Ring Lardner
d. the Book of Kells
e. Gospels
f. Rapunzel
g. the Goose Girl
h. the *Thousand and One Nights*
i. *The Origin of Species*
j. the King James Version of the Bible

2. Write definitions and your own sentences for the following words:
   a. initiating (par. 10)
   b. enchanted-looking (par. 11)
   c. treadmill (par. 11)
   d. holiness (par. 11)
   e. enlightenment (par. 14)
   f. opulence (par. 15)
   g. radiance (par. 15)
   h. reposing (par. 15)
   i. deprived (par. 18)
   j. cadence (par. 18)

THINKING CRITICALLY ABOUT THE ESSAY

Understanding the Writer's Ideas

1. Where did Welty's grandmother come from? Where was Welty herself brought up? Why did Welty's grandparents want to cut off their daughter's hair?
2. For what reason did Welty's mother receive a set of Charles Dickens's works? What does this tell you about the attitude toward reading in Welty's family? What happened to the set of Dickens? Although Welty doesn't say so, what do you think she did with the books? Why?
3. How did the way Welty's mother felt toward books affect her child's attitude toward reading? In what ways did the conditions in Welty's home contribute to her attitude toward books?
4. Why does the writer say of her mother, "I must have given her no peace" (par. 6)?

5. Why was it "startling and disappointing" for Welty to find out that storybooks were written by *people?* Where did she think they came from? Aside from the stories themselves, what is it that the author loves so much about books?
6. For what reasons does the writer feel that learning the alphabet is so important? To what other learning processes does she compare it? Before she learned to recite her alphabet, why was it so important to her?
7. Explain in your own words what the writer considers to be the relation between physical sensations and learning words. According to the author why is it important for parents to read to their children?
8. For what reason was the young Welty taken out of school? How did this affect her attitude toward reading? How did her mother influence her at this time?
9. At the time of writing this piece, the writer was in her mid-seventies. Explain what she sees as the relation between the Bible and Southern writers of her generation. By what descriptions and references in the essay does she indicate her feelings for the Bible?
10. Identify the source of the final sentence. Why is it especially significant to this essay?

Understanding the Writer's Techniques

1. What is the main idea of Welty's essay? Is there any point at which she directly states that main idea? Explain.
2. Why does the writer use an *image* (see Glossary) for her title instead of choosing a more straightforward one, such as William Zinsser's "Simplicity" (pages 34–39), or William Saroyan's "Why I Write" (pages 14–17)? What effect does Welty achieve with the title? What does the title mean?
3. A *reminiscence* is a narrative account of a special memory. How does the writer use reminiscence in this essay?
4. The *tone* (see Glossary) of an essay is the expression of the writer's attitude toward the topic. State the tone of this essay. What specifically about the writing contributes to that tone?
5. *Description* helps the reader to "see" objects and scenes and to feel their importance through the author's eyes. *Narra-*

tion—the telling of a story—helps the reader follow a sequence of events. (See Chapters 3 and 4.) Both techniques rely on the writer's skill in choosing and presenting details. In what way does Welty make use of description and narration in this essay? How would you evaluate her use of details?

6. Placing words in italics emphasizes them. Where does the author use italics in this essay? Why does she use them?

7. What does the writer mean by the italicized phrase in the statement "Those books had been *through fire and water* before I was born" (par. 5)? How does the image contribute to the point she's making?

8. The writing of *dialogue* (see Glossary), often used as part of a narration, is the technique whereby a writer either reproduces words actually spoken or invents speech that logically fits into the essay or story. How does Welty use dialogue here? In what ways does it affect your understanding or enjoyment of the writing?

9. *Similes* (see Glossary) are imaginative comparisons using the word "like" or "as." Use of similes often enlivens the writing and makes it memorable.

In your own words, explain what is being compared in the following similes (in italics) drawn from Welty's essay, and tell how they contribute to the essay:

a. . . . we were in her rocker together, which ticked in rhythm as we rocked, *as though we had a cricket accompanying the story.* (par. 6)

b. The word "moon" came into my mouth *as though fed to me out of a silver spoon.* (par. 12)

c. Listening children know stories are *there.* When their elders sit and begin, children are just waiting and hoping for one to come out, *like a mouse from its hole.* (par. 13)

10. Throughout this essay, the writer refers to "the word." Is she referring to a specific word or to a more abstract concept? Explain. Reread the essay, and find and list all references to "the word." What is the relation between them all? How do they work to keep the essay *coherent* and *unified* (see Glossary)? How do they build to the reference in the final sentence? Why is "the Word" capitalized there?

Exploring the Writer's Ideas

1. The writer believes that it is very important for parents to read to their children. Some specialists in child development even advocate reading to infants still in the womb and to babies before they've spoken their first words. For what reasons might such activities be important? Do you personally feel they are important or useful? Would you read to an unborn infant? Why or why not? If you would, *what* would you read?
2. Welty was born in 1909 and obviously belongs to a different generation from the vast majority of college students today. Do you feel that her type of love and advocacy of reading are as valid for the current generation, raised on television, video, cassettes, VCRs, CDs, satellite dishes, and MTV? Explain.
3. Welty describes her love of books as going beyond the words and stories they contain to their physical and visual attributes. What objects—not other people—do you love or respect with that intensity? Tell a little about why and how you have developed this feeling.

IDEAS FOR WRITING

Prewriting

In the visual and auditory age in which we live—we watch and listen to television, tune in the radio, see movies regularly—what is the proper role for reading? Talk to friends, teachers, and fellow students about the matter. Record their observations and try to classify their responses.

Guided Writing

Write an essay that describes your own attitude toward reading.

1. In order to set the stage for the discussion of your attitude, begin by recalling details about a moment with a parent or other adult.
2. Use dialogue as part of this scene.
3. Go as far back in your childhood as you can possibly remember, and narrate two or three incidents that help explain the formation of your current attitude toward reading.

4. Use sensory language (color, sound, smell, touch, and taste) to show how the environment of the home where you grew up helped shape your attitude.
5. Tell about a particular, special childhood fascination with something you *saw*—not read—in a book.
6. Try to describe the first time you were conscious of the *meaning* of a particular word.
7. Use at least one *simile* in your essay.
8. Create and keep a consistent *tone* throughout the essay.
9. End your essay with an explanation of how a particular book has been continually influential to you as well as to others of your generation.
10. Give your essay an unusual title that derives from some description in your essay.

Thinking and Writing Collaboratively

Form groups of three to five students, and read the essays you each prepared for the Guided Writing assignment. Together, make a list of the various attitudes expressed about reading by group members. Report to the class as a whole on the reading attitudes of your group.

More Writing Projects

1. Enter in your journal early memories of people who read to you or of books that you read on your own. Try to capture the sensation and importance of these early reading experiences.
2. Return to question 2 in Exploring the Writer's Ideas, and write a one-paragraph response to it.
3. Write an essay on the person who most influenced your childhood education. Did this person read to you, give you books, make you do your homework? Assess the impact of this person on your life.

Prison Studies

Malcolm X

Born Malcolm Little in Omaha, Nebraska, Malcolm X (1925–1965) was a charismatic leader of the black power movement and founded the Organization of Afro-American Unity. In prison, he became a Black Muslim. (He split with this faith in 1963 to convert to orthodox Islam.) "Prison Studies" is excerpted from the popular and fascinating *Autobiography of Malcolm X,* which he cowrote with *Roots* author Alex Haley. The essay describes the writer's struggle to learn to read as well as the joy and power he felt when he won that struggle.

PREREADING: THINKING ABOUT THE ESSAY IN ADVANCE

Reflect on what you know about prison life. Could someone interested in reading and learning find a way to pursue his or her interests in such a setting? Why or why not?

Words to Watch

emulate (par. 2) imitate, especially from respect
motivation (par. 2) reason to do something
tablets (par. 3) writing notebooks
bunk (par. 9) small bed
rehabilitation (par. 10) the process of restoring to a state of usefulness or constructiveness
inmate (par. 10) prisoner
corridor (par. 13) hallway; walkway
vistas (par. 15) mental overviews
confers (par. 15) bestows; gives ceremoniously
alma mater (par. 15) the college that one has attended

1 Many who today hear me somewhere in person, or on television, or those who read something I've said, will think I went to school

far beyond the eighth grade. This impression is due entirely to my prison studies.

It had really begun back in the Charlestown Prison, when 2
Bimbi first made me feel envy of his stock of knowledge. Bimbi had always taken charge of any conversation he was in, and I had tried to emulate him. But every book I picked up had few sentences which didn't contain anywhere from one to nearly all of the words that might as well have been in Chinese. When I just skipped those words, of course, I really ended up with little idea of what the book said. So I had come to the Norfolk Prison Colony still going through only book-reading motions. Pretty soon, I would have quit even these motions, unless I had received the motivation that I did.

I saw that the best thing I could do was get hold of a 3
dictionary—to study, to learn some words. I was lucky enough to reason also that I should try to improve my penmanship. It was sad. I couldn't even write in a straight line. It was both ideas together that moved me to request a dictionary along with some tablets and pencils from the Norfolk Prison Colony school.

I spent two days just riffling uncertainly through the dictio- 4
nary's pages. I'd never realized so many words existed! I didn't know which words I needed to learn. Finally, to start some kind of action, I began copying.

In my slow, painstaking, ragged handwriting, I copied into 5
my tablet everything printed on that first page, down to the punctuation marks.

I believe it took me a day. Then, aloud, I read back, to 6
myself, everything I'd written on the tablet. Over and over, aloud, to myself, I read my own handwriting.

I woke up the next morning, thinking about those words— 7
immensely proud to realize that not only had I written so much at one time, but I'd written words that I never knew were in the world. Moreover, with a little effort, I also could remember what many of these words meant. I reviewed the words whose meanings I didn't remember. Funny thing, from the dictionary first page right now, that "aardvark" springs to my mind. The dictionary had a picture of it, a long-tailed, long-eared, burrowing African mammal, which lives off termites caught by sticking out its tongue as an anteater does for ants.

8 I was so fascinated that I went on—I copied the dictionary's next page. And the same experience came when I studied that. With every succeeding page, I also learned of people and places and events from history. Actually the dictionary is like a miniature encyclopedia. Finally the dictionary's A section had filled a whole tablet—and I went on into the B's. That was the way I started copying what eventually became the entire dictionary. It went a lot faster after so much practice helped me to pick up handwriting speed. Between what I wrote in my tablet, and writing letters, during the rest of my time in prison I would guess I wrote a million words.

9 I suppose it was inevitable that as my word-base broadened, I could for the first time pick up a book and read and now begin to understand what the book was saying. Anyone who has read a great deal can imagine the new world that opened. Let me tell you something; from then until I left that prison, in every free moment I had, if I was not reading in the library, I was reading on my bunk. You couldn't have gotten me out of books with a wedge. Between Mr. Muhammad's teachings, my correspondence, my visitors—usually Ella and Reginald—and my reading of books, months passed without my even thinking about being imprisoned. In fact, up to then, I never had been so truly free in my life. . . .

10 As you can imagine, especially in a prison where there was heavy emphasis on rehabilitation, an inmate was smiled upon if he demonstrated an unusually intense interest in books. There was a sizable number of well-read inmates, especially the popular debaters. Some were said by many to be practically walking encyclopedias. They were almost celebrities. No university would ask any student to devour literature as I did when this new world opened to me, of being able to read and *understand.*

11 I read more in my room than in the library itself. An inmate who was known to read a lot could check out more than the permitted maximum number of books. I preferred reading in the total isolation of my own room.

12 When I had progressed to really serious reading, every night at about ten P.M. I would be outraged with the "lights out." It always seemed to catch me right in the middle of something engrossing.

Fortunately, right outside my door was a corridor light that cast a glow into my room. The glow was enough to read by, once my eyes adjusted to it. So when "lights out" came, I would sit on the floor where I could continue reading in that glow. 13

At one-hour intervals the night guards paced past every room. Each time I heard the approaching footsteps, I jumped into bed and feigned sleep. And as soon as the guard passed, I got back out of bed onto the floor area of that light-glow, where I would read for another fifty-eight minutes—until the guard approached again. That went on until three or four every morning. Three or four hours of sleep a night was enough for me. Often in the years in the streets I had slept less than that. 14

I have often reflected upon the new vistas that reading opened to me. I knew right there in prison that reading had changed forever the course of my life. As I see it today, the ability to read awoke inside me some long dormant craving to be mentally alive. I certainly wasn't seeking any degree, the way a college confers a status symbol upon its students. My homemade education gave me, with every additional book that I read, a little bit more sensitivity to the deafness, dumbness, and blindness that was afflicting the black race in America. Not long ago, an English writer telephoned me from London, asking questions. One was, "What's your alma mater?" I told him, "Books." You will never catch me with a free fifteen minutes in which I'm not studying something I feel might be able to help the black man. . . . 15

Every time I catch a plane, I have with me a book that I want to read—and that's a lot of books these days. If I weren't out here every day battling the white man, I could spend the rest of my life reading, just satisfying my curiosity—because you can hardly mention anything I'm not curious about. I don't think anybody ever got more out of going to prison than I did. In fact, prison enabled me to study far more intensively than I would have if my life had gone differently and I had attended some college. I imagine that one of the biggest troubles with colleges is there are too many distractions, too much panty-raiding, fraternities, and boola-boola and all of that. Where else but in prison could I have attacked my ignorance by being able to study intensely sometimes as much as fifteen hours a day? 16

BUILDING VOCABULARY

1. Throughout the selection, the writer uses *figurative* and *colloquial language* (see Glossary). As you know, figurative language involves imaginative comparisons, which go beyond plain or ordinary statements. Colloquial language involves informal or conversational phrases and expressions.

   The following are examples of some of the figurative and colloquial usages in this essay. Explain each italicized word group in your own words.

   a. *going through* only *book-reading motions* (par. 2)
   b. I was *lucky enough* (par. 3)
   c. *Funny thing* (par. 7)
   d. can imagine *the new world that opened* (par. 9)
   e. *You couldn't have gotten me out of books with a wedge* (par. 9)
   f. an inmate was *smiled upon* (par. 10)
   g. to be practically *walking encyclopedias* (par. 10)
   h. ask any student *to devour literature* (par. 10)
   i. changed forever *the course of my life* (par. 15)
   j. *some long dormant craving* to be *mentally alive* (par. 15)
   k. *the deafness, dumbness, and blindness that was afflicting* the black race in America (par. 15)
   l. Every time I *catch a plane* (par. 16)
   m. every day *battling the white man* (par. 16)
   n. just *satisfying my curiosity* (par. 16)
   o. *boola-boola and all of that* (par. 16)
   p. I have *attacked my ignorance* (par. 16)

2. Find the following words in the essay. Write brief definitions for them without using a dictionary. If they are unfamiliar to you, try to determine their meaning based on the context in which they appear.

   a. riffling (par. 4)
   b. painstaking (par. 5)
   c. ragged (par. 5)
   d. burrowing (par. 7)
   e. inevitable (par. 9)
   f. emphasis (par. 10)
   g. distractions (par. 16)

THINKING CRITICALLY ABOUT THE ESSAY

Understanding the Writer's Ideas

1. What was the highest level of formal education that the writer achieved? How is this different from the impression most people got from him? Why?
2. Who was Bimbi? Where did Malcolm X meet him? How was Bimbi important to the writer?
3. What does the writer mean by stating that when he tried to read, most of the words "might as well have been in Chinese"? What happened when he skipped over such words? What motivated him to change his way of reading?
4. Why did Malcolm X start trying to improve his handwriting? How was it connected to his desire to improve his reading ability? Briefly describe how he went about this dual process. How did he feel after the first day of this process? Why?
5. How is the dictionary "like a miniature encyclopedia"?
6. Judging from this essay and his description of his "homemade education," how much time did Malcolm X spend in prison? Does the fact that he was in prison affect your appreciation of his learning process? How?
7. What is a "word-base" (par. 9)? What happened once the author's word-base expanded? How did this give him a sense of freedom?
8. Who is "Mr. Muhammad"?
9. Why did the prison officials like Malcolm X? What special privileges came to him as a result of this favorable opinion?
10. Why was Malcolm X angered with the "lights out" procedure? How did he overcome it?
11. What does the following sentence tell you about Malcolm X's life: "Often in the years in the streets I had slept less than that" (par. 14)?
12. Characterize the writer's opinion of a college education. How does he compare his education to a college degree? How did his education influence his understanding of his place and role in American society?

13. In your own words, describe the writer's attitude toward American blacks. Toward the relation between blacks and whites?
14. To what main purpose in life does the writer refer? What was the relation between this purpose and his feelings about reading? Use one word to describe Malcolm X's attitude toward reading.
15. What does the conclusion mean?

Understanding the Writer's Techniques

1. What is the thesis? Where does the writer place it?
2. In Chapters 9 and 10, you will learn about the techniques of *process analysis* and *cause-and-effect analysis.* Briefly, process analysis tells the reader *how* something is done; cause-and-effect analysis explains *why* one thing leads to or affects another.

   For this essay, outline step by step the process whereby Malcolm X developed his ability to read and enthusiasm for reading. Next, for each step in your outline, explain why one step led to the next.
3. *Narration* (see Chapter 4) is the telling of a story or the orderly relating of a series of events. How does Malcolm X use narration in this essay? How does he order the events of his narration?
4. What is the effect of the words "Let me tell you something" in paragraph 9?
5. How is the writer's memory of the first page of the dictionary like a dictionary entry itself? What does this say about the importance of this memory to the author?
6. *Tone* (see Glossary) is a writer's attitude toward his or her subject. Characterize the tone of this essay. What elements of the writing contribute to that tone? Be specific.
7. Which paragraphs make up the conclusion of this essay? How does the author develop his conclusion? How does he relate it to the main body of the essay? Do you feel that there is a change in tone (see question 6) in the conclusion? Explain, using specific examples.
8. What is Malcolm X's main purpose in writing this essay? For whom is it intended? How do you know?

Exploring the Writer's Ideas

1. Malcolm X writes about his newly found love of reading and ability to read: "In fact, up to then, I never had been so truly free in my life." Has learning any particular skill or activity ever given you such a feeling of freedom or joy? Explain.
2. What do you feel was the source of Malcolm X's attitude toward a college education? Do you think any of his points here are valid? Why? What are your opinions about the quality of the college education you are receiving?
3. The writer also implies that, in some ways, the educational opportunities of prison were superior to those he would have had at college. What is his basis for this attitude? Have you ever experienced a circumstance in which being restricted actually benefited you? Explain.
4. Malcolm X held very strong opinions about the relations between blacks and whites in America. Do some library research on him to try to understand his opinions. You might begin by reading *The Autobiography of Malcolm X,* from which this essay was excerpted. Do you agree or disagree with his feelings? Why?
5. Following Malcolm X's example, handwrite a page from a dictionary (a pocket dictionary will be fine), copying everything—including punctuation—*exactly!*

   How long did it take you? How did it make you feel? Did you learn anything from the experience?

IDEAS FOR WRITING

Prewriting

Brainstorm on a difficult activity that you learned how to perform. What problems did the activity present? Why did you want to learn how to do it?

Guided Writing

Write an essay in which you tell about an activity that you can now perform but that once seemed impossible to you.

1. Open your essay with an example in which you compare what most people assume about your skill or background in the activity to what the reality is.
2. Mention someone who especially influenced you in your desire to master this activity.
3. Tell what kept you from giving up on learning this activity.
4. Explain, step by step, the *process* by which you learned more and more about the activity. Explain how and why one step led to the next.
5. Use *figurative* and *colloquial* language where you think it appropriate in your essay.
6. Describe in some detail how you overcame an obstacle, imposed by others, which could have impeded your learning process.
7. Use your conclusion to express a deeply felt personal opinion and to generalize your learning of this skill to the population at large.

Thinking and Writing Collaboratively

Exchange a draft version of your Guided Writing essay with another writer in the class. After you read your partner's essay, make recommendations for helping the writer produce the next draft. Use the items numbered 1–7 above to guide your discussion.

More Writing Projects

1. Select any page of a standard dictionary and copy in your journal at least ten words, with definitions, that are new or somewhat unfamiliar to you. Then jot down some thoughts on the process.
2. Ask yourself formal, journalistic questions about Malcolm X's essay: *What* happened? *Who* was involved? *How* was it done? *Where* did it occur? *When* did it occur? *Why* did it happen? Write out answers to these questions, and then assemble them in a unified, coherent paragraph.
3. Form a group with three other classmates. Focus on the context of Malcolm X's essay and on his comment on "the deafness, dumbness, and blindness that was afflicting the black race in America" (par. 15). Discuss this issue and its connection to education. Then prepare a collaborative essay on the topic.

"See Spot Run": Teaching My Grandmother to Read

Ellen Tashie Frisina

Ellen Tashie Frisina writes about her "secret" project to teach her 70-year-old grandmother, who came to the United States from Greece in 1916, to read English. Frisina's narrative reveals the pleasures of reading and illustrates the importance of reading no matter what age the reader.

PREREADING: THINKING ABOUT THE ESSAY IN ADVANCE

What do you think it would be like to be an adult who, living in America today, cannot read or write English? What problems would such a person face? Do you know or have you read about anyone who cannot read?

Words to Watch

differentiated (par. 1) separated from; distinguished from
stealthily (par. 2) secretly
monosyllabic (par. 3) one syllable; short in length
vehemently (par. 8) severely; intensely; angrily
phonetically (par. 14) pronounced by sound
afghan (par. 15) a blanket or shawl
crocheting (par. 15) a type of needlework

When I was 14 years old, and very impressed with my teenage status (looking forward to all the rewards it would bring), I set for myself a very special goal—a goal that so differentiated me from my friends that I don't believe I told a single one. As a teenager, I was expected to have deep, dark secrets, but I was not supposed to keep them from my friends. 1

My secret was a project that I undertook every day after school for several months. It began when I stealthily made my way into the local elementary school—horror of horrors should I 2 be seen; I was now in junior high. I identified myself as a *graduate* of the elementary school, and being taken under wing by a favorite fifth grade teacher, I was given a small bundle from a locked storeroom—a bundle that I quickly dropped into a bag, lest anyone see me walking home with something from the "little kids" school.

3 I brought the bundle home—proudly now, for within the confines of my home, I was proud of my project. I walked into the living room, and one by one, emptied the bag of basic reading books. They were thin books with colorful covers and large print. The words were monosyllabic and repetitive. I sat down to the secret task at hand.

4 "All right," I said authoritatively to my 70-year-old grandmother, "today we begin our first reading lesson."

5 For weeks afterward, my grandmother and I sat patiently side by side—roles reversed as she, with a bit of difficulty, sounded out every word, then read them again, piece by piece, until she understood the short sentences. When she slowly repeated the full sentence, we both would smile and clap our hands—I felt so proud, so grown up.

6 My grandmother was born in Kalamata, Greece, in a rocky little farming village where nothing much grew. She never had the time to go to school. As the oldest child, she was expected to take care of her brother and sister, as well as the house and meals, while her mother tended to the gardens, and her father scratched out what little he could from the soil.

7 So, for my grandmother, schooling was out. But she had big plans for herself. She had heard about America. About how rich you could be. How people on the streets would offer you a dollar just to smell the flower you were carrying. About how everyone lived in nice houses—not stone huts on the sides of mountains—and had nice clothes and time for school.

8 So my grandmother made a decision at 14—just a child, I realize now—to take a long and sickening 30-day sea voyage alone to the United States. After lying about her age to the passport officials, who would shake their heads vehemently at anyone under 16 leaving her family, and after giving her favorite gold earrings to her cousin, saying "In America, I will have all the gold I want," my young grandmother put herself on a ship. She landed in New York in 1916.

No need to repeat the story of how it went for years. The streets were not made of gold. People weren't interested in smelling flowers held by strangers. My grandmother was a foreigner. Alone. A young girl who worked hard doing piecework to earn enough money for meals. No leisure time, no new gold earrings—and no school. 9

She learned only enough English to help her in her daily business as she traveled about Brooklyn. Socially, the "foreigners" stayed in neighborhoods where they didn't feel like foreigners. English came slowly. 10

My grandmother had never learned to read. She could make out a menu, but not a newspaper. She could read a street sign, but not a shop directory. She could read only what she needed to read as, through the years, she married, had five daughters, and helped my grandfather with his restaurant. 11

So when I was 14—the same age that my grandmother was when she left her family, her country, and everything she knew—I took it upon myself to teach my grandmother something, something I already knew how to do. Something with which I could give back to her some of the things she had taught me. 12

And it was slight repayment for all she taught me. How to cover the fig tree in tar paper so it could survive the winter. How to cultivate rose bushes and magnolia trees that thrived on her little piece of property. How to make baklava, and other Greek delights, working from her memory. ("Now we add some milk." "How much?" "Until we have enough.") Best of all, she had taught me my ethnic heritage. 13

First, we phonetically sounded out the alphabet. Then, we talked about vowels—English is such a difficult language to learn. I hadn't even begun to explain the different sounds "gh" could make. We were still at the basics. 14

Every afternoon, we would sit in the living room, my grandmother with an afghan covering her knees, giving up her crocheting for her reading lesson. I, with the patience that can come only from love, slowly coached her from the basic reader to the second-grade reader, giving up my telephone gossiping. 15

Years later, my grandmother still hadn't learned quite enough to sit comfortably with a newspaper or magazine, but it felt awfully good to see her try. How we used to laugh at her pronunciation mistakes. She laughed more heartily than I. I never 16 knew whether I should laugh. Here was this old woman slowly and carefully sounding out each word, moving her lips, not saying anything aloud until she was absolutely sure, and then, loudly, proudly, happily saying, "Look at Spot. See Spot run."

17 When my grandmother died and we faced the sad task of emptying her home, I was going through her night-table drawer and came upon the basic readers. I turned the pages slowly, remembering. I put them in a paper bag, and the next day returned them to the "little kids" school. Maybe someday, some teenager will request them again, for the same task. It will make for a lifetime of memories.

BUILDING VOCABULARY

Put the following phrases into your own words and explain what the writer means in the context of the essay.

a. "very impressed with my teenage status" (par. 1)
b. "No need to repeat the story of how it went for years." (par. 9) Why not? What is the implication of this sentence?
c. "doing piecework to earn enough money for meals." (par. 9) What was piecework?
d. "Best of all, she had taught me my ethnic heritage." (par. 13)
e. "First, we phonetically sounded out the alphabet." (par. 14)

THINKING CRITICALLY ABOUT THE ESSAY

Understanding the Writer's Ideas

1. The author begins by saying that her project was a secret from her junior high school peers. Explain why a 14-year-old would not want to be seen carrying basic readers. What further reasons might the author have had for keeping her project a secret?
2. In paragraph 3, the author uses the words "proudly" and "proud." Why has her attitude changed?
3. How does teaching her grandmother to read change the relation between the two? How does Frisina speak to her grandmother in paragraph 4?

4. What are the myths about America that cause the grandmother to make her difficult decision to leave her family in Greece? How does the real America live up to the stories the grandmother had heard before she arrived? How common are experiences like the grandmother's for other immigrants?
5. What does Frisina imply in paragraph 10 about the daily life of immigrants in the early twentieth century? How is language usually acquired? What limits the grandmother's ability to learn English?
6. The author provides details of what her grandmother taught her for which the author is grateful. How do the specific details help the reader understand the kind of woman the grandmother was? What kind of life did the grandmother lead?
7. In paragraph 14, the author describes how hard it is to learn English. What in particular makes English a hard language to read? What can you tell from paragraph 17 about how the grandmother felt about her reading? Why does the grandmother keep the schoolbooks in her night-table drawer? What does this tell you about how she felt about learning to read?

Understanding the Writer's Techniques

1. Where does the author place her thesis statement? Why does she put it where she does? Explain the thesis in your own words.
2. *Diction* (see Glossary) refers to a writer's choice and use of words. We classify *levels of diction*—"informal," "academic," "low-class," "snobbish," "conversational," and so forth. How would you describe the general level of diction in this essay? Does the level suit the subject matter? Why?
3. Why does the author rely on short paragraphs throughout her narrative? What does the paragraph length and diction tell you about the intended audience for this piece?
4. The writer assumes that the reader is familiar with the history of immigration in America in the early twentieth century. How do we know that she makes this assumption? Should she provide readers with more historical detail? Why or why not?
5. Describe the method the author uses to teach her grandmother to read. Is this the way you remember learning to read?

Describe the first book you remember reading. How did your experience compare with the grandmother's?

Exploring the Writer's Ideas

1. The author uses the story of her grandmother's life to illustrate the experiences of many immigrants who came to America in the early twentieth century. How do those experiences compare with the arrival of immigrants to America today? Is it easier or more difficult to immigrate here now? What evidence can you provide to support your position?
2. Though the grandmother could barely read a newspaper, even her limited literacy seemed to give her pleasure. Why should learning to read be so important to an adult who cannot read? In a world of television, movies, and other visual sources of information, is learning to read truly important for illiterate adults? Why or why not?
3. The effort to teach and learn reading helps bridge the gap between generations. Do you see any practical applications here for bringing old and young people together for more harmonious relations? How else can young people and old people be united?

IDEAS FOR WRITING

Prewriting

Teaching someone to do something—anything—is fraught with problems and, at the same time, alive with possibilities and rewards. What do you see as the positive and negative aspects of teaching someone to do something? Use free association to indicate as many pluses and minuses as you can.

Guided Writing

Write an essay titled "Teaching __________ to __________." Fill in the blanks after considering your own experience with teaching someone something. You might choose one of these topics:

Teaching my daughter/son to read
Reading English as a second language (about your own experience or someone else's)
Working as a volunteer in a neighborhood literacy program

1. Begin your essay with a general discussion about the expectations you had when you started this learning project and the feelings you had when you accomplished it.
2. Define yourself as a reader. What age were you when you started the project? What kind of reading did you do? How did you feel about reading? Why?
3. Explain why you started the project of teaching someone to read or of changing the level of your own reading skill. What situation encouraged or required you to change or act?
4. Use examples and illustrations to show how you began the task. Give examples of words and sentences you worked with. Give the steps you used to carry out your project.
5. Describe the moment when a change happened—the first time your son or daughter read to you or the first time a difficult English sentence became clear. Use dialogue to capture the moment.
6. Analyze how you changed as a result of this moment, and why you remember it so vividly.
7. Conclude by describing your present status as a reader, or the skills level of the person you taught to read. Was the project worthwhile?

Thinking and Writing Collaboratively

Form groups of three students each, and read aloud drafts of each other's essays for the Guided Writing activity. Then discuss the essays. Was the writer's experience clear to you? Do you know why the writer started his or her teaching project? Do the illustrations show how the task was performed? Did the writer make clear the moment of change?

More Writing Projects

1. In your journal, write down your ideas about what the difference is between reading "See Spot run" and reading a science

textbook or a technical manual or a play by Shakespeare. Give steps by which a reader can increase his or her reading skills.

2. Write a paragraph in which you consider whether or not it is important to be a "good" reader to succeed in life.
3. Can teaching someone else, like a son or daughter, to read teach you to read better as well? Write an essay in which you discuss a parent's role in teaching his or her child to read. Consider what the child learns at school and what he or she learns at home about reading.

Wordstruck

Robert MacNeil

Robert MacNeil is co-anchor of public television's *MacNeil/ Lehrer NewsHour.* He was born in Montreal in 1931 and reared in the smaller city of Halifax, Nova Scotia. In this selection, MacNeil writes about the books that shaped his imagination and introduced him to "everything wise and wonderful," especially the magic of words which allowed him to expand the boundaries of his childhood world.

PREREADING: THINKING ABOUT THE ESSAY IN ADVANCE

Books can provide children with a rich fantasy world where they can escape reality, make imaginary friends, and visit imaginary worlds. But can a child become too involved with the imaginary and lose touch with reality? Or, do you think the more imaginative play through books the better for a child?

Words to Watch

time zone (par. 1) any of the twenty-four longitudinal divisions of the Earth's surface in which a standard time is kept

cosmopolitan (par. 1) so sophisticated as to be at home in all parts of the world

gossamer (par. 7) a soft, sheer, gauzy fabric

vestiges (par. 11) evidence of something that once existed but exists or appears no more

colonialism (par. 11) a policy by which a nation maintains or extends its control over foreign dependencies

psyche (par. 14) the spirit or soul

archaic language (par. 20) words once common but now used chiefly to suggest an earlier style or period

bourgeois (par. 23) a person belonging to the middle class

template (par. 28) a pattern or gauge used as a guide in making something accurately

matrix (par. 29) a situation or surrounding substance within which something else originates, develops, or is contained

placenta (par. 29) a membranous vascular organ that develops in female mammals during pregnancy

1 Nova Scotia lies one time zone closer to England than most of North America, but in the days of my childhood it was spiritually closer still. Psychologically, the province I grew up in was still in large measure a British colony. Halifax society was conditioned by the presence of generations of well-born, sometimes aristocratic, British officers and showed it. The higher up the social pecking order in that small but cosmopolitan seaport town, the more people identified with England. We looked to England for the real juice of our patriotism, our ideals of dress and manners, codes of honour, military dash, and styles of drill, marmalade and gin, pipe tobacco and tweed. We drew spiritual values from the Church of England and humour from *Punch.* It was natural, therefore, that from that fountainhead of everything wise and wonderful came the books that shaped my imagination. When the magic of words first ensnared me, they were words for the most part written in England and intended for English ears: nursery rhymes, Beatrix Potter, *Winnie-the-Pooh, Peter Pan, The Water Babies,* and *The Wind in the Willows.*

2 Obviously I must have been steeped in British middle-class idiom. After all, Canadian boys didn't say *Oh, bother!* when something annoyed them, or wear *Wellingtons* or *mackintoshes,* as Christopher Robin did, yet I knew them well. They became as familiar as the rubber boots and raincoats we wore. In spite of all this concentrated exposure to English writing, I didn't pick up and use such expressions. They accumulated in a reserve store, a second vocabulary; my dictionary of vicarious literary experience.

3 What did consciously affect me was the literary landscape. I was, and remain today, highly susceptible to the physical setting described in books. Starting with the Milne stories, part of me began inhabiting or wishing to be in the places they depicted, both the landscape and the emotional climate.

4 With a few exceptional moments, my life was unclouded and serene. There was the row over the taxi window. At the age of five I was sitting on the curb throwing stones into the street. A

taxi passed and one of my stones broke a window. The taxi stopped, the driver grabbed me and marched me up to the house. My mother reacted so strongly that he began pleading with her, "No, don't beat him. It's all right! It was just an accident."

Nothing like that ever happened to Christopher Robin. 5
Nobody threw sand in his eyes, which happened once to me, followed by an agonizing session of having them flushed out with boric acid. Nobody required him to eat everything on the plate—the liver or the scrambled egg which had long gone cold and clammy—down to the last bite, because of the starving Chinese or my moral character. The emotional climate was irresistible, I suppose, because Christopher Robin seemed to be totally in command of his world, as I manifestly was not of mine. He seemed, from a child's perspective, free from arbitrary orders. He decided when to put on his Wellingtons and when to visit his friends. He seemed to live to please himself as long as he bore the tedium of being polite to his elders.

The backdrop to the serenity of this emotional landscape 6
was a physical world which also drew me strongly. It was something else first experienced in these books. The land in a book is a magic land: the author may tell you that it is ugly and barren, devastated by storms or wars, but it will fascinate me as real landscapes often cannot. The mere fact that they form the setting for a story that draws you in, for characters you identify with, casts an enchantment over that place. So it was with the meadows, the woods, the brooks inhabited by Winnie-the-Pooh, Rabbit, Owl, Kanga, and Tigger.

This was my first experience of being drawn into the spell 7
cast by a storyteller whose words spin gossamer bonds that tie your heart and hopes to him. It was the discovery that words make another place, a place to escape to with your spirit alone. Every child entranced by reading stumbles on that blissful experience sooner or later.

For this Canadian child in the thirties there was some- 8
thing more at work. Somehow the idea was planted in me that the English landscape had a spiritual legitimacy that our Canadian landscape did not, because it was always the English landscape we read about. England was where stories were set, where people had adventures: England became the land of story books for me.

9 English woods, meadows, lanes, and villages stirred feelings that ours did not, as did the words for features of the English landscape not encountered in Canada: *commons, dells, dingles, downs, moors, fells, tarns, burns,* and *becks*—the words were heavy with the promise of adventure.

10 That played subtly into other Anglophile influences working on me and I grew up putting a special value on things English. The forces drawing me there were irresistible, like a strong elastic band pulling me to the British Isles.

11 Lots of Americans feel that. For Canadians of my generation struggling, and often losing the struggle, for a national and psychic identity, England became more real than our own world, because of the books we lived in from childhood. It has taken another generation to throw off the vestiges of that psychic colonialism I grew up with, although there are a few shreds of it still left in the Canadian psyche. The seeds of my personal struggle, my personal strain of the virus, must have been planted by the words of Milne, Stevenson, Dickens, and Barrie.

12 In the garden of the small apartment house we lived in was a very big tree. One day, filled with visions of hollow trees that people could enter, even live in, I attacked the trunk of this tree. The power of imagination or wishful thinking was so strong that it by-passed any sense of physical reality. I actually believed I could cut rooms inside the tree; or, if I made a little effort, a staircase would magically appear. I would ascend the tree into an enchanted storybook world. Under my puny hatchet, the tree suffered no more than a few nicks and I retired very disappointed. I must have been thinking of Owl's tree with its curved steps in the Hundred Acre Wood or the hollow-tree entrances to the homes of the Lost Boys in *Peter Pan.*

13 That book made a strong impression at the age of four or five. *Peter Pan* was the first story that actually frightened me a little, just enough fear to make it pleasurable. The snatching of the Lost Boys by the pirates was a moment I could laugh off only when Captain Hook got it from the crocodile which had swallowed the alarm clock, but it left a shadow of anxiety. As for Peter, I never shared his desire not to grow up. I was less moved by the pathetic need to have his shadow sewn back on than by the hard-to-define attractions I felt for Wendy, who did the sewing.

Wendy jumped into my psyche as though there had been a template for her already cut out: the sister I did not have; a subtle blend of comforting maternalism and other vaguely intuited but desirable feminine attributes. 14

(No sister, but by now I had a brother, Hugh, almost four years younger. He arrived home just before the Christmas on which we had one of the last trees with real lighted candles on the tips of its branches, as memorable for its warm wax smell as for the sight.) 15

In *Peter Pan* I do not recall being consciously aware of the language, just the stories and the characters. What surprises me now is to find how facetious Barrie's style is, full of coy nudges and arch asides, which, if I had ever noticed them, were forgotten. Even more surprising is the level of the language: 16

> Next comes Nibs, the gay and debonair, followed by Slightly, who cuts whistles out of the trees and dances ecstatically to his own tunes.

Debonair and *ecstatically* are not nowadays considered vocabulary for children under ten. But then that is true of many of the books considered appropriate to read to us fifty years ago, and probably even truer fifty years before that. 17

Certainly, *Robinson Crusoe* and *Gulliver's Travels,* written for adults, make no concessions to twentieth-century children. This is Gulliver's scene setting for the naval attack by Blefuscu on Lilliput: 18

> . . . upon this notice of an intended invasion, I avoided appearing on that side of the coast, for fear of being discovered by some of the enemy's ships, who had received no intelligence of me, all intercourse between the two empires having been strictly forbidden during the war, upon pain of death, and an embargo laid by our Emperor upon all vessels whatsoever.

What happened when I heard words I did not understand? I may have asked occasionally, but I remember clearly never wanting to interrupt the story. Either I got the drift from the context or ignored the words I did not know until some later time. That is how I find myself dealing with foreign languages: asking for translations of some words, guessing at others, remembering, forgetting, but, in net terms, the word command growing by the day. 19

20 Archaic language did not put me off. The stories had such compelling narrative ideas—Crusoe marooned alone, Gulliver in a land of people six inches tall—that I listened past the older words, listened harder. When I was aware of them they gave the stories a pleasant flavour, a little additional mystery, part of the atmosphere, like the illustrations of period costumes and weapons. It did not discourage me that Robin Hood said *methinks* and *sooth.*

> "Ah, Little John, methinks care for thine own appetite hath a share in that speech, as well as care for me. But in sooth I care not to dine alone. I would have a stranger guest, some abbot or bishop or baron, who would pay us for our hospitality. I will not dine till a guest be found, and I leave it to you three to find him."

21 In the *Just So Stories* and *The Jungle Books,* which we read in the same years, Kipling pushed his language right in front of me; I couldn't ignore it, the exotic Indian words, like *Bandarlog* and *dhak* tree, that seemed to have a taste as well as a sound; the strong names for the characters like Tabaqui the jackal, Nag the cobra, and Rikki-Tikki-Tavi, the mongoose. There were also his rhetorical devices, borrowed from the oral storytellers, repetitions like *the great grey-green, greasy Limpopo River, all set about with fever trees.* They are funny to a child and they grow hypnotic like magic incantations. The repetitions, the sing-song rhythms, and the exotic vocabulary were so suggestive that I imagined I could smell things like the perfumed smoke from the dung fire or the mysterious odour of sandalwood.

22 Kipling could make me sense a world totally beyond my experience: the heat, the dust, the smells, the clamour, the cries and noises of men and animals. The dark natural forces, like the snakes, were never sentimentalized but in Kipling's hands became both more menacing and yet more tolerable because you were permitted to know their thoughts, too.

> Nag waved to and fro, and then Rikki-Tikki heard him drinking from the biggest water jar that was used to fill the bath. "That is good," said the snake. "Now, when Karait was killed, the big man had a stick. He may have that stick still, but when he comes to bathe in the morning he will not have a stick. I shall wait here till he comes." . . . Nag coiled himself down, coil by coil, round the bulge at the bottom of the water jar, and Rikki-Tikki stayed still as death.

Robinson Crusoe was my first full-blooded adult hero and his story enthralled me. I did not know until I got to college and heard about Defoe's place in the social history of England that what I absorbed so avidly was really an exemplar of right values—a model for the emerging British middle class—God-fearing, devout, honest, hard-working, sober, and obsessively protective of property. Something quite bourgeois in me must have responded, because I felt a deepening satisfaction and security as the poor devil retrieved each useful tool or cask of gunpowder from his wrecked ship. 23

Crusoe was another fictional character instantly congenial to me. I knew that I could cope with being the lone survivor of such a disaster. Crusoe made his isolation so cosy that I envied his being alone to fend for himself so cheerfully. 24

All these stories were laying down little lessons in psychology, as well as language, and this material was not being laid down in an empty place. New pieces triggered responses from material that was already there, for example, the pleasure it gave me as Crusoe provisioned his cave. 25

Laid down is a term with many associations—the keel of a ship to be built; fruits preserved for the winter; wine laid down to age. It is the term they use in sound and videotape editing when one track or sequence has been recorded and others will be added and mixed together. 26

It must be with words as it is with music. Music heard early in life lays down a rich bed of memories against which you evaluate and absorb music encountered later. Each layer adds to the richness of your musical experience; it ingrains expectations that will govern your taste for future music and perhaps change your feelings about music you already know. Certain harmonic patterns embed themselves in your consciousness and create yearnings for repetition, so that you can relive that pleasurable disturbance of the soul. Gradually, your head becomes an unimaginably large juke box, with instantaneous recall and cross-referencing, far more sophisticated than anything man-made. 27

It is so with words and word patterns. They accumulate in layers, and as the layers thicken they govern all use and appreciation of language thenceforth. Like music, the patterns of melody, rhythm, and quality of voice become templates against which we judge the sweetness and justness of new patterns and 28 rhythms; and the patterns laid down in our memories create expectations and hungers for fulfillment again. It is the same for the bookish person and for the illiterate. Each has a mind programmed with language—from prayers, hymns, verses, jokes, patriotic texts, proverbs, folk sayings, clichés, stories, movies, radio, and television.

29 I picture each of those layers of experience and language gradually accumulating and thickening to form a kind of living matrix, nourishing like a placenta, serving as a mini-thesaurus or dictionary of quotations, yet more retrievable and interactive and richer because it is so one's own, steeped in emotional colour and personal associations.

BUILDING VOCABULARY

In groups, use these words in sentences. Then, rewrite the sentences using words that are opposite in meaning (antonyms).

a. steeped (par. 2)
b. serene (par. 4)
c. arbitrary (par. 5)
d. tedium (par. 5)
e. ascend (par. 12)
f. coy (par. 16)

THINKING CRITICALLY ABOUT THE ESSAY

Understanding the Writer's Ideas

1. Why did MacNeil find that part of him "began inhabiting or wishing to be in places" (par. 3) that the books he read depicted?
2. What does MacNeil mean when he says "words make another place"? (par. 7)
3. How would MacNeil describe vestiges of psychic colonialism?
4. MacNeil claims he attacked a tree trunk. What was behind this odd behavior?
5. Summarize MacNeil's analysis of the language level considered appropriate for children today as compared to that of the

language used in pre-twentieth-century children's stories.
6. MacNeil feels that word repetitions "borrowed from the oral storytellers" had a special effect on him. Why did they?
7. In the statement, "All these stories were laying down little lessons in psychology," what is MacNeil referring to?
8. MacNeil uses the term *laid down* to make a connection between words and music. Explain his point.
9. How does reading culminate in a "kind of living matrix," according to MacNeil? Use your own words to state the point.

Understanding the Writer's Techniques

1. State the essay's thesis in your own words.
2. Why does MacNeil's opening comparison of Halifax and England help focus this essay's main idea?
3. How does the transition word *therefore* at the end of paragraph 1 connect the essay's thesis to MacNeil's historical references to Halifax and England?
4. How are paragraphs 4 to 9 an illustration of a statement MacNeil makes at the end of paragraph 3? Identify the sentence in paragraph 3 that sets up this elaboration.
5. What comparisons does MacNeil make between his childhood experiences and those of Christopher Robin?
6. What purpose does paragraph 10 serve in relationship to the essay's thesis? Could paragraph 10 be cut from the essay?
7. Is the example MacNeil uses in paragraph 12 to define what he means by "power of imagination" convincing? Why or why not?
8. Why didn't MacNeil define all the vocabulary not commonly found in children's stories today?

Exploring the Writer's Ideas

1. Have you ever found yourself wishing to inhabit a place described in a story or shown in a movie? Why or why not?
2. Sometimes young people want to be like the characters in the fictions that they read, see, or hear. Have you ever wanted to be like someone you read about or someone in the movies or on television?

3. MacNeil found himself using British words that Canadian boys didn't use. How in your experience have you used certain words or phrases that are not commonly used in your community or home?
4. Given that America, like Canada, was a British colony and American children still read *Winnie-the-Pooh,* do you think we too are "losing the struggle for a national and psychic identity," as MacNeil claims? Do American children have a literature of their own? Why or why not?
5. Do you believe that children's stories can overpower a young person's imagination to the extent that the stories can lead children to bypass a sense of physical reality? Explain.
6. Try reading a story that is on a language level well above your own, or try reading something that uses archaic language like Middle English or Elizabethan English. Then reflect on whether or not MacNeil is right that such difficult words can give the reader a "pleasant flavour."
7. Do you believe that word repetitions, sing-song rhythms, and exotic language can really make us (the readers) smell and experience things in a story? Why or why not?
8. What is your understanding of MacNeil's idea that interactions with language can create a "large juke box" or "living matrix" in the reader's head. Do you agree or disagree?

IDEAS FOR WRITING

Prewriting

Make a list of children's stories that you read or heard as a child and note the feelings you still have about these stories.

Guided Writing

Write an essay that explores your experiences with children's stories and how these stories have affected your feelings about language and words.

1. In the beginning, describe the kind of language used in your community or social group and contrast it with the kind of language (and community) found in the children's stories

you've read (or heard). What are the similarities and differences?

2. Elaborate on whether or not you found the emotional lives of the characters in your children's stories meaningful to you. Why or why not?
3. Reflect on how the physical landscape of your storybook world was similar to or different from your physical world. Tell if you would rather have lived in the storybook landscape as opposed to your own. For example, if you read about castles, did you want to live in a castle instead of your two-bedroom apartment? Why?
4. Elaborate on whether or not any of the children's stories you've read captured your imagination to the extent that you lost all sense of physical reality.
5. Tell if any children's story ever frightened you or helped you solve a problem.
6. Analyze the language level of the children's stories you read. Were they written with a pre-twentieth-century vocabulary? Why or why not? Give examples.
7. Conclude with an examination of whether or not your experiences with children's stories have laid down associations with words and word patterns that now govern your taste or interest in certain kind of literature. Did your early experiences with children's literature make you "hunger" for more experiences with language and reading? Explain.

Thinking and Writing Collaboratively

Form groups of three students each, and read drafts of each other's essays for the Guided Writing activity. Has the writer analyzed the vocabulary clearly? What suggestions can you make to improve the next draft?

More Writing Projects

1. In your journal, describe an experience you've had doing something that required using your imagination, such as an art project, a problem-solving activity, or the decoration in your room.

2. Write a paragraph that argues the pros and cons of allowing children to escape into fantasy worlds.
3. Write an essay that answers this question: If you could escape into a fantasy word of your own making, what would it be and why?

SUMMING UP: CHAPTER 2

1. In one way or another, all the writers in this chapter explain how reading has provided them with emotional ease or intellectual stimulation at some point in their lives. Which of these writers, alone or in combination, best reflects your own view of reading? Write an essay in which you address this question.
2. On the average, Americans are said to read less than one book per person annually. Take a survey of several people who are not students to find out how often and what kind of books they read. In an essay, analyze the results. Indicate the types of people you interviewed, and explain why your results either conformed to or differed from the norm. Indicate the types of books each person read.
3. List all the books you have read in the past six months. For each, write a brief two- or three-sentence reaction. Compare your list with those of your classmates. What reading trends do you notice? From these lists, what generalizations can you draw about college students' reading habits?
4. The United States ranks forty-ninth among nations in literacy. People often ask, "Why is there such a low rate of literacy in such an advanced nation?" What is your answer to this question? How do you think the writers in this chapter would respond to the question? Write an essay that explains your response by drawing on Welty, Malcolm X, Frisina, and MacNeil. Suggest some ways to improve the rate of literacy in this country. You might want to consider this fact: By the time the average American finishes high school, he or she has spent 18,000 hours in front of a television set as compared to 12,000 hours in the classroom.
5. Using Welty or MacNeil as an example, write an essay in which you reflect on your early memories of reading. Describe when you learned to read, when you experienced pleasure at being read to, or when you started appreciating a particular kind of reading. Call your essay "Reading When I Was Young."

CHAPTER 3

Description

WHAT IS DESCRIPTION?

Description is a technique for showing readers what the writer sees: objects, scenes, characters, ideas, and even emotions and moods. Good description relies on the use of *sensory language*—that is, language that evokes our five senses of sight, touch, taste, smell, and sound. In writing, description uses specific *nouns* and *adjectives* to create carefully selected vivid details. The word "vehicle" is neutral, but a "rusty, green 1959 Pontiac convertible" creates a picture. Description is frequently used to make *abstract* ideas more *concrete.* While the abstract word "liberty" may have a definition for each reader, a description of the Statue of Liberty gleaming in New York's harbor at twilight creates an emotional description of liberty. Description, then, is used by writers who want their readers to *see* what they are writing about. A writer like Louise Erdrich uses description of the natural world to reflect on being a parent. A physician, like Richard Selzer, uses description to re-create the experience of a dying patient. Maxine Hong Kingston uses vivid description of her mother's collection of turtles, catfish, pigeons, skunks, and other unexpected food sources to re-create for her readers a culture different from their own. Akira Kurosawa relies on description to capture the concrete details of childhood. Each writer, then, uses description to help us, as readers, *see* the material about which he or she is writing. As writers, we can study their techniques to improve our own essays.

HOW DO WE READ DESCRIPTION?

Reading a descriptive essay requires us to

- Identify what the writer is describing, and ask why he or she is describing it.
- Look for the concrete nouns, supportive adjectives, or other sensory words that the writer uses to create vivid pictures.
- Find the perspective or angle from which the writer describes: Is it top to bottom, left to right, front to back? Or is it a mood description that relies on feelings? How has the writer *selected* details to create the mood?
- Determine how the writer has organized the description. Here we must look for a "dominant impression." This arises from the writer's focus on a single subject and the feelings that the writer brings to that subject. Each one should be identified.
- Identify the purpose of the description. What is the *thesis* of the writing?
- Determine what audience the writer is aiming toward. How do we know?

HOW DO WE WRITE DESCRIPTION?

After reading some of the selections of descriptive writing in this chapter, you should be ready to write your own description. Don't just read about Kingston's animals, though, or Erdrich's blue jay. Think critically about how you can adapt their methods to your needs.

Select a topic and begin to write a thesis statement, keeping in mind that you will want to give the reader information about what you are describing and what angle you are taking on the topic.

Sample thesis sentence:

> For a first-time tourist in New York City, the subway trains can seem confusing and threatening, but the long-time resident finds the train system a clever, speedy network for traveling around the city.

Here, we see the thesis statement sets out a purpose and an audience. The purpose is to demonstrate the virtues of the New

York transit system, and the audience is not the well-traveled New Yorker, but a visitor.

Collect a list of sensory words.

> New York City's subway trains are noisy and crowded, labeled with brightly colored letters, made of shiny corrugated stainless steel, travel at 90 miles per hour, display colorful graffiti and advertising signs, run on electricity.

Use the five senses:

What are subways sounds? Music by street musicians, the screech of brakes, conductors giving directions over scratchy loudspeakers, people talking in different languages.

What are subway smells? Pretzels roasting, the sweaty odor of human bodies crowded together on a hot summer day.

What are subway textures? Colored metal straps and poles for balance, the crisp corner of a newspaper you're reading.

What are subway tastes? A candy bar or chewing gum you buy at the newsstand.

What are subway sights? Crowds of people rushing to work; the colorful pillars freshly painted in each station; the drunk asleep on a bench; the police officer in a blue uniform; the litter on the ground; the subway system maps near each token booth; the advertising posters on the walls and trains.

Plan a dominant impression and an order for arranging details. You might look at the subway from a passenger's point of view and describe the travel process from getting onto the train to arriving at the destination. Your impression might be that to the uninitiated, the subway system seems confusing, but to the experienced New Yorker, trains are the fastest and safest way to get around town.

Express a *purpose* for the description. The purpose might be to prepare a visitor from out of town for her first subway ride by writing a letter to her before she arrives in New York.

Identify the audience: Who will read the essay?

If you were writing to the Commissioner of Transportation in New York, or to a cousin from Iowa whom you know well, you would write differently in each case. Awareness of audience can help you choose a level of diction and formality. Knowing your audience can also help you decide which details to include and which your readers might know. It is always best to assume that the audience knows less than you do and to include details even if they seem obvious to you.

For example, even if you, as a native New Yorker, know that subway trains run twenty-four hours a day, your cousin from Iowa would not be expected to know this, so you should include it as part of your description of how efficient the system is.

Writing the Draft

Use the thesis statement to set up an introductory paragraph. Then plan the body paragraphs so that they follow the order you decided on—from beginning the journey to arriving, from the top of a subway car to the bottom, or from the outside of the train to the inside. Include as many details in the first draft as possible; it is easier to take them out in a second or third draft than to add them later. Then plan the conclusion to help the reader understand what the purpose of the description has been.

Reading and Revising the Draft

Read your first draft, circling each description word. Then go back and add *another* description word after the ones already in the essay. If you can't think of any more words, use a *thesaurus* to find new words.

If possible, read your essay aloud to a classmate. Ask him or her to tell you if the details are vivid. Have your classmate suggest where more details are needed. Check to see that you have included some description in each sensory category: sight, sound, taste, touch, and smell.

Proofread your essay for correctness.

Make a clean, neat final copy.

The Blue Jay's Dance

Louise Erdrich

Louise Erdrich, the daughter of a German immigrant and a Chippewa Indian, is best known for her novels *Love Medicine* (1984) and *Beet Queen* (1986). Note in this descriptive essay how she uses images of a hawk and a blue jay to reflect on parents' responsibilities in protecting their children.

PREREADING: THINKING ABOUT THE ESSAY IN ADVANCE

What are a parent's responsibilities to a child? What struggles do you see a parent enduring to keep a child safe from harm? When does the parent's obligation to protecting the child stop? Does it ever stop?

Words to Watch

raucous (par. 2) rough-sounding and harsh

feints (par. 3) attacks in a manner designed to draw defensive action away from an intended target

manic (par. 4) excessively intense or enthusiastic

clench (par. 4) close tightly

differentiating (par. 4) to show the difference in or between

1 The hawk sweeps over, light shining through her rust red tail. She makes an immaculate cross in flight, her shadow running along the ground behind her as I'm walking below. Our shadows join, momentarily, and then separate, both to our appointed rounds. Always, she hunts flying into the cast of the sun, making a pass east to west. Once inside, I settle baby, resettle baby, settle and resettle myself, and have just lowered my head into my hands to proofread a page when a blur outside my vision causes me to look up.

The hawk drops headfirst out of a cloud. She folds her wings hard against her and plunges into the low branches of the apple tree, moving at such dazzling speed I can barely follow. She strikes at one of the seven blue jays who make up the raucous gang and it tumbles before her, head over feet, end over end. She plunges after it from the branches, flops in the sun. They both light on the ground and square off, about a foot apart in the snow. 2

The struck jay thrusts out its head, screams, raises its wings, and dances *toward* the gray hawk. The plain of snow must seem endless, an arena without shelter, and the bird gets no help from the other six jays except loud encouragement at a safe distance. I hardly breathe. The hawk, on the ground, its wings clattering against the packed crust, is so much larger than its shadow, which has long brushed in and out of mine. It screams back, eyes filled with yellow light. Its hooked beak opens and it feints with its neck. Yet the jay, ridiculous, continues to dance, hopping forward, hornpiping up and down with tiny leaps, all of its feathers on end to increase its size. Its crest is sharp, its beak open in a continual shriek, its eye-mask fierce. It pedals its feet in the air. The hawk steps backward. She seems confused, cocks her head, and does not snap the blue jay's neck. She watches. Although I know nothing of the hawk and cannot imagine what moves her, it does seem to me that she is fascinated, that she puzzles at the absurd display before she raises her wings and lifts off. 3

Past the gray moralizing and the fierce Roman Catholic embrace of suffering and fate that so often clouds the subject of suicide, there is the blue jay's dance. Beyond the impossible corners, stark cliffs, dark wells of trapped longing, there is that manic, successful jig—cocky, exuberant, entirely a bluff, a joke. That dance makes me clench down hard on life. But it is also a dance that in other circumstances might lead me, you, anyone, to choose a voluntary death. I see in that small bird's crazy courage some of what it took for my grandparents to live out the tough times. I peer around me, stroke my own skin, look into this baby's eyes that register me as a blurred self-extension, as a function of her will. I have made a pact with life: if I were to die now it would be a form of suicide for her. Since the two of us are still in the process of differentiating, since my acts are hers and I do 4 not even think, yet, where I stop for her or where her needs, exactly, begin, I must dance for her. I must be the one to dip and twirl in the cold glare and I must teach her, as she grows, the unlikely steps.

BUILDING VOCABULARY

Denotation refers to the dictionary definition of a word; *connotation* refers to the various shades of meaning and feelings readers bring to a word or phrase (see Glossary). Look up and write the dictionary definition for each of the words in italics. Then explain in your own words the connotative meaning of each sentence or phrase.

a. She makes an *immaculate* cross in flight (par. 1)
b. They both *light* on the ground and square off (par. 2)
c. The *struck* jay . . . dances toward the gray hawk. (par. 3)
d. Past the gray *moralizing* . . . there is the blue jay's dance. (par. 4)
e. *twirl* in the cold glare (par. 4)

THINKING CRITICALLY ABOUT THE ESSAY

Understanding the Writer's Ideas

1. What was the writer doing when she first looked up at the hawk? What does this tell us about the observer?
2. Why does the writer say the blue jay is "ridiculous" in paragraph 3?
3. What is Erdrich referring to in paragraph 4—the "Roman Catholic embrace of suffering and fate that so often clouds the subject of suicide"?
4. What tough times might Erdrich's grandparents have had to endure?
5. What does Erdrich mean when she says "I must dance for her"? To whom does she refer? To what dance? What is the dance's connection to the hawk?
6. What are the "unlikely steps" Erdrich concludes that she needs to teach her child? Explain.

Understanding the Writer's Techniques

1. What is the essay's thesis? How is it implied in the descriptive details of the hawk?
2. For the first three paragraphs Erdrich focuses purely on descriptive detail, but in paragraph 4 she shifts to first person narration. What impact does this have on the reader?
3. In the first sentence of paragraph 4, Erdrich writes about "gray moralizing." Can moralizing be gray or any color? (Look up the word *moralizing* in a dictionary.) Why is Erdrich using color in this way?
4. How does the essay's conclusion actually refer back to the beginning?

Exploring the Writer's Ideas

1. This essay begins with a powerful predator, the hawk, flying over a mother (the writer) settling her baby. Do you think the writer wants the reader to get the idea that the hawk might actually swoop down on this woman's child and not just the blue jay? Why or why not?
2. When the blue jay confronts the more powerful hawk, Erdrich says the jay is "ridiculous." Do you agree?
3. How would you explain the hawk's quick retreat after confronting the weaker blue jay, who "dances"?
4. Where does Erdrich get the idea that Roman Catholics embrace "suffering and fate"? What does she mean? Is she accurate?
5. Erdrich takes the position that if a mother chooses death (when confronting a stronger foe), this would be a form of suicide, and it would leave the child without protection. Is Erdrich overstating this situation? What do you think?
6. If you were to create a different title for the essay, what would it be? Explain.

IDEAS FOR WRITING

Prewriting

Make a list of the various ways that you think parents or guardians must protect children under their care.

Guided Writing

Write an essay on what you think is the single greatest threat to children today and what parents can do about it.

1. As an image to start your essay, choose a creature (the threat) that preys on smaller creatures (the child) and explore the image in at least two descriptive paragraphs. Follow Erdrich's lead and do not make the link until later in the essay between these creatures and the idea of protecting the child.
2. Rely on concrete sensory detail to paint vivid pictures of the creatures you are describing. Use verbs that indicate precise actions; use specific nouns as opposed to too many adjectives.
3. Use a transition to bring together your view of how the creature's attack is similar to or different from the threat to children that you are writing about.
4. Explain why a caregiver should (or should not) intervene to protect a child from this threat.
5. Take a final position on how far you think a parent or guardian should go to protect his or her child. Should parents or guardians sacrifice their own lives to protect their children?

Thinking and Writing Collaboratively

Form groups of three or four students, and read your essays aloud. As a group, write a summary review of the main threats your group thinks face children today. Was there agreement on the dangers? How would the group rank these threats by importance?

More Writing Projects

1. Use your journal to record your worst or best dreams.
2. Write a descriptive paragraph that uses sensory detail to recreate one of your best or worst dreams.
3. Do the following: Imagine you are standing on the edge of the universe. You look over the edge and what you see is the ideal place to raise a child. Write an essay that describes that place.

Catfish in the Bathtub

Maxine Hong Kingston

In this selection from her best-selling *The Woman Warrior* (1976), Chinese-American author Maxine Hong Kingston describes various strange eating habits of her childhood. The author skillfully blends techniques of personal narration and rich sensory detailing to create a fascinating impression of another culture's daily lifestyle.

PREREADING: THINKING ABOUT THE ESSAY IN ADVANCE

What unusual foods have you eaten? What unusual dish can you remember one of your relatives preparing when you were a child? How did you feel about eating this food?

Words to Watch

dromedaries (par. 1) one-humped camels
sensibility (par. 1) ability to receive sensations
perched (par. 1) resting on a bird's roost
scowls (par. 1) expressions of displeasure
dismembering (par. 1) taking apart bodily limbs and innards
sprains (par. 2) sudden twists of joints such as ankles or wrists
unsettle (par. 3) make uneasy or uncomfortable
tufts (par. 4) forms into small patches of hair
awobble (par. 6) unsteady; teetering
toadstools (par. 7) mushrooms
revulsion (par. 8) a strong reaction away from something

1 My mother has cooked for us: raccoons, skunks, hawks, city pigeons, wild ducks, wild geese, black-skinned bantams, snakes, garden snails, turtles that crawled about the pantry floor and sometimes escaped under refrigerator or stove, catfish that swam in the bathtub. "The emperors used to eat the peaked hump of purple

dromedaries," she would say. "They used chopsticks made from rhinoceros horn, and they ate ducks' tongues and monkeys' lips." She boiled the weeds we pulled up in the yard. There was a tender plant with flowers like white stars hiding under the leaves, which were like the flower petals but green. I've not been able to find it since growing up. It had no taste. When I was as tall as the washing machine, I stepped out on the back porch one night, and some heavy, ruffling, windy, clawed thing dived at me. Even after getting chanted back to sensibility, I shook when I recalled that perched everywhere there were owls with great hunched shoulders and yellow scowls. They were a surprise for my mother from my father. We children used to hide under the beds with our fingers in our ears to shut out the bird screams and the thud, thud of the turtles swimming in the boiling water, their shells hitting the sides of the pot. Once the third aunt who worked at the laundry ran out and bought us bags of candy to hold over our noses; my mother was dismembering skunk on the chopping block. I could smell the rubbery odor through the candy.

2 In a glass jar on a shelf my mother kept a big brown hand with pointed claws stewing in alcohol and herbs. She must have brought it from China because I do not remember a time when I did not have the hand to look at. She said it was a bear's claw, and for many years I thought bears were hairless. My mother used the tobacco, leeks, and grasses swimming about the hand to rub our sprains and bruises.

3 Just as I would climb up to the shelf to take one look after another at the hand, I would hear my mother's monkey story. I'd take my fingers out of my ears and let her monkey words enter my brain. I did not always listen voluntarily, though. She would begin telling the story, perhaps repeating it to a homesick villager, and I'd overhear before I had a chance to protect myself. Then the monkey words would unsettle me; a curtain flapped loose inside my brain. I have wanted to say, "Stop it. Stop it," but not once did I say, "Stop it."

4 "Do you know what people in China eat when they have the money?" my mother began. "They buy into a monkey feast. The eaters sit around a thick wood table with a hole in the middle. Boys bring in the monkey at the end of a pole. Its neck is in a collar at the end of the pole, and it is screaming. Its hands are tied behind it. They clamp the monkey into the table; the whole table fits like

another collar around its neck. Using a surgeon's saw, the cooks cut a clean line in a circle at the top of its head. To loosen the bone, they tap with a tiny hammer and wedge here and there with a silver pick. Then an old woman reaches out her hand to the monkey's face and up to its scalp, where she tufts some hairs and lifts off the lid of the skull. The eaters spoon out the brains."

Did she say, "You should have seen the faces the monkey made"? Did she say, "The people laughed at the monkey screaming"? It was alive? The curtain flaps closed like merciful black wings. 5

"Eat! Eat!" my mother would shout at our heads bent over bowls, the blood pudding awobble in the middle of the table. 6

She had one rule to keep us safe from toadstools and such: "If it tastes good, it's bad for you," she said. "If it tastes bad, it's good for you." 7

We'd have to face four- and five-day-old leftovers until we ate it all. The squid eye would keep appearing at breakfast and dinner until eaten. Sometimes brown masses sat on every dish. I have seen revulsion on the faces of visitors who've caught us at meals. 8

"Have you eaten yet?" the Chinese greet one another. 9

"Yes, I have," they answer whether they have or not. "And you?" 10

I would live on plastic. 11

BUILDING VOCABULARY

1. Go through this essay again and list every animal mentioned. Then, write a short description of each, using the dictionary or encyclopedia if necessary.
2. Use any five of the Words to Watch in sentences of your own.

THINKING CRITICALLY ABOUT THE ESSAY

Understanding the Writer's Ideas

1. What is Kingston saying about her childhood? How does her opening catalogue of foods that her mother prepared, combined with further descriptions of foods, support this point?

What are some of the "strange" foods that she ate but that are not mentioned in this first paragraph?

2. Who are "the emperors" mentioned in paragraph 1? What were some of their more unusual dishes?
3. What attacks and frightens the young Kingston on her back porch? Where did they come from? How do we know that she was a young girl at the time? Explain the meaning of "even after getting chanted back to sensibility."
4. At the end of the first paragraph, the author mentions methods she and her siblings used to shut out unpleasant sensory input. What were they?
5. For what purpose did her mother keep a bear's claw in a glass jar? Where did Kingston think it came from? Why?
6. What are the "monkey words"? Summarize the "monkey words" in your own language. Kingston says that she wanted to say "Stop it" to the monkey words, but didn't. Why didn't she?
7. What was Kingston's mother's attitude toward the taste of things in relation to their healthfulness?
8. Why would there sometimes be "revulsion on the faces of visitors" who watched the author's family eating?
9. What is the traditional Chinese greeting?
10. What is the author's overall attitude toward her mother? Explain.

Understanding the Writer's Techniques

1. Does Kingston ever make a direct *thesis statement?* Why or why not?
2. In this essay, Kingston seems to shift in and out of various tenses deliberately. For example, in paragraph 3, she writes: ". . . a curtain *flapped* loose inside my brain. I *have wanted* to say. . . ." Why do you think that Kingston uses such a technique? List three other examples of such tense shifts.
3. Comment on Kingston's use of transitions. How do they contribute to the overall *coherence* (see Glossary) of the essay?
4. How does Kingston use the five senses to create descriptive imagery? Give examples of her use of sounds, tastes, smells, sights, and feelings. Which are the most effective?

5. Eliminating the specific references to China, how do we know that the author is of Chinese background? Which details or references contribute to this understanding?
6. Evaluate the use of *dialogue* (records of spoken words or conversations) in this essay. What effect does it have on the flow of the writing? On our understanding of Kingston's main point?
7. In paragraph 1, why does the author give so much attention to the white flower stars with no taste? Is she merely describing yet another thing she ate, or does she have some other purpose? Explain.
8. Although other incidents or ideas are described rather briefly, Kingston devotes a full, detailed paragraph to a description of the monkey feast. Why?
9. Throughout the essay, Kingston combines very realistic description (the bear's claw, the turtles thudding against the cook pot, the monkey feast) with various *similes* and *metaphors* (see Glossary). Explain the meaning of the following uses of *figurative language* (see Glossary):
   a. a curtain flapped loose inside my brain (par. 3)
   b. The curtain flaps closed like merciful black wings. (par. 5)
   c. Sometimes brown masses sat on every dish. (par. 8)
10. What is the effect of the series of questions in paragraph 5? Why are some in quotations and others not?
11. Explain the meaning of the last sentence. How does it relate to Kingston's *purpose* (see Glossary) in this essay?

Exploring the Writer's Ideas

1. Kingston certainly describes some "strange" foods and eating habits in this essay. But, what makes particular foods "strange"? What are some of the strangest foods you have ever eaten? Where did they come from? Why did you eat them? How did you react to them? What foods or eating habits that are common to your everyday life might be considered strange by people from other cultures?
2. In this essay, Kingston concentrates on her mother, mentioning her father only once. Speculate on why she excludes her father in this way, but base your speculation on the material of the essay.

3. As we all know, different cultures have very different customs. In this essay, for example, the author describes the Chinese way of greeting one another as well as the monkey feast, both of which are quite foreign to American culture. Describe different cultural customs that you have observed in your school, among your friends, in places around your city or town. How do you feel when you observe customs different from the ones you are familiar with? Do you believe that any particular custom is "right" or "wrong"? Why? Which custom among your own culture's would you most like to see changed? Why?
4. Describe your reaction to the monkey feast description.
5. For what reason do you think the Chinese greet each other with the words "Have you eaten yet?" Attempt to do further research on this custom. List as many different ways as you know of people greeting one another.

IDEAS FOR WRITING

Prewriting

Write the words *Family Food* on top of a sheet of paper and write everything that comes to mind about the topic. Give yourself about five minutes or so. Do not edit your writing: put as many of your ideas as you can on paper.

Guided Writing

Write an essay entitled "Food" in which you describe its importance to you, your family, and your cultural background.

1. Begin with a list of important foods related to your family's life-style.
2. Show the role of your parents or other relatives in relation to these foods.
3. Briefly tell about an incident involving food that affected you deeply.
4. Create strong sensory imagery. Attempt to use at least one image for each of the five senses.

5. If possible, relate food customs to your family's ethnic or cultural background.
6. Use dialogue in your essay, including some of the dialogue of your "inner voice."
7. Use transitions to make the parts of your essay cohere.
8. Mention how outsiders experienced this custom.
9. End your essay with a direct statement to summarize your current attitude toward the food you have described and those times in your life.

Thinking and Writing Collaboratively

Read a draft of the Guided Writing essay by one of your classmates. Then, write a paragraph to indicate what you learned about the importance of food to the writer and to his or her family and cultural background. What parts of the essay stand out most in your mind? Where do you think the writer might have included further details?

More Writing Projects

1. In your journal, write a description of an interesting custom or activity that you witnessed, a custom coming from outside your own cultural or social background. Include vivid sensory details.
2. Describe in detail the most wonderful meal you have ever eaten.
3. Research and write a short report about the food and eating customs of a culture other than your own.

The Discus Thrower

Richard Selzer

Richard Selzer, a surgeon, gives his readers vivid insights into the excitement as well as the pathos of the world of medicine. His books include *Rituals of Surgery* (1974) and *Mortal Lessons* (1977). His essays are widely published in magazines, including *Esquire, Harper's,* and *Redbook.* In this essay, Selzer dramatically describes a patient's final day.

PREREADING: THINKING ABOUT THE ESSAY IN ADVANCE

What experiences have you had with hospital patients? Have you ever visited anyone in a hospital? What was the experience like? What did the patient look like?

Words to Watch

furtive (par. 1) sly

pruned (par. 2) cut back; trimmed

facsimile (par. 2) an exact copy

forceps (par. 19) an instrument used in operations for holding or pulling

shard (par. 19) a broken piece; fragment

athwart (par. 20) across

probes (par. 32) investigates thoroughly

hefts (par. 32) tests the weight of by lifting; heaves

1 I spy on my patients. Ought not a doctor to observe his patients by any means and from any stance, that he might the more fully assemble evidence? So I stand in the doorways of hospital rooms and gaze. Oh, it is not all that furtive an act. Those in bed need only look up to discover me. But they never do.

2 From the doorway of Room 542 the man in the bed seems deeply tanned. Blue eyes and close-cropped white hair give him

the appearance of vigor and good health. But I know that his skin is not brown from the sun. It is rusted, rather, in the last stage of containing the vile repose within. And the blue eyes are frosted, looking inward like the windows of a snowbound cottage. This man is blind. This man is also legless—the right leg missing from midthigh down, the left from just below the knee. It gives him the look of a bonsai, roots and branches pruned into the dwarfed facsimile of a great tree.

Propped on pillows, he cups his right thigh in both hands. 3 Now and then he shakes his head as though acknowledging the intensity of his suffering. In all of this he makes no sound. Is he mute as well as blind?

The room in which he dwells is empty of all possessions— 4 no get-well cards, small, private caches of food, day-old flowers, slippers, all the usual kick-shaws of the sickroom. There is only the bed, a chair, a nightstand, and a tray on wheels that can be swung across his lap for meals.

"What time is it?" he asks. 5

"Three o'clock." 6

"Morning or afternoon?" 7

"Afternoon." 8

He is silent. There is nothing else he wants to know. 9

"How are you?" I say. 10

"Who is it?" he asks. 11

"It's the doctor. How do you feel?" 12

He does not answer right away. 13

"Feel?" he says. 14

"I hope you feel better," I say. 15

I press the button at the side of the bed. 16

"Down you go," I say. 17

"Yes, down," he says. 18

He falls back upon the bed awkwardly. His stumps, 19 unweighted by legs and feet, rise in the air, presenting themselves. I unwrap the bandages from the stumps, and begin to cut away the black scabs and the dead, glazed fat with scissors and forceps. A shard of white bone comes loose. I pick it away. I wash the wounds with disinfectant and redress the stumps. All this while, he does not speak. What is he thinking behind those lids that do not blink? Is he remembering a time when he was whole? Does he dream of feet? Of when his body was not a rotting log?

20 He lies solid and inert. In spite of everything, he remains impressive, as though he were a sailor standing athwart a slanting deck.

21 "Anything more I can do for you?" I ask.

22 For a long moment he is silent.

23 "Yes," he says at last and without the least irony. "You can bring me a pair of shoes."

24 In the corridor, the head nurse is waiting for me.

25 "We have to do something about him," she says. "Every morning he orders scrambled eggs for breakfast, and, instead of eating them, he picks up the plate and throws it against the wall."

26 "Throws his plate?"

27 "Nasty. That's what he is. No wonder his family doesn't come to visit. They probably can't stand him any more than we can."

28 She is waiting for me to do something.

29 "Well?"

30 "We'll see," I say.

31 The next morning I am waiting in the corridor when the kitchen delivers his breakfast. I watch the aide place the tray on the stand and swing it across his lap. She presses the button to raise the head of the bed. Then she leaves.

32 In time the man reaches to find the rim of the tray, then on to find the dome of the covered dish. He lifts off the cover and places it on the stand. He fingers across the plate until he probes the eggs. He lifts the plate in both hands, sets it on the palm of his right hand, centers it, balances it. He hefts it up and down slightly, getting the feel of it. Abruptly, he draws back his right arm as far as he can.

33 There is the crack of the plate breaking against the wall at the foot of his bed and the small wet sound of the scrambled eggs dropping to the floor.

34 And then he laughs. It is a sound you have never heard. It is something new under the sun. It could cure cancer.

35 Out in the corridor, the eyes of the head nurse narrow.

36 "Laughed, did he?"

37 She writes something down on her clipboard.

38 A second aide arrives, brings a second breakfast tray, puts it on the nightstand, out of his reach. She looks over at me shaking her head and making her mouth go. I see that we are to be accomplices.

"I've got to feed you," she says to the man. 39

"Oh, no you don't," the man says. 40

"Oh, yes I do," the aide says, "after the way you just did. 41
Nurse says so."

"Get me my shoes," the man says. 42

"Here's oatmeal," the aide says. "Open." And she touches 43
the spoon to his lower lip.

"I ordered scrambled eggs," says the man. 44

"That's right," the aide says. 45

I step forward. 46

"Is there anything I can do?" I say. 47

"Who are you?" the man asks. 48

In the evening I go once more to that ward to make my 49
rounds. The head nurse reports to me that Room 542 is deceased. She has discovered this quite by accident, she says. No, there had been no sound. Nothing. It's a blessing, she says.

I go into his room, a spy looking for secrets. He is still there 50
in his bed. His face is relaxed, grave, dignified. After a while, I turn to leave. My gaze sweeps the wall at the foot of the bed, and I see the place where it has been repeatedly washed, where the wall looks very clean and very white.

BUILDING VOCABULARY

1. In this essay, Selzer uses a few words that derive from languages other than English. Look up the following words and tell what language they come from. Then, write a definition for each.
   a. bonsai (par. 2)
   b. caches (par. 4)
   c. kick-shaws (par. 4)
2. Use these words from the essay in complete sentences of your own.
   a. vile (par. 2)
   b. repose (par. 2)
   c. dwarfed (par. 2)
   d. glazed (par. 19)
   e. inert (par. 20)
   f. accomplices (par. 38)

THINKING CRITICALLY ABOUT THE ESSAY

Understanding the Writer's Ideas

1. What reason does Selzer give for a doctor's spying on his patients?
2. What does the man in Room 542 look like? Why is his skin brown? How does Selzer know he is blind? Why does Selzer think the patient may be mute? When do we know that he is not mute?
3. What is the author's meaning of the phrase "vile repose" (par. 2)?
4. How do we know that this patient does not receive many visitors?
5. Aside from wanting to know the time of day, what is the patient's one request? Do you think he is serious about his request? Why?
6. Why does the patient hurl his food tray against the wall?
7. For what reason does the head nurse complain about the patient?
8. What does Selzer feel and think about the patient? How do you know?

Understanding the Writer's Techniques

1. What is the author's thesis? Where is it stated?
2. Throughout the essay, Selzer asks a number of questions. Locate at least three of these questions that are not a part of the dialogue. To whom do you think they are addressed? What is their effect on the reader?
3. Selzer heightens the description by making vivid and unusual comparisons. Locate and explain in your own words three comparisons that you feel are especially descriptive and intriguing.
4. Selzer uses some very short sentences interspersed among longer ones. Locate at least four very short sentences. How do they draw your attention to the description?
5. Locate in Selzer's essay at least five examples of vivid description (imagery) relating to illness. What is their emotional effect on the reader?

6. How does Selzer use *dialogue* to reveal the personality of the patient? of the doctor? of the head nurse?
7. In paragraph 23, Selzer states that the patient delivers his request "without the least irony." *Irony* (see Glossary) is saying what is opposite to what one means. Why might Selzer have expected irony from the patient? Why might someone in the sick man's condition use irony? What do you think the man means by his request "You can bring me a pair of shoes"—if, in fact, the remark is not an ironical one?
8. What does the title of the essay mean? What is a discus thrower? Why has Selzer chosen an ancient image of an athlete as the title of this essay? In what way is the title ironic?
9. Why does Selzer use such an unusual word as *kick-shaws* (par. 4)?
10. *Double entendre* is a French expression that indicates that something has a double meaning, each equally valid. What might be the two meanings of the nurse's words "It's a blessing"?
11. In this essay, the author uses a *framing* device: that is, he opens and closes the essay with a similar image or idea. What is that idea? Why is it effective? What are the differences in the use of this idea in the opening and closing paragraphs?
12. The heart of this essay is the patient's insistence upon throwing his breakfast plate at the wall, and yet Selzer does not attempt to explain the man's reasons for such an act. Why do you think the man hurls his breakfast across the room each morning—and why does he laugh? Why does Selzer not provide an analysis of the action? How does the title help us see Selzer's attitude toward the man's act?

Exploring the Writer's Ideas

1. In the beginning of the essay Selzer asks, "Ought not a doctor to observe his patients by any means from any stance, that he might the more fully assemble evidence?" Do you feel that a doctor should have this right? Why? What rights do you believe patients should have in a hospital?
2. The head nurse in Selzer's description seems fed up with the patient in Room 542. Why do you think she feels this

way? Do you think that a person in her position has the right to express this feeling on his or her job? Why or why not?

3. The patient's attitude is influenced by his physical state and his nearness to death. How have physical ailments or handicaps changed the attitudes of people you have known? Has an illness influenced your thoughts at any time?

IDEAS FOR WRITING

Prewriting

How can you tell when a person is ill or under stress? Make a list of the behavioral qualities that tell you that the person is not him- or herself.

Guided Writing

Describe a person you have observed who was seriously ill, in danger, or under great stress.

1. Base your description on close observation of the person during a short but concentrated span of time: a morning or afternoon, an hour or two, even a few minutes.
2. Begin with a short, direct paragraph in which you introduce the person and the critical situation he or she faces.
3. Include yourself ("I") in the description.
4. Describe the vantage point from which you are "spying" or observing, and focus on the particular subject of the scene.
5. Throughout your essay, ask key questions.
6. Use imagery and original comparisons to highlight the description of your subject.
7. Include some dialogue with either the subject or another person.
8. Describe at least one very intense action performed by your subject.
9. Tell how the subject and scene had changed when you next saw them.

Thinking and Writing Collaboratively

Assisted suicide for terminally ill patients has received a great deal of attention in the national press recently. Form discussion groups of about five students and consider the issue. Then, have the group write a paragraph summarizing its views on a patient's "right to die."

More Writing Projects

1. In your journal, describe a hospital room in which you stayed or visited some other person. Focus on your sensory perceptions of the place.
2. Describe in an extended paragraph an interaction you had with a person who was blind or deaf or was disabled in some other way. In your description, focus closely on the person's features. Write about your reactions during and after the interaction.
3. Using both description and commentary, analyze the people you observe in one of the following situations: a bus or train during rush hour; breakfast at a diner or restaurant; a sports event or concert. Incorporate the description and observation into a five-paragraph essay.

Babyhood

Akira Kurosawa

Akira Kurosawa is the most famous Japanese film director in the West. Born in 1910, his reputation soared with a series of sword-fight epic movies such as *The Seven Samurai* (1954). "Babyhood," however, is a side of Kurosawa that he has never explored in his films: his very first memories of himself.

PREREADING: THINKING ABOUT THE ESSAY IN ADVANCE

What are the earliest memories you have of yourself as an infant or child? What do you remember of your first room? a bath? a family member?

Words to Watch

kimono (par. 3) a long, wide-sleeved Japanese robe worn as an outer garment

Rolls-Royce (par. 5) a very expensive British car

Tokyo (par. 8) the capital and most important city in Japan

Sherlock Holmes (par. 9) the most famous detective in literature

1 I was in the washtub naked. The place was dimly lit, and I was soaking in hot water and rocking myself by holding on to the rims of the tub. At the lowest point the tub teetered between two sloping boards, the water making little splashing noises as it rocked. This must have been very interesting for me. I rocked the tub with all my strength. Suddenly it overturned. I have a very vivid memory of the strange feeling of shock and uncertainty at that moment, of the sensation of that wet and slippery space between the boards against my bare skin, and of looking up at something painfully bright overhead.

2 After reaching an age of awareness, I would occasionally recall this incident. But it seemed a trivial thing, so I said nothing about it until I became an adult. It must have been after I had

passed twenty years of age that for some reason I mentioned to my mother that I remembered these sensations. For a moment she just stared at me in surprise; then she informed me that this could only have been something that occurred when we went to my father's birthplace up north in Akita Prefecture to attend a memorial service for my grandfather. I had been one year old at the time.

The dimly lit place where I sat in a tub lodged between two 3
boards was the room that served as both kitchen and bath in the house where my father was born. My mother had been about to give me a bath, but first she put me in the tub of hot water and went into the next room to take off her kimono. Suddenly she heard me start wailing at the top of my lungs. She rushed back and found me spilled out of the tub on the floor crying. The painfully bright, shiny thing over head, my mother explained, was probably a hanging oil lamp of the type still used when I was a baby.

This incident with the washtub is my very first memory of 4
myself. Naturally, I do not recall being born. However, my oldest sister, now deceased, used to say, "You were a strange baby." Apparently I emerged from my mother's womb without uttering a sound, but with my hands firmly clasped together. When at last they were able to pry my hands apart, I had bruises on both palms.

I think this story may be a lie. It was probably made up to 5
tease me because I was the youngest child. After all, if I really had been born such a grasping person, by now I would be a millionaire and surely would be riding around in nothing less than a Rolls-Royce.

After the washtub incident of my first year, I can now recall 6
only a few other events from my babyhood, in a form resembling out-of-focus bits of film footage. All of them are things seen from my infant's vantage point on my nurse's shoulders.

One of them is something seen through a wire net. People 7
dressed in white flail at a ball with a stick, run after it as it dances and flies through the air, and pick it up and throw it around. Later I understood that this was the view from behind the net of the baseball field at the gymnastics school where my father was a teacher. So I must say that my liking for baseball today is deep-rooted; apparently I've been watching it since babyhood.

8 Another memory from babyhood, also a sight viewed from my nurse's back, comes to mind: a fire seen from a great distance. Between us and the fire stretches an expanse of dark water. My home was in the Ōmori district of Tokyo, so this was probably the Ōmori shore of Tokyo Bay, and since the fire appeared very far away, it must have taken place somewhere near Haneda (now the site of one of Tokyo's international airports). I was frightened by this distant fire and cried. Even now I have a strong dislike of fires, and especially when I see the night sky reddened with flames I am overcome by fear.

9 One last memory of babyhood remains. In this case, too, I am on my nurse's back, and from time to time we enter a small dark room. Years later I would occasionally recall this frequent occurrence and wonder what it was. Then one day all at once, like Sherlock Holmes solving a mystery, I understood: my nurse, with me still on her back, was going to the toilet. What an insult!

10 Many years later my nurse came to see me. She looked up at this person who had reached nearly six feet and more than 150 pounds and just said, "My dear, how you've grown," as she clasped me around the knees and broke into tears. I had been ready to reproach her for the indignities she had caused me to suffer in the past, but suddenly I was moved by this figure of an old woman I no longer recognized, and all I could do was stare vacantly down at her.

BUILDING VOCABULARY

Write definitions for the following words. Then use each word in a sentence.

a. vivid (par. 1)
b. vantage (par. 6)
c. flail (par. 7)
d. indignities (par. 10)
e. vacantly (par. 10)

THINKING CRITICALLY ABOUT THE ESSAY

Understanding the Writer's Ideas

1. What is the essay's thesis?
2. Kurosawa's first memory of himself is the sensation of a "wet and slippery space." Is there any truth to this memory?

3. Why did Kurosawa's oldest sister believe he was a strange baby (par. 4)? Does Kurosawa agree with her memory of him?
4. What *metaphor* (see Glossary) does the writer use to describe how he recalls events from his babyhood?
5. Why does the writer believe his liking for baseball may be "deep-rooted"?
6. From what vantage point does Kurosawa recall his experiences?
7. What does Kurosawa suspect is behind his fear of fires?
8. Why many years later did this writer's nurse break down in tears and clasp him around the knees?

Understanding the Writer's Techniques

1. Most readers expect a thesis statement to occur at the beginning of an essay. Why is this essay's thesis unusual?
2. This writer says he recalls his babyhood like film footage. How is this essay's first sentence like a bit of film?
3. Besides visual detail, Kurosawa places a great deal of emphasis on another kind of detail. What? And why?
4. Given that the writer is a filmmaker, how does he construct a memories vantage point for his camera? What is it?
5. How would you describe the functions of the first couple of words of paragraphs 7, 8, and 9? What would be synonyms for each word?
6. In what ways does the essay end like a movie?

Exploring the Writer's Ideas

1. Kurosawa describes the very first memory of himself as an infant in a washtub. Do you think it's possible to have such an early memory? Why or why not?
2. The writer's sister suggests that Kurosawa might be a grasping personality because he was born with his hands "firmly clasped"? Do you think she is right? Do infants reveal their personalities at birth? Explain.
3. Can infants watching a sports event grow to like that sport as adults? This is Kurosawa's idea. Why would you agree or disagree?
4. This writer believes in the notion of fears inspired at babyhood. What fears, if any, do you have that you think may be

traced to babyhood? Or are there other explanations? Give examples to support your answer.

5. If you could solve a mystery from your babyhood, what would it be? What memory would you like to know more about? Why?
6. What stories have you heard about yourself as a baby or child? Do you think these stories are accurate? Explain.

IDEAS FOR WRITING

Prewriting

Make a drawing of yourself as a baby and write notes next to each component of the picture to express what memory the picture triggers.

Guided Writing

Write an essay that explores your earliest memories of yourself as a baby or child.

1. Describe the most striking memory from your babyhood, detailing an incident you recall.
2. As an adult looking back, what does the incident mean to you today? How do you feel about it?
3. Tell what traits you think you exhibit as an adult that might be traced back to the incident.
4. Describe two or more other early memories you have and explain how you think they may affect something in your life today.
5. Describe the primary person who took care of you and tell what you would say to this person today about the care the person gave you.

Thinking and Writing Collaboratively

If the care we receive as infants affects who we become as adults, what do you think is the ideal kind of baby care we should all get to make us the best possible adults we can be? Share your ideas in groups and write an essay to address the issue.

More Writing Projects

1. Observe babies in your community in stores, buses, or in strollers. In your journal, record impressions and feelings about what you see.
2. Using observations from your journal, write a paragraph describing what you see as the good and/or bad aspects of being an infant.
3. Write an essay describing why you think being a baby is better or worse than being an adult.

SUMMING UP: CHAPTER 3

1. As you have discovered in this chapter, one of the keys to writing effective description is the selection and creation of vivid and relevant images. How do the writers in this chapter use imagery? Which writer's images do you find most concrete, original, vivid, and creative? For each of the four essays of description in this chapter, write a paragraph in which you evaluate the writer's use of imagery.
2. Kurosawa and Selzer provide vivid descriptions of people. What general guidelines for describing people do you derive from these writers? Write a short essay called "How to Describe People," basing your observations on Kurosawa's and Selzer's techniques.
3. Maxine Hong Kingston and Louise Erdrich both write from their experience as members of a multicultural society. Is there any evidence that their ethnic backgrounds shape their choice of subject or method of description? Write a short essay on the relation between the writers' backgrounds and the nature of their descriptions.
4. The essays by Erdrich and Selzer are, each in its own way, meditations on life and death. What did you learn about life and death from these two writers?

CHAPTER 4

Narration

WHAT IS NARRATION?

Narration is the telling of a story. As a technique in essay writing, it normally involves a discussion of events that are "true" or real, events that take place over a period of time. Narration helps a writer explain things and, as such, it is an important skill for the kind of writing often required of you.

Narration often includes the use of *description* in order to make the *purpose* of the story clear. A good narrative, then, must have a *thesis.* The thesis tells the reader that the narrative goes beyond just telling a story for entertainment. Like description, the narrative has a purpose, and an audience. The writer puts forth a main idea through the events and details of the story. For example, a writer might decide to *narrate* the events that led her to leave her native country and come to the United States as an immigrant. She would establish her thesis—her main point—quickly, and then use the body of the essay to tell about the event itself. She would use narration as the means to an end—to make a significant statement about the important decision that changed her life.

Writer Elizabeth Wong uses narrative to explore the pitfalls of divorcing herself from her cultural heritage as she tells about events in her youth with the purpose of pointing out the dangers of becoming "All-American." In his comic narrative "Salvation," Langston Hughes reveals his disillusionment as he cannot find Jesus as his family expects him to. Nicholas Weinstock uses the narrative of a basketball game to raise larger issues of friendship and fellowship. The renowned writer George Orwell narrates events at a hanging he witnessed in Burma to call attention to how all too often we can take the value of life for granted. Each writer, then, whose work you will read in this chapter, uses narrative to tell a story of events that take place over a period of time, but also to put forward a thesis or main idea that comes directly out of events in the story.

HOW DO WE READ NARRATIVE?

Reading narrative requires us to look for more than the story, but not to overlook the story. So, as we read, we should ask ourselves:

- What are the main events in the narrative or story?
- What is the writer's purpose in telling us about these events, as stated in the thesis?
- How is the story organized? Is it chronological? Does the writer use *flashback* (see Glossary)? How much time is covered in the narrative?
- Does the author use description to make the narrative more vivid for a reader?
- What point of view does the author use? Are events told through his or her own eyes, or from a detached and objective point of view? Why did the writer make this choice about point of view? How would altering the point of view alter the purpose of the narrative?
- What transitions of time does the writer use to connect events? Look for expressions that link events: *next, soon after, a day later, suddenly, after two years.* These expressions act like bridges to connect the various moments in the narrative pattern.
- Does the writer use dialogue? What is the effect of dialogue in the narrative?
- What audience is the author aiming at? How do we know?

HOW DO WE WRITE NARRATIVE?

After reading the selections of narrative writing in this chapter, you should be ready to try narrative writing on your own. Fortunately, most individuals have a basic storytelling ability and know how to develop stories that make a point. Once you master narration as a writing pattern, you will be able to use it in a variety of situations.

Select the event you want to tell a story about. Begin with a thesis statement that gives the reader the purpose of the narrative.

Sample thesis statement:

> My year studying abroad in Paris was an adventure that taught me not only skills in a foreign language but a new respect for people with cultural values different from my own.

Decide which point of view you will use: first person? third person? Think about who your audience is, and choose the point of view best suited for that audience. If you are writing to a friend, first person may be more informal. If you are writing to address a wider public audience, as Orwell is, third person might be more effective.

First person: I saw a man hanged, and the experience changed my views on capital punishment.

Third person: Spending a day at a Planned Parenthood clinic would help opponents of abortion understand the other side's fervent commitment to choice.

Determine the purpose of the narrative in relation to your audience. If you were writing for a Roman Catholic newspaper, for instance, your audience would be different from the audience you'd address in a feminist magazine like *Ms.:* the purpose would be different as well. In one case, you might be trying to get readers to change their views through your description. In another case, you might be showing how weak the opposition was by the way you described them.

Plan the scope of the piece: How much time will events cover? Can you describe all the events within the required length of the essay? Notice that Nicholas Weinstock's narrative, for instance, concentrates on one incident—a basketball game on a court at the University of Botswana.

Plan to include dialogue. Here, you might include a few fragments of conversation between lost or confused freshmen to give our "first day at school" story real-life flavor:

"Did you buy your books yet?"

"No, I couldn't find the bookstore!"

"Well, I already spent $125, and that was only for two courses. I'm going to have to ask my Mom for more money."

"Yeah, I'm thinking maybe I'm going to need a part-time job."

"Yeah, maybe we can work in the bookstore and get a discount."

Make a list of *transitions* that show the passage of time and use as many as you need to help your reader follow the sequence of events in the narrative. Check that there are transitions between events: *after that, a few hours later, by the time the day ended.*

State your *thesis.* Write out the thesis statement so that you know the *subject* and the *purpose* of the essay. Then make a list of the major events in the story. You might begin with why you chose the college you did, and how you felt when you got accepted. Or, you might begin with your arrival on the first day of classes, and go through the main events of the day—going to class, buying books, meeting other new students, evaluating teachers, having lunch, and so forth.

Plan an arrangement of events. Most narratives benefit from a clear chronological sequence. All the writers here pay careful attention to the march of events over time, and you should follow their lead. As in Orwell's focused narrative, integrate commentary, analysis, or assessment, but keep your eye on the order of events.

Writing the Draft

Once you have structured your essay, build your ideas by including descriptive details. Insert as many descriptive words as possible to help a reader *see* the campus, the students, the cafeteria, and so on:

the bright-colored sofas in the student lounge, filled with cigarette burns

the smells of french fries from the cafeteria, with its long rows of orange tables

the conversations of the biology majors at the next table, who were talking about cutting up frogs the large, imposing library, with its rows of blue computer terminals and its hushed whispered noises

Discuss how these events made you feel about your decision. Did you choose the right college?

Write a conclusion that reinforces the purpose of the essay. Make a direct statement of the way the events in the narrative changed you, or how your expectations for the day compare with what really happened.

Reading and Revising the Draft

Read the essay aloud to a classmate who is also a new freshman. Ask your listener if his or her day was the same as yours. Did you put the events in a logical sequence? Can your listener suggest more ideas to add? Have you included enough details so that a reader who was not a member of the college community could see the events as you saw them?

Proofread carefully for correctness and make a neat final copy.

The Struggle to Be an All-American Girl

Elizabeth Wong

In this poignant remembrance, Elizabeth Wong tells of the hurts and sorrows of her bicultural upbringing. Wong effectively blends concrete description and imaginative comparisons to give a vivid look into the life of a child who felt she had a Chinese exterior but an American interior.

PREREADING: THINKING ABOUT THE ESSAY IN ADVANCE

America prides itself on its ability to assimilate cultures, yet the process of assimilation is not without difficulties, particularly for children. What problems do you foresee for a child of one cultural background growing up in the midst of another culture?

Words to Watch

stoically (par. 1) without showing emotion
dissuade (par. 2) to talk out of doing something
ideographs (par. 7) Chinese picture symbols used to form words
disassociate (par. 8) to detach from association
vendors (par. 8) sellers of goods
gibberish (par. 9) confused, unintelligible speech or language
pidgin (par. 10) simplified speech that is usually a mixture of two or more languages

1 It's still there, the Chinese school on Yale Street where my brother and I used to go. Despite the new coat of paint and the high wire fence, the school I knew 10 years ago remains remarkably, stoically the same.

2 Every day at 5 P.M., instead of playing with our fourth- and fifth-grade friends or sneaking out to the empty lot to hunt ghosts

and animal bones, my brother and I had to go to Chinese school. No amount of kicking, screaming, or pleading could dissuade my mother, who was solidly determined to have us learn the language of our heritage.

Forcibly, she walked us the seven long, hilly blocks from our home to school, depositing our defiant tearful faces before the stern principal. My only memory of him is that he swayed on his heels like a palm tree, and he always clasped his impatient twitching hands behind his back. I recognized him as a repressed maniacal child killer, and knew that if we ever saw his hands we'd be in big trouble. 3

We all sat in little chairs in an empty auditorium. The room smelled like Chinese medicine, an imported faraway mustiness. Like ancient mothballs or dirty closets. I hated that smell. I favored crisp new scents. Like the soft French perfume that my American teacher wore in public school. 4

There was a stage far to the right, flanked by an American flag and the flag of the Nationalist Republic of China, which was also red, white and blue but not as pretty. 5

Although the emphasis at the school was mainly language—speaking, reading, writing—the lessons always began with an exercise in politeness. With the entrance of the teacher, the best student would tap a bell and everyone would get up, kowtow, and chant, "Sing san ho," the phonetic for "How are you, teacher?" 6

Being ten years old, I had better things to learn than ideographs copied painstakingly in lines that ran right to left from the tip of a *moc but,* a real ink pen that had to be held in an awkward way if blotches were to be avoided. After all, I could do the multiplication tables, name the satellites of Mars, and write reports on "Little Women" and "Black Beauty." Nancy Drew, my favorite book heroine, never spoke Chinese. 7

The language was a source of embarrassment. More times than not, I had tried to disassociate myself from the nagging loud voice that followed me wherever I wandered in the nearby American supermarket outside Chinatown. The voice belonged to my grandmother, a fragile woman in her seventies who could outshout the best of the street vendors. Her humor was raunchy, her Chinese rhythmless, patternless. It was quick, it was loud, it was unbeautiful. It was not like the quiet, lilting romance of French or 8 the gentle refinement of the American South. Chinese sounded pedestrian. Public.

9 In Chinatown, the comings and goings of hundreds of Chinese on their daily tasks sounded chaotic and frenzied. I did not want to be thought of as mad, as talking gibberish. When I spoke English, people nodded at me, smiled sweetly, said encouraging words. Even the people in my culture would cluck and say that I'd do well in life. "My, doesn't she move her lips fast," they would say, meaning that I'd be able to keep up with the world outside Chinatown.

10 My brother was even more fanatical than I about speaking English. He was especially hard on my mother, criticizing her, often cruelly, for her pidgin speech—smatterings of Chinese scattered like chop suey in her conversation. "It's not 'What it is,' Mom," he'd say in exasperation. "It's 'What *is* it, what *is* it, what *is* it!'" Sometimes Mom might leave out an occasional "the" or "a," or perhaps a verb of being. He would stop her in mid-sentence: "Say it again, Mom. Say it right." When he tripped over his own tongue, he'd blame it on her: "See, Mom, it's all your fault. You set a bad example."

11 What infuriated my mother most was when my brother cornered her on her consonants, especially "r." My father had played a cruel joke on Mom by assigning her an American name that her tongue wouldn't allow her to say. No matter how hard she tried, "Ruth" always ended up "Luth" or "Roof."

12 After two years of writing with a *moc but* and reciting words with multiples of meanings, I finally was granted a cultural divorce. I was permitted to stop Chinese school.

13 I thought of myself as multicultural. I preferred tacos to egg rolls; I enjoyed Cinco de Mayo more than Chinese New Year.

14 At last, I was one of you; I wasn't one of them.

15 Sadly, I still am.

BUILDING VOCABULARY

For each of the words in italics, choose the letter of the word or expression that most closely matches its meaning.

1. the *stern* principal (par. 3)
a. military **b.** very old **c.** immoral **d.** strict

2. *repressed* maniacal child killer (par. 3)
   a. quiet **b.** ugly **c.** held back **d.** retired
3. an imported faraway *mustiness* (par. 4)
   a. country **b.** moth balls **c.** chair **d.** staleness
4. a *fragile* woman (par. 8)
   a. elderly **b.** frail **c.** tall **d.** inconsistent
5. her humor was *raunchy* (par. 8)
   a. obscene **b.** unclear **c.** childish **d.** very funny
6. quiet *lilting* romance of French (par. 8)
   a. musical **b.** tilting **c.** loving **d.** complicated
7. thought of as *mad* (par. 9)
   a. foreign **b.** angry **c.** stupid **d.** crazy
8. what *infuriated* my mother most (par. 11)
   a. angered **b.** humiliated **c.** made laugh **d.** typified

THINKING CRITICALLY ABOUT THE ESSAY

Understanding the Writer's Ideas

1. What did Elizabeth Wong and her brother do every day after school? How did that make them different from their friends? What was their attitude toward what they did? How do you know?
2. What does Wong mean when she says of the principal "I recognized him as a repressed maniacal child killer"? Why were she and her brother afraid to see his hands?
3. What was the main purpose of going to Chinese school? What did Wong feel she had learned at "regular" American school? Which did she feel was more important? What are *Little Women, Black Beauty,* and Nancy Drew?
4. In the first sentence of paragraph 8, what language is "the language"?
5. What was Wong's grandmother like? What was Wong's attitude toward her? Why?
6. When Wong spoke English in Chinatown, why did the others think it was good that she moved her lips quickly?
7. What was her brother's attitude toward speaking English? How did he treat their mother when she tried to speak Eng-

lish? Why was it unfortunate that the mother had the American name *Ruth?* Who gave her that name? Why?

8. Explain the expression "he tripped over his own tongue" (par. 10).

9. In paragraph 13, Wong states, "I thought of myself as multicultural." What does that mean? What are tacos, egg rolls, and Cinco de Mayo? Why is it surprising that Wong includes those items as examples of her multiculturalism?

10. Who are the "you" and "them" of paragraph 14? Explain the significance of the last sentence. What does it indicate about Wong's attitude toward Chinese school from the vantage point of being an adult?

Understanding the Writer's Techniques

1. Wong does not state a thesis directly in a thesis sentence. How does her title imply a thesis? If you were writing a thesis sentence of your own for this essay, what would it be?

2. What is Wong's purpose in writing this narrative? Is the technique of narration an appropriate one to her purpose? Why or why not?

3. This narrative contains several stories. The first one ends after paragraph 7 and tells about Wong's routine after 5 P.M. on school days. Paragraphs 8 and 9, 10 and 11, and 12 and 13 offer other related narratives. Summarize each of these briefly. How does Wong help the reader shift from story to story?

4. The writer of narration will present *time* in a way that best fulfills the purpose of the narration. This presentation may take many forms: a single, personal event; a series of related events; a historical occurrence; an aging process. Obviously Wong chose a series of related events. Why does she use such a narrative structure to make her point? Could she have chosen an alternative plan, do you think? Why or why not?

5. Writers of narration often rely upon descriptive details to flesh out their stories. Find examples of sensory language here that makes the scene come alive for the reader.

6. Writers often use figurative comparisons to enliven their writing and to make it more distinctive. A *simile* is an imaginative form of figurative comparison using "like" or "as" to connect two items. One thing is similar to another in this figure. A *metaphor* is a figure of speech in which the writer compares two items not normally thought of as similar, but unlike in a simile, the comparison is direct—that is, it does not use "like" or "as." In other words, one thing is said to be the other thing, not merely to be like it. For example, if you wanted to compare love to a rose, you might use these two comparisons:

Simile:
My love is *like* a red, red rose.
Metaphor:
My love *is* a red, red rose.

In Wong's essay, find the similes and metaphors in paragraphs 2, 3, 4, 10, and 12. For each, name the two items compared and explain the comparison in your own words.

7. Narratives often include lines of spoken language—that is, one person in the narrative talking alone or to another. Wong uses quoted detail sparsely here. Why did she choose to limit the dialogue? How effective is the dialogue that appears here? Where do you think she might have used more dialogue to advance the narrative?
8. The last two paragraphs are only one sentence each. Why do you think the author chose this technique?
9. What is the *irony* (see Glossary) in the last sentence of the essay? How would the meaning of the last sentence change if you eliminated the word "sadly"? What is the irony in the title of the essay?
10. What is the *tone* (see Glossary) of this essay? How does Wong create that tone?

Exploring the Writer's Ideas

1. Wong and her brother deeply resented being forced to attend Chinese school. When children very clearly express displeasure or unhappiness, should parents force them to do things anyway? Why or why not?
2. On one level this essay is about a clash of cultures, here the ancient Chinese culture of Wong's ancestry and the culture of twentieth-century United States. Is it possible for someone to maintain connections to his or her ethnic or cultural back-

ground and at the same time to become an all-American girl or boy? What do people of foreign backgrounds gain when they become completely Americanized? What do they lose?

3. Because of their foreign ways, the mother and grandmother clearly embarrassed the Wong children. Under what other conditions that you can think of do parents embarrass children? Children, parents?

IDEAS FOR WRITING

Prewriting

Do timed writing—that is, write nonstop for fifteen or twenty minutes without editing or correcting your work—on the topic of your grade school or high school. What experience stands out most in your mind? What moment taught you most about yourself?

Guided Writing

Write a narration in which you tell about some difficult moment that took place in grade school or high school, a moment that taught you something about yourself, your needs, or your cultural background.

1. Provide a concrete description of the school.
2. Tell in correct sequence about the event.
3. Identify people who play a part in this moment.
4. Use concrete, sensory description throughout your essay.
5. Use original similes and metaphors to make your narrative clearer and more dramatic.
6. Use dialogue (or spoken conversation) appropriately in order to advance the narrative.
7. In your conclusion, indicate what your attitude toward this moment is now that you are an adult.
8. Write a title that implies your thesis.

Thinking and Writing Collaboratively

In groups of two or three, read aloud drafts of each other's essays, looking particularly at the use of concrete sensory detail and figures of speech—metaphors and similes. Which images strike you as most clear, original, and easy to visualize?

More Writing Projects

1. Did you have any problems in grade school or high school because of your background or ancestry? Did you know someone who had such problems? Record a specific incident in your journal.
2. Write a narrative paragraph explaining some basic insights about your heritage or culture.
3. Get together with other classmates in a small group and brainstorm or bounce ideas off one another on troubling ethnic, racial, or cultural issues on campus. Write down all the incidents. Then write a narrative essay tracing one episode or connecting a series of them.

Salvation

Langston Hughes

For more than forty years, Langston Hughes (1902–1967) was a major figure in American literature. In poetry, essays, drama, and fiction he attempted, as he said himself, "to explain and illuminate the Negro condition in America." This selection from his autobiography, *The Big Sea* (1940), tells the story of his "conversion" to Christ. Salvation was a key event in the life of his community, but Hughes tells comically how he bowed to pressure by permitting himself to be "saved from sin."

PREREADING: THINKING ABOUT THE ESSAY IN ADVANCE

What is the role of religion today in the lives of most Americans? What role does religion play in your life? In what ways do the religious values of your family compare and contrast with your own?

Words to Watch

dire (par. 3) terrible; disastrous

gnarled (par. 4) knotty; twisted

rounder (par. 6) watchman; policeman

deacons (par. 6) members of the clergy or laypersons who are appointed to help the minister

serenely (par. 7) calmly; tranquilly

knickerbockered (par. 11) dressed in short, loose trousers that are gathered below the knees

1 I was saved from sin when I was going on thirteen. But not really saved. It happened like this. There was a big revival at my Auntie Reed's church. Every night for weeks there had been much preaching, singing, praying, and shouting, and some very hardened sinners had been brought to Christ, and the membership of the church had grown by leaps and bounds. Then just before the

revival ended, they held a special meeting for children, "to bring the young lambs to the fold." My aunt spoke of it for days ahead. That night I was escorted to the front row and placed on the mourners' bench with all the other young sinners, who had not yet been brought to Jesus.

My aunt told me that when you were saved you saw a light, 2
and something happened to you inside! And Jesus came into your life! And God was with you from then on! She said you could see and hear and feel Jesus in your soul. I believed her. I had heard a great many old people say the same thing and it seemed to me they ought to know. So I sat there calmly in the hot, crowded church, waiting for Jesus to come to me.

The preacher preached a wonderful rhythmical sermon, all 3
moans and shouts and lonely cries and dire pictures of hell, and then he sang a song about the ninety and nine safe in the fold, but one little lamb was left out in the cold. Then he said: "Won't you come? Won't you come to Jesus? Young lambs, won't you come?" And he held out his arms to all us young sinners there on the mourners' bench. And the little girls cried. And some of them jumped up and went to Jesus right away. But most of us just sat there.

A great many old people came and knelt around us and 4
prayed, old women with jet-black faces and braided hair, old men with work-gnarled hands. And the church sang a song about the lower lights are burning, some poor sinners to be saved. And the whole building rocked with prayer and song.

Still I kept waiting to *see* Jesus. 5

Finally all the young people had gone to the altar and were 6
saved, but one boy and me. He was a rounder's son named Westley. Westley and I were surrounded by sisters and deacons praying. It was very hot in the church, and getting late now. Finally Westley said to me in a whisper: "God damn! I'm tired o' sitting here. Let's get up and be saved." So he got up and was saved.

Then I was left all alone on the mourners' bench. My aunt 7
came and knelt at my knees and cried, while prayers and songs swirled all around me in the little church. The whole congregation prayed for me alone, in a mighty wail of moans and voices. And I kept waiting serenely for Jesus, waiting, waiting—but he didn't come. I wanted to see him, but nothing happened to me. Nothing! I wanted something to happen to me, but nothing happened.

8 I heard the songs and the minister saying: "Why don't you come? My dear child, why don't you come to Jesus? Jesus is waiting for you. He wants you. Why don't you come? Sister Reed, what is this child's name?"

9 "Langston," my aunt sobbed.

10 "Langston, why don't you come? Why don't you come and be saved? Oh, Lamb of God! Why don't you come?"

11 Now it was really getting late. I began to be ashamed of myself, holding everything up so long. I began to wonder what God thought about Westley, who certainly hadn't seen Jesus either, but who was now sitting proudly on the platform, swinging his knickerbockered legs and grinning down at me, surrounded by deacons and old women on their knees praying. God had not struck Westley dead for taking his name in vain or for lying in the temple. So I decided that maybe to save further trouble, I'd better lie, too, and say that Jesus had come, and get up and be saved.

12 So I got up.

13 Suddenly the whole room broke into a sea of shouting, as they saw me rise. Waves of rejoicing swept the place. Women leaped in the air. My aunt threw her arms around me. The minister took me by the hand and led me to the platform.

14 When things quieted down, in a hushed silence, punctuated by a few ecstatic "Amens," all the new young lambs were blessed in the name of God. Then joyous singing filled the room.

15 That night, for the last time in my life but one—for I was a big boy twelve years old—I cried. I cried, in bed alone, and couldn't stop. I buried my head under the quilts, but my aunt heard me. She woke up and told my uncle I was crying because the Holy Ghost had come into my life, and because I had seen Jesus. But I was really crying because I couldn't bear to tell her that I had lied, that I had deceived everybody in the church, that I hadn't seen Jesus, and that now I didn't believe there was a Jesus any more, since he didn't come to help me.

BUILDING VOCABULARY

1. Throughout this essay, Hughes selects words dealing with religion to emphasize his ideas. Look the following words up in

a dictionary. Then tell what *connotations* (see Glossary) the words have for you.
   a. sin (par. 1)
   b. mourner (par. 1)
   c. lamb (par. 3)
   d. salvation (title)
2. Locate additional words that deal with religion.
3. When Hughes talks about lambs in the fold—and lambs in general—he is using a figure of speech, a comparison (see Chapter 6). What is being compared? How does religion enter into the comparison? Why is it useful as a figure of speech?

THINKING CRITICALLY ABOUT THE ESSAY

Understanding the Writer's Ideas

1. According to Hughes's description, what is a revival meeting like? What is the effect of the "preaching, singing, praying, and shouting" on the "sinners" and the "young lambs"?
2. Why does Westley "see" Jesus? Why does Langston Hughes come to Jesus?
3. How does the author feel after his salvation? Does Hughes finally believe in Christ after his experience? How do you know?

Understanding the Writer's Techniques

1. Is there a thesis statement in the essay? Where is it located?
2. How does the first paragraph serve as an introduction to the narrative?
3. What is the value of description in this essay? List several instances of vivid description that contribute to the narrative.
4. Where does the main narration begin? How much time passes in the course of the action?
5. In narration, it is especially important to have effective *transitions*—or word bridges—from stage to stage in the action. Transitions help the reader shift easily from idea to idea, event to event. List several transition words that Hughes uses.

6. A piece of writing has *coherence* if all its parts relate clearly and logically to one another. Each sentence grows naturally from the sentence before it; each paragraph grows naturally from the paragraph before it. Is Hughes's essay coherent? Which transitions help advance the action and relate the parts of a single paragraph to one another? Which transitions help connect paragraphs together? How does the way Hughes organized this essay help establish coherence?
7. A story (whether it is true or fiction) has to be told from the first-person ("I, we"), second-person ("you"), or third-person ("he, she, it, they") *point of view.* Point of view in narration sets up the author's position in regard to the action, making the author either a part of the action or an observer of it.
   a. What is the point of view in "Salvation"—is it first, second, or third person?
   b. Why has Hughes chosen this point of view instead of any other? Can you think of any advantages to this point of view?
8. What is your opinion about the last paragraph, the conclusion of this selection? What does it suggest about the mind of a twelve-year-old boy? What does it say about adults' misunderstanding of the activities of children?
9. What does the word "conversion" mean? What conversion really takes place in this piece? How does that compare with what people usually mean when they use "conversion" in a religious sense?

Exploring the Writer's Ideas

1. Hughes seems to suggest that we are forced to do things because of social pressures. Do you agree with his suggestion? Do people do things because their friends or families expect them to? To what extent are we part of the "herd"? Is it possible for a person to retain individuality under pressure from a group? When did you bow to group pressures? When did you resist?
2. Do you find the religious experience in Hughes's essay unusual or extreme? Why or why not? How do *you* define religion?
3. Under what circumstances might a person lie in order to satisfy others? Try to recall a specific episode in which you or someone you know was forced to lie in order to please others.

IDEAS FOR WRITING

Prewriting

Write a few sentences to define *group pressure*. Then give an example or two of a time when you gave in to group pressure or were forced to lie in order to impress others.

Guided Writing

Narrate an event in your life where you (or someone you know) gave in to group pressure or were forced to lie in order to please those around you.

1. Start with a thesis statement.
2. Set the stage for your narrative in the opening paragraph by telling where and when the incident took place. Use specific names for places.
3. Try to keep the action within as brief a time period as possible. If you can write about an event that took no more than a few minutes, so much the better.
4. Use description to sketch in the characters around you. Use colors, actions, sounds, smells, sensations of touch to fill in details of the scene.
5. Use effective transitions of time to link sentences and paragraphs.
6. Use the last paragraph to explain how you felt immediately after the incident.

Thinking and Writing Collaboratively

Exchange drafts of your Guided Writing essay with one other person in the class. Then, write out a brief outline of the events the writer has presented in the narrative. Is the sequence clear? Do the introduction and thesis set the stage appropriately for the sequence of events? Do the transitions link paragraphs and sentences effectively? Return the paper with your written response.

More Writing Projects

1. Explain in a journal entry an abstract word like "salvation," "sin," "love," or "hatred" by narrating an event that reveals the meaning of the word to you.
2. Write an extended paragraph on an important event that affected your relationship with family, friends, or your community during your childhood.
3. Make a list of all the important details that you associate with some religious occasion in your life. Then write a narrative essay on the experience.

Ghost Legs

Nicholas Weinstock

Nicholas Weinstock is a book editor and freelance writer. Here he portrays his experiences overcoming cultural as well as language barriers to forge new friendships with African men in Botswana through the game of basketball. Basketball, he claims, is a way for all men to "reach each other."

PREREADING: THINKING ABOUT THE ESSAY IN ADVANCE

How can everyday street or playground sports contribute to building friendships? Discuss this question with students in the class.

Words to Watch

rickety (par. 2)   likely to break
beckoned (par. 7)   attracted with gestures
fast-break (par. 11)   quick
crack up (par. 19)   to laugh
D. (par. 19)   a slang term for defense

Echoing across the sandbox campus of the University of Botswana was the unmistakable *pong* of a basketball on concrete. For a month, ever since my arrival as the African university's first Rotary Scholar, and only white student, I'd been checking the court for some sign of a game. 1

My graduate work in African literature had been the easiest part. It was far tougher outside the classrooms' sun-warmed cement walls, where I still stumbled over singular and plural greetings and never got the dirty jokes in Setswana that cracked up the cafeteria. Basketball was a language I spoke. Until this afternoon the court had remained empty, two rickety, netless hoops and their shadows beneath the angry sun. *Pong. Pong-pong.* Today, at last, guys were running. 2

3 The ball carrier was the last to notice my entrance. The other dozen players had straightened up to stare, but he continued to dribble furiously around and between them, zigzagging toward the basket, until one of the crowd of local kids on the sideline announced, *"Lekgowa le tla go tshameka"*—the white guy's coming to play. Then he held the ball and whirled toward me.

4 "Fine," he managed after a moment. "Let us choose it up."

5 I was selected first. *I'm not that good,* I thought of confessing to my captain as I hitched my shorts and jogged into place behind him. But that was not something you said at the start of a pickup game. *Check it up!* That was more like it. *Bring it on now.* Ceremonial chants the world over.

6 "I will guard Ghost Legs," the young man opposite me said with a smile.

7 "No, no," the other captain said. He beckoned to the tallest player, shirtless, sweating through dirty jeans. "*You* take on this, this Larry Bird." From the sideline crowd there were murmurs of pleasure.

8 My captain pinned the ball against my chest and guided me to the far side of the court.

9 "I'm not sure you want me bringing it up," I laughed to him. "I'm not much of a guard." And I *hated* Larry Bird, then still helping the Celtics beat the Knicks. I stepped over the base line and bounced the ball in to him.

10 "You are from America, isn't it," he said conclusively, flipping it back and loping downcourt to join the rest of my team.

11 For as long as I can remember, basketball has served me as a unique arena for pickup, fast-break friendships. Where else can men progress from strangers to jostling, hand-slapping companions in the course of an hour?

12 So many times I'd watched a newcomer enter a game unknown, distrusted—too fat to run the offense, too short to rebound, dark socks a sure sign of awkwardness—only to earn the full-throated cheers of men who'd have sneered at him in the street or office. Now, that was me, the alien who glowed pale, who spoke only a crumpled American English, who'd shown up on some scholarship nobody understood from a country no one wanted to understand. I needed the game, my game, its powers and mine.

I dribbled up carefully to where the teams were bumping 13
past each other, the defense waving their arms. I was already sweating so much that the ball slipped each time my hand pushed it to the concrete. A teammate broke into the open toward a sideline. I passed and made for the hoop. He zipped it back to me, and I jumped past a late-arriving defender to lay the ball in. Brief cheers erupted from the crowd.

A few teammates slapped my hand as we settled back on 14
defense. "Good take, Nicholas," one barked from behind. "Way to go up *strong*." I was so startled to hear both my name and the familiar lingo that I would have turned, had our opponents not already crossed the halfcourt line.

"Got ball," I yelled, stepping forward. In sudden panic the 15
point guard turned protectively sideways and launched a blind hook shot over his shoulder. It cleared the basket by six feet and bounced once, dead in the sand. I laughed, expecting an avalanche of jeers, but the ball had already been collected and lobbed in to me.

I dribbled slowly, scanning our offense before whipping the 16
ball straight ahead to someone wide open under the basket. As he bent forward it ricocheted off his knee and straight up, gonging the underside of the rim and coming back down into an opponent's hands. The sideline collapsed in glee, and hooted with color commentary in Setswana. My teammate beamed, rubbing his knee as we returned to defense.

The other team accidentally kicked the ball out of bounds 17
and I was presented with the ball at halfcourt. My captain broke to the basket. I led him with a crisp one-bouncer, which he caught and released in stride, curling an underhanded layup straight through the hoop from below. As everyone exploded in merry chorus, he jumped up and down, grinning, hands on his head.

"Backward basket!" someone yelled from the crowd. The 18
laughter swelled.

I wanted to laugh too, but it seemed absurd. They were 19
terrible. You didn't crack up at your own slapstick mistakes; you clapped once and cursed. Or shook your head and hustled back on D. Our spectators were still doubled over, calling weakly for the ball to be given back to me so that we could repeat the spectacle. It wasn't success they'd come to watch; it was a game.

20 The game ended with a score like a soccer game's, but my legs burned with fatigue and sunburn as they churned over the sand in the darkness. Walking next to me, my captain confirmed "Yes-yes, it is good fun."

21 "Yeah, I love basketball."

22 "You know, it is a *new* sport here in Botswana," he lamented. "We do not know how to play like Americans."

23 *Doesn't matter,* I wanted to tell him. *This has so little to do with basketball.* But that wasn't true. This was friendship, with its monotonous pounding and awkward elbows, its strict rules, fleeting grace and glory. I wanted to be good at it. But true fellowship, unlike the fellowship that had landed me here, wasn't anything I could easily win. It could only be played, over and over, making teammates of men and games of their efforts to reach each other.

BUILDING VOCABULARY

The words below either name actions or depict emotions. Define the words, then classify each in one of the two groups.

a. loping (par. 10)
b. sneered (par. 12)
c. lobbed (par. 15)
d. ricocheted (par. 16)
e. glee (par. 16)
f. lamented (par. 22)

THINKING CRITICALLY ABOUT THE ESSAY

Understanding the Writer's Ideas

1. What does Weinstock mean when he says, "Basketball was a language I spoke"?
2. What does the title "Ghost Legs" refer to?
3. What is Weinstock doing in Botswana? How does he feel living in another culture?
4. Weinstock is selected first among the players choosing up teams. Why did the players believe Weinstock would be an excellent basketball player?

5. After playing ball with the team for a short while, Weinstock is called something other than Larry Bird. What is he called and why?
6. What does Weinstock mean when he says, "It wasn't success they'd come to watch; it was a game" (par. 19)?
7. After the game is over, why does Weinstock believe playing basketball "has so little to do with basketball" (par. 23)?

Understanding the Writer's Techniques

1. What is the thesis of this essay?
2. Notice how the narrative begins with a little story, a scene—to grab the reader's attention. But where does the scene end and the thesis begin? Which one of the five senses does this narrative begin with and what is its impact on the reader?
3. Why does Weinstock's narrative re-create (quote) the actual words his teammates spoke in Setswana—*"Lekgowa le tla go tshameka"* (par. 3)? What does this suggest about narration?
4. What is the effect of Weinstock's putting his thoughts, "I'm not that good," in italics (par. 5)?
5. How does the writer's opening scene use *chronology* (see Glossary)?
6. After the opening scene, what function do paragraphs 11 and 12 serve?
7. What is the relation of paragraph 13 to the narrative's opening scene?
8. After the game is over, the action stops, but this is not the end of Weinstock's story. How is the narrative concluded?

Exploring the Writer's Ideas

1. Weinstock claims that playing basketball creates communication between people from different cultures who don't speak the same language. Do you agree or disagree? Why?
2. When African players refer to the writer as "Ghost Legs" are they insulting him? Why or why not?
3. Because basketball is new in Botswana, the men want to learn to play it like Americans. But is adopting a sport from another culture a good idea? What if it replaces a country's traditional sport?

4. Weinstock suggests that the basketball court is the one place where men can earn the respect of other men. Is this true? Can women, do you think, earn the respect of other women on the basketball court? Where else can men earn men's respect and women earn women's, other than on a court or a field for games?
5. When one player makes a mistake the others laugh, but Weinstock thinks that this is "absurd." How do you feel about Weinstock's reaction to his teammates' laughter?
6. What distinction does Weinstock make between friendship and fellowship? Do you concur with this distinction? Why or why not?

IDEAS FOR WRITING

Prewriting

Freewrite for ten minutes, recording your associations and memories with this idea in mind: making new friends.

Guided Writing

Write a narrative that explores a strategy you used to make a new friend(s).

1. In a few paragraphs, use a chronological scene to show *only* how and where you first met your friend(s).
2. Try to use one of the five senses to attract the reader's attention. Also, make sure that the opening scene focuses on the strategy that you will introduce in your thesis statement.
3. After the opening scene is over, present your thesis sentence.
4. Elaborate on your thesis in a following paragraph that gives the reader a little history about how you developed this strategy or how it has worked in situations other than the one in this narrative.
5. Continue with the opening scene of this narrative, but progress chronologically (five or six short paragraphs) from the point where you left off in the opening scene—the point of just meeting the new friend(s)—to a point where you feel you are first accepted by the person(s). By the end of this scene,

make clear how and when you know you have been fully accepted by the new person or people. Is it something someone says to you? Is it something that someone does?

6. Use exact dialogue from the scene—even expressions in a foreign language if the moment produced them.
7. Conclude the narrative with a summary that reflects on why you think your strategy worked in the situation described.

Thinking and Writing Collaboratively

In small groups, read aloud your Guided Writing essays. Using the points made by writers in your group, create a manual called "How to Meet New People and Make Friends." What would your six most important points be and why?

More Writing Projects

1. In your journal, record your interactions with someone you think is a friend.
2. Write two paragraphs. In one, explain why you think someone was a good friend. In another, describe a situation where you learned that someone was *not* a good friend.
3. Write a narrative that focuses on an incident wherein you learned that someone was (or was not) a good friend.

A Hanging

George Orwell

One of the masters of English prose, George Orwell (1903–1950) often used narration of personal events to explore important social issues. Notice here how he involves the reader in a simple yet fascinating and tragic story, almost as if he were writing fiction. Orwell takes a brief time span and expands that moment with specific language. At one point, as you will see, the purpose of the narrative comes into sharp focus.

PREREADING: THINKING ABOUT THE ESSAY IN ADVANCE

The number of people executed through the system of justice in the United States has increased dramatically over the past few years. How do you explain the growth of executions by hanging, lethal injection, and the electric chair? Why does U.S. society provide for capital punishment? Under what circumstances is a person sentenced to capital punishment?

Words to Watch

sodden (par. 1) heavy with water

absurdly (par. 2) ridiculously

desolately (par. 3) gloomily; lifelessly; cheerlessly

prodding (par. 3) poking or thrusting at something

Dravidian (par. 4) any member of a group of intermixed races of southern India and Burma

pariah (par. 6) outcast; a member of a low caste of southern India and Burma

servile (par. 11) slavelike; lacking spirit or independence

reiterated (par. 12) repeated

abominable (par. 13) hateful; disagreeable; unpleasant

timorously (par. 15) fearfully

oscillated (par. 16) moved back and forth between two points

garrulously (par. 20) in a talkative manner

refractory (par. 22) stubborn

amicably (par. 24) in a friendly way; peaceably

It was in Burma, a sodden morning of the rains. A sickly light, like yellow tinfoil, was slanting over the high walls into the jail yard. We were waiting outside the condemned cells, a row of sheds fronted with double bars, like small animal cages. Each cell measured about ten feet by ten and was quite bare within except for a plank bed and a pot of drinking water. In some of them brown silent men were squatting at the inner bars, with their blankets draped round them. These were the condemned men, due to be hanged within the next week or two. 1

One prisoner had been brought out of his cell. He was a Hindu, a puny wisp of a man, with a shaven head and vague liquid eyes. He had a thick, sprouting moustache, absurdly too big for his body, rather like the moustache of a comic man on the films. Six tall Indian warders were guarding him and getting him ready for the gallows. Two of them stood by with rifles with fixed bayonets, while the others handcuffed him, passed a chain through his handcuffs and fixed it to their belts, and lashed his arms tight to his sides. They crowded very close about him, with their hands always on him in a careful, caressing grip, as though all the while feeling him to make sure he was there. It was like men handling a fish which is still alive and may jump back into the water. But he stood quite unresisting, yielding his arms limply to the ropes, as though he hardly noticed what was happening. 2

Eight o'clock struck and a bugle call, desolately thin in the wet air, floated from the distant barracks. The superintendent of the jail, who was standing apart from the rest of us, moodily prodding the gravel with his stick, raised his head at the sound. He was an army doctor, with a grey toothbrush moustache and a gruff voice. "For God's sake hurry up, Francis," he said irritably. "The man ought to have been dead by this time. Aren't you ready yet?" 3

Francis, the head jailer, a fat Dravidian in a white drill suit and gold spectacles, waved his black hand. "Yes sir, yes sir," he bubbled. "All iss satisfactorily prepared. The hangman iss waiting. We shall proceed." 4

"Well, quick march, then. The prisoners can't get their breakfast till this job's over." 5

We set out for the gallows. Two warders marched on either side of the prisoner, with their files at the slope; two others marched close against him, gripping him by arm and shoulder, as 6 though at once pushing and supporting him. The rest of us, magistrates and the like, followed behind. Suddenly, when we had gone ten yards, the procession stopped short without any order or warning. A dreadful thing had happened—a dog, come goodness knows whence, had appeared in the yard. It came bounding among us with a loud volley of barks, and leapt round us wagging its whole body, wild with glee at finding so many human beings together. It was a large woolly dog, half Airedale, half pariah. For a moment it pranced round us, and then, before anyone could stop it, it had made a dash for the prisoner, and jumping up tried to lick his face. Everyone stood aghast, too taken aback even to grab at the dog.

7 "Who let that bloody brute in here?" said the superintendent angrily. "Catch it, someone!"

8 A warder, detached from the escort, charged clumsily after the dog, but it danced and gambolled just out of his reach, taking everything as part of the game. A young Eurasian jailer picked up a handful of gravel and tried to stone the dog away, but it dodged the stones and came after us again. Its yaps echoed from the jail walls. The prisoner, in the grasp of the two warders, looked on incuriously, as though this was another formality of the hanging. It was several minutes before someone managed to catch the dog. Then we put my handkerchief through its collar and moved off once more, with the dog still straining and whimpering.

9 It was about forty yards to the gallows. I watched the bare brown back of the prisoner marching in front of me. He walked clumsily with his bound arms, but quite steadily, with that bobbing gait of the Indian who never straightens his knees. At each step his muscles slid neatly into place, the lock of hair on his scalp danced up and down, his feet printed themselves on the wet gravel. And once, in spite of the men who gripped him by each shoulder, he stepped slightly aside to avoid a puddle on the path.

10 It is curious, but till that moment I had never realised what it means to destroy a healthy, conscious man. When I saw the prisoner step aside to avoid the puddle, I saw the mystery, the unspeakable wrongness, of cutting a life short when it is in full tide. This man was not dying, he was alive just as we were alive. All the organs of his body were working—bowels digesting food, skin renewing itself, nails growing, tissues forming—all toiling away in solemn foolery. His nails would still be growing when he

stood on the drop, when he was falling through the air with a tenth of a second to live. His eyes saw the yellow gravel and the grey walls, and his brain still remembered, foresaw, reasoned—reasoned even about puddles. He and we were a party of men walking together, seeing, hearing, feeling, understanding the same world; and in two minutes, with a sudden snap, one of us would be gone—one mind less, one world less.

The gallows stood in a small yard, separate from the main 11 grounds of the prison, and overgrown with tall prickly weeds. It was a brick erection like three sides of a shed, with planking on top, and above that two beams and a crossbar with the rope dangling. The hangman, a grey-haired convict in the white uniform of the prison, was waiting beside his machine. He greeted us with a servile crouch as we entered. At a word from Francis the two warders, gripping the prisoner more closely than ever, half led, half pushed him to the gallows and helped him clumsily up the ladder. Then the hangman climbed up and fixed the rope round the prisoner's neck.

We stood waiting, five yards away. The warders had formed 12 in a rough circle round the gallows. And then, when the noose was fixed, the prisoner began crying out on his god. It was a high, reiterated cry of "Ram! Ram! Ram! Ram!", not urgent and fearful like a prayer or a cry for help, but steady, rhythmical, almost like the tolling of a bell. The dog answered the sound with a whine. The hangman, still standing on the gallows, produced a small cotton bag like a flour bag and drew it down over the prisoner's face. But the sound, muffled by the cloth, still persisted, over and over again: "Ram! Ram! Ram! Ram! Ram!"

The hangman climbed down and stood ready, holding the 13 lever. Minutes seemed to pass. The steady, muffled crying from the prisoner went on and on, "Ram! Ram! Ram!" never faltering for an instant. The superintendent, his head on his chest, was slowly poking the ground with his stick; perhaps he was counting the cries, allowing the prisoner a fixed number—fifty, perhaps, or a hundred. Everyone had changed colour. The Indians had gone grey like bad coffee, and one or two of the bayonets were wavering. We looked at the lashed, hooded man on the drop, and listened to his cries—each cry another second of life; the same thought was in all our minds: oh, kill him quickly, get it over, stop that abominable noise!

14 Suddenly the superintendent made up his mind. Throwing up his head he made a swift motion with his stick. "Chalo!" he shouted almost fiercely.

15 There was a clanking noise, and then dead silence. The prisoner had vanished, and the rope was twisting on itself. I let go of the dog, and it galloped immediately to the back of the gallows; but when it got there it stopped short, barked, and then retreated into a corner of the yard, where it stood among the weeds, looking timorously out at us. We went round the gallows to inspect the prisoner's body. He was dangling with his toes pointed straight downwards, very slowly revolving, as dead as a stone.

16 The superintendent reached out with his stick and poked the bare body; it oscillated, slightly. "*He's* all right," said the superintendent. He backed out from under the gallows, and blew out a deep breath. The moody look had gone out of his face quite suddenly. He glanced at his wristwatch. "Eight minutes past eight. Well, that's all for this morning, thank God."

17 The warders unfixed bayonets and marched away. The dog, sobered and conscious of having misbehaved itself, slipped after them. We walked out of the gallows yard, past the condemned cells with their waiting prisoners, into the big central yard of the prison. The convicts, under the command of warders armed with lathis, were already receiving their breakfast. They squatted in long rows, each man holding a tin pannikin, while two warders with buckets marched round ladling out rice; it seemed quite a homely, jolly scene, after the hanging. An enormous relief had come upon us now that the job was done. One felt an impulse to sing, to break into a run, to snigger. All at once everyone began chattering gaily.

18 The Eurasian boy walking beside me nodded towards the way we had come, with a knowing smile: "Do you know, sir, our friend (he meant the dead man), when he heard his appeal had been dismissed, he pissed on the floor of his cell. From fright—Kindly take one of my cigarettes, sir. Do you not admire my new silver case, sir? From the boxwallah, two rupees eight annas. Classy European style."

19 Several people laughed—at what, nobody seemed certain.

20 Francis was walking by the superintendent, talking garrulously: "Well, sir, all hass passed off with the utmost satisfactori-

ness. It wass all finished—flick! like that. It iss not always so—oah, no! I have known cases where the doctor wass obliged to go beneath the gallows and pull the prisoner's legs to ensure decease. Most disagreeable!"

"Wriggling about, eh? That's bad," said the superintendent. 21

"Ach, sir, it iss worse when they become refractory! One 22
man, I recall, clung to the bars of hiss cage when we went to take him out. You will scarcely credit, sir, that it took six warders to dislodge him, three pulling at each leg. We reasoned with him. 'My dear fellow,' we said, 'think of all the pain and trouble you are causing to us!' But no, he would not listen! Ach, he wass very troublesome!"

I found that I was laughing quite loudly. Everyone was laugh- 23
ing. Even the superintendent grinned in a tolerant way. "You'd better all come out and have a drink," he said quite genially. "I've got a bottle of whisky in the car. We could do with it."

We went through the big double gates of the prison, into the 24
road. "Pulling at his legs!" exclaimed a Burmese magistrate suddenly, and burst into a loud chuckling. We all began laughing again. At that moment Francis's anecdote seemed extraordinarily funny. We all had a drink together, native and European alike, quite amicably. The dead man was a hundred yards away.

BUILDING VOCABULARY

1. Use *context clues* (see Glossary) to make an "educated guess" about the definitions of the following words in italics. Before you guess, look back to the paragraph for clues. Afterward, check your guess in a dictionary.

a. *condemned* men (par. 1)
b. puny *wisp* of a man (par. 2)
c. Indian *warders* (par. 2)
d. careful, *caressing* grip (par. 2)
e. stood *aghast* (par. 6)
f. it danced and *gambolled* (par. 8)
g. *solemn* foolery (par. 10)
h. armed with *lathis* (par. 17)
i. a tin *pannikin* (par. 17)
j. quite *genially* (par. 23)

2. What are definitions for the words below? Look at words within them, which you may be able to recognize.
   a. moodily
   b. dreadful
   c. Eurasian
   d. incuriously
   e. formality

THINKING CRITICALLY ABOUT THE ESSAY

Understanding the Writer's Ideas

1. The events in the essay occur in Burma, a country in Asia. Describe in your own words the specific details of the action.
2. Who are the major characters in this essay? Why might you include the dog as a major character?
3. In a narrative essay the writer often tells the events in chronological order. Examine the following events from "A Hanging." Arrange them in the order in which they occurred.
   a. A large woolly dog tries to lick the prisoner's face.
   b. A Eurasian boy talks about his silver case.
   c. The superintendent signals "Chalo!" to the hangman.
   d. One prisoner, a Hindu, is brought from his cell.
   e. Francis discusses with the superintendent a prisoner who had to be pulled off the bars of his cage.
   f. The prisoner steps aside to avoid a puddle as he marches to the gallows.
4. What is the author's opinion of *capital punishment* (legally killing someone who has disobeyed the laws of society)? How does the incident with the puddle suggest that opinion, even indirectly?

Understanding the Writer's Techniques

1. What is the main point that the writer wishes to make in this essay? Which paragraph tells the author's thesis most clearly? Which sentence in that paragraph best states the main idea of the essay?

2. In the first paragraph of the essay, we see clear images such as "brown silent men were squatting at the inner bars, with their blankets draped around them." The use of color and action make an instant appeal to our sense of sight.

a. What images in the rest of the essay do you find most vivid?

b. Which sentence gives the best details of sound?

c. What word pictures suggest action and color?

d. Where do you find words that describe a sensation of touch?

3. In order to make their images clearer, writers use *figurative language* (see Glossary). "A Hanging" is especially rich in *similes,* which are comparisons using the word "like" or "as."

a. What simile does Orwell use in the first paragraph in order to let us see how the light slants over the jail yard walls? How does the simile make the scene clearer?

b. What other simile does Orwell use in the first paragraph?

c. Discuss the similes in the paragraphs listed below. What are the things being compared? Are the similes, in your opinion, original? How do they contribute to the image the author intends to create?

(1) It was like men handling a fish (par. 2)

(2) a thick sprouting moustache . . . rather like the moustache of a comic man on the films (par. 2)

(3) It was a high, reiterated cry . . . like the tolling of a bell. (par. 12)

(4) The Indians had gone grey like bad coffee (par. 13)

(5) He was dangling with his toes pointed straight downwards, slowly revolving, as dead as a stone. (par. 15)

4. You know that an important feature of narration is the writer's ability to look at a brief span of time and to expand that moment with specific language.

a. How has Orwell limited the events in "A Hanging" to a specific moment in time and place?

b. How does the image "a sodden morning of the rains" in paragraph 1 set the mood for the main event portrayed in the essay? What is the effect of the image "brown silent men"? Why does Orwell describe the prisoner as "a puny wisp of a man, with a shaven head and vague liquid eyes" (par. 2)? Why does the author present him in almost a comic way?

c. What is the effect of the image about the bugle call in paragraph 3? Why does Orwell create the image of the dog trying to lick the prisoner's face (par. 6)? How does it contribute to his main point? In paragraph 12, Orwell tells us that the dog whines. Why does he give that detail? Discuss the value of the images about the dog in paragraphs 15 and 17.

d. Why does Orwell offer the image of the prisoner stepping aside "to avoid a puddle on the path"? How does it advance the point of the essay? What is the effect of the image of the superintendent poking the ground with his stick (par. 13)?

e. What is the importance of the superintendent's words in paragraph 3? What is the value of the Eurasian boy's conversation in paragraph 18? How does the dialogue in paragraphs 20 to 24 contribute to Orwell's main point?

f. Why has Orwell left out information about the crime the prisoner committed? How would you feel about the prisoner if you knew he were, say, a rapist, a murderer, a molester of children, or a heroin supplier?

5. Analyze the point of view in the essay. Is the "I" narrator an observer, a participant, or both? Is he neutral or involved? Support your opinion.

6. In "A Hanging," Orwell skillfully uses several forms of *irony* to support his main ideas. Irony, in general, is the use of language to suggest the opposite of what is said. First, there is *verbal irony,* which involves a contrast between what is said and what is actually meant. Second, there is *irony of situation,* where there is a contrast between what is expected or thought appropriate and what actually happens. Then, there is *dramatic irony,* in which there is a contrast between what a character says and what the reader (or the audience) actually knows or understands.

   a. In paragraph 2, why does Orwell describe the prisoner as a *comic* type? Why does he emphasize the prisoner's *smallness?* Why does Orwell write that the prisoner "hardly noticed what was happening"? Why might this be called ironic?

   b. When the dog appears in paragraph 6, how is its behavior described? How do the dog's actions contrast with the situation?

c. What is the major irony that Orwell analyzes in paragraph 10?
d. In paragraph 11, how does the fact that one prisoner is being used to execute another prisoner strike you?
e. Why is the superintendent's remark in paragraph 16—"*He's* all right"—a good example of verbal irony?
f. After the hanging, the men engage in seemingly normal actions. However, Orwell undercuts these actions through the use of irony. Find at least three examples of irony in paragraphs 17 to 24.

Exploring the Writer's Ideas

1. Orwell is clearly against capital punishment. Why might you agree or disagree with him? Are there any crimes for which capital punishment is acceptable to you? If not, what should society do with those convicted of serious crimes?
2. Do you think the method used to perform capital punishment has anything to do with the way we view it? Is death by hanging or firing squad worse than death by gas or by the electric chair? Or are they all the same? Socrates—a Greek philosopher convicted of conspiracy—was forced to drink *hemlock,* a fast-acting poison. Can you accept that?
3. Orwell shows a variety of reactions people have to an act of execution. Can you believe the way the people behave here? Why? How do you explain the large crowds that gathered to watch public executions in Europe in the sixteenth and seventeenth centuries?

IDEAS FOR WRITING

Prewriting

Make two columns on a sheet of paper that you have headed *Capital Punishment.* In one column, jot down all the reasons you can think of in favor of capital punishment. In the other column, indicate all the reasons you can think of against it.

Guided Writing

Write a narrative essay in which you tell about a punishment you either saw or received. Use sensory language, selecting your details carefully. At one point in your paper—as Orwell does in paragraph 10—state your opinion or interpretation of the punishment clearly.

1. Use a number of images that name colors, sounds, smells, and actions.
2. Try to write at least three original similes. Think through your comparisons carefully. Make sure they are logical. Avoid overused comparisons like "He was white as a ghost."
3. Set your narrative in time and place. Tell the season of the year and the place in which the event occurred.
4. Fill in details of the setting. Show what the surroundings look like.
5. Name people by name. Show details of their actions. Quote some of their spoken dialogue.
6. Use the first-person point of view.

Thinking and Writing Collaboratively

In small groups, read drafts of each other's essays for the Guided Writing activity. Look especially at the point at which the writer states an opinion about or interprets the punishment received. Does the writer adequately explain the event? What insights has the writer brought to the moment by analyzing it? How could either the narrative itself or the interpretation be made clearer or more powerful?

More Writing Projects

1. Narrate in your journal an event that turned out differently from what you expected—a blind date, a picnic, a holiday. Try to stress the irony of the situation.
2. Write a narrative paragraph that describes a vivid event in which you hid your true feelings about the event, such as a

postelection party, the wedding of someone you disliked, a job interview, a visit to the doctor.

3. Write an editorial for your college newspaper supporting or attacking the idea of capital punishment. Communicate your position through the use of real or hypothetical narration of a relevant event.

SUMMING UP: CHAPTER 4

1. Orwell's essay has remained one of the outstanding essays of the century, widely anthologized and frequently taught in English writing classes. How do you account for its popularity? Would you consider it the best essay in this chapter or in the four chapters you have read so far? Why or why not? Write an essay in which you analyze and evaluate "A Hanging."
2. Elizabeth Wong and Nicholas Weinstock both challenge cultural assumptions about fitting into other societies. Use their narratives as a starting point, and write an essay about a particular time in your childhood when you tried to accept, ignore, or defy a given cultural or social expectation.
3. You are Richard Selzer (author of "The Discus Thrower," pages 106–109) and you have been asked by a local newspaper to write a short review of George Orwell's "A Hanging." Basing your insights on the philosophy of "The Discus Thrower," write the review. Or, if you choose, be George Orwell and write a review of Selzer's "The Discus Thrower."
4. What have you learned about writing strong narratives from the writers in this chapter? What generalizations can you draw? What "rules" can you derive? Write an essay called "How to Write Narratives" based on what you have learned from Wong, Hughes, Weinstock, and (or) Orwell. Make specific references to the writer(s) of your choice.
5. Hughes's essay highlights the role of religion in life. Write an essay in which you narrate an important religious experience that you remember. You might want to narrate the story of your own "conversion."

CHAPTER 5

Illustration

WHAT IS ILLUSTRATION?

One convenient way for writers to present and to support a point is through *illustration*—that is, by means of several examples to back up an idea. Illustration (or *exemplification*) helps a writer put general or abstract thoughts into specific examples. As readers, we often find that we are able to understand a writer's point more effectively because we respond to the concrete examples. We are familiar with illustration in everyday life. If a police officer is called a racist, the review board will want *illustrations* of the racist behavior. The accuser will have to provide concrete examples of racist language, or present arrest statistics that show the officer was more likely to arrest Koreans, for instance, than white Americans.

Writing that uses illustration is most effective if it uses *several* examples to support the thesis. A single, isolated example might not convince anyone easily, but a series of examples builds up a stronger case. Writers can also use an *extended example,* which is one example that is developed at length.

For instance, you might want to illustrate your thesis that American patchwork quilts are an important record of women's history. Since your reader might not be familiar with quilts, you would have to illustrate your argument with examples such as these:

- Baltimore album quilts were given to eastern women heading west in the nineteenth century, and contain signatures and dates stitched in the squares to mark the event.

- Women used blue and white in quilt patterns to show their support for the temperance movement that opposed sale of alcohol.
- Women named patterns after geographic and historical events, creating such quilts as Rocky Road to Kansas and Abe Lincoln's Platform.
- African-American quilters adapted techniques from West Africa to make blankets for slave quarters.
- One quilter from Kentucky recorded all the deaths in her family in her work. The unusual quilt contains a pattern of a cemetery and coffins with names for each family member!

If you visited a museum and there was only one painting on the wall, you would probably feel that you hadn't gotten your money's worth. You expect a museum to be a *collection* of paintings, so that you can study a variety of types of art or several paintings by the same painter in order to understand the whole field of art. In the same way, through the accumulation of illustrations, the writer builds a case for the thesis.

In this chapter, Brent Staples, an African-American journalist, illustrates the ways in which some people perceive his mere presence on a street at night as a threat. Mike Lupica uses humorous examples to illustrate the fall of the great American sports hero. James Popkin with Katia Hetter looks at America's gambling craze. Finally, Lewis Thomas uses examples from his experience as a surgeon to illustrate how death is a natural part of the life cycle. Each writer knows that one example is insufficient to create a case, but that multiple examples yield a convincing essay.

HOW DO WE READ ILLUSTRATION?

Reading illustration requires us to ask ourselves these questions:

- What is the writer's thesis? What is the *purpose* of the examples?
- What audience is the writer addressing? How do we know?
- What other techniques is the writer using? Is there narration? description? How are these used to help the illustration?
- In what order has the writer arranged the examples? Where is the most important example placed?

- How does the writer use *transitions?* Often, transitions in illustration essays enumerate: *first, second, third; one, another.*

HOW DO WE WRITE WITH ILLUSTRATIONS?

Read the selections critically to see the many ways in which writers can use illustrations to support an idea. Notice how many illustrations each writer provides, and plan to do the same in your essay.

Select your topic and write a thesis sentence that tells the reader what you are going to illustrate and what your main idea is about the subject.

Sample thesis statement:

> Quilts have long been cherished for their beautiful colors and patterns, but few collectors recognize the history stitched into the squares.

Make a list of *examples* to support the thesis.

Examples by quilt types: Baltimore album quilts, political quilts, suffrage quilts, slave quilts, graveyard quilts

Examples by quilt pattern names: Radical Rose; Drunkard's Path; Memory Blocks; Old Maid's Puzzle; Wheel of Mystery; Log Cabin; Rocky Road to Kansas; Slave Chain; Underground Railroad; Delectable Mountains; Union Star; Jackson Star; Old Indian Trail; Trip around the World

Determine who the audience will be; a group of experienced quilters? museum curators? a PTA group? Each is a different audience with different interests and needs.

Plan an arrangement of the examples. Begin with the least important and build up to the most important. Or arrange the examples in chronological order.

Plan to use other techniques (such as description), especially if your audience is unfamiliar with your subject. If you are writing the quilt paper and using the example of the Baltimore album quilt, you would then have to *describe* it for readers who do not know what such a quilt looks like.

Be sure that the *purpose* of the illustrations is clearly stated, especially in the conclusion. In the quilt essay, for instance, different quilt patterns might be illustrated in order to encourage readers to preserve and study quilts.

Writing and Revising the Draft

Use the first paragraph to introduce the subject and to set up a clear thesis. You might introduce an *abstract* idea, such as forgotten history, that will be *illustrated* in the examples.

Plan the body to give the reader lots of examples, and to develop the examples if necessary. Use narration, description, and dialogue to enhance the illustrations. Write a conclusion that returns to the abstract idea you began with in the introduction.

Write a second draft for reading aloud.

Revise, based on your listener's comments. Proofread the essay carefully. Check spelling and grammar. Make a final copy.

Night Walker

Brent Staples

Brent Staples is an editorial writer for *The New York Times* and holds a Ph.D. in psychology from the University of Chicago. Yet, since his youth, he has instilled fear and suspicion in many just by taking nighttime walks to combat his insomnia. In this essay, which appeared in the *Los Angeles Times* in 1986, Staples explains how others perceive themselves as his potential victim simply because he is a black man in "urban America."

PREREADING: THINKING ABOUT THE ESSAY IN ADVANCE

Imagine this scene: you are walking alone at night in a relatively wealthy neighborhood and you hear footsteps behind you that you believe are the footsteps of someone of a different race from yours. How do you feel? What do you do? Why?

Words to Watch

affluent (par. 1) wealthy
discreet (par. 1) showing good judgment; careful
quarry (par. 2) prey; object of a hunt
dismayed (par. 2) discouraged
taut (par. 4) tight; tense
warrenlike (par. 5) like a crowded tenement district
bandolier (par. 5) gun belt worn across the chest
solace (par. 5) relief; consolation; comfort
retrospect (par. 6) review of past event
ad hoc (par. 7) unplanned; for the particular case at hand
labyrinthine (par. 7) like a maze
skittish (par. 9) nervous; jumpy
constitutionals (par. 10) regular walks

1 My first victim was a woman—white, well dressed, probably in her early 20s. I came upon her late one evening on a deserted street in Hyde Park, a relatively affluent neighborhood in an otherwise mean, impoverished section of Chicago. As I swung onto the avenue behind her, there seemed to be a discreet, uninflammatory distance between us. Not so. She cast back a worried glance. To her, the youngish black man—a broad six feet two inches with a beard and billowing hair, both hands shoved into the pockets of a bulky military jacket—seemed menacingly close. She picked up her pace and was soon running in earnest. Within seconds she disappeared into a cross street.

2 That was more than a decade ago. I was 22 years old, a graduate student newly arrived at the University of Chicago. It was in the echo of that terrified woman's footfalls that I first began to know the unwieldy inheritance I'd come into—the ability to alter public space in ugly ways. It was clear that she thought herself the quarry of a mugger, a rapist, or worse. Suffering a bout of insomnia, however, I was stalking sleep, not defenseless wayfarers. As a softy who is scarcely able to take a knife to a raw chicken—let alone hold one to a person's throat—I was surprised, embarrassed, and dismayed all at once. Her flight made me feel like an accomplice in tyranny. It also made it clear that I was indistinguishable from the muggers who occasionally seeped into the area from the surrounding ghetto. I soon gathered that being perceived as dangerous is a hazard in itself: Where fear and weapons meet—and they often do in urban America—there is always the possibility of death.

3 In that first year, my first away from my hometown, I was to become thoroughly familiar with the language of fear. At dark, shadowy intersections, I could cross in front of a car stopped at a traffic light and elicit the *thunk, thunk, thunk, thunk* of the driver—black, white, male, female—hammering down the door locks. On less traveled streets after dark, I grew accustomed to but never comfortable with people crossing to the other side of the street rather than pass me. Then there were the standard unpleasantries with policemen, doormen, bouncers, cabdrivers, and others whose business it is to screen out troublesome individuals *before* there is any nastiness.

4 I moved to New York nearly two years ago and I have remained an avid night walker. In central Manhattan, the near-

constant crowd covers the tense one-on-one street encounters. Elsewhere, things can get very taut indeed.

After dark, on the warrenlike streets of Brooklyn where I 5
live, I often see women who fear the worst from me. They seem to have set their faces on neutral, and with their purse straps strung across their chests bandolier-style, they forge ahead as though bracing themselves against being tackled. I understand, of course, that the danger they perceive is not a hallucination. Women are particularly vulnerable to street violence, and young black males are drastically overrepresented among the perpetrators of that violence. Yet these truths are no solace against the alienation that comes of being ever the suspect, an entity with whom pedestrians avoid making eye contact.

It is not altogether clear to me how I reached the ripe old 6
age of 22 without being conscious of the lethality nighttime pedestrians attributed to me. Perhaps it was because in Chester, Pa., the small, angry industrial town where I came of age in the 1960s, I was scarcely noticeable against a backdrop of gang warfare, street knifings, and murders. I grew up one of the good boys, had perhaps a half-dozen fistfights. In retrospect, my shyness of combat has clear sources. As a boy, I saw countless tough guys locked away; I have since buried several, too. They were babies, really—a teen-age cousin, a brother of 22, a childhood friend in his mid-20s—all gone down in episodes of bravado played out in the streets. I chose, perhaps unconsciously, to remain a shadow—timid, but a survivor.

The fearsomeness mistakenly attributed to me in public 7
places often has a perilous flavor. The most frightening of these confusions occurred in the late 1970s and early 1980s, when I worked as a journalist in Chicago. One day, rushing into the office of a magazine I was writing for with a deadline story in hand, I was mistaken for a burglar. The office manager called security and, with an ad hoc posse, pursued me through the labyrinthine halls, nearly to my editor's door. I had no way of proving who I was. I could only move briskly toward the company of someone who knew me.

Relatively speaking, however, I never fared as badly as 8
another black male journalist. He went to nearby Waukegan, Ill., a couple of summers ago to work on a story about a murderer who was born there. Mistaking the reporter for the killer, police

officers hauled him from his car at gunpoint and but for his press credentials would probably have tried to book him. Such episodes are not uncommon. Black men trade tales like this all the time.

9 Over the years, I learned to smother the rage I felt at so often being mistaken for a criminal. Not to do so would surely have led to madness. I now take precautions to make myself less threatening. I move about with care, particularly late in the evening. I give a wide berth to nervous people on subway platforms during the wee hours. If I happen to be entering a building behind some people who appear skittish, I may walk by, letting them clear the lobby before I return, so as not to seem to be following them. I have been calm and extremely congenial on those rare occasions when I've been pulled over by the police.

10 And on late-evening constitutionals I employ what has proved to be an excellent tension-reducing measure: I whistle melodies from Beethoven and Vivaldi and the more popular classical composers. Even steely New Yorkers hunching toward nighttime destinations seem to relax, and occasionally they even join in the tune. Virtually everybody seems to sense that a mugger wouldn't be warbling bright, sunny selections from Vivaldi's "Four Seasons." It is my equivalent of the cowbell that hikers wear when they are in bear country.

BUILDING VOCABULARY

1. Use context clues to determine the meaning of each word in italics. Return to the appropriate paragraph in the essay for more clues. Then, if necessary, check your definitions in a dictionary and compare the dictionary meaning with the meaning you derived from the context.
   - **a.** seemed *menacingly* close (par. 1)
   - **b.** I was *indistinguishable* from the muggers who occasionally *seeped* into the area (par. 2)
   - **c.** I have remained an *avid* night walker (par. 4)
   - **d.** they *forge* ahead (par. 5)
   - **e.** Women are particularly *vulnerable* to street violence (par. 5)
   - **f.** the *lethality* nighttime pedestrians attributed to me (par. 6)
   - **g.** episodes of *bravado* played out in the streets (par. 6)

h. I learned to *smother* the rage I felt . . . so often (par. 9)
i. I now take *precautions* to make myself less threatening (par. 9)
j. Even *steely* New Yorkers *hunching* toward nighttime destinations (par. 10)

2. Reread paragraph 1. List all the words suggesting action and all the words involving emotion. What is the cumulative effect?

THINKING CRITICALLY ABOUT THE ESSAY

Understanding the Writer's Ideas

1. Explain in your own words the incident Staples narrates in paragraph 1. Where does it take place? When? How old was the author at the time? What was he doing? During the incident, why did the woman "cast back a worried glance"? Was she really his "victim"? Explain. What was Staples's reaction to the incident?
2. How does Staples describe himself in paragraph 1? What point is he making by such a description?
3. What is the "unwieldy inheritance" mentioned in paragraph 2? What is Staples's definition of it? What is the implied meaning?
4. How would you describe Staples's personality? What does he mean when he describes himself as "a softy"? How does he illustrate the fact that he is "a softy"? Why did he develop this personality?
5. Explain the meaning of the statement, "I soon gathered that being perceived as dangerous is a hazard in itself" (par. 2).
6. What is "the language of fear" (par. 3)? What examples does Staples provide to illustrate this "language"?
7. Why did car drivers lock their doors when the author walked in front of their cars? How did Staples feel about that?
8. Where did Staples grow up? Did he experience the same reactions there to his nighttime walks as he did in Chicago? Why? How was Manhattan different from Chicago for the author? How was Brooklyn different from Manhattan?
9. What has been Staples's reaction to the numerous incidents of mistaken identity? How has he dealt with that reaction?

What "precautions" does he take to make himself "less threatening"?
10. Summarize the example Staples narrates about the black journalist in Waukegan.
11. What has been the author's experiences with the police? Explain.
12. Does the author feel that all the danger people attribute to him when he takes night walks is unfair or unwarranted? Explain.
13. Why does his whistling selections from Beethoven and Vivaldi seem to make people less afraid of the author?

Understanding the Writer's Techniques

1. What is Staples's thesis in this essay?
2. How do the title and opening statement of this essay grasp and hold the reader's interest?
3. Reread the first paragraph. What *mood* or *tone* does Staples establish here? How? Does he sustain that mood? Is there a shift in tone? Explain.
4. How does the author use *narration* in paragraph 1 as a way to illustrate a point? What point is illustrated? Where else does he use narration?
5. What is the effect of the two-word sentence "Not so" in paragraph 1?
6. Staples uses *description* in this essay. Which descriptions serve as illustrations? Explain what ideas they support.
7. *Onomatopoeia* is the use of words whose sounds suggest their sense or action. Where in the essay does Staples use this technique? What action does the sound represent? Why does the author use this technique instead of simply describing the action?
8. What examples from Staples's childhood illustrate why he developed his particular adult personality?
9. Explain the meaning of the final sentence in the essay.
10. *Stereotypes* are oversimplified, uncritical judgments about people, races, issues, events, and so forth. Where in this essay does the author present stereotypes? For what purpose?

11. For whom was this article intended? Why do you think so? Is it written primarily for a white or black audience? Explain.

Exploring the Writer's Ideas

1. In this essay, Staples gives not only examples of his own experiences but also those of other black men. It is interesting, however, that he does not include examples of the experiences of black women. Why do you think he omitted these references? How do you feel about the omission? Are there any recent news stories, either in your city or in others, which might be included as such illustrations?
2. What prejudices and stereotypes about different racial and cultural groups do people in your community hold? Where do these prejudices and stereotypes come from? Do you think any are justified?
3. What everyday situations do you perceive as most dangerous? Why do you perceive them as such? How do you react to protect yourself? Do you feel your perceptions and reactions are realistic? Explain.

IDEAS FOR WRITING

Prewriting

Write down a few of your personality traits, and then jot down ways in which people identify those traits. Also, indicate how people misperceive you—that is, how they reach wrong conclusions about your personality.

Guided Writing

Write an essay that illustrates how something about your personality has been incorrectly perceived at some time or over a period of time.

1. Begin your essay by narrating a single incident that vividly illustrates the misperception. Begin this illustration with a statement.

2. Explain the time context of this incident as it fits into your life or into a continuing misperception.
3. Describe and illustrate "who you really are" in relation to this misperception.
4. Explain how this misperception fits into a larger context outside your immediate, personal experience of it.
5. Write a series of descriptive illustrations to explain how this misperception has continued to affect you over time.
6. Explain how you first became aware of the misperception.
7. If possible, offer illustrations of others who have suffered the same or similar misperceptions of themselves.
8. Write about your emotional reaction to this overall situation.
9. Illustrate how you have learned to cope with the situation.
10. Give your essay a "catchy" title.

Thinking and Writing Collaboratively

Form groups of four or five, and recommend productive ways to solve the key problems raised by Staples in his essay. Take notes, and then as a group write down the problems and their possible solutions. Share the group's writing with the rest of the class.

More Writing Projects

1. Usually stereotypes are thought of as negative. Illustrate at least three *positive* stereotypes in your latest journal entry.
2. Write a paragraph in which you illustrate your family's or friends' misconceptions about your girlfriend/boyfriend, wife/husband, or best friend.
3. What tension reducing measures do you use in situations that might frighten you or in which you might frighten others? Write an essay to address the issue.

Fall of the Legends

Mike Lupica

Mike Lupica, a well-known sports journalist, looks at the history of sports heroes. His essay takes the position that America's sports fans no longer see their heroes as larger than life. Rather, he believes, the new American pastime is watching sports heroes, like O. J. Simpson, fall from grace.

PREREADING: THINKING ABOUT THE ESSAY IN ADVANCE

Think about a comic strip you would create for kids who are sports fans. Who would be the hero for this sports comic strip? What kinds of things would the sports hero be doing in the strip?

Words to Watch

Beowulf (par. 4) hero of Old English epic

mythical (par. 5) fictitious

landscape (par. 17) an expanse of scenery that can be seen in a single view

preconceived (par. 17) to form (as an opinion) before having full knowledge

scrutiny (par. 18) a close, careful examination or study

The most remarkable cheers in sports this year did not come from an arena. They came from the side of a freeway in Los Angeles, from the people who applauded O. J. Simpson as he rode, gun to his head, in the back of a white Ford Bronco, a stream of police cars not far behind. Go, O. J., go! 1

Once it was common—the most normal thing in the world—to put the stars of sports up on pedestals. Now the national pastime seems to be watching them fall one after another. 2

The memorable pictures in sports no longer catch Emmitt Smith running for a touchdown or Barry Bonds at the plate, another baseball on its way out of the park. They show Simpson's 3 mug shot or Mike Tyson in handcuffs or Magic Johnson announcing his retirement from basketball because he has contracted the AIDS virus after years of promiscuity. You can put Michael Jordan, the most famous athlete in the world, on that list, too: Jordan in sunglasses on national television, addressing allegations of million-dollar gambling losses; Jordan on the golf course, wagering a thousand dollars per hole; Jordan on ESPN's SportsCenter almost every night of the summer, striking out as a Double-A baseball player struggling to hit .200.

4 We are not talking about real heroes here, policemen or firemen or soldiers fighting for something important. The great heroes of sports are more like those of movies or fiction. They are larger than life. In a way, Babe Ruth was no more real than Beowulf. But now, forty years after Ruth's death, even the idea of the sports hero in this country is dead, as dead as the Game of the Week in baseball or the Friday Night Fights, dead as the Polo Grounds or Ebbets Field. The list of casualties is long and storied, from blue-collar champion Pete Rose to Hall of Fame ace Steve Carlton. In 1994 alone, Dwight Gooden, the most luminous baseball pitcher since Sandy Koufax, tested positive for drugs (his second offense); Darryl Strawberry, one of Gooden's closest friends, checked himself into rehab (his second visit); Scottie Pippen refused to take the court in an NBA playoff game; Jack Nicklaus served up a few uncensored thoughts on race and golf; Tonya Harding, one of America's darling figure skaters, looked the other way while her husband planned an assault on her closest rival; and John Daly, a golfer who came out of nowhere to win the PGA a few years ago, capturing the imagination of everyone who follows sports, updated his troubled history of alcohol abuse and domestic disputes to include a parking-lot scuffle with an elderly man.

5 Legends are not made by game footage or file tape. They are born in memory and imagination and by word of mouth. Mickey Mantle is a legend. In his playing days and beyond, he was the kind of mythical star Ruth had been. He played the second half of his career on ruined knees, but he always seemed larger than life. Now the Mantle of legend, the Mantle of memory, has been replaced by Mantle the recovering alcoholic, a February graduate of the Betty Ford Clinic.

6 Looking frail and human, more so than he was ever supposed to look, Mantle admitted this year that he had a drinking

problem. After he returned from rehab, I sent a note to his New York hotel, wishing him luck, telling him I was rooting harder for him now than I ever did as a kid. At the bottom of the note, I asked Mantle to give me a call. I thought I might write a column about his experience.

Later that night, I was watching the Yankees on television 7
when the phone rang.

"Mike?" 8

I smiled. "Hey, Mickey, thanks for calling." 9

There was a pause at the other end of the line, and then in 10
a quiet voice Mantle said, "How'd you know it was me?"

If you grew up in Upstate New York in the Fifties and Six- 11
ties—as I did—you rooted for the Yankees, listened to them on the radio, and watched them on television. Mel Allen and Red Barber and Phil Rizzuto brought you the games. Mantle was the sports hero. I tried to explain that to him. "If I don't know your voice by now . . ." I said, letting the thought drift away, back toward the time when Mantle hit those balls out of sight, the ones Mel Allen described as going . . . going . . . gone.

There was another pause. "Thanks for the note," Mantle 12
said.

I told him I meant it. 13

"I get a lot of notes just like it these days," he said. "My 14
mail's so different now you wouldn't believe it. You can't even call it fan mail anymore. It's more like letters from close friends. It's so unbelievable it touches my heart. It makes me cry."

Cheers never did that. 15

There is no one thing that killed the American sports hero. Some 16
got sick and some were arrested. Some got drunk and some got high. Some of them beat up women. And some blew it all on gambling. The only real culprit, it seems, is time. In a different age, Magic Johnson would have been able to screw himself into a coma and face no physical consequences. In another era of sports and life, Desiree Washington might not have had the courage to charge Mike Tyson with rape. Still, it's hard to imagine Roberto Clemente charging fifteen bucks for an autograph or Y. A. Tittle skipping camp to up his paycheck.

If the athletes have changed, it's because the landscape has 17
changed. Today's players come to the big time with their wallets

full and some preconceived idea of what a sports hero should be, how they should play things, and how they should be marketed. They are handed $60 million contracts when they leave college. You have to wonder how many of the heroes of the past could have taken that kind of hit and had the same careers. Would it have gone as well for Willie Mays if he had been rich beyond imagination at the age of twenty? Or Jack Kramer? Or even Jack Nicklaus?

18 There is more to this than money, though. The fan has changed as well. He wants to know too much. And those of us in the media are only too willing to give him what he wants. With each passing year, it seems the fan gets closer to the field. He gets into the action, then all the way into the locker room. And soon he discovers what I found out a long time ago: A seat in the stands is still the best seat in sports. The athletes may look small from high up in the stadium, but you can still make them out to be big. It's safe to assume, though, that Willie Mays's public relations would have been no better today than those of his godson Barry Bonds, who is known to be prickly himself and occasionally—at least in his dealings with the media—to be just a prick. And I do not believe Joe DiMaggio, one of the few enduring sports heroes, would have stood up to the day-to-day scrutiny that modern ballplayers face. He would not enjoy being staked out by autograph hunters in a hotel lobby; he would not like hiding from the reporters and talk-show producers who stalk today's stars.

19 It's true. Sports heroes have destroyed themselves, but we have helped them off the pedestal. We love their skills but hate the money they make. We demand that they reveal themselves, and then when we see them as they really are, we blame *them* for letting us down. That is why most fans react with such viciousness when one of their heroes turns out to be a drunk or an addict. We don't ever want to hear how sick these guys are. After all, they are rich and talented and, by God, they should know better.

20 The best chance an athlete has is to be someone from the past. Mantle, who comes from a time when sports heroes were still gods, was greeted as warmly as ever when he showed himself to the world as just another aging, beat-up ex-drunk. He was celebrated for his recovery from alcoholism at the very time that Gooden was vilified by the angry children of sports journalism for having the nerve to act like an addict.

When Mantle and I spoke on the telephone, I told him that 21
he might hear the biggest cheer of his life when he returned to Yankee Stadium for Oldtimer's Day.

"If that is true," Mantle said, "it would have to be some 22
cheer, wouldn't it?"

As it turned out, the reception he got was not the greatest of 23
his life. Just another one. They cheered Mickey Mantle at Yankee Stadium because he is still around. In a time when the sports hero is dead, he is a survivor.

BUILDING VOCABULARY

Separate the words below into two lists: (1) those words that refer to positive aspects of sports heroes and (2) those words that refer to negative aspects. Define the terms using the dictionary or context clues.

a. pedestals (par. 2)
b. promiscuity (par. 3)
c. luminous (par. 4)
d. legend (par. 5)
e. to be a prick (par. 18)
f. vilified (par. 20)

THINKING CRITICALLY ABOUT THE ESSAY

Understanding the Writer's Ideas

1. According to this writer, what do the cheers for O. J. Simpson fleeing police in his white Bronco say about Americans and their relation to sports heroes?
2. Who would be this writer's real heroes? Why?
3. What has caused the death of the American sports hero for Lupica?
4. How did Mickey Mantle become a baseball legend?
5. What does Mickey Mantle mean when he says he gets fan mail that seems "more like letters from close friends"?
6. What killed the American sports hero, besides crimes committed?

7. The writer says that sports fans just aren't what they used to be. Why does he feel this way?
8. How are fans partly responsible for the death of the American sports hero?
9. For Lupica, what is the only way for an athlete today to become a sports hero?

Understanding the Writer's Techniques

1. What is the thesis of this essay?
2. What detail does Lupica use in the opening paragraph to illustrate his thesis?
3. Of all the sports heroes in the essay, Lupica focuses on Mickey Mantle more than anyone else. How does this focus support the thesis?
4. Lupica claims that fans want to get too close to sports stars. Yet in his own essay, he tells of a private phone conversation he had with Mickey Mantle. Why does the writer contradict the essay's main point?
5. Is this essay written for sports fans or the general public? How do you know?

Exploring the Writer's Ideas

1. Do you agree with this writer's thesis that Americans enjoying watching sports heroes fall? Why or why not?
2. According to Lupica, real heroes are police officers and fire fighters. Why are they more important than sports stars? Do you agree or disagree?
3. O. J. Simpson, Mike Tyson, and Tonya Harding are only a few examples used by Lupica of fallen stars. Do you think that there are enough fallen sports figures to make this thesis stick, or is Lupica overstating his thesis? Why or why not?
4. Who is your hero? Is this person on a pedestal for you, or fallen? Explain.
5. If, as the writer believes, police officers and fire fighters are more important than sports figures, shouldn't they get more money than the sports star? What's your position?
6. The media plays a big role in bringing the private lives of fallen sports heroes into America's living rooms. Should the

media give the fans what they want, or should the media try to restore sports heroes to their pedestals? Explain.

IDEAS FOR WRITING

Prewriting

Imagine that you are put on a pedestal of fame. What would your claim to fame be? Would you keep your private life away from the media? Would you be a role model? Freewrite on this possibility.

Guided Writing

Fill in the blank in the following sentence: "I should be a hero because __________." Then write an essay that illustrates your reasons.

1. To fill in the blank: Select some important aspect of your life to elaborate on. Consider a time you helped your community clean up a park, or a time you helped a friend in trouble.
2. Use the above sentence as your thesis. Work it into the introduction like Lupica—after you describe a scene to illustrate some aspect of your heroic effort.
3. Provide at least two or three detailed illustrations of your heroic deed to support your thesis. With each illustration, show why what you did was heroic.
4. Focus on how or why you could have fallen from your pedestal but didn't. (If you did fall from your pedestal, elaborate here.)
5. Conclude the essay by suggesting the best way for others to become heroic themselves.

Thinking and Writing Collaboratively

In groups, contribute specific illustrations of people who you think should be considered heroes in your community and why. Then use what the group has gathered to survey potential heroes in America.

More Writing Projects

1. In your journal, illustrate ways people you've felt were important have disappointed you.
2. Focus a paragraph to illustrate one person who has disappointed you the most.
3. Write an essay using all the notes from above to illustrate the ways in which people have disappointed you.

America's Gambling Craze

James Popkin with Katia Hetter

James Popkin and Katia Hetter explore the growth and history of gambling in America. They look at its impact on cities and suburbs seeking to raise tax money from gambling revenues, as well as the increasing social problems associated with gambling. They use compelling statistics and facts to illustrate their point.

PREREADING: THINKING ABOUT THE ESSAY IN ADVANCE

What are your views on gambling? Should it be legal? Why or why not? Should states use any form of gambling to raise money for services and reduce taxes? Why or why not?

Words to Watch

sanctioned (par. 3) gave approval or consent to

jai alai (par. 4) an extremely fast court game in which players use a long, hand-shaped basket strapped to the wrist to propel the ball against a wall

Prohibition (par. 5) a period in American history (1920–33) during which laws prohibited the sale, manufacture, transport, or possession of alcoholic beverages

revenue (par. 8) all the income produced by a particular source

No one howled in protest last month when H&R Block set up makeshift tax-preparation offices in four Nevada casinos and offered gamblers same-day "refund-anticipation loans." And few people cared recently when a Florida inventor won a U.S. patent that could someday enable television audiences to legally bet on game shows, football games and even beauty pageants from their homes. 1

What's the deal? Not that long ago, Americans held gambling in nearly the same esteem as heroin dealing and applauded 2 when ax-wielding police paid a visit to the corner dice room. But moral outrage has become as outmoded as a penny slot machine. In 1955, for example, baseball commissioner Ford Frick considered wagering so corrupt he prohibited major leaguers from overnighting in Las Vegas. Last year, by contrast, Americans for the first time made more trips to casinos than they did to Major League ballparks—some 92 million trips, according to one study.

3 It took six decades for gambling to become America's Pastime, from the legalization of Nevada casinos in 1931 to April Fool's Day 1991, when Davenport, Iowa, launched the Diamond Lady, the nation's first legal riverboat casino. The gradual creation of 37 state lotteries broke down the public's mistrust, conveying a clear message that the government sanctioned gambling; indeed, is even coming to depend on it as a tax-revenue source. Corporate ownership of casinos helped in its own way, too, replacing shady operators with trusted brand names like Hilton and MGM. Casinos now operate or are authorized in 23 states, and 95 percent of all Americans are expected to live within a three- or four-hour drive of one by the year 2000.

4 Today, the Bible Belt might as well be renamed the Blackjack Belt, with floating and land-based casinos throughout Mississippi and Louisiana and plans for more in Florida, Texas, Alabama and Arkansas. Meanwhile, the Midwest is overrun with slot hogs, none of the porcine variety. Iowa, Illinois, Indiana and Missouri allow riverboat gambling, and a 50,000-square-foot land-based casino is scheduled to open in mid-May just outside Detroit, in Windsor, Ontario. Low-stakes casinos attract visitors to old mining towns in Colorado and South Dakota, and Indian tribes operate 225 casinos and high-stakes bingo halls nationwide. Add church bingo, card rooms, sports wagering, dog and horse racing and jai alai to the mix and it becomes clear why Americans legally wagered $330 billion in 1992—a 1,800 percent increase over 1976.

5 **Calling for new games.** Like the first bars that opened after Prohibition, modern gambling halls are enormously successful. "It will be impossible not to make a lot of money," one executive in New Orleans bragged before his casino had even opened. "It's like spitting and missing the floor." Such boasts—and the real possibility that the boom will create 500,000 jobs nationwide this decade—have not been lost on federal, state and local lawmak-

ers. In the first six weeks of this year alone they introduced more than 200 bills regarding gambling.

But casinos and lotteries may not guarantee the jackpots many politicians expect. When urban-planning professor Robert Goodman reviewed the economic-impact studies that 14 government agencies relied upon before deciding to embrace casino gambling, he found that most were written with a pro-industry spin and only four were balanced and factored in gambling's hidden costs. Goodman's two-year study, due out next week, concludes that newly opened casinos "suck money out of the local economy," away from existing movie theaters, car dealerships, clothing shops and sports arenas. In Atlantic City, for example, about 100 of 250 local restaurants have closed since the casinos debuted in 1978, says Goodman, who teaches at the University of Massachusetts at Amherst. 6

"Slum by the sea." States that get hooked on gambling revenues soon suffer withdrawal symptoms when local competition kicks in. Although pioneering casinos and lotteries typically are profitable, gambling grosses decline when lotteries or casinos open in neighboring states. In Biloxi, Miss., for example, slot revenues at first topped about $207 per machine per day. A year later when competitors moved in, however, the daily win-per-machine figure dipped to $109. 7

States frequently overestimate the financial impact of gambling revenues, too. "Legalized gambling is never large enough to solve any social problems," says gambling-law professor and paid industry consultant I. Nelson Rose. In New Jersey, for example, horse racing alone accounted for about 10 percent of state revenue in the 1950s. Today, despite the addition of a lottery and 12 casinos, the state earns only 6 percent of its revenue through gambling. "Atlantic City used to be a slum by the sea," says Rose. "Now it's a slum by the sea with casinos." 8

America's love affair with dice and cards has always been a fickle romance, and some academics predict a breakup soon. Legalized gambling in America has been running on a 70-year boom-and-bust cycle since the colonists started the first lotteries. "We're now riding the third wave of legal gambling" that began with the Depression, says Rose, who has written extensively on the subject and teaches at Whittier Law School in Los Angeles. The trend self-destructs after a few decades, when the public sim- 9 ply gets fed up and embraces more-conservative values. Rose believes a cheating or corruption scandal will trigger the next crash in about 35 years, an idea that most casino officials think is ludicrous.

10 The sky is not falling yet. Apart from a handful of academics and the odd politician, few Americans are seriously questioning the morality of an industry that is expected to help gamblers lose a record $35 billion in 1995 alone. Religious leaders have been oddly silent, perhaps because so many churches and synagogues rely on bingo revenues. "The biggest things we have to help people are churches and temples and the government," says Arnie Wexler, executive director of the Council on Compulsive Gambling of New Jersey. "And now they're all in the gambling business."

11 **Getting hooked.** The consequences can be damaging. Wexler says he got a phone call late last week from a man in his 70s who ran up $150,000 in debt just by buying lottery tickets. Although most gambling experts believe that only 1 percent to 3 percent of Americans have a serious gambling problem at any given time, a July 1993 Gallup Poll funded by Wexler's group suggests that the figure may be closer to 5 percent. Regardless, now that casinos are no longer located just in Atlantic City and Nevada it's reasonable to assume that the total number of problem gamblers will soar. "If you put a guy who wouldn't cheat on his wife in a room with a gorgeous nude woman, some guys would fall by the wayside," Wexler says. "When you make gambling legal and socially acceptable, people will try it and some of them will get hooked."

12 But try telling that to a gambler happily feeding a slot machine and waiting for a multimillion-dollar payoff. Fifty-one percent of American adults now find casino gambling "acceptable for anyone," and 35 percent describe it as "acceptable for others but not for me," according to a recent Yankelovich Inc. survey paid for by Harrah's Casinos. The attraction is simple. "The action for them is the thrill of what's going to happen in the next pull of that slot-machine handle," explains Harrah's president, Phil Satre.

BUILDING VOCABULARY

Write sentences in which you use the following words correctly. Use a dictionary.

a. spin (par. 6)
b. factored (par. 6)
c. debuted (par. 6)
d. fickle (par. 9)
e. ludicrous (par. 9)

THINKING CRITICALLY ABOUT THE ESSAY

Understanding the Writer's Ideas

1. How do Americans view gambling today as opposed to forty years ago?
2. What eventually broke down the public's mistrust of gambling?
3. Gambling enthusiasts claim that gambling has economic benefits other than tax revenues. What are they? Do you think this claim is accurate? Why or why not?
4. What do the writers mean when they refer to the "slum by the sea"? Explain.
5. Why, according to this article, are religious leaders silent about the ills of gambling?
6. What is the theory about the history of gambling?
7. According to the essay, can someone who gambles get hooked and ruin his or her life? Do you see the potential of getting hooked as a serious objection to gambling? Why or why not?
8. If most people don't get rich on gambling, why do so many do it, according to the writers?

Understanding the Writer's Techniques

1. What is unusual about the way the writers introduce the thesis? What is the thesis?
2. How does the word "howled" (par. 1) set the tone of the essay?
3. Before paragraphs 5, 7, and 11 there are subheads (the words in bold print). How are these related to topic sentences?

4. These writers use different kinds of detail to support their thesis. What kinds do they use? Give examples.
5. What is unusual about the topic sentence of the concluding paragraph 12?
6. Will this analysis of gambling find readers who are pro- or anti-gambling? Explain.
7. There are quotes that illustrate the writers' point. But what do you note about the people who are quoted? Are they people who are knowledgeable about the topic? Why? And what does this say about choosing people to quote in an essay?

Exploring the Writer's Ideas

1. Should gambling be considered as morally corrupt as the writers explain? Why or why not?
2. The writers claim that by the year 2000, 95 percent of all Americans will live within a short drive to a gambling casino. Is there any reason to slow such growth? Why or why not?
3. If gamblers wagered $330 billion in 1992, how is it possible for casinos to "suck money from the economy" as the writers suggest? Are the casinos or the gamblers at fault for the implied waste? Explain your answers.
4. Is there something unethical about or wrong with so many churches and synagogues using gambling to raise revenues? Why or why not?
5. Given that gambling is addictive and leads to serious debt problems, why is the government sponsoring it in the form of lotteries? Should governments be more responsible? Explain your position.
6. What does Harrah's Casinos president mean by the fact that the attraction to gambling is simple: "The thrill of what's going to happen . . . next"? Do you agree or disagree?
7. If, as these writers suggest, TV audiences will one day be able to bet on games from the home, should Americans rethink the future of such technology given the problems with gambling stated in this essay? Use examples to illustrate your view.

IDEAS FOR WRITING

Prewriting

Write a letter to your local political leader in which you outline reasons that gambling as a source of revenue would be good or bad for your community.

Guided Writing

Illustrate a problem in your community that could be solved with money (i.e., building repair, new schools, etc.). Look at whether or not gambling would be a good way for your community to obtain this money.

1. Begin the essay by illustrating the problem in your community.
2. Give the details of how money could solve this problem.
3. Illustrate the kinds of problems and benefits associated with gambling that might occur in your community.
4. Take a position on why gambling is or is not the best way for your community to raise money to solve its problem.
5. Offer other ways of raising money in your community without resorting to gambling.
6. In conclusion, take a final position on gambling and its place in your community.

Thinking and Writing Collaboratively

Exchange essays with another student in the class and, after you read the paper, make an outline to show the writer's thesis and the different examples provided to support the thesis. Then discuss with the writer the clarity and force of his or her essay, using the outline you prepared.

More Writing Projects

1. In your journal, reflect on your earliest experiences with some type of gambling. If you've never been exposed to gambling, why is that?

2. Write a paragraph about why you find the kind of gambling described in the above essay acceptable or against your moral code.
3. Write an essay that uses illustration to detail your own experience with gambling, highlighting your personal views on the issue.

Death in the Open

Lewis Thomas

Dr. Lewis Thomas was president of the Memorial Sloan-Kettering Cancer Center in New York City. He wrote numerous articles about science, medicine, and life structures and cycles geared for the lay reader. His observations often bring fascinating clarity to the cycles of life and death on our planet. The following essay, a brilliant inquiry into the "natural marvel" of death, appears in his book *Lives of a Cell* (1974), which won the National Book Award for Arts and Letters in 1975.

PREREADING: THINKING ABOUT THE ESSAY IN ADVANCE

A familiar phenomenon that many of us have witnessed is an animal's dead body—a squirrel, a mouse, a bird, a cat or dog—on a street or highway, dead either as roadkill or from natural causes. Reflect a moment on such a phenomenon. What do you think of and feel when you witness such a scene?

Words to Watch

voles (par. 1) the members of any one of several species of small rodents

impropriety (par. 2) an improper action or remark

progeny (par. 4) descendants or offspring

mutation (par. 4) a sudden genetic change

amebocytes (par. 4) one-celled organisms

stipulated (par. 6) made a special condition for

incongruity (par. 6) something which is not consistent with its environment

conspicuous (par. 7) very obvious

inexplicably (par. 7) unexplainably

anomalies (par. 10) irregularities

notion (par. 11) an idea

detestable (par. 11) hateful

synchrony (par. 11) simultaneous occurrence

1 Most of the dead animals you see on highways near the cities are dogs, a few cats. Out in the countryside, the forms and coloring of the dead are strange; these are the wild creatures. Seen from a car window they appear as fragments, evoking memories of woodchucks, badgers, skunks, voles, snakes, sometimes the mysterious wreckage of a deer.

2 It is always a queer shock, part a sudden upwelling of grief, part unaccountable amazement. It is simply astounding to see an animal dead on a highway. The outrage is more than just the location; it is the impropriety of such visible death, anywhere. You do not expect to see dead animals in the open. It is the nature of animals to die alone, off somewhere, hidden. It is wrong to see them lying out on the highway; it is wrong to see them anywhere.

3 Everything in the world dies, but we only know about it as a kind of abstraction. If you stand in a meadow, at the edge of a hillside, and look around carefully, almost everything you can catch sight of is in the process of dying, and most things will be dead long before you are. If it were not for the constant renewal and replacement going on before your eyes, the whole place would turn to stone and sand under your feet.

4 There are some creatures that do not seem to die at all; they simply vanish totally into their own progeny. Single cells do this. The cell becomes two, then four, and so on, and after a while the last trace is gone. It cannot be seen as death; barring mutation, the descendants are simply the first cell, living all over again. The cycles of the slime mold have episodes that seem as conclusive as death, but the withered slug, with its stalk and fruiting body, is plainly the transient tissue of a developing animal; the free-swimming amebocytes use this organ collectively in order to produce more of themselves.

5 There are said to be a billion billion insects on the earth at any moment, most of them with very short life expectancies by our standards. Someone has estimated that there are 25 million assorted insects hanging in the air over every temperate square mile, in a column extending upward for thousands of feet, drifting through the layers of the atmosphere like plankton. They are dying steadily, some by being eaten, some just dropping in their tracks, tons of them around the earth, disintegrating as they die, invisibly.

6 Who ever sees dead birds, in anything like the huge numbers stipulated by the certainty of the death of all birds? A dead

bird is an incongruity, more startling than an unexpected live bird, sure evidence to the human mind that something has gone wrong. Birds do their dying off somewhere, behind things, under things, never on the wing.

Animals seem to have an instinct for performing death 7
alone, hidden. Even the largest, most conspicuous ones find ways to conceal themselves in time. If an elephant missteps and dies in an open place, the herd will not leave him there; the others will pick him up and carry the body from place to place, finally putting it down in some inexplicably suitable location. When elephants encounter the skeleton of an elephant out in the open, they methodically take up each of the bones and distribute them, in a ponderous ceremony, over neighboring acres.

It is a natural marvel. All of the life of the earth dies, all of 8
the time, in the same volume as the new life that dazzles us each morning, each spring. All we see of this is the odd stump, the fly struggling on the porch floor of the summer house in October, the fragment on the highway. I have lived all my life with an embarrassment of squirrels in my backyard, they are all over the place, all year long, and I have never seen, anywhere, a dead squirrel.

I suppose it is just as well. If the earth were otherwise, and 9
all the dying were done in the open, with the dead there to be looked at, we would never have it out of our minds. We can forget about it much of the time, or think of it as an accident to be avoided, somehow. But it does make the process of dying seem more exceptional than it really is, and harder to engage in at the times when we must ourselves engage.

In our way, we conform as best we can to the rest of nature. 10
The obituary pages tell us of the news that we are dying away, while the birth announcements in finer print, off at the side of the page, inform us of our replacements, but we get no grasp from this of the enormity of scale. There are 3 billion of us on the earth, and all 3 billion must be dead, on a schedule, within this lifetime. The vast mortality, involving something over 50 million of us each year, takes place in relative secrecy. We can only really know of the deaths in our households, or among our friends. These, detached in our minds from all the rest, we take to be unnatural events, anomalies, outrages. We speak of our own dead in low voices; struck down, we say, as though visible death can only occur for cause, by disease or violence, avoidably. We send off for flowers, grieve, make cere-

monies, scatter bones, unaware of the rest of the 3 billion on the same schedule. All of that immense mass of flesh and bone and consciousness will disappear by absorption into the earth, without recognition by the transient survivors.

11 Less than a half century from now, our replacements will have more than doubled the numbers. It is hard to see how we can continue to keep the secret, with such multitudes doing the dying. We will have to give up the notion that death is catastrophe, or detestable, or avoidable, or even strange. We will need to learn more about the cycling of life in the rest of the system, and about our connection to the process. Everything that comes alive seems to be in trade for something that dies, cell for cell. There might be some comfort in the recognition of synchrony, in the information that we all go down together, in the best of company.

BUILDING VOCABULARY

1. Thomas makes imaginative and often unique use of adjectival expressions. Explain the meaning of each adjective in the phrases below:
   - **a.** *queer* shock (par. 2)
   - **b.** *unaccountable* amazement (par. 2)
   - **c.** *visible* death (pars. 2 and 10)
   - **d.** *transient* tissue (par. 4)
   - **e.** *ponderous* ceremony (par. 7)
   - **f.** *neighboring* acres (par. 7)
   - **g.** *natural* marvel (par. 8)
   - **h.** *vast* mortality (par. 10)
   - **i.** *relative* secrecy (par. 10)
   - **j.** *transient* survivors (par. 10)
2. An *idiom* is an expression that has a special meaning only when taken as a whole; taken separately, the words may not make sense. What are the meanings of the following idioms?
   - **a.** upwelling of grief (par. 2)
   - **b.** catch sight of (par. 3)
   - **c.** on the wing (par. 6)
   - **d.** in time (par. 7)
   - **e.** no grasp . . . of (par. 10)
   - **f.** for cause (par. 10)

THINKING CRITICALLY ABOUT THE ESSAY

Understanding the Writer's Ideas

1. Why does Thomas feel that it is strange to see dead animals in the countryside? How are dead animals more varied in the country than in the city? According to Thomas, for what reason is it a shock to see a dead animal on the road?
2. In paragraph 3, Thomas suggests that death is often an "abstraction." What does he mean by this statement? How does he suggest we can make death something more real? In your own words, for what reasons does he suggest we accept the life-death cycle as a more concrete idea?
3. Why, according to Thomas, do single cells seem not to die?
4. What is the meaning of the question at the beginning of paragraph 6? How does it relate to the theme of the essay? To what does the author compare seeing a dead bird? Why does he call it an "incongruity"? How is it "sure evidence . . . that something has gone wrong"?
5. Explain the process of death among elephants as Thomas describes it.
6. Explain the meaning of "the odd stump" in paragraph 8. What two examples of "the odd stump" does Thomas offer?
7. What example from personal experience does Thomas give to show that dead animals seem "to disappear"?
8. Explain the meaning of the first sentence of paragraph 9. In your own words, tell why Thomas feels the way he does.
9. What is the "secret" in paragraph 11?
10. In paragraph 10 Thomas says, "In our way, we conform as best we can to the rest of nature." What does he mean? What supporting examples does he offer? What is the result? What examples does Thomas give of our reactions to the death of other human beings?
11. Why does Thomas say we must change our attitude toward death? How does he suggest that we do so?

Understanding the Writer's Techniques

1. What is Thomas's thesis in this essay? In what way is it reinforced by the concluding paragraph?

2. Study the introductory paragraphs. Why does the author offer several examples? Why is "the mysterious wreckage of a deer" an especially effective example?
3. Are there any clear illustrations in paragraph 2? Why or why not? What is the effect? Explain the connection between paragraphs 2 and 3.
4. Paragraphs 4 to 8 use illustrations to support a series of generalizations or topic sentences. Put a check mark by the topic sentence in these paragraphs and identify the generalization. Then analyze the illustrations used to support each one. Which examples are the most specific? the most visual? the most personal? Are there any extended examples?
5. How does paragraph 9 serve as a transition to the topic of paragraph 10? Why does Thomas use statistics in paragraph 10? How do they drive his point home?
6. Examine the author's use of pronouns in this essay. First, trace the use of first-person pronouns ("I," "we," "my," "our"). Why does Thomas use such pronouns? Why is their use in paragraph 8 especially effective? Next, consider Thomas's frequent use of the pronoun *it.* (Beginning writers are often instructed to minimize their use of such pronouns as *it, this,* and *that* because they are not specific and may leave the reader confused.) Explain what the word *it* stands for in paragraphs 2, 4, 8, and 9. Why does Thomas use a word whose meaning may be confusing?
7. Thomas uses *figurative language* (see Glossary) in this essay, particularly *similes* and *metaphors* (see Glossary). Explain in your own words the meanings of the following similes and metaphors:
   a. *the mysterious wreckage* of a deer (par. 1)
   b. episodes that seem *as conclusive as death* (par. 4)
   c. drifting through the layers of the atmosphere *like plankton* (par. 5)
8. We may say that the expression "dropping in their tracks" in paragraph 5 is a kind of pun. (A *pun* is a humorous use of a word or an expression that suggests two meanings.) What is the popular expression using the words *dropping* and *flies* that Thomas's phrase puns on?
9. Thomas makes use of a technique called "repetition with a difference"—that is, saying *almost* the same thing for added

emphasis. Explain how repetition with a difference adds effectiveness to the sentences in which each of the following expressions is used:

a. alone, hidden (par. 7)

b. each morning, each spring (par. 8)

c. unnatural events, anomalies, outrages (par. 10)

d. catastrophe, or detestable, or avoidable, or even strange (par. 11)

10. *Parallelism* (see Glossary) is a type of sentence structure within a paragraph that creates a balance in the presentation of ideas and adds emphasis. It often uses a repeating pattern of subjects and verbs, prepositional phrases, questions, and so on. How does Thomas use parallelism in paragraph 3? paragraph 10? paragraph 11?

Exploring the Writer's Ideas

1. We might say that Thomas's title, "Death in the Open," is a double entendre (that is, has a double meaning). In what two ways may we interpret the phrase "in the open" as it relates to the contents of the essay? How do the two meanings relate to the philosophical points Thomas makes, especially in the two opening paragraphs and in the conclusion? Do you feel it is important to be more "open" about death? Why?

2. In paragraph 10, Thomas writes, "We speak of our own dead in low voices; struck down, we . . ." "Struck down" is used here as a *euphemism* (see Glossary) in place of other words that might be upsetting or distasteful. What other euphemisms do we have for death? Euphemisms for dying are often used to explain death to children. Do you think it is right, or necessary, to use such "guarded language" with youngsters? Why? For what other words or expressions do we commonly use euphemisms?

3. At the end of the essay, Thomas suggests that we might be more comfortable with death if we understood it as a natural, common occurrence. What are your feelings about this philosophy?

4. According to Thomas's views in paragraph 9, because we don't often see dead animals "in the open," we are less prepared when we do encounter death. Do you think this reasoning is correct? Why or why not?

5. In paragraph 7 Thomas explains the process of death among elephants. What is your impression of the elephant herd's behavior at the death of one of its members? Why does Thomas call it "a natural marvel"? Have you ever heard the expression "the elephant dying grounds"? What does it mean?
6. Reread Louise Erdrich's "The Blue Jay's Dance" (pages 94–96). What similarities do you find between Thomas's and Erdrich's visions of nature? Discuss them with specific references to the essays. How are the visions different? alike? Which author's ideas most closely resemble your own view of nature?

IDEAS FOR WRITING

Prewriting

Brainstorm for five to ten minutes on the phrase "in the open." What does it mean? What does it mean to you? What various ways can you apply it to elements in your life? What other acts "in the open" surprise, puzzle, stir, or shock you?

Guided Writing

Write an essay in which you illustrate "__________ in the Open." Fill in the blank with a word of your choice, a word that reflects some phenomenon, emotion, or idea whose features are often hard to understand. You might write about birth in the open, concerts in the open, love in the open, fear in the open, or war in the open, for example.

1. Develop an introduction with general examples that are relevant to your topic.
2. Add one or two paragraphs in which you speculate or philosophize on the phenomenon you are writing about.
3. Point out how the topic is most common throughout nature, society, or the world.
4. Give at least three extended examples that illustrate your topic.
5. Use the first-person pronouns "I" and "we" to add emphasis.

6. Illustrate ways in which people are generally unaware of certain features of the topic or tend to hide these features.
7. Try to include at least one statistic in your essay.
8. Use some idiomatic expressions in your essay.
9. Conclude your essay with some examples of how and why we can become more "open" about the topic.

Thinking and Writing Collaboratively

Form small groups, and read the drafts of each other's Guided Writing essays. After general comments about how to take the essay to the next draft, concentrate on the conclusions in each piece. Does the writer give appropriate examples in the conclusion? Do you see how and why the writer feels that we can become more open about the topic at hand?

More Writing Projects

1. For a journal entry, use examples to tell of your first experiences with death. You may want to write about the death of a relative, a friend, an acquaintance, a celebrity, or a pet.
2. Visit a place in the countryside (or a park) for one hour. Make a written record as you walk around detailing all evidence of natural death that you come across. Then write an illustrative paragraph on natural death as you observed it.
3. In your library, explore various burial practices among different races, religions, or ethnic groups and write an essay in which you illustrate several of these practices.

SUMMING UP: CHAPTER 5

1. Richard Selzer ("The Discus Thrower," pages 106–109), Lewis Thomas ("Death in the Open," pages 189–192), and George Orwell ("A Hanging," pages 148–153) all deal with death and dying. Write your own essay about the issue, drawing on points from these three authors to illustrate your own position.
2. From this chapter select the essay that you think best uses the mode of illustration. Write an essay in which you analyze the writer's techniques and strategies. Make specific references to the text.
3. The world of the night, the environment of Staples's "Night Walker," challenges our senses and our perceptions, simply because it is so different from the typical daytime worlds we usually inhabit. What unusual nighttime experiences have you had? How do you feel about the night? Write an essay of illustration to address these questions.
4. The sports arena draws considerable attention from gamblers. What do you think should be the appropriate relation between sports and gambling? What insights from Lupica and Popkin inform your thoughts about betting on the outcomes of games or matches—baseball, football, basketball, boxing? Write an essay using illustration to make your point.

CHAPTER 6

Comparison and Contrast

WHAT IS COMPARISON AND CONTRAST?

When we compare two things, we look for similarities. When we contrast, we look for differences. The comparison-contrast writing strategy, then, is a way of analyzing likenesses and differences between two or more subjects. Usually, the purpose is to evaluate or judge which is superior. Thus we might appreciate soccer if we compare it with football; we understand Roman Catholicism better if we see it in light of Buddhism.

Writers who use the comparison-contrast technique know that careful planning is required to *organize* the likenesses and differences into logical patterns. Some authors might use only *comparison,* to look at the similarities between subjects. Others might use only *contrast.* Often, writers combine the two in a carefully structured essay that balances one with the other.

Like many of the writing and reading strategies you have learned, comparison and contrast is familiar from everyday life. If you were about to buy a new car, for instance, you would look at several models before you made a choice. You might consider price, size, horsepower, options, safety features, status, and dependability before you spent such a large amount of money. If you were deciding whether to send your daughter to a public school or a private school, you would compare and contrast the features of each type of institution: cost, teacher quality, class size, location, curriculum, and composition of the student body might all be considered. If you were an art historian, you might compare and contrast an early picture by Matisse with one he completed late in life in order to understand his development as an artist.

Writing a comparison-contrast essay requires more careful planning, however, than the everyday life application technique. Both call for common sense. You wouldn't compare parochial schools with an Oldsmobile, for instance; they simply don't relate. But you would compare The Dalton School with Public School 34, or a Cutlass Supreme with a Volvo, a Matisse with a Cezanne. Clearly, any strong pattern of comparison and contrast treats items that are in the same category or class. Moreover, there always has to be a basis for comparison; in other words, you compare or contrast two items in order to try to deal with all-important aspects of the things being compared before arriving at a final determination. These commonsense characteristics of comparison and contrast apply to our pattern of thought as well as our pattern of writing.

Author Rachel Carson, for instance, contrasts two visions of the future for planet Earth: a flourishing environment or a devastated landscape. Thus she has a common category: the condition of the global ecology. She can use *contrast* because she has a common ground for her analysis. Ellen Goodman looks at friendships, Alice Walker at two landscapes, and Michele Ingrassia at the different body images of black girls and white girls. Each author sets up a formal pattern for contrasting and comparing subjects within a related class. One side of the pattern helps us understand the other. Finally, we may establish a preference for one or the other subject.

HOW DO WE READ COMPARISON AND CONTRAST?

Reading comparison and contrast requires us to ask ourselves these questions:

- What subjects has the author selected? Are they from a similar class or category?
- What is the basis for the comparison or contrast? What is the writer's *thesis?*
- What is the arrangement of topics? How has the writer organized each paragraph? Notice where transitional expressions

(on the one hand, on the other hand, similarly, in contrast) are used to help the reader follow the writer's train of thought.
- Is the writer fair to each subject, devoting an equal amount of space to each side? Make an outline of one of the reading selections to see how the writer has balanced the two subjects.
- Has the writer used narration, description, or illustration to develop the comparison? What other techniques has the author used?
- Does the conclusion show a preference for one subject over the other? Is the conclusion justified by the evidence in the body?

HOW DO WE WRITE COMPARISON AND CONTRAST?

After reading the professional writers in this chapter, you will be better prepared to organize your own essay. Begin by clearly identifying the subjects of your comparison and by establishing the basis for it. The thesis sentence performs this important function for you.

Sample thesis statement:

> Living in a small town is better than living in a big city because life is safer, friendlier, and cheaper.

Plan a strategy for the comparison and contrast. Writers can use one of three main techniques: block, alternating, or combination. The *block method* requires that the writer put all the points about one side (the small town in this case) in one part of the essay, and all the points about the other side (big city life) together in another part of the essay. In the *alternating method,* the writer explains one point about small-town life and then immediately gives the contrasting point about big-city life. The *combination* pattern allows the writer to use both alternating and block techniques.

Make a careful outline. For each point about one side, try to find a balancing point about the other. If, for instance, you write about the housing available in a small town, write about housing in the big city. Although it may be impossible to manage exact matches, try to be as fair as possible to each side.

Writing and Revising the Draft

Set up a purpose for the comparison and contrast in the thesis sentence.

Write an outline using paragraph blocks to indicate subject A and subject B. For instance, if you were going to write in the block form, your outline would look like this:

Introduction (with thesis)
Block A: Small Town
1. housing
2. jobs
3. social life
Block B: Big City
1. housing
2. jobs
3. social life
Conclusion

If you were going to use the alternating form, the outline would look as follows:

Introduction (with thesis)
Block A: Housing
1. big city
2. small town
Block B: Jobs
1. big city
2. small town
Block C: Social Life
1. big city
2. small town
Conclusion

Use transitional devices, especially with the alternating form. Each time you shift from one subject to the other, use a transition as needed: *like, unlike, on the one hand, on the other hand, in contrast, similarly.*

In the conclusion, offer your view of the two subjects.

Proofread carefully. Check the draft for clarity and correctness and make a final copy.

A Fable for Tomorrow

Rachel Carson

Rachel Carson wrote a number of books and articles in the 1950s and 1960s that alerted Americans to dangers facing our natural environment. In this section from *Silent Spring* (1962), look for the ways in which Carson establishes a series of contrasts for her imaginary American town.

PREREADING: THINKING ABOUT THE ESSAY IN ADVANCE

What dangers do you see affecting our environment over the next decades? How can we as a society address these environmental problems?

Words to Watch

migrants (par. 2) people, animals, or birds that move from one place to another

blight (par. 3) a disease or condition that kills or checks growth

maladies (par. 3) illnesses

moribund (par. 4) dying

pollination (par. 5) the transfer of pollen (male sex cells) from one part of the flower to another

granular (par. 7) consisting of grains

specter (par. 9) a ghost; an object of fear or dread

stark (par. 9) bleak; barren; standing out in sharp outline

There was once a town in the heart of America where all life 1
seemed to live in harmony with its surroundings. The town lay in the midst of a checkerboard of prosperous farms, with fields of grain and hillsides of orchards where, in spring, white clouds of bloom drifted above the green fields. In autumn, oak and maple and birch set up a blaze of color that flamed and flickered across

a backdrop of pines. Then foxes barked in the hills and deer silently crossed the fields, half hidden in the mists of the fall mornings.

2 Along the roads, laurel, viburnum and alder, great ferns and wildflowers delighted the traveler's eye through much of the year. Even in winter the roadsides were places of beauty, where countless birds came to feed on the berries and on the seed heads of the dried weeds rising above the snow. The countryside was, in fact, famous for the abundance and variety of its bird life, and when the flood of migrants was pouring through in spring and fall people traveled from great distances to observe them. Others came to fish the streams, which flowed clear and cold out of the hills and contained shady pools where trout lay. So it had been from the days many years ago when the first settlers raised their houses, sank their wells, and built their barns.

3 Then a strange blight crept over the area and everything began to change. Some evil spell had settled on the community: mysterious maladies swept the flocks of chickens; the cattle and sheep sickened and died. Everywhere was a shadow of death. The farmers spoke of much illness among their families. In the town the doctors had become more and more puzzled by new kinds of sickness appearing among their patients. There had been several sudden and unexplained deaths not only among adults but even among children, who would be stricken suddenly while at play and die within a few hours.

4 There was a strange stillness. The birds, for example—where had they gone? Many people spoke of them, puzzled and disturbed. The feeding stations in the backyards were deserted. The few birds seen anywhere were moribund; they trembled violently and could not fly. It was a spring without voices. On the mornings that had once throbbed with the dawn chorus of robins, catbirds, doves, jays, wrens, and scores of other bird voices there was now no sound; only silence lay over the fields and woods and marsh.

5 On the farms the hens brooded, but no chicks hatched. The farmers complained that they were unable to raise any pigs—the litters were small and the young survived only a few days. The apple trees were coming into bloom but no bees droned among the blossoms, so there was no pollination and there would be no fruit.

The roadsides, once so attractive, were now lined with browned and withered vegetation as though swept by fire. These, too, were silent, deserted by all living things. Even the streams were now lifeless. Anglers no longer visited them, for all the fish had died. 6

In the gutters under the eaves and between the shingles of the roofs, a white granular powder still showed a few patches; some weeks before it had fallen like snow upon the roofs and the lawns, the fields and streams. 7

No witchcraft, no enemy action had silenced the rebirth of new life in this stricken world. The people had done it themselves. 8

This town does not actually exist, but it might easily have a thousand counterparts in America or elsewhere in the world. I know of no community that has experienced all the misfortunes I describe. Yet every one of these disasters has actually happened somewhere, and many real communities have already suffered a substantial number of them. A grim specter has crept upon us almost unnoticed, and this imagined tragedy may easily become a stark reality we all shall know. 9

BUILDING VOCABULARY

1. In the second paragraph, find at least five concrete words that relate to trees, birds, and vegetation. How many of these objects could you identify? Look in a dictionary for the meanings of those words you do not know.

2. Try to identify the italicized words through the *context clues* (see Glossary) provided by the complete sentence.

   a. half-hidden in the *mists* (par. 1)

   b. when the first settlers *raised* their houses (par. 2)

   c. *stricken* suddenly while at play (par. 3)

   d. the hens *brooded,* but no chicks hatched (par. 5)

   e. *Anglers* no longer visited them, for all the fish had died. (par. 6)

THINKING CRITICALLY ABOUT THE ESSAY

Understanding the Writer's Ideas

1. What is the quality of the world that Carson describes in her opening paragraph? If you had to describe it in just one or two words, which would you use?
2. What are some of the natural objects that Carson describes in her first two paragraphs? Why does she not focus on simply one aspect of nature—like animals, trees, or flowers?
3. How does Carson describe the "evil spell" that settles over the countryside?
4. What does Carson mean when she declares, "It was a spring without voices" (par. 4)? Why does she show that the critical action takes place in the springtime?
5. What do you think is the "white granular powder" that Carson refers to in paragraph 7? Why does she not explain what it is or where it came from?
6. In paragraph 9, the author states her basic point. What is it? Does she offer a solution to the problem that she poses?

Understanding the Writer's Techniques

1. A *fable* is a story with a moral; in other words, a fable is a form of teaching narrative. How does Carson structure her narrative in this essay? What is the "moral" or thesis?
2. What is the purpose of the description in this essay? Why does the writer use such vivid and precise words?
3. Where in this essay does Carson begin to shift from an essentially optimistic tone to a negative one?
4. Does Carson rely on comparison or contrast in this essay?
5. In the *block method* of comparison and contrast, the writer presents all information about one subject, and then all information about a second subject, as in the following:

A

B

a. How does Carson use this pattern in her essay?
b. Are there actually two subjects in this essay, or two different aspects of one subject? How does chronology relate to the block structure?
c. Are the two major parts of Carson's essay equally weighted? Why or why not?
d. In the second part of the essay, does Carson ever lose sight of the objects introduced in the first part? What new terms does she introduce?

6. How can you explain paragraphs 8 and 9—which do not involve narration, description, or comparison and contrast—in relation to the rest of the essay? What is the nature of Carson's conclusion?

Exploring the Writer's Ideas

1. Today chemicals are used to destroy crop insects, to color and preserve food, and to purify our water, among other things. Would Carson term this "progress"? Would you? Do you think that there are inadequate safeguards and controls in the use of chemicals? What recent examples of chemical use have made the news?

2. Why would you agree or disagree that factories and corporations should protect the environment that they use? Should a company, for example, be forced to clean up an entire river that it polluted? What about oil spills?

3. Have there been any problems with the use of chemicals and the environment in your own area? Describe them. How do local citizens feel about these problems?

4. Do you think that it will be possible in the future for Americans to "live in harmony" with their natural surroundings? Why do you believe what you do?

IDEAS FOR WRITING

Prewriting

Define the word *fable*. List the various elements that you think contribute to successful fables.

Guided Writing

Write a fable (an imaginary story with a moral) in which you contrast one aspect of the life of a person, community, or nation with another.

1. Begin with a phrase similar to Carson's "There was once . . ." so that the reader knows you are writing a narrative fable.
2. Relate your story to an American problem.
3. Use the block method in order to establish your contrast. Write first about one aspect of the topic and then about the other.
4. Use sensory detail in order to make your narrative clear and interesting.
5. Make certain that you establish an effective transition as you move into the contrast.
6. In the second part of your essay, be sure to refer to the same points you raised in the first part.
7. Use the conclusion to establish the "moral" of your fable.

Thinking and Writing Collaboratively

Exchange Guided Writing essays with another member of the class. Has the writer produced a successful fable? Why or why not? Is the moral clear? Is the American problem well defined? Finally, discuss the structure of the essay. Has the writer used the block method of development appropriately? Does an effective transition link the contrast with the stated problem?

More Writing Projects

1. In a journal entry, describe a place you know well, one that has changed for better or worse. Contrast the place as it once was with the way it is now. Use concrete images that appeal to color, action, sound, smell, taste, and touch.
2. Examine in two block paragraphs the two sides of a specific ecological issue today—for instance, acid rain, the global warming trend, or the use of nuclear energy.
3. Using the block method, compare and contrast Carson's fable with the fable you wrote in Guided Writing.

The Place Where I Was Born

Alice Walker

Alice Walker is a novelist, poet, essayist, short story writer, and, in her own term, a "womanist." She has won both the American Book Award and the Pulitzer Prize for her novel *The Color Purple* (1982). As her essay reveals, she grew up in Eatonton, Georgia, but now lives in northern California. In comparing and contrasting her birthplace with her adopted home, Walker examines the persistence of racism in American society, and the decisions it forces victims of racial oppression to make.

PREREADING: THINKING ABOUT THE ESSAY IN ADVANCE

Think back to the city or town you first remember living in. What was it like? Describe some of its features. What did you like best about it? least?

Words to Watch

displaced (par. 1) cast out from; removed from
expanse (par. 1) large stretch or space
discreet (par. 1) careful in speech; tactful
enigmatic (par. 1) puzzling; mysterious
nostalgic (par. 3) meditative; longing for what is not present
dell (par. 5) small, secluded valley
bustles (par. 9) moves about briskly

I am a displaced person. I sit here on a swing on the deck of my house in northern California admiring how the fog has turned the valley below into a lake. For hours nothing will be visible below me except this large expanse of vapor; then slowly, as the sun rises and gains in intensity, the fog will start to curl up and begin its slow rolling drift toward the ocean. People here call it the dragon; and, indeed, a dragon is what it looks like, puffing and coiling, winged, flaring and in places thin and discreet, as it races 1 before the sun, back to its ocean coast den. Mornings I sit here in awe and great peace. The mountains across the valley come and go in the mist; the redwoods and firs, oaks and giant bays appear as clumpish spires, enigmatic shapes of green, like the stone forests one sees in Chinese paintings of Guilin.

2 It is incredibly beautiful where I live. Not fancy at all, or exclusive. But from where I sit on my deck I can look down on the backs of hawks, and the wide, satiny wings of turkey vultures glistening in the sun become my present connection to ancient Egyptian Africa. The pond is so still below me that the trees reflected in it seem, from this distance, to be painted in its depths.

3 All this—the beauty, the quiet, the cleanliness, the peace—is what I love. I realize how lucky I am to have found it here. And yet, there are days when my view of the mountains and redwoods makes me nostalgic for small rounded hills easily walked over, and for the look of big-leaf poplar and the scent of pine.

4 I am nostalgic for the land of my birth, the land I left forever when I was 13—moving first to the town of Eatonton, Georgia, and then, at 17, to the city of Atlanta.

5 I cried one day as I talked to a friend about a tree I loved as a child. A tree that had sheltered my father on his long cold walk to school each morning: It was midway between his house and the school and because there was a large cavity in its trunk, a fire could be made inside it. During my childhood, in a tiny, overcrowded house in a tiny dell below it, I looked up at it frequently and felt reassured by its age, its generosity despite its years of brutalization (the fires, I knew, had to hurt), and its tall, old-growth pine nobility. When it was struck by lightning and killed, and then was cut down and made into firewood, I grieved as if it had been a person. Secretly. Because who among the members of my family would not have laughed at my grief?

6 I have felt entirely fortunate to have had this companion, and even today remember it with gratitude. But why the tears? my friend wanted to know. And it suddenly dawned on me that perhaps it *was* sad that it was a tree and not a member of my family to whom I was so emotionally close.

7 As a child I assumed I would always have the middle Georgia landscape to live in, as Br'er Rabbit, a native also, and relative, had his brier patch. It was not to be. The pain of racist oppression, and its consequence, economic impoverishment,

drove me to the four corners of the earth in search of justice and peace, and work that affirmed my whole being. I have come to rest here, weary from travel, on a deck—not a southern front porch—overlooking another world.

I am content; and yet, I wonder what my life would have 8
been like if I had been able to stay home.

I remember early morning fogs in Georgia, not so dramatic 9
as California ones, but magical too because out of the southern fog of memory tramps my dark father, smiling and large, glowing with rootedness, and talking of hound dogs, biscuits and coons. And my equally rooted mother bustles around the corner of our house preparing to start a wash, the fire under the black wash pot extending a circle of warmth in which I, a grave-eyed child, stand. There is my sister Ruth, beautiful to me and dressed elegantly for high school in gray felt skirt and rhinestone brooch, hurrying up the road to catch the yellow school bus which glows like a large glowworm in the early morning fog.

BUILDING VOCABULARY

1. Walker uses many references to nature as she describes and compares her two places. Identify the following natural elements in her scenes:
   a. redwoods
   b. firs
   c. oaks
   d. giant bays
   e. hawks
   f. turkey vultures
   g. big-leaf poplar
   h. pine
2. Walker alludes to other cultures and traditions in her essay. What does she mean by each of the following:
   a. Chinese paintings of Guilin
   b. Egyptian Africa
   c. Br'er Rabbit

THINKING CRITICALLY ABOUT THE ESSAY

Understanding the Writer's Ideas

1. Why does the author consider herself a "displaced person"? What is the difference between being displaced and buying a new home?
2. What are the features of Walker's California home that make her content to live there?
3. Why does she cry when she remembers her childhood in Georgia? Why is the tree so important?
4. In paragraph 7, what does the author list as the consequences of her being an African American? Why did she have to leave Georgia?
5. Walker uses the natural world, particularly landscape, to create images of her past and present life. Why does she look so closely at the trees? Why does she use the metaphors of "rooted" and "rootedness" to describe her parents (par. 9)?

Understanding the Writer's Techniques

1. Where does the author place her thesis statement? What is her thesis?
2. Does Walker use *contrast* or *comparison* in her essay as her primary mode? What key words does she use to indicate that she is dealing primarily with similarities or differences?
3. Examine the structure of Walker's essay. How does she use the block method (see page 206) to organize her essay? Create an outline of Walker's essay.
4. What is the purpose of paragraph 8? Why is it so short? What key transition words does Walker use?
5. As well as presenting the two physical worlds of California and Georgia, Walker describes the two emotional worlds of the present time, and her nostalgia for the past. How does the memory of her sister, presented in the conclusion, contrast with the tone of the first sentence of the essay?
6. How is the structure of Walker's essay similar to or different from that used by Rachel Carson in "A Fable for Tomorrow" (pages 203–205)?

7. Reread paragraph 7. How does Walker introduce the *cause* of her being "displaced" by using contrast? Why is she "on a deck," and not "a southern front porch"? How do these two contrasting sites make concrete her political experience?
8. Note Walker's use of both abstract and concrete language. In paragraph 7, she relies on abstract words: "racist oppression," "economic impoverishment," "justice and peace." In paragraph 9, she uses concrete words: "hound dogs, biscuits and coons." Why does she include both types of language?

Exploring the Writer's Ideas

1. Walker implies that landscape is an essential part of our identity. She suggests that where we have lived, or where we live now, is a clue to who we are. Do you agree with her? Can we always control our landscape? Can we live where we choose? Do we ever outgrow our childhood landscapes, and leave them, not like Walker because we are compelled to, but because they seem too confining?
2. Walker describes herself as "nostalgic" (par. 3). In what ways might nostalgia be a false key to the past? Is nostalgia the same as memory? What are the *connotations* (see Glossary) of the word "nostalgic"?
3. As an African-American woman writer, Walker is keenly aware of the history of "displacement" of oppressed peoples. She has written, for instance, about Native Americans who were displaced from their ancestral lands by European settlers. What other racial or ethnic groups might be considered "displaced"? How can the idea of displacement be applied to urban dwellers? Because of her success as a writer, Walker was able to find a new home. What happens to displaced people who do not have her talent?
4. Do you think Walker would be content, as an adult, to return to Eatonton if circumstances were different, and she did not feel that the racism would make her life painful? Can we return to our "home" of childhood?

IDEAS FOR WRITING

Prewriting

Make two columns on a sheet of paper. In one column, make a list of the outstanding features of one place that you know well. In the other column, indicate the outstanding features of a contrasting place.

Guided Writing

Write an essay in which you contrast two places you know very well.

1. In your first paragraph, write a clear thesis statement that uses key words to indicate the contrast your essay will make.
2. Give the two places names and define the special quality of each place by comparing it with a familiar painting or story.
3. Write an outline using the block method of organization.
4. Base your essay on your personal associations with the two places. Don't write a tourist brochure.
5. Make sure each paragraph has only one main point.
6. Use transitions between paragraphs.
7. Write one paragraph in which you reveal which place you prefer, and why. Why have you moved from one place to the other?

Thinking and Writing Collaboratively

Form groups of three or four students, and read your essays aloud while group members take notes. How can the writer improve the comparison and contrast? Does the thesis sentence make the terms of the contrast obvious? Has the writer made clear which place he or she prefers?

More Writing Projects

1. In your journal, develop characteristics of two places: where you are now, and your ideal place. Label the lists as "real" and "ideal."
2. In two paragraphs, compare and contrast two experiences, one in which you experienced prejudice or were discriminated

against, and the other in which an incident took place that overcame prejudice or discrimination.

3. Using the comparison-contrast method, write an essay in which you examine your attitudes to a particular "ism"—racism, sexism, ageism—and the attitudes of another generation, such as your parents' or grandparents' generation. Or compare your attitudes with those of someone you recently met, attitudes that either surprised or offended you.

The Tapestry of Friendships

Ellen Goodman

Syndicated columnist for the *Boston Globe, Washington Post,* and other newspapers, Ellen Goodman presents a thought-provoking comparison of two categories of human relations in this selection from her book *Close to Home.* Notice especially how she blends personal experience with a clipped, direct journalistic style to examine the ways in which "friends" and "buddies" relate to one another.

PREREADING: THINKING ABOUT THE ESSAY IN ADVANCE

How do you define "friendship"? Does this definition apply to both your female and male friends? Is there a difference between your male and female friendships, and if so, how do you explain it?

Words to Watch

slight (par. 1) not having much substance
fragility (par. 2) condition of being easily broken or harmed
resiliency (par. 2) condition of being able to recover easily from misfortune or change
binge (par. 4) spree; indulgence
atavistic (par. 5) manifesting a throwback to the past
culled (par. 5) chosen from
palpably (par. 8) in a way that can be touched or felt
loathsome (par. 10) detestable; hateful
wretched (par. 13) miserable; woeful
claustrophobic (par. 16) uncomfortable at being confined in small places

1 It was, in many ways, a slight movie. Nothing actually happened. There was no big-budget chase scene, no bloody shoot-out. The story ended without any cosmic conclusions.

Yet she found Claudia Weill's film *Girlfriends* gentle and affecting. Slowly, it panned across the tapestry of friendship—showing its fragility, its resiliency, its role as the connecting tissue between the lives of two young women. 2

When it was over, she thought about the movies she'd seen this year—*Julia, The Turning Point* and now *Girlfriends.* It seemed that the peculiar eye, the social lens of the cinema, had drastically shifted its focus. Suddenly the Male Buddy movies had been replaced by the Female Friendship flicks. 3

This wasn't just another binge of trendiness, but a kind of *cinéma vérité.* For once the movies were reflecting a shift, not just from men to women but from one definition of friendship to another. 4

Across millions of miles of celluloid, the ideal of friendship had always been male—a world of sidekicks and "pardners," of Butch Cassidys and Sundance Kids. There had been something almost atavistic about these visions of attachments—as if producers culled their plots from some pop anthropology book on male bonding. Movies portrayed the idea that only men, those direct descendants of hunters and Hemingways, inherited a primal capacity for friendship. In contrast, they portrayed women picking on each other, the way they once picked berries. 5

Well, that duality must have been mortally wounded in some shoot-out at the You're OK, I'm OK Corral. Now, on the screen, they were at least aware of the subtle distinction between men and women as buddies and friends. 6

About 150 years ago, Coleridge had written, "A woman's friendship borders more closely on love than man's. Men affect each other in the reflection of noble or friendly acts, whilst women ask fewer proofs and more signs and expressions of attachment." 7

Well, she thought, on the whole, men had buddies, while women had friends. Buddies bonded, but friends loved. Buddies faced adversity together, but friends faced each other. There was something palpably different in the way they spent their time. Buddies seemed to "do" things together; friends simply "were" together. 8

Buddies came linked, like accessories, to one activity or another. People have golf buddies and business buddies, college buddies and club buddies. Men often keep their buddies in these categories, while women keep a special category for friends. 9

10 A man once told her that men weren't real buddies until they'd been "through the wars" together—corporate or athletic or military. They had to soldier together, he said. Women, on the other hand, didn't count themselves as friends until they'd shared three loathsome confidences.

11 Buddies hang tough together; friends hang onto each other.

12 It probably had something to do with pride. You don't show off to a friend; you show need. Buddies try to keep the worst from each other; friends confess it.

13 A friend of hers once telephoned her lover, just to find out if he were home. She hung up without a hello when he picked up the phone. Later, wretched with embarrassment, the friend moaned, "Can you believe me? A thirty-five-year-old lawyer, making a chicken call?" Together they laughed and made it better.

14 Buddies seek approval. But friends seek acceptance.

15 She knew so many men who had been trained in restraint, afraid of each other's judgment or awkward with each other's affection. She wasn't sure which. Like buddies in the movies, they would die for each other, but never hug each other.

16 She'd reread *Babbitt* recently, that extraordinary catalogue of male grievances. The only relationship that gave meaning to the claustrophobic life of George Babbitt had been with Paul Riesling. But not once in the tragedy of their lives had one been able to say to the other: You make a difference.

17 Even now men shocked her at times with their description of friendship. Does this one have a best friend? "Why, of course, we see each other every February." Does that one call his most intimate pal long distance? "Why, certainly, whenever there's a real reason." Do those two old chums ever have dinner together? "You mean alone? Without our wives?"

18 Yet, things were changing. The ideal of intimacy wasn't this parallel playmate, this teammate, this trenchmate. Not even in Hollywood. In the double standard of friendship, for once the female version was becoming accepted as the general ideal.

19 After all, a buddy is a fine life-companion. But one's friends, as Santayana once wrote, "are that part of the race with which one can be human."

BUILDING VOCABULARY

1. The first six paragraphs of this essay use many words and expressions related to film. Explain the meaning or connotation of each of the following words and expressions. Pay special attention to their context in Goodman's article.
   a. big-budget chase scene (par. 1)
   b. bloody shoot-out (par. 1)
   c. it panned (par. 2)
   d. the peculiar eye (par. 3)
   e. the social lens of the cinema (par. 3)
   f. shifted its focus (par. 3)
   g. flicks (par. 3)
   h. *cinéma vérité* (par. 4)
   i. millions of miles of celluloid (par. 5)
   j. plots (par. 5)
   k. on the screen (par. 6)
2. Write an *antonym* (word with an opposite meaning) for each of the following words from the Words to Watch section. Then use each antonym in a sentence.
   a. slight
   b. fragility
   c. resiliency
   d. atavistic
   e. palpably
   f. loathsome
   g. wretched

THINKING CRITICALLY ABOUT THE ESSAY

Understanding the Writer's Ideas

1. What does the author mean when she writes that the movie "ended without any cosmic conclusions" (par. 1)? Is she being critical or descriptive in this statement? Explain.
2. Who is the "she" first mentioned at the beginning of paragraph 2 and referred to throughout the essay?
3. What pattern of change does the author note in the same-year releases of the films *Julia, The Turning Point,* and *Girl-*

friends? Does she feel this is a superficial or real change? How do you know?

4. What is the author's main complaint about the ways in which movies have traditionally portrayed friendships? What example does she offer? Explain the meaning of the sentence, "Movies portrayed the idea that only men, those direct descendants of hunters and Hemingway, inherited a primal capacity for friendship" (par. 5). What is "male bonding"?
5. What two allusions does Goodman combine to produce the expression "the You're OK, I'm OK Corral"? Explain the full meaning of the sentence in which that expression appears.
6. According to Goodman, what is the main difference between male and female friendships? Which type do you think she prefers? Why?
7. What quality of friendships is suggested by the title?
8. What is meant by "the double standard of friendship"?
9. How does Goodman's conclusion support her preference for male or female types of friendships?

Understanding the Writer's Techniques

1. What is the main idea of this essay? Which sentence serves as the thesis statement? What two subjects form the basis for comparison in this essay?
2. Like most well-constructed essays, this one has three clear sections: introduction, body, conclusion. Specify which paragraphs make up each section. Does this seem a good balance? Explain.
3. How would you describe the effect of the writing in the opening paragraph? Does it give you a clear idea of the subject of this essay? Is that important in this essay? Why?
4. In the beginning, Goodman uses a number of *metaphors* (see Glossary), including the title. Explain the following metaphors in your own words:
   a. The Tapestry of Friendships (title and par. 2)
   b. the connecting tissue between the lives of two young women (par. 2)

   In what ways do the two metaphors convey similar ideas? Which do you prefer? Why?

5. What is the effect of the use of the pronoun "she" throughout the essay? Why do you suppose Goodman chose to use "she" rather than "I"?
6. Among the main purposes of a comparison-contrast essay are (a) *to explain* something unfamiliar in terms of something already familiar, (b) *to understand* better two things already known by comparing them point for point, (c) *to evaluate* the relative value of two things. Which of these objectives most closely describes Goodman's purpose? Explain.
7. Which of the three methods of writing comparison essays—block, alternating, or combination—dominates in this essay? Explain.
8. Who is the intended audience for this essay? Why?
9. There are four literary *allusions* (see Glossary) in this essay: (a) Hemingway, (b) Coleridge, (c) *Babbitt,* and (d) Santayana. Identify each and explain why Goodman chose to include it.
10. Throughout the essay, Goodman uses short, direct sentences and relatively short paragraphs. What is her purpose for that? Does it allow for adequate development of this subject matter? Why or why not?
11. At what points does Goodman make use of relatively *extended illustrations?*
12. Goodman chooses to point out the contrasts between her two subjects in short, directly opposing sentences or clauses, beginning with paragraph 8: ". . . men had buddies, while women had friends. Buddies bonded, but friends loved."

    Go through the essay and list all such opposing statements. How do these statements affect your reading of the essay?
13. How does Goodman use *repetition* as a transitional device in the essay?
14. What is the effect of the series of questions that comprise paragraph 17? How is it like a dialogue? Why are some of the questions in quotation marks and others not?
15. A good conclusion for an essay of comparison or contrast will either (a) restate the main idea, (b) offer a solution, or (c) set a new frame of reference by generalizing from the thesis. Which approach or combination of approaches does Goodman use? How effective is her conclusion? Why?

Exploring the Writer's Ideas

1. Do you agree with Goodman's basic distinction between female and male friendships? How closely does it relate to your own experiences? Do you have any friendships that don't fit into either of the two categories she describes?
2. In the beginning of this essay, Goodman refers to the "binge of trendiness" toward pop anthropology and psychology. Such periodicals, books, and syndicated columns as *Psychology Today, Men Are from Mars, Women Are from Venus,* and Dr. Joyce Brothers—to name just a few—are widely read. What's more, radio call-in shows offering on-the-air advice are nationally syndicated and immensely popular.

   What are your feelings about such media presentations? Do you think they are useful? Are there instances when they might be harmful? Why do you think they are so popular?
3. Why does Goodman avoid any discussion of friendship between men and women? Do you feel this omission in any way affects the forcefulness or completeness of her essay? Explain.

IDEAS FOR WRITING

Prewriting

Draw a line down a sheet of paper, labeling the left side *Women* and the right side *Men.* Then identify a topic—for example, dating—that you think men and women approach differently. Next, jot down a few points of contrast that help to explain the precise nature of the differences you plan to investigate.

Guided Writing

Write an essay that contrasts the ways in which men and women perceive or approach some aspect of interpersonal relationships. You might choose, for example, dating, parenting, expressing affection, or divorce.

1. Begin with a description of some depiction of the subject in the contemporary media (for example, a film, TV program, book, video, commercial).

2. Staying with the same medium, give other examples that illustrate how the medium is shifting away from the old, established ways of viewing the subject. Use language specific to that medium.
3. In the rest of your introductory section, use a few metaphors.
4. As a transitional device, cite a statement from a well-known authority (not necessarily on the particular subject).
5. State the main idea of your essay at the beginning of the body section.
6. Develop your contrast using short, direct, opposing statements that summarize the different approaches of men and women.
7. Develop at least two of these opposing statements through extended personal examples.
8. Make your preference for either approach *implicit* (subtle) rather than *explicit* (obvious) throughout.
9. Make the last paragraph of the body of your essay a series of questions that form an internal dialogue.
10. Conclude with a statement that generalizes the main differences and your evaluation of the two approaches.

Thinking and Writing Collaboratively

Working in groups of four, examine the opening paragraphs of your Guided Writing essays. Which of the four introductory paragraphs encourage you to read more of the essay? Which, if any, need revision for stronger effect? Suggest specific ways to improve each introductory paragraph. Revise your own introduction based on readers' responses.

More Writing Projects

1. Compare and contrast in a journal entry two films or books, plays, or television programs that portray contrasting views of friendship, love, or marriage.
2. Compare in one or two paragraphs the ways you relate to two close friends.
3. Write an essay that compares and/or contrasts what was considered physically attractive in two different time periods in America. You may either focus your essay on one sex or attempt to discuss both.

The Body of the Beholder

Michele Ingrassia

Newsweek writer Michele Ingrassia takes a look at a study that shows why white girls dislike their bodies, but black girls are proud of theirs. Why do some find that being fat can also mean being fit?

PREREADING: THINKING ABOUT THE ESSAY IN ADVANCE

Look in the mirror. What do you see? How do you feel about your body?

Words to Watch

dissect (par. 1) to cut apart or separate (tissue), especially for anatomical study

anthropologist (par. 3) a scientist who studies the origin, behavior, and physical, social, and cultural development of human beings

superwaif (par. 4) a slang phrase meaning a model who makes a lot of money because she looks gaunt, like an orphaned child (waif)

magnetism (par. 5) unusual power to attract, fascinate, or influence

1 When you're a teenage girl, there's no place to hide. Certainly not in gym class, where the shorts are short, the T shirts revealing and the adolescent critics eager to dissect every flaw. Yet out on the hardwood gym floors at Morgan Park High, a largely African-American school on Chicago's Southwest Side, the girls aren't talking about how bad their bodies are, but how good. Sure, all of them compete to see how many sit-ups they can do—Janet Jackson's washboard stomach is their model. But ask Diane Howard about weight, and the African-American senior, who carries 133 pounds on her 5-foot 7½-inch frame, says she'd happily add 15 pounds—if she could ensure they'd land on her hips. Or La'Taria Stokes, a stoutly built junior who takes it as high praise when boys remark, "Your hips are screaming for twins!" "I know I'm fat," La'Taria says. "I don't care."

In a society that worships at the altar of supermodels like Claudia, Christy and Kate, white teenagers are obsessed with staying thin. But there's growing evidence that black and white girls view their bodies in dramatically different ways. The latest findings come in a study to be published in the journal *Human Organization* this spring by a team of black and white researchers at the University of Arizona. While 90 percent of the white junior-high and high-school girls studied voiced dissatisfaction with their weight, 70 percent of African-American teens were satisfied with their bodies. 2

In fact, even significantly overweight black teens described themselves as happy. That confidence may not carry over to other areas of black teens' lives, but the study suggests that, at least here, it's a lifelong source of pride. Asked to describe women as they age, two thirds of the black teens said they get more beautiful, and many cited their mothers as examples. White girls responded that their mothers may have been beautiful—back in their youth. Says anthropologist Mimi Nichter, one of the study's coauthors, "In white culture, the window of beauty is so small." 3

What is beauty? White teens defined perfection as 5 feet 7 and 100 to 110 pounds—superwaif Kate Moss's vital stats. African-American girls described the perfect size in more attainable terms—full hips, thick thighs, the sort of proportions about which Hammer ("Pumps and a Bump") and Sir Mix-Alot ("Baby Got Back") rap poetic. But they said that true beauty—"looking good"—is about more than size. Almost two thirds of the black teens defined beauty as "the right attitude." 4

The disparity in body images isn't just in kids' heads. It's reflected in fashion magazines, in ads, and it's out there, on TV, every Thursday night. On NBC, the sitcom "Friends" stars Courteney Cox, Jennifer Aniston and Lisa Kudrow, all of them white and twentysomething, classically beautiful and reed thin. Meanwhile, Fox Television's "Living Single," aimed at an African-American audience, projects a less Hollywood ideal—its stars are four twentysomething black women whose bodies are, well, *real.* Especially the big-boned, bronze-haired rapper Queen Latifah, whose size only adds to her magnetism. During a break at the Lite Nites program at the Harlem YMCA, over the squeal of sneakers on the basketball court, Brandy Wood, 14, describes 5

Queen Latifah's appeal: "What I like about her is the way she wears her hair and the color in it and the clothes she wears."

6 Underlying the beauty gap are 200 years of cultural differences. "In white, middle-class America, part of the great American Dream of making it is to be able to make yourself over," says Nichter. "In the black community, there is the reality that you might not move up the ladder as easily. As one girl put it, you have to be realistic—if you think negatively about yourself, you won't get anywhere." It's no accident that Barbie has long embodied a white-adolescent ideal—in the early days, she came with her own scale (set at 110) and her own diet guide ("How to Lose Weight: Don't Eat"). Even in this postfeminist era, Barbie's tight-is-right message is stronger than ever. Before kindergarten, researchers say, white girls know that Daddy eats and Mommy diets. By high school, many have split the world into physical haves and have-nots, rivals across the beauty line. "It's not that you hate them [perfect girls]," says Sarah Immel, a junior at Evanston Township High School north of Chicago. "It's that you're kind of jealous that they have it so easy, that they're so perfect-looking."

7 In the black community, size isn't debated, it's taken for granted—a sign, some say, that after decades of preaching black-is-beautiful, black parents and educators have gotten across the message of self-respect. Indeed, black teens grow up equating a full figure with health and fertility. Black women's magazines tend to tout NOT TRYING TO BE SIZE 8, not TEN TIPS FOR THIN THIGHS. And even girls who fit the white ideal aren't necessarily comfortable there. Supermodel Tyra Banks recalls how, in high school in Los Angeles, she was the envy of her white girlfriends. "They would tell me, 'Oh, Tyra, you look so good'," says Banks. "But I was like, 'I want a booty and thighs like my black girlfriends'."

8 Men send some of the strongest signals. What's fat? "You got to be *real* fat for me to notice," says Muhammad Latif, a Harlem 15-year-old. White girls follow what they *think* guys want, whether guys want it or not. Sprawled across the well-worn sofas and hard-back chairs of the student lounge, boys at Evanston High scoff at the girls' idealization of Kate Moss. "Sickly," they say, "gross." Sixteen-year-old Trevis Milton, a blond swimmer, has no interest in dating Kate wanna-bes. "I

don't want to feel like I'm going to break them." Here, perfection is a hardbody, like Linda Hamilton in "Terminator II." "It's not so much about eating broccoli and water as running," says senior Kevin Mack.

And if hardbodies are hot, girls often need to diet to achieve 9 them, too. According to the Arizona study, which was funded by the National Institute of Child Health and Human Development, 62 percent of the white girls reported dieting at least once in the past year. Even those who say they'd rather be fit than thin get caught up. Sarah Martin, 16, a junior at Evanston, confesses she's tried forcing herself to throw up but couldn't. She's still frustrated: ". . . have a big appetite, and I feel so guilty when I eat."

Black teens don't usually go to such extremes. Anorexia 10 and bulimia are relatively minor problems among African-American girls. And though 51 percent of the black teens in the study said they'd dieted in the last year, follow-up interviews showed that far fewer were on sustained weight-and-exercise programs. Indeed, 64 percent of the black girls thought it was better to be "a little" overweight than underweight. And while they agreed that "very overweight" girls should diet, they defined that as someone who "takes up two seats on the bus."

The black image of beauty may seem saner, but it's not nec- 11 essarily healthy. Black women don't obsess on size, but they do worry about other white cultural ideals that black men value. "We look at Heather Locklear and see the long hair and the fair, pure skin," says *Essence* magazine senior editor Pamela Johnson. More troubling, the acceptance of fat means many girls ignore the real dangers of obesity. Dieting costs money—even if it's not a fancy commercial program; fruits, vegetables and lean meats are pricier than high-fat foods. Exercise? Only one state—Illinois—requires daily physical education for every kid. Anyway, as black teenagers complain, exercise can ruin your hair—and, if you're plunking down $35 a week at the hairdresser, you don't want to sweat out your 'do in the gym. "I don't think we should obsess about weight and fitness, but there is a middle ground," says the well-toned black actress Jada Pinkett. Maybe that's where Queen Latifah meets Kate Moss.

BUILDING VOCABULARY

These words have medical denotations. What are they? Check a medical dictionary.

a. anorexia (par. 10)
b. bulimia (par. 10)
c. obsess (par. 11)

THINKING CRITICALLY ABOUT THE ESSAY

Understanding the Writer's Ideas

1. What does the writer mean when she says teenage girls generally have "no place to hide" (par. 1)?
2. What did the findings of a study by the journal *Human Organization* reveal about the way young girls see their bodies?
3. How did black and white teens view the bodies of their mothers?
4. How does superwaif Kate Moss serve as a role model for teenage girls?
5. Television seems to reflect the different attitudes about body image of black and white teenage girls. How?
6. What may account for the differing views of beauty for black and white girls?
7. How are full-figured black women viewed in their community? Why?
8. Dieting is an American obsession. But is this true for black teens? Explain.
9. Are attitudes about black women's bodies potentially harmful, leading to an increase in obesity in black girls?

Understanding the Writer's Techniques

1. Where does the writer state her thesis? How does the statement make the essay's plan clear?
2. How are the essay's paragraphs ordered around the comparison-contrast structure?
3. How does the writer use statistics to support the comparison-contrast paragraph technique?
4. What audience does the writer have in mind? Do you think this essay is written for men or women? Explain.

5. What makes the transition sentences in paragraph 4 different from the others?
6. Do all the paragraphs (including par. 4) have a topic sentence? Give examples.
7. In the concluding paragraph of the comparison-contrast essay, it is common to bring the two subjects together for a final observation. How does this writer follow that strategy?

Exploring the Writer's Ideas

1. Do you agree with the writer's premise that white girls are mostly obsessed with being thin? Explain.
2. Given the reported differences in the way black and white girls see their bodies, whose view do you prefer and why?
3. Is there a connection between how girls see their mothers' bodies and how they see their own, as the essay suggests? What is your feeling?
4. Television is blamed for many of society's ills. Should television be more responsible for the body types it chooses if it influences the way young girls see their own bodies? Explain.
5. In the black community, "there is the reality that you might not move up the ladder as easily." How do you feel about this statement? What does it mean and how does it relate to body image?
6. If the "black-is-beautiful" movement helped black women avoid negative body images, do white women need a similar movement? Give examples in your response.
7. How do men in your community communicate what they think constitutes a beautiful body? What is a beautiful man's body?
8. Despite the positive aspects of liking yourself (even if you are heavy), can an acceptance of weight lead to ill health? Why or why not? What do you propose?

IDEAS FOR WRITING

Prewriting

Make a list of your body features, explaining what you like or dislike about yourself (and/or others).

Guided Writing

Compare your attitudes about your body to those examined in Ingrassia's essay.

1. Begin with a description that shows how your attitudes about your body are shared (or not) by your community.
2. Make sure your thesis reflects the comparison your essay plans to make between your body image and those discussed in the above essay.
3. Focus on how your ideas of beauty differ from (or are the same as) the ideas in the essay. Try to make at least three comparisons (paragraphs).
4. Tell how your culture has historically looked at beauty.
5. How (and what) do men make clear about feminine (or masculine) beauty in your community?
6. Conclude by evaluating what the ideal body type should be for you (and/or men and women).

Thinking and Writing Collaboratively

Working in a group of four, use what you know about body image and the ways it can hurt some people, and research ways society can change to make people of all body types feel more comfortable with themselves. Then write an essay using what the group has gathered to compare ways society can change to help all people develop a positive body image.

More Writing Projects

1. Watch television commercials for women's and men's products. Reflect in your journal on what beauty messages the television commercials are communicating.
2. Look at the body images of men and women in magazine ads. Then write a paragraph that compares the beauty messages you find in television commercials and magazine ads.
3. Write an essay that compares the images of men and women in television commercials and magazine ads. Take a position on which ones are acceptable or not acceptable. Consider which ones have the most harmful affects on young people or society in general.

SUMMING UP: CHAPTER 6

1. In the essays you have read thus far in this book, you have learned much about the personal lives of many of the authors. Select two whose lives seem very different, and write an essay in which you contrast their lives. In your essay, use only illustrations that you can cite or derive from the selections; that is, do not do research or use other outside information about the authors.
2. In this chapter, Carson deals with a very old fictional form: the fable. Check the definition of this term. Then, write an essay in which you explore the author's use of the word.
3. Which author in this chapter do you think most successfully uses the comparison-contrast form? Write an essay in which you analyze the best comparison-contrast essay as you see it. Indicate the techniques and strategies that you feel work best. Make specific references to the essay you have chosen as a model.
4. In the manner of Rachel Carson, write your own "Fable for Tomorrow," in which you show how today's indifference to the environment will affect the future. Remember: *Silent Spring* was written in 1962, and many scholars believe that the way people abuse the environment today is even more serious than it was then.
5. Examine the essays by Ellen Goodman ("The Tapestry of Friendships") and Michele Ingrassia ("The Body of the Beholder"). Compare and contrast the ways in which they discuss men and women, and white and black Americans, respectively.
6. Obtain a copy of Alice Walker's essay, "Beauty: When the Other Dancer Is the Self." Then compare her views on beauty with Michele Ingrassia's presentation of the subject in "The Body of the Beholder."

CHAPTER 7

Definition

WHAT IS DEFINITION?

We are used to opening a dictionary when we want to *define* a word. Often, however, the dictionary definition is brief, and does not fully explain the meaning of a word as an individual writer sees it. An *extended definition* is necessary when a writer wishes to convey the full meaning of a word that is central to the writer's or a culture's thought. When an entire essay focuses on the meaning of a key word or group of related words, extended definition becomes the primary method of organization.

Definition can look at the *denotation* of a word, which is its literal meaning, or at the *connotations,* which are the variety of meanings associated with the word through common use (see Glossary). Denotation is generally available in the dictionary. Connotation, on the other hand, requires that the writer examine not only the denotation but also the way the word is used. In defining, a writer can also explore levels of *diction* (see Glossary), such as standard English, colloquial expressions, and slang. The word "red," for example, denotes a primary color. The connotations, however, are varied: In the early twentieth century Communists were called "Reds" because of the color of the Russian flag. We also associate red with the color of Valentine's cards, with passion and romance. "Redneck" derives from the sunburned skin of a white person who works outdoors and connotes a life-style associated with outdoor living and conservative political views. "Redskin" was a pejorative term used by European settlers to describe Native Americans.

We need extended definition to help us fully understand the complexity of our language. Most often, we use definition when words are abstract, controversial, or complex. Terms like "freedom," "pornography," "affirmative action," "bisexual," and "feminism" demand extended definition because they are often confused with some other word or term; because they are so easily misunderstood; or because they are of special importance to the writer, who chooses to redefine the term for his or her own purposes.

Although we can, of course, offer an extended definition just for the sake of definition, we usually go through the trouble of defining because we have strong opinions about complex and controversial words; consequently, we try to provide an extended definition for the purpose of illuminating a thesis for readers. Writer Alice Walker, for instance, once wrote an essay about feminism and African-American women. In her extended definition, she said that the meaning of "feminism" was restricted to white, upper- and middle-class women. As a result, the word did not apply to black women. She created the term "womanist," and wrote her essay to define it. Because of the controversial nature of her definition of "feminist," Walker relied on extended definition to support her thesis that the women's movement needed to pay more attention to women of color.

It *is* possible to give an objective definition of "feminism," with the writer tracing its history, explaining its historic applications, and describing its various subdivisions, such as "radical feminism." However, most of the time, writers have strong opinions. They would want to develop a thesis about the term, perhaps covering much of the same ground as the objective account but taking care that the reader understands the word as they do. It is normal for us to have our own opinions about any word, but in all instances we must make the reader understand fully what we mean by it.

In this chapter Gloria Naylor, an African-American woman, uses extended definition to confront the hate word "nigger." Her many *illustrations* of how and where the word is used show how definition is often determined by context. Janice Castro, with Dan Cook and Cristina Garcia, tackle the issue of what is English as they define a new American language, "Spanglish." In a more humorous vein, Jack Denton Scott provides an extended definition of "bagel," and Suzanne Britt Jordan has fun defining "fun."

HOW DO WE READ DEFINITION?

Reading definition requires us to ask ourselves these questions:

- What is the writer's thesis? Determine if the definition is *objective* or *subjective* (see Glossary).
- Does the writer state the definition directly, or expect the reader to understand it from the information the writer gives? When you finish reading the essay, write out a one-sentence definition of the term the writer has defined.
- What are the various techniques the writer uses, such as illustration with examples, description, narrative? The writer may also use *negation,* a technique of defining a word by what it does *not* mean. In addition, a writer may use a strategy of defining some general group to which the subject belongs (for instance, an orange is a member of the larger group of citrus), and to show how the word differs from all other words in the general group (by its color, acid content, size, and so forth).
- What is the writer's tone? Is the definition comic or serious? Does it rely on *irony* (see Glossary)?

HOW DO WE WRITE A DEFINITION?

Reading the variety of *definitions* in this chapter will prepare you to write your own. The skill required in good definition writing is to make abstract ideas concrete. Writing good definitions allows you to practice many of the other writing strategies you already know, including narration, description, and illustration.

The thesis for your definition does not have to appear in the introduction, but it is helpful to write it out for yourself before you begin.

- Select the word: for example, *multiculturalism.*
- Place it in a class: Multiculturalism is a *belief,* or *system of values,* or *philosophy.*
- Distinguish it from other members of that class: Multiculturalists favor recognition and celebration of differences among various social groups instead of seeking similarities.
- Use negation: Multiculturalism is not the "melting pot" metaphor of how American society is constituted.

By arranging these pieces, and revising the language, you can create a working thesis.

Sample thesis statement:

> Multiculturalism supports the preservation and celebration of differences among people of diverse cultures rather than urging them to replace their ethnic identities with one single "American" identity.

Select support to illustrate, narrate, and describe the term. The selection of evidence can demonstrate the writer's *point of view* on the term. Is multiculturalism splitting the nation into separate groups, or is it affirming the identity of both minority and majority citizens? Look at how the term is used in a variety of settings, such as education, government, social services agencies, and religious institutions.

You might want to visit the library to see how a reference book's definition compares with your own. Libraries have a variety of dictionaries. Depending on the kind of word you are researching, you might want to look at a dictionary of slang, or even a dictionary of quotations to read some famous opinions about abstract words like "love," "hope," and "truth."

What is the *purpose* of the definition? Decide whether you want to show support for the policy or argue against its effectiveness.

Who is the audience? The writer would choose different language for addressing a PTA meeting than for writing to Congress.

Plan an arrangement of the supporting evidence. Unlike comparison and contrast, for instance, definition does not require a formal method of outlining. Examples can be arranged to suit the kind of word being defined, and the mood of the writer. Because so many methods can be applied effectively in an essay of extended definition, you should be able to organize and develop this type of composition easily.

Review the *transitions* you have used in other essays and see which ones apply here. You might want to focus on transitions that show addition: *another, in addition, furthermore.*

Writing and Revising the Draft

Think about where to put the thesis. What is the effect of placing it at the end rather than at the beginning?

Plan your strategy. Arrange the examples so that they most effectively create the extended definition you want. Your essay should have *coherence.* Avoid an unrelated collection of definitions.

Read your essay to a classmate who has defined a similar word. Decide whose definition is more successful, and why.

Revise. Revision may require that you reorganize, moving the examples and other supporting evidence to different sentences and paragraphs to make your argument more effective for a reader.

Proofread for correctness and make a final copy of your work.

Spanglish

Janice Castro with Dan Cook and Cristina Garcia

Janice Castro and her co-authors Dan Cook and Cristina Garcia are staff writers for *Time* magazine. This essay explores hybrid languages, such as the free-form blend of English and Spanish known as "Spanglish." They survey this hybrid language's growing influence on American English.

PREREADING: THINKING ABOUT THE ESSAY IN ADVANCE

Some people think America should be an English-only country. For example, they object to government tax forms or road signs in languages like Spanish or Chinese. What do you think?

Words to Watch

bemused (par. 1) caused to be bewildered; confused

melting pot (par. 3) a place where immigrants of different cultures or races form an integrated society

transplanted (par. 5) transferred from one place or residence to another; resettled or relocated

luxuriant (par. 10) excessively elaborate

mangled (par. 10) butchered; deformed

In Manhattan a first-grader greets her visiting grandparents, happily exclaiming, "Come here, *siéntate!*" Her bemused grandfather, who does not speak Spanish, nevertheless knows she is asking him to sit down. A Miami personnel officer understands what a job applicant means when he says, "*Quiero un* part time." Nor do drivers miss a beat reading a billboard alongside a Los Angeles street advertising CERVEZA—SIX-PACK! 1

This free-form blend of Spanish and English, known as Spanglish, is common linguistic currency wherever concentrations of Hispanic Americans are found in the U.S. In Los Ange- 2 les, where 55% of the city's 3 million inhabitants speak Spanish, Spanglish is as much a part of daily life as sunglasses. Unlike the broken-English efforts of earlier immigrants from Europe, Asia and other regions, Spanglish has become a widely accepted conversational mode used casually—even playfully—by Spanish-speaking immigrants and native-born Americans alike.

3 Consisting of one part Hispanicized English, one part Americanized Spanish and more than a little fractured syntax, Spanglish is a bit like a Robin Williams comedy routine: a crackling line of cross-cultural patter straight from the melting pot. Often it enters Anglo homes and families through the children, who pick it up at school or at play with their young Hispanic contemporaries. In other cases, it comes from watching TV; many an Anglo child watching *Sesame Street* has learned *uno dos tres* almost as quickly as one two three.

4 Spanglish takes a variety of forms, from the Southern California Anglos who bid farewell with the utterly silly "*hasta la* bye-bye" to the Cuban-American drivers in Miami who *parquean* their *carros.* Some Spanglish sentences are mostly Spanish, with a quick detour for an English word or two. A Latino friend may cut short a conversation by glancing at his watch and excusing himself with the explanation that he must "*ir al* supermarket."

5 Many of the English words transplanted in this way are simply handier than their Spanish counterparts. No matter how distasteful the subject, for example, it is still easier to say "income tax" than *impuesto sobre la renta.* At the same time, many Spanish-speaking immigrants have adopted such terms as VCR, microwave and dishwasher for what they view as largely American phenomena. Still other English words convey a cultural context that is not implicit in the Spanish. A friend who invites you to *lonche* most likely has in mind the brisk American custom of "doing lunch" rather than the languorous afternoon break traditionally implied by *almuerzo.*

6 Mainstream Americans exposed to similar hybrids of German, Chinese or Hindi might be mystified. But even Anglos who speak little or no Spanish are somewhat familiar with Spanglish. Living among them, for one thing, are 19 million Hispanics. In addition, more American high school and university students sign up for Spanish than for any other foreign language.

Only in the past ten years, though, has Spanglish begun to turn into a national slang. Its popularity has grown with the explosive increases in U.S. immigration from Latin American countries. English has increasingly collided with Spanish in retail stores, offices and classrooms, in pop music and on street corners. Anglos whose ancestors picked up such Spanish words as *rancho, bronco, tornado* and *incommunicado,* for instance, now freely use such Spanish words as *gracias, bueno, amigo* and *por favor.* 7

Among Latinos, Spanglish conversations often flow easily from Spanish into several sentences of English and back. 8

Spanglish is a sort of code for Latinos: the speakers know Spanish, but their hybrid language reflects the American culture in which they live. Many lean to shorter, clipped phrases in place of the longer, more graceful expressions their parents used. Says Leonel de la Cuesta, an assistant professor of modern languages at Florida International University in Miami: "In the U.S., time is money, and that is showing up in Spanglish as an economy of language." Conversational examples: *taipiar* (type) and *winshiwiper* (windshield wiper) replace *escribir a máquina* and *limpiaparabrisas.* 9

Major advertisers, eager to tap the estimated $134 billion in spending power wielded by Spanish-speaking Americans, have ventured into Spanglish to promote their products. In some cases, attempts to sprinkle Spanish through commercials have produced embarrassing gaffes. A Braniff airlines ad that sought to tell Spanish-speaking audiences they could settle back *en* (in) luxuriant *cuero* (leather) seats, for example, inadvertently said they could fly without clothes *(encuero).* A fractured translation of the Miller Lite slogan told readers the beer was "Filling, and less delicious." Similar blunders are often made by Anglos trying to impress Spanish-speaking pals. But if Latinos are amused by mangled Spanglish, they also recognize these goofs as a sort of friendly acceptance. As they might put it, *no problema.* 10

BUILDING VOCABULARY

The words below all refer to language use. Write definitions for the words. Then use each word in a sentence.

a. linguistic (par. 2)
b. syntax (par. 3)
c. patter (par. 3)
d. implicit (par. 5)
e. hybrids (par. 6)
f. gaffes (par. 10)

THINKING CRITICALLY ABOUT THE ESSAY

Understanding the Writer's Ideas

1. A street advertisement "CERVEZA—SIX PACK," is an example of what type of language?
2. How do many youngsters (Hispanics and Anglos) pick up cross-cultural speech?
3. What are the different forms of Spanglish?
4. Why is Spanglish sometimes handier for Hispanics than their Spanish language?
5. What makes Spanglish easier to understand for most Americans than, say, a hybrid of English and Hindi?
6. For Anglos, Spanglish can result in some embarrassing gaffes. Why and how? Give an example.

Understanding the Writer's Techniques

1. What is the thesis of the essay?
2. How does the title reflect the essay's thesis?
3. These writers give a clear definition of Spanglish. Where and what is it, precisely?
4. What statistics do the writers present to help inform readers about Spanglish? What effect does the use of statistics have on the essay? Would this essay be as instructive without them? Explain.
5. In the essay the writer makes use of many of the other expository techniques. Explain where the writer uses these techniques: illustration; process; comparison and contrast.
6. Some information in this essay is highlighted by the use of italics. Why is the material set off from the main text of the essay? Explain.
7. Is this essay written for English or Spanish speakers? Why?

Exploring the Writer's Ideas

1. What attitudes do Americans have about those who speak "broken" English?
2. Do you believe Spanglish, as this essay suggests, is more accepted by Americans who studied a foreign language in school, especially Spanish?
3. What in your high school experience was the language most studied? Was it Spanish? Why or why not?
4. What is your experience with a hybrid language? Describe. What is your feeling about hybrid languages? Are they a threat to the purity of our national language—English? Explain.
5. Teachers often tell students to learn proper English in order to get a job. According to this essay, advertisers and people in business have found it worthwhile to use Spanglish to sell their products. Why do schools emphasize proper language when businesses are trying to learn and use hybrid languages? What is going on?

IDEAS FOR WRITING

Prewriting

Freewrite for fifteen minutes about whatever comes to mind when you think of the word "language." Consider social, political, and cultural elements as well as the obvious linguistic elements.

Guided Writing

Write an extended definition of the term "language," focusing on the key element or elements that you think are most important for someone to understand about the word. Address social, political, or cultural features that help explain the importance of language as a human phenomenon.

1. Begin with a short anecdote from personal experience to introduce the concept of language.
2. Write a thesis sentence to link language with the concept you are addressing. For example, you might write, "Because the idea of language is so connected to cultural identity, under-

standing a culture can help us understand why certain groups resist learning the language of a new country." Or, you might write, "Teenagers have a distinct language all their own."

3. Define "language" from your particular perspective, drawing on the element you have chosen for your focus.
4. Give some examples of the language element that you are focusing on.
5. Explain how people understand or do not understand the element you are exploring. What problems are created because people do not understand or appreciate that element?
6. Propose the results if, in fact, people did come to understand the language feature you are dealing with.
7. Give your essay a lively title that blends the elements you are considering in the way that Castro has blended them in her title "Spanglish."

Thinking and Writing Collaboratively

In groups of three, read drafts of each other's essays and write a one-paragraph critique for each of the two papers you have read. What language element does the writer focus on? Does the thesis sentence explain the writer's position clearly? Do the examples illustrate the point effectively? Then, read the critiques of your own essay, and use them to help you think your essay through before you do your next revision.

More Writing Projects

1. In your journal, reflect on the possible advantages and problems that result when cultures come in close contact with each other.
2. Write a paragraph to define the word "slang."
3. Select any cultural group that you think has had a major impact on American culture, and write an essay to examine that impact. Consider linguistic, social, and economic contributions.

Fun, Oh Boy. Fun. You Could Die from It.

Suzanne Britt Jordan

Most of us never really consider exactly what it means to have a good time. Suzanne Britt Jordan, a writer who claims she "tries to have fun, but often fails," offers an extended definition of the word "fun" by pointing out what it is *not.*

PREREADING: THINKING ABOUT THE ESSAY IN ADVANCE

What expectations do you bring to an article entitled "Fun, Oh Boy. Fun. You Could Die from It"? Can "fun" actually harm or kill you? In what ways? Do you think that we are too much of a "fun" culture? Why or why not?

Words to Watch

puritan (par. 3) one who practices or preaches a stricter moral code than that which most people now follow

selfless (par. 4) unselfish; having no concern for oneself

fetish (par. 5) something regarded with extravagant trust or respect

licentiousness (par. 9) a lack of moral restraints

consumption (par. 9) act of taking in or using up a substance; eating or drinking

epitome (par. 11) an ideal; a typical representation

capacity (par. 12) the ability to hold something

damper (par. 13) something that regulates or that stops something from flowing

reverently (par. 13) respectfully; worshipfully

blaspheme (par. 13) to speak of without reverence

weary (par. 14) tired; worn-out

horizon (par. 14) the apparent line where the earth meets the sky

scan (par. 14) to examine something carefully

1 Fun is hard to have.

2 Fun is a rare jewel.

3 Somewhere along the line people got the modern idea that fun was there for the asking, that people deserved fun, that if we didn't have a little fun every day we would turn into (sakes alive!) puritans.

4 "Was it fun?" became the question that overshadowed all other questions: good questions like: Was it moral? Was it kind? Was it honest? Was it beneficial? Was it generous? Was it necessary? And (my favorite) was it selfless?

5 When the pleasure got to be the main thing, the fun fetish was sure to follow. Everything was supposed to be fun. If it wasn't fun, then by Jove, we were going to make it fun, or else.

6 Think of all the things that got the reputation of being fun. Family outings were supposed to be fun. Sex was supposed to be fun. Education was supposed to be fun. Work was supposed to be fun. Walt Disney was supposed to be fun. Church was supposed to be fun. Staying fit was supposed to be fun.

7 Just to make sure that everybody knew how much fun we were having, we put happy faces on flunking test papers, dirty bumpers, sticky refrigerator doors, bathroom mirrors.

8 If a kid, looking at his very happy parents traipsing through that very happy Disney World, said, "This ain't fun, ma," his ma's heart sank. She wondered where she had gone wrong. Everybody told her what fun family outings to Disney World would be. Golly gee, what was the matter?

9 Fun got to be such a big thing that everybody started to look for more and more thrilling ways to supply it. One way was to step up the level of danger or licentiousness or alcohol or drug consumption so that you could be sure that, no matter what, you would manage to have a little fun.

10 Television commercials brought a lot of fun and fun-loving folks into the picture. Everything that people in those commercials did looked like fun: taking Polaroid snapshots, swilling beer, buying insurance, mopping the floor, bowling, taking aspirin. We all wished, I'm sure, that we could have half as much fun as those rough-and-ready guys around the locker room, flicking each other with towels and pouring champagne. The more commercials people watched, the more they wondered when the fun would start in their own lives. It was pretty depressing.

Big occasions were supposed to be fun. Christmas, Thanksgiving and Easter were obviously supposed to be fun. Your wedding day was supposed to be fun. Your wedding night was supposed to be a whole lot of fun. Your honeymoon was supposed to be the epitome of fundom. And so we ended up going through every Big Event we ever celebrated, waiting for the fun to start. 11

It occurred to me, while I was sitting around waiting for the fun to start, that not much is, and that I should tell you just in case you're worried about your fun capacity. 12

I don't mean to put a damper on things. I just mean we ought to treat fun reverently. It is a mystery. It cannot be caught like a virus. It cannot be trapped like an animal. The god of mirth is paying us back for all those years of thinking fun was everywhere by refusing to come to our party. I don't want to blaspheme fun anymore. When fun comes in on little dancing feet, you probably won't be expecting it. In fact, I bet it comes when you're doing your duty, your job, or your work. It may even come on a Tuesday. 13

I remember one day, long ago, on which I had an especially good time. Pam Davis and I walked to the College Village drug store one Saturday morning to buy some candy. We were about 12 years old (fun ages). She got her Bit-O-Honey. I got my malted milk balls, chocolate stars, Chunkys, and a small bag of M & M's. We started back to her house. I was going to spend the night. We had the whole day to look forward to. We had plenty of candy. It was a long way to Pam's house but every time we got weary Pam would put her hand over her eyes, scan the horizon like a sailor and say, "Oughta reach home by nightfall," at which point the two of us would laugh until we thought we couldn't stand it another minute. Then after we got calm, she'd say it again. You should have been there. It was the kind of day and friendship and occasion that made me deeply regretful that I had to grow up. 14

It was fun. 15

BUILDING VOCABULARY

1. *Trite language* refers to words and expressions that have been overused and, consequently, have lost much of their effective-

ness. People do rely on trite language in their conversations, but writers usually avoid overused expressions. However, a good writer will be able to introduce such vocabulary at strategic points. Examples of trite language in Jordan's essay appear below. Explain in your own words what they mean.
   a. a rare jewel (par. 2)
   b. by Jove (par. 5)
   c. his ma's heart sank (par. 8)
   d. golly gee (par. 8)
2. For each of the following words drawn from Jordan's essay, write a denotative definition. Then list four *connotations* (see Glossary) that each word has for you.
   a. overshadowed (par. 4)
   b. flunking (par. 7)
   c. traipsing (par. 8)
   d. swilling (par. 10)
   e. mirth (par. 13)
3. Select five words from the Words to Watch section and use them in sentences of your own.

THINKING CRITICALLY ABOUT THE ESSAY

Understanding the Writer's Ideas

1. What are some of the things Jordan says fun is not?
2. What does Jordan suggest we did to something if it wasn't already fun? Identify some of the things she says are "supposed" to be fun.
3. In paragraph 6, Jordan lists some familiar things that seem empty of fun. How does she say people made them fun anyway?
4. What are some of the ways people make fun even more thrilling?
5. What does Jordan list as looking like fun on television commercials?
6. Discuss the relationship between big occasions and the experience of fun. Explain the meaning of the statement, "It may even come on a Tuesday" (par. 13).
7. Describe Jordan's attitude concerning how much in life really is fun. According to Jordan, how should we treat fun? Why?

Is it something she says can be experienced only at special times?

8. How old was Jordan at the time she remembers having an especially good time with her friend Pam? Describe in your own words why she had such a good time that day. What are some of the candies she remembers buying? Why was it especially funny when Pam would say, "Oughta reach home by nightfall"?
9. For what reason does Jordan feel regretful at the end of the essay? Although she is regretful, do you think she is actually sad? Why?

Understanding the Writer's Techniques

1. What is the author's thesis? Where is it placed?
2. Does Jordan ever offer a single-sentence definition of "fun"? Where? Is that sentence sufficient to define the concept? Why?
3. Jordan employs the technique of *negation*—defining a term through showing what it is *not*—so strongly in this essay that the writing verges on *irony.* Irony is using language to suggest the opposite of what is said (see Glossary). Explain the irony in paragraphs 9, 10, and 11.
4. Why does the author continually point out things that are supposed to be fun? What is she trying to tell us about these things?
5. Writers usually avoid vague language such as "everything" and "everybody" in their writing, yet Jordan uses these words frequently in her essay. Explain her purpose in deliberately avoiding concrete terms.
6. What is the *tone* (see Glossary) of this essay? Is it fun? How does Jordan create the tone? Much of the writing in this essay has a very conversational quality to it, as though the author were speaking directly to the reader. Locate five words or phrases that have this quality.
7. Why does Jordan use so many examples and illustrations in this essay? Which paragraphs use multiple illustrations with special effectiveness?
8. There is a definite turning point in this essay where Jordan switches from an ironic to an affirmative point of view and

begins to explain what fun *can be* rather than what it *is not.* One paragraph in particular serves as the transition between the two attitudes. Which one is it? Which is the first paragraph to be mostly affirmative? What is the result of this switch?

9. Jordan uses specific brand names in the essay. Locate at least four of them. Why do you think she uses these brand names instead of names that simply identify the object?
10. What is the function of narration in the development of this essay? Where does the author *narrate* an imagined incident? Where does she use a real incident? Why does Jordan use narration in this paper?
11. Compare the effects of the two simple, direct statements that begin and end the essay. Why does Jordan not develop a more elaborate introduction and conclusion?

Exploring the Writer's Ideas

1. Jordan begins her essay by stating, "Fun is hard to have." At one point she indicates, "Fun got to be such a big thing that everybody started looking for more and more thrilling ways to supply it" (par. 9). Do you think that fun is hard to have? Why or why not? What relationship does the epidemic use of drugs and alcohol have to our difficulties in having fun today?
2. The author raises the question of how at big events we are sometimes left "waiting for the fun to start" (par. 11). What functions do events or occasions such as holidays, weddings, or birthdays play in our society? Why is there an emphasis placed on having fun at those events? Do you think there should be such an emphasis? Why?
3. This essay appeared as a guest editorial in *The New York Times.* We do not usually think of *The New York Times* as a "fun" newspaper, but rather as one that deals with serious issues of international significance. Jordan's article might be considered popular writing or light reading. Do you feel there is a place in the media—newspapers, magazines, radio, television—for a mixture of "heavy" and "light" attitudes? What well-respected newspapers or magazines that you know include articles on popular topics? What subjects do you think would currently be most appealing to popular audiences?

4. At the end of the essay, Jordan seems to imply that it is easier for children to have fun than it is for grownups. Do you agree? Is the basic experience of fun any different for kids or for adults? Do you feel it was any easier for people to have fun in days past than it is now? Why?

IDEAS FOR WRITING

Prewriting

Words like "fun," "love," and "prejudice" have strong connotations—many shades of meaning—associated with them. Select your own highly connotative word, and then make a list of words and phrases that help to define it.

Guided Writing

Select one of the following highly connotative terms for various types of experiences and write an extended definition about it: love, creativity, alienation, prejudice, fidelity.

1. Prepare for your essay by consulting a good dictionary for the lexical definition (denotation) of the term. However, instead of beginning with this definition, start with some catchy, interesting opening statements related to the definition.
2. Write a thesis sentence that names the word you will define and that tells the special opinion, attitude, or point of view you have about the word.
3. Attempt to establish the importance of your subject by considering it in terms of our current understanding of fun.
4. Use the technique of negation (see page 234) by providing various examples and illustrations of what your topic *is not* in order to establish your own viewpoint of what it *is*.
5. Use other strategies—description, narration, comparison and contrast, and so forth—to aid in clearly establishing an extended definition of your topic.
6. At the end of your essay dramatize through narration at least one personal experience that relates the importance of the topic to your life.

Thinking and Writing Collaboratively

Exchange a draft version of your Guided Writing definition essay with another class member, and review your partner's paper carefully. Does it follow the recommendations in the Guided Writing exercise? Which strategies for writing an extended definition have been used? Does the essay incorporate personal experience? Write a one-paragraph evaluation of your classmate's essay.

More Writing Projects

1. Sit someplace on campus and observe people having fun. Record in your journal their behavior—actions, gestures, noises, and so forth. Then turn these notes into a definition of "campus fun."
2. Write a brief one-paragraph definition of a "funny person." Use vivid details to create this portrait.
3. From a book of popular quotations *(Bartlett's Familiar Quotations,* the *Oxford Dictionary of Quotations)* check under the heading "fun" and select a number of statements about fun by professional writers. Then write an essay in which you expand one of those definitions. Draw upon your own experiences or readings to support the definition you choose to expand.

A Word's Meaning

Gloria Naylor

Gloria Naylor is best known for her novel *The Women of Brewster Place* (1982). She has also published *Mama Day* (1986) and *Bailey's Cafe* (1992) to critical acclaim. As an African-American woman and a writer, Naylor has found that words can change their meaning, depending on who defines them. Telling of a confrontation with an angry classmate who called her a "nigger" in the third grade, Naylor develops an extended definition of the word and its multiple meanings. As you read, think about other words that depend on context for their meaning.

PREREADING: THINKING ABOUT THE ESSAY IN ADVANCE

Naylor suggests that different words—even offensive words—mean different things to different people. Would you agree or disagree, and why? Can you think of a word that you personally find very offensive but others might find acceptable?

Words to Watch

transcendent (par. 1) rising above
fleeting (par. 1) moving quickly
intermittent (par. 2) alternate; repeated
consensus (par. 2) agreement
verified (par. 3) confirmed
gravitated (par. 4) moved toward
inflections (par. 5) pitch or tone of voice
endearment (par. 9) expression of affection
disembodied (par. 9) separated from the body
unkempt (par. 10) messy
social stratum (par. 14) status

1 Language is the subject. It is the written form with which I've managed to keep the wolf away from the door and, in diaries, to keep my sanity. In spite of this, I consider the written word inferior to the spoken, and much of the frustration experienced by novelists is the awareness that whatever we manage to capture in even the most transcendent passages falls far short of the richness of life. Dialogue achieves its power in the dynamics of a fleeting moment of sight, sound, smell and touch.

2 I'm not going to enter the debate here about whether it is language that shapes reality or vice versa. That battle is doomed to be waged whenever we seek intermittent reprieve from the chicken and egg dispute. I will simply take the position that the spoken word, like the written word, amounts to a nonsensical arrangement of sounds or letters without a consensus that assigns "meaning." And building from the meanings of what we hear, we order reality. Words themselves are innocuous; it is the consensus that gives them true power.

3 I remember the first time I heard the word nigger. In my third-grade class, our math tests were being passed down the rows, and as I handed the papers to a little boy in back of me, I remarked that once again he had received a much lower mark than I did. He snatched his test from me and spit out that word. Had he called me a nymphomaniac or a necrophiliac, I couldn't have been more puzzled. I didn't know what a nigger was, but I knew that whatever it meant, it was something he shouldn't have called me. This was verified when I raised my hand, and in a loud voice repeated what he had said and watched the teacher scold him for using a "bad" word. I was later to go home and ask the inevitable questions that every black parent must face—"Mommy, what does 'nigger' mean?"

4 And what exactly did it mean? Thinking back, I realize that this could not have been the first time the word was used in my presence. I was part of a large extended family that had migrated from the rural South after World War II and formed a close-knit network that gravitated around my maternal grandparents. Their ground-floor apartment in one of the buildings they owned in Harlem was a weekend mecca for my immediate family, along with countless aunts, uncles and cousins who brought along assorted friends. It was a bustling and open house with assorted neighbors and tenants popping in and out to exchange bits of gos-

sip, pick up an old quarrel or referee the ongoing checkers game in which my grandmother cheated shamelessly. They were all there to let down their hair and put up their feet after a week of labor in the factories, laundries and shipyards of New York.

Amid the clamor, which could reach deafening propor- 5
tions—two or three conversations going on simultaneously, punctuated by the sound of a baby's crying somewhere in the back rooms or out on the street—there was still a rigid set of rules about what was said and how. Older children were sent out of the living room when it was time to get into the juicy details about "you-know-who" up on the third floor who had gone and gotten herself "p-r-e-g-n-a-n-t!" But my parents, knowing that I could spell well beyond my years, always demanded that I follow the others out to play. Beyond sexual misconduct and death, everything else was considered harmless for our young ears. And so among the anecdotes of the triumphs and disappointments in the various workings of their lives, the word nigger was used in my presence, but it was set within contexts and inflections that caused it to register in my mind as something else.

In the singular, the word was always applied to a man who 6
had distinguished himself in some situation that brought their approval for his strength, intelligence or drive:

"Did Johnny *really* do that?" 7

"I'm telling you, that nigger pulled in $6,000 of overtime 8
last year. Said he got enough for a down payment on a house."

When used with a possessive adjective by a woman—"my 9
nigger"—it became a term of endearment for husband or boyfriend. But it could be more than just a term applied to a man. In their mouths it became the pure essence of manhood—a disembodied force that channeled their past history of struggle and present survival against the odds into a victorious statement of being: "Yeah, that old foreman found out quick enough—you don't mess with a nigger."

In the plural, it became a description of some group within 10
the community that had overstepped the bounds of decency as my family defined it: Parents who neglected their children, a drunken couple who fought in public, people who simply refused to look for work, those with excessively dirty mouths or unkempt households were all "trifling niggers." This particular circle could forgive hard times, unemployment, the occasional bout of depres-

sion—they had gone through all of that themselves—but the unforgivable sin was a lack of self-respect.

11 A woman could never be a "nigger" in the singular, with its connotation of confirming worth. The noun "girl" was its closest equivalent in that sense, but only when used in direct address and regardless of the gender doing the addressing. "Girl" was a token of respect for a woman. The one-syllable word was drawn out to sound like three in recognition of the extra ounce of wit, nerve or daring that the woman had shown in the situation under discussion.

12 "G-i-r-l, stop. You mean you said that to his face?"

13 But if the word was used in a third-person reference or shortened so that it almost snapped out of the mouth, it always involved some element of communal disapproval. And age became an important factor in these exchanges. It was only between individuals of the same generation, or from an older person to a younger (but never the other way around), that "girl" would be considered a compliment.

14 I don't agree with the argument that use of the word nigger at this social stratum of the black community was an internalization of racism. The dynamics were the exact opposite: the people in my grandmother's living room took a word that whites used to signify worthlessness or degradation and rendered it impotent. Gathering there together, they transformed "nigger" to signify the varied and complex human beings they knew themselves to be. If the word was to disappear totally from the mouths of even the most liberal of white society, no one in that room was naïve enough to believe it would disappear from white minds. Meeting the word head-on, they proved it had absolutely nothing to do with the way they were determined to live their lives.

15 So there must have been dozens of times that the "nigger" was spoken in front of me before I reached the third grade. But I didn't "hear" it until it was said by a small pair of lips that had already learned it could be a way to humiliate me. That was the word I went home and asked my mother about. And since she knew that I had to grow up in America, she took me in her lap and explained.

BUILDING VOCABULARY

1. In paragraph 3, Naylor says the word "nigger" is as puzzling to her as "nymphomaniac" and "necrophiliac." Using a dictionary, find both the meanings of these two terms and find their etymology, or roots.
2. In paragraph 14, Naylor writes, "I don't agree with the argument that use of the word nigger at this social stratum of the black community was an internalization of racism." Put Naylor's idea into your own words. Use the context of the sentence to understand key terms such as "social stratum" and "internalization."

THINKING CRITICALLY ABOUT THE ESSAY

Understanding the Writer's Ideas

1. What is the original situation in which Naylor recognizes that "nigger" can be a hate word? What clues from outside the dictionary meaning of the word help her to recognize this meaning? What confirms her suspicion that the word is "bad"?
2. In paragraph 4, Naylor gives us information about her family and background. In your own words, what kind of family did Naylor come from? Where did she grow up? What economic and social class did her family come from? How do you know?
3. In paragraph 5, Naylor explains the values of her group. What was considered appropriate and what was inappropriate for children to hear? What kind of behavior was condemned by the group?
4. Naylor defines at least five contexts in which the word "nigger" might be used. Make a list giving the five contexts, and write a sentence putting the use of the word into your own definition.
5. Explain one context in which Naylor says "nigger" was never used (par. 11). How are age and gender important in determining how the word was used?
6. When Naylor says in paragraph 14 that blacks' use of the word "nigger" about themselves rendered the word "impo-

tent," what does she mean? How do they "transform" the meaning of the word?

7. In the last paragraph, Naylor recalls her mother's reaction to the experience of hearing a third-grade classmate use the word to humiliate her. What do you think the mother explained?

Understanding the Writer's Techniques

1. Where is the thesis statement of Naylor's essay? How do you know?
2. Why does Naylor begin with two paragraphs about language, in a very general or theoretical way? Explain what these two paragraphs tell us about the writer's authority to define words. How does she use her introduction to make herself sound like an expert on the problem of defining words?
3. In paragraph 3, the author shifts tone. She moves from the formal language of the introduction to the personal voice as she retells her childhood experience. What is the effect of this transition on the reader? Why?
4. Look closely at the examples of usage Naylor provides in paragraphs 8, 9, 10, and 11. Why does she give dialogue to illustrate the various contexts in which she heard the word "nigger" used? In what way is this variety of speakers related to her thesis statement?
5. Naylor uses grammatical terms to clarify differences in meaning, such as "in the singular" (par. 6), "possessive adjective" (par. 9), "plural" (par. 10), and "third-person reference" (par. 13). Why does she use these technical terms? What does it reveal about the audience for whom she is writing? What does it reveal about Naylor's understanding of that audience?
6. What do you think about the last sentence of the essay? Why does the author return to the simple and direct language of her childhood experience in order to conclude rather than using the theoretical and technical language of other parts of the essay?

Exploring the Writer's Ideas

1. Naylor chooses to define a difficult and controversial word in her essay. Does she define it in a way that makes you think

again about the meaning of the word "nigger"? Have you used the word in any of the ways she defines? How have contemporary rap musicians used the word in ways to suggest that Naylor's definition is accurate?

2. Naylor argues that the definition of words emerges from consensus. So, if the third-grader used "nigger" to humiliate his classmate, we must draw the conclusion that that little boy's society consented to the racism he intended by using the word. How does this idea get reinforced in the last paragraph of the essay? What attitude toward racism does the mother seem to reveal when she picks up her daughter? Does Naylor's definition essay offer any solutions to the negative meaning the word carries?
3. The classic American novel *The Adventures of Huckleberry Finn* by Mark Twain uses the word "nigger" almost 200 times. For this reason, some school libraries want to ban the book. Does Naylor's definition essay offer any solutions to this censorship debate?
4. In what way does Naylor's discussion of language raise issues similar to those discussed by Amy Tan in "Mother Tongue" (pages 22–28)? While Tan is dealing with language among immigrants and Naylor is addressing the varieties of meaning of words to native speakers of English, both writers deal with the politics of language. How does each writer define the relationship between language and power?

IDEAS FOR WRITING

Prewriting

Select an objectionable or offensive word, and for five minutes freewrite on the subject, trying to cover as many ways in which the word is used as possible.

Guided Writing

Choose a word that you have recently heard used that offended you because it was sexist, racist, homophobic, or otherwise objectionable. Write a definition essay in which you define the word, show examples of its power to offend, and conclude by offering alternate words.

1. Use an anecdote to show whom you heard using the word, where it was used, and how you felt when you heard it used. Explain who you are, and who the other speaker was in your introduction.
2. In your thesis give the word and give an expanded definition of what the word means to you.
3. Explain the background of the word's negative use. Who uses it? What is the dictionary meaning of the word? How do you think the word got corrupted?
4. Give examples to expand your thesis that the word has negative meanings. Show who uses it, and for what purpose. Draw your examples from people at work, the media, or historical figures.
5. Use another example to show how the word can change meaning if the speaker deliberately uses it in order to mock its usual meaning or "render it impotent" as Naylor says.
6. If possible, try to define the word by negation—that is, by what it does not mean.
7. Connect your paragraphs with transitions that relate one idea thoughtfully to the next.
8. In your conclusion, place the term in a broader perspective, one that goes beyond the specific word to the power of language to shape reality or control behavior.

Thinking and Writing Collaboratively

Many colleges and universities are trying to find ways to discourage or prevent hate speech by writing codes of conduct. In groups of five or six, discuss possible approaches to this issue, and then draft a policy statement that defines what unacceptable language is and how your campus will respond to it.

More Writing Projects

1. In your journal, record an incident in which someone addressed you with an offensive word. Explain how you reacted and why.

2. Write a one-paragraph definition of a word or phrase by which you would feel comfortable being labeled. Are you a single parent? an Italian-American? an honor student? Write a sharp thesis to define the term, and then expand the definition with examples.
3. The term "multicultural" refers to a perspective on society that values the differences among people of varying ethnic origin, religious belief, sexual preference, and social class. In an essay, write an extended definition of the term "multicultural society." Draw upon your own experiences and (or) your readings to support your definition.

What's a Bagel?

Jack Denton Scott

Author and bagel lover Jack Denton Scott combines a variety of expository techniques, statistics, and citations from experts to define what has now become one of America's most popular foods. In the process of definition, he explains why the bagel can no longer be considered only an East Coast ethnic food as America becomes "bagelized."

PREREADING: THINKING ABOUT THE ESSAY IN ADVANCE

What is your favorite food or dish? How much do you know about this food—its origin and history, preparation, and overall popularity in American culture?

Words to Watch

aficionados (par. 1) ans; devotees
phenomenon (par. 2) observable fact or event
consumers (par. 2) users of goods
croissant (par. 4) French crescent-shaped pastry
hearth (par. 5) brick fireplace or oven
automated (par. 6) mechanical
quirky (par. 7) peculiar; eccentric
tutus (par. 9) short skirts worn by ballerinas
spirited (par. 14) lively

1 If bread is the staff of life, the bagel may be the laugh of life. "Brooklyn jawbreakers," "crocodile teething rings," even "doughnuts with rigor mortis" are affectionate terms invoked by bagel aficionados.

2 For those who haven't tried one, the flavorful bagel is a shiny, hard, crisp yet chewy roll with a hole in the middle, and it is booming in popularity. Eight million are consumed daily in the

United States—worth about $400 million a year. Bakery experts call the phenomenon "the Americanization of the bagel." To bagel believers it's "the bagelization of America." In the past four years retail sales of bagels have about doubled. Over 80 percent of these sales are now to non-Jewish consumers, a dramatic sociological switch. Moreover, the "bagel belt," always on the East Coast, is starting to stretch across the country. In fact, the world's largest bagel bakery is now located in Mattoon, Ill., producing over a million rolls a day.

Walter Heller of *Progressive Grocer* magazine calls the 3
bagel's rise to stardom an example of "America's current love affair with ethnic foods." Yet, unless sliced in half, toasted and eaten warm, the bagel isn't easy to handle. It may make messy sandwiches and challenge the teeth. What's more, bagels become stale and hard after 12 hours—"something you can fight wars with," as one bagel expert said.

For the health-conscious, however, the bagel has a lot going 4
for it. The plain, two-ounce toaster-size has just 150 calories and one gram of fat. (The popular buttery croissant, by comparison, contains 235 calories and 12 grams of fat.) Furthermore, the plain bagel has no cholesterol, preservatives, or artificial color.

Bagels are made with unbleached, protein-rich, high-gluten 5
flour, lightly seasoned with malt, salt and sugar, and raised with yeast. They then get a brief bath in boiling water. This results in the shiny surface after they are baked. (Most are hearth-baked to give them a crusty exterior and chewy interior.)

Some U.S. bakeries still use the Old World method of 6
rolling and shaping the stiff dough by hand. This requires about six months to learn, but one expert bagel baker can whip out about 700 an hour. (One automated machine can turn out up to 9000 an hour.)

Where did this quirky roll originate? One version has the 7
bagel created by an Austrian baker in 1683, honoring the king of Poland who had defeated Turkish invaders. It was first formed to resemble a stirrup *(beugel,* from the German *bügel,* for stirrup), because the king's favorite hobby was riding.

Another account puts the bagel in Cracow, Poland, in 1610, 8
where poor Jews, who normally ate coarse black bread, considered their uncommon white-flour roll a delicacy. Bagels were officially approved as presents for women after childbirth, and

mothers used them as teething rings for their children. In the 1600s in Russia, bagels were looped on strings, and were thought to bring good luck and have magical powers.

9 Bagels were brought to New York City and New Jersey by Jewish immigrants about 1910. Among the most successful immigrant bagel bakers was Harry Lender, who arrived from Lublin, Poland, in 1927 and settled in New Haven, Conn. His sons—Sam, Murray and Marvin—have almost made Lender's Bagels household words by using humor to push sales. For their bakery's 55th anniversary party, Murray and the executive staff attended a ballet class for two months; then, dressed in orange leotards and yellow tutus, they gracefully tiptoed to what was announced as "The Dance of the Bagels."

10 Today the baffling bagel surge to the top is even inspiring bagel restaurants. They offer as many as 17 flavors, from raisin and honey to zippy onion, plus bagel sandwiches, burgers, clubs, grilled cheese, French toast, salad sandwich combos, an egg-and-sausage bagelwich and a rancher's bagel breakfast. Big also are bagelettes—one-inch bagels—served by the basket with dinners. Then there are hero, hoagie, pizza and taco bagels—even Bagel Dogs. Where there's a bagel, there's a way.

11 Bagel bakeries are opening in Alaska, England, Japan and Israel. Ron Stieglitz, founder of the New York Bagels bakery in London, where few people had ever seen a bagel, had trouble raising money from banks. "A lot of them thought we were a football team," he said. But the bakery now supplies four large retail chains and many small shops and restaurants.

12 Lyle Fox, from Chicago sees more potential for the bagel in Japan than in the United States. Young Japanese view the bagel as trendy and upscale—so much so that he easily sells 6000 a day. Fox discovered that the Japanese associate the bagel with New York, and New York with fashion. Thus, a lot of his customers are young women who consider the bagel as "sort of another accessory." A long-time bagel lover, Fox says his stomach does a sickly flip when Japanese customers ask for lox and cream cheese on a cinnamon-raisin bagel.

13 Cashing in on the new bagel awareness, innovators have come up with some really neat twists. Three Philadelphians started Bagels in Bed, a home-delivery business. Mike Bretz, owner of Simon Brothers Bakery in Skokie, Ill., has borrowed an

idea from Chinese fortune cookies. He stuffs slips with Yiddish wisdom into his Schlepper Simon's Yiddish Fortune Bagels. One cheerfully advises, "Smile, bubeleh, success is assured."

A spirited cookbook, *The Bagels' Bagel Book* (Acropolis Books), has recipes like "Mexicali Bagel Fondue," the "Kojak Bagel" with feta cheese and Greek olives, "Tofu Bagels," and "Delhi Bagels" with whipped cream cheese, curry and chutney. The book also captures some of the laughter inspired by baking's most remarkable roll. Here's comedienne Phyllis Diller: "President Reagan was so gung-ho to get ethnic votes, he went into a deli and ordered a bagel. The waiter asked, 'How would you like that?' Ronnie said, 'On rye.'" 14

What's a bagel? Fun you can eat. 15

BUILDING VOCABULARY

1. Scott uses a variety of informal expressions that are fairly common in daily conversation and media talk or writing. Explain the following expressions in your own words.
   a. it is booming in popularity (par. 2)
   b. whip out (par. 6)
   c. household words (par. 9)
   d. to push sales (par. 9)
   e. trendy and upscale (par. 12)
   f. cashing in on (par. 13)
   g. gung-ho (par. 14)
2. List all the ethnic foods (other than bagels) mentioned in this essay and explain what they are.

THINKING CRITICALLY ABOUT THE ESSAY

Understanding the Writer's Ideas

1. In paragraph 1, Scott uses a number of very colorful phrases to define bagels. Try to explain the following in your own words.
   a. Brooklyn jawbreakers
   b. crocodile teething rings
   c. doughnuts with rigor mortis

2. What ethnic group is traditionally associated with bagels? What "dramatic sociological switch" has occurred over the past few years?
3. What is meant by the "bagel belt"? Where has it traditionally been located? How is that location changing? Where is the world's largest bagel factory? Why is that surprising?
4. What are "ethnic foods"? How does the bagel figure in "America's current love affair with ethnic foods"?
5. For what reasons can a bagel be considered a food for the health conscious?
6. What is the process of making bagels? Explain the phrase "the Old World method"? What is the "Old World"?
7. In your own words, summarize the two stories concerning the origin of the bagel. What accounts for the shape of the modern bagel? Why were bagels considered delicacies among the poor Jews of Cracow? Does Scott seem to favor either story about the bagel's origins? Explain.
8. Where, when, and by whom were bagels first brought to the United States? How have these "bagel pioneers" continued to promote bagels?
9. Identify the origins of these take-offs on familiar sayings:
   a. If bread is the staff of life, the bagel may be the laugh of life. (par. 1)
   b. Where there's a bagel, there's a way. (par. 10)
10. In what other parts of the world are bagel factories operating? What was the problem in starting up a bagel business in London? Why are bagels so popular in Japan? Why does bagel manufacturer Lyle Fox get a little sick when the Japanese ask for lox and cream cheese on a cinnamon-raisin bagel?
11. Explain the meaning of the joke that concludes the essay. What serious point does it make about the bagel business?
12. Explain the meaning of the last paragraph: "What's a bagel? Fun you can eat."

Understanding the Writer's Techniques

1. What are Scott's *purpose* and *thesis* in this essay? How does the title indicate his purpose? Who is his *intended audience?* Explain.

2. Does Scott ever give a simple definition of a bagel? If so, where? Is it an objective or a subjective definition? Explain.
3. What is the general *tone* (see Glossary) of this essay? What is it about Scott's writing style that creates this tone? Is the tone appropriate to the subject and audience? Why?
4. Even a lighthearted essay can benefit from the use of *statistics* and *authorities* on the subject at hand. What statistics concerning bagels and their manufacture does Scott present? What authorities does he cite? What effect does the use of statistics and authorities have on the essay? Would the essay have been as effective without them? Explain.
5. Throughout the essay, Scott makes use of many of the other expository techniques discussed in this book. Explain where Scott uses each of the techniques below.
   a. definition (Chapter 7)
   b. process analysis (Chapter 9)
   c. comparison and contrast (Chapter 6)
   d. narration (Chapter 4)
   e. illustration (Chapter 5)

   What is the effect of using all these techniques in the essay?
6. Some information in this essay is contained in parentheses. Identify all the parenthetical information. Why does Scott choose to set off this material from the main text? Is it necessary to do so? Explain.
7. Scott uses various *allusions* (see Glossary). Explain or identify the origin of each allusion below.
   a. "The Dance of the Bagels"
   b. Yiddish
   c. Kojak
   d. Delhi
   e. Phyllis Diller
   f. President Reagan

Exploring the Writer's Ideas

1. Over the past few years, a wide diversity of foods has become available to Americans all over the country. Most supermarkets carry a full complement of ethnic foods, and even small towns are likely to have at least one "ethnic" restaurant. Like Scott, some believe this is a positive trend because it allows

Americans to enjoy and learn about other cultures. Others bemoan the demise of regional American foods. What is your opinion? How has the increased availability of ethnic foods affected your area?

2. Discuss with your classmates some of the most exotic foods you've ever eaten.
3. Eating habits are among the most deeply rooted of all cultural behaviors. What may be perfectly acceptable in one culture may be considered quite rude in another. Research some of the eating habits of other cultures and compare them with those of your own culture. Discuss this issue with your classmates.
4. When did you eat your first bagel? Describe the situation. What did you eat with it? Did you like it? Which of Scott's descriptions conform with your own feelings about bagels? Do you regularly eat bagels now? Why or why not?

IDEAS FOR WRITING

Prewriting

Think of something—a food or a type of music or an article of clothing—that you identify with as a member of your family or culture. Then list five reasons why this item or subject is so important to you.

Guided Writing

Write a definition essay entitled "What's a _________?" Fill in the blank with the name of something which was once thought to belong exclusively to a particular ethnic, cultural, or social group but now has become "Americanized" or "standardized." You might choose an article of clothing, a type of music, a cooking utensil, and so forth. (You may also choose a type of food.)

1. Begin your essay with some colorful definitions of your subject. (These may be definitions you've heard or ones you make up.)
2. Give a straightforward, objective definition of this item.
3. Explain how the item has become "Americanized." In your explanation, try to use at least three expository techniques other than definition.

4. Include some references to statistics and (or) authorities on the subject.
5. Describe the origin of this item. If possible, find out how and when it first appeared in the United States.
6. Keep an amusing tone throughout your essay.
7. Include several allusions to other cultures.
8. Conclude with a subjective definition that derives from the material presented throughout your essay.

Thinking and Writing Collaboratively

In small groups, consider strategies that Scott used in his extended definition of a bagel that class members were able to employ in their own definition essays. As a group, make a list of these strategies. Review the entries on the list, and then select one strategy that you may have overlooked to add to the draft of your extended definition essay.

More Writing Projects

1. Record in your journal all the associations connected with your favorite color. Then, using this list, write a definition of it.
2. Write an extended one-paragraph definition of a particular emotion.
3. Discuss with other class members all connotations related to the word "pizza." List all these associations on the chalkboard. Select the most appropriate items on the list and write an essay defining pizza.

SUMMING UP: CHAPTER 7

1. In her essay on fun in this chapter, Suzanne Britt Jordan defines a term we all understand but might have difficulty explaining. One way she approaches this definition is through negation—that is, explaining what fun *is not.* Write an essay that defines by negation a similar, understood but difficult-to-explain term—for example "privacy," "the blues," "class," "happiness," or "success."
2. Working with another class member, make a comparative analysis of the Jordan and Scott pieces. Give consideration to theme, subject matter, tone, and language. Then decide how both essays would help a visitor to the United States understand something about American culture. After you have discussed your findings, write your own essay on how the Jordan and Scott selections help to define American culture.
3. Both Gloria Naylor and Janice Castro define words that relate to values placed on language within an ethnic community. Think of a word that has troubled you or been used against you in your early life. It might be a word you associate, for example, with ethnicity, economic status, or personal appearance. Write an essay in which you define this word, considering both how the people who aimed it meant it to be interpreted and how an outsider might define it.
4. Gloria Naylor argues that a word is defined by "consensus." That is, a community agrees among its members on how the word will be used, despite outside definitions. On your campus find examples of current words, defined by "consensus" in the college community, whose meanings would be surprising to outsiders like your parents.
5. Look back over the titles of all the essays in this chapter and previous chapters of this book. Choose one term from any title (for example, "All-American Girl," "Salvation," or "Night Walker"), and write an essay defining that term *subjectively* (from a personal viewpoint).

CHAPTER 8

Classification

WHAT IS CLASSIFICATION?

Classification is the arrangement of information into groups or categories in order to make clear the relations among members of the group. In a supermarket, the soups are together in one aisle, the frozen foods in another. In a record, tape, and disc store, all the jazz is in one section while the rap music is in a separate section. You wouldn't expect to find a can of tomato soup next to the butter pecan ice cream any more than you'd look for a CD of George Gershwin's *An American in Paris* in the same section as a CD by Ice-T.

Writers need to classify, because it helps them present a mass of material by means of some orderly system. Related bits of information seem clearer when presented together as parts of a group. Unlike writing narrative, for example, developing classification requires a different level of analysis and planning. The writer not only is presenting a single topic or event, but is placing the subject into a complex network of relations. In a narrative, we can tell the story of a single event from start to finish, such as the time we saw a Van Gogh painting in an art museum. In classification, we have to think beyond the personal experience to try to place that Van Gogh painting in a wider context. Where does Van Gogh "fit" in the history of painting? Why is he different from other painters? How does his style relate to other work of the same period? In pursuing these questions, we seek not only to *record* our experience in looking at the painting but to *understand* it more fully.

Classification, then, begins by thinking about a body of material and trying to break it down into distinct parts, or categories. Called *division* or *analysis,* this first task helps split an idea or object into usable components. Then, some of the parts can serve as categories into which the writer can fit individual pieces that share some common qualities.

For example, if the writer wanted to *analyze* the Van Gogh painting, she might begin with the large subject of painting. Then she could *divide,* or break the subject down, into two groups.

traditional painting
modern painting

Then, she could further *divide* the types of modern painting:

impressionist
postimpressionist
fauvist
art nouveau
cubist
art deco
abstract expressionist
op art
minimalist art

The purpose is to determine what the parts of the whole are. If we know what the components of *modern painting* are, then we can place or locate the Van Gogh painting in relation to other paintings. We would know whether it belonged in the soup aisle or the freezer section, so to speak. In this case, we would decide that it is *not* traditional painting, so that we would separate it from that group. We would place it in the modern group. Now we know which aisle it belongs in. But is it tomato or chicken soup? Now we relate it to the other modern types of painting, and place it in the postimpressionist group. Our decision is based on an analysis of the painter's use of color, his style, and the ways he differs from painters in the other groups.

Our analysis does not mean that the Van Gogh has nothing in common with traditional painting. Van Gogh, for instance, shares an interest in landscape and self-portraits with Rembrandt. But the bright, bold colors of his *Starry Night* are so dramatically different from the somber colors of the older Dutch painter's *Nightwatch* that we are inclined to emphasize their *division*. We could, for instance, set up a supermarket on the basis of what color the food labels were: all the red labels in one aisle, all the yellow labels together. But such a system would make it much harder to find what we wanted unless we were experts in package design. Similarly, our classification of painting is based on the most sensible method of division.

HOW DO WE READ CLASSIFICATION?

Reading classification involves the following steps:

- Identify what the author is classifying. Find the thesis to determine what the purpose or basis of the classification is.
- Make an outline of the essay. Find the divisions and the classifications into which the author has sorted the subject.
- Determine whether the categories are clearly defined. Do they overlap?
- Be alert for stereotypes. Has the author used them in order to build the groups? If so, see if the groups are oversimplified and thus unreliable.
- Identify the intended audience. How do we know who the audience is?

In this chapter, Judith Viorst classifies friends into eight groups, and even numbers them to make it is easy to follow her divisions. E. B. White analyzes three New Yorks, first separating its various strands for a close look at the city, but then weaving them back together to create the "whole" city he loved so much. Andrew R. Rooney takes a humorous look at people who are and aren't handy around the house. James T. Baker brings together a variety of writing techniques to analyze the world of education with some humor. Each writer has a different purpose for classification, but each uses the same basic system of organization.

HOW DO WE WRITE CLASSIFICATION?

These four essayists should provide you with enough examples of how to classify to make your writing task easy. Classification resembles outlining. Whether the subject is personal, technical, simple, complex, or abstract, the writer can organize material into categories, and can move carefully from one category to another in developing an essay.

Select your topic and begin to divide it into categories. Try drawing a tree with branches or use a model from a biology book that shows the division of life into genus, species, phyla, and so on. Or make lists. Think about how your library classifies books. Arranging books by the color of the covers might look attractive, but it would presume that all library users already knew what a book looked like before they came to the library. Instead, libraries divide books by type. They generally begin with two large groups: fiction and nonfiction. Within these categories, they create small ones: English fiction, Mexican fiction, Australian fiction. Within nonfiction, they divide books into history, religion, geography, mathematics, and so on. In this way, a reader can find a book based on need, and not prior knowledge. Keeping the library in mind, make a list of categories for your topic.

Make an outline and arrange the groups to avoid overlap from one group to the next.

Decide on a system of classification. Don't force objects into arbitrary slots, though. Don't ignore differences that violate your categories. Try to create a legitimate system that avoids stereotyping or oversimplification; don't classify invalidly. Be sure your categories are legitimate.

Write a thesis that identifies the purpose of your system of classification. Think of the ways in which your system can broaden a reader's understanding of the subject rather than narrow it.

Sample thesis statement:

> At least three groups of immigrants reach the United States today—political refugees seeking asylum, economic refugees looking for a better life, and religious dissidents looking for freedom to practice their chosen beliefs.

Writing the Draft

Write a rough draft. Be sure that you explain the categories and give examples for each one.

For each category, use definition, description, illustration, or narrative to help the reader see the distinct nature of the division you have created. Use transitions between each category or group.

Proofread for correctness. Make a final copy.

Friends, Good Friends—and Such Good Friends

Judith Viorst

In this essay Judith Viorst, who writes for numerous popular magazines, examines types of friends in her life. Her pattern of development is easy to follow, because she tends to stay on one level in the process of classification. As you read this essay, try to keep in mind the similarities and distinctions that Viorst makes among types of friends, as well as the principles of classification that she uses.

PREREADING: THINKING ABOUT THE ESSAY IN ADVANCE

Take a few moments to think about the types of friends that play various roles in your life. How many distinct varieties of friends can you identify? Do you act differently with each type or have different expectations? How does each type of friend make you feel?

Words to Watch

nonchalant (par. 3) showing an easy unconcern or disinterest

endodontist (par. 14) a dentist specializing in diseases of dental pulp and root canals

sibling (par. 16) brother or sister

dormant (par. 19) as if asleep; inactive

self-revelation (par. 22) self-discovery; self-disclosure

calibrated (par. 29) measured; fixed; checked carefully

Women are friends, I once would have said, when they totally love and support and trust each other, and bare to each other the secrets of their souls, and run—no questions asked—to help each other, and tell harsh truths to each other (no, you can't wear that dress unless you lose ten pounds first) when harsh truths must be told. 1

2 Women are friends, I once would have said, when they share the same affection for Ingmar Bergman, plus train rides, cats, warm rain, charades, Camus, and hate with equal ardor Newark and Brussels sprouts and Lawrence Welk and camping.

3 In other words, I once would have said that a friend is a friend all the way, but now I believe that's a narrow point of view. For the friendships I have and the friendships I see are conducted at many levels of intensity, serve many different functions, meet different needs and range from those as all-the-way as the friendship of the soul sisters mentioned above to that of the most nonchalant and casual playmates.

4 Consider these varieties of friendship:

5 1. Convenience friends. These are the women with whom, if our paths weren't crossing all the time, we'd have no particular reason to be friends: a next-door neighbor, a woman in our car pool, the mother of one of our children's closest friends or maybe some mommy with whom we serve juice and cookies each week at the Glenwood Co-op Nursery.

6 Convenience friends are convenient indeed. They'll lend us their cups and silverware for a party. They'll drive our kids to soccer when we're sick. They'll take us to pick up our car when we need a lift to the garage. They'll even take our cats when we go on vacation. As we will for them.

7 But we don't, with convenience friends, ever come too close or tell too much; we maintain our public face and emotional distance. "Which means," says Elaine, "that I'll talk about being overweight but not about being depressed. Which means I'll admit being mad but not blind with rage. Which means I might say that we're pinched this month but never that I'm worried sick over money."

8 But which doesn't mean that there isn't sufficient value to be found in these friendships of mutual aid, in convenience friends.

9 2. Special-interest friends. These friendships aren't intimate, and they needn't involve kids or silverware or cats. Their value lies in some interest jointly shared. And so we may have an office friend or a yoga friend or a tennis friend or a friend from the Women's Democratic Club.

10 "I've got one woman friend," says Joyce, "who likes, as I do, to take psychology courses. Which makes it nice for me—and nice for her. It's fun to go with someone you know and it's fun to

discuss what you've learned, driving back from the classes." And for the most part, she says, that's all they discuss.

"I'd say that what we're doing is *doing* together, not being together," Suzanne says of her Tuesday-doubles friends. "It's mainly a tennis relationship, but we play together well. And I guess we all need to have a couple of playmates." 11

I agree. 12

My playmate is a shopping friend, a woman of marvelous taste, a woman who knows exactly *where* to buy *what,* and furthermore is a woman who always knows beyond a doubt what one ought to be buying. I don't have the time to keep up with what's new in eyeshadow, hemlines and shoes and whether the smock look is in or finished already. But since (oh, shame!) I care a lot about eyeshadow, hemlines and shoes, and since I don't *want* to wear smocks if the smock look is finished, I'm very glad to have a shopping friend. 13

3. Historical friends. We all have a friend who knew us when . . . maybe way back in Miss Meltzer's second grade, when our family lived in that three-room flat in Brooklyn, when our dad was out of work for seven months, when our brother Allie got in that fight where they had to call the police, when our sister married the endodontist from Yonkers and when, the morning after we lost our virginity, she was the first, the only, friend we told. 14

The years have gone by and we've gone separate ways and we've little in common now, but we're still an intimate part of each other's past. And so whenever we go to Detroit we always go to visit this friend of our girlhood. Who knows how we looked before our teeth were straightened. Who knows how we talked before our voice got unBrooklyned. Who knows what we ate before we learned about artichokes. And who, by her presence, puts us in touch with an earlier part of ourself, a part of ourself it's important never to lose. 15

"What this friend means to me and what I mean to her," says Grace, "is having a sister without sibling rivalry. We know the texture of each other's lives. She remembers my grandmother's cabbage soup. I remember the way her uncle played the piano. There's simply no other friend who remembers those things." 16

4. Crossroads friends. Like historical friends, our crossroads friends are important for *what was*—for the friendship we shared at a crucial, now past, time of life. A time, perhaps, when 17

we roomed in college together; or worked as eager young singles in the Big City together; or went together, as my friend Elizabeth and I did through pregnancy, birth and that scary first year of new motherhood.

18 Crossroads friends forge powerful links, links strong enough to endure with not much more contact than once-a-year letters at Christmas. And out of respect for those crossroads years, for those dramas and dreams we once shared, we will always be friends.

19 5. Cross-generational friends. Historical friends and crossroads friends seem to maintain a special kind of intimacy—dormant but always ready to be revived—and though we may rarely meet, whenever we do connect, it's personal and intense. Another kind of intimacy exists in the friendships that form across generations in what one woman calls her daughter-mother and her mother-daughter relationships.

20 Evelyn's friend is her mother's age—"but I share so much more than I ever could with my mother"—a woman she talks to of music, of books and of life. "What I get from her is the benefit of her experience. What she gets—and enjoys—from me is a youthful perspective. It's a pleasure for both of us."

21 I have in my own life a precious friend, a woman of 65 who has lived very hard, who is wise, who listens well; who has been where I am and can help me understand it; and who represents not only an ultimate ideal mother to me but also the person I'd like to be when I grow up.

22 In our daughter role we tend to do more than our share of self-revelation; in our mother role we tend to receive what's revealed. It's another kind of pleasure—playing wise mother to a questing younger person. It's another very lovely kind of friendship.

23 6. Part-of-a-couple friends. Some of the women we call our friends we never see alone—we see them as part of a couple at couples' parties. And though we share interests in many things and respect each other's views, we aren't moved to deepen the relationship. Whatever the reason, a lack of time or—and this is more likely—a lack of chemistry, our friendship remains in the context of a group. But the fact that our feeling on seeing each other is always, "I'm *so* glad she's here" and the fact that we spend half the evening talking together says that this too, in its own way, counts as a friendship.

(Other part-of-a-couple friends are the friends that came with the marriage, and some of these are friends we could live without. But sometimes, alas, she married our husband's best friend; and sometimes, alas, she *is* our husband's best friend. And so we find ourself dealing with her, somewhat against our will, in a spirit of what I'll call *reluctant* friendship.) 24

7. Men who are friends. I wanted to write just of women friends, but the women I've talked to won't let me—they say I must mention man-woman friendships too. For these friendships can be just as close and as dear as those that we form with women. Listen to Lucy's description of one such friendship: 25

"We've found we have things to talk about that are different from what he talks about with my husband and different from what I talk about with his wife. So sometimes we call on the phone or meet for lunch. There are similar intellectual interests—we always pass on to each other the books that we love—but there's also something tender and caring too." 26

In a couple of crises, Lucy says, "he offered himself, for talking and for helping. And when someone died in his family he wanted me there. The sexual, flirty part of our friendship is very small, but *some*—just enough to make it fun and different." She thinks—and I agree—that the sexual part, though small, is always *some,* is always there when a man and a woman are friends. 27

It's only in the past few years that I've made friends with men, in the sense of a friendship that's *mine,* not just part of two couples. And achieving with them the ease and the trust I've found with women friends has value indeed. Under the dryer at home last week, putting on mascara and rouge, I comfortably sat and talked with a fellow named Peter. Peter, I finally decided, could handle the shock of me minus mascara under the dryer. Because we care for each other. Because we're friends. 28

8. There are medium friends, and pretty good friends, and very good friends indeed, and these friendships are defined by their level of intimacy. And what we'll reveal at each of these levels of intimacy is calibrated with care. We might tell a medium friend, for example, that yesterday we had a fight with our husband. And we might tell a pretty good friend that this fight with our husband made us so mad that we slept on the couch. And we might tell a very good friend that the reason we got so mad in that fight that we slept on the couch had something to do with 29

that girl who works in his office. But it's only to our very best friends that we're willing to tell all, to tell what's going on with that girl in his office.

30 The best of friends, I still believe, totally love and support and trust each other, and bare to each other the secrets of their souls, and run—no questions asked—to help each other, and tell harsh truths to each other when they must be told.

31 But we needn't agree about everything (only 12-year-old girl friends agree about *everything*) to tolerate each other's point of view. To accept without judgment. To give and to take without ever keeping score. And to *be* there, as I am for them and as they are for me, to comfort our sorrows, to celebrate our joys.

BUILDING VOCABULARY

1. Find *antonyms* (words that mean the opposite of given words) for the following entries.
 a. harsh (par. 1)
 b. mutual (par. 8)
 c. crucial (par. 17)
 d. intimacy (par. 29)
 e. tolerate (par. 31)

2. The *derivation* of a word—how it originated and where it came from—can make you more aware of meanings. Your dictionary normally lists abbreviations (for instance, L. for Latin, Fr. for French) for word origins, and sometimes explains fully the way a word came into use. Look up the following words to determine their origins.
 a. psychology (par. 10)
 b. historical (par. 14)
 c. sibling (par. 16)
 d. Christmas (par. 18)
 e. sexual (par. 27)

THINKING CRITICALLY ABOUT THE ESSAY

Understanding the Writer's Ideas

1. What is Viorst's definition of friendship in the first two paragraphs? Does she accept this definition? Why or why not?
2. Name and describe in your own words the types of friends that Viorst mentions in her essay.
3. In what way are "convenience friends" and "special-interest friends" alike? How are "historical friends" and "crossroads friends" alike?
4. What does Viorst mean when she writes, "In our daughter role we tend to do more than our share of self-revelation; in our mother role we tend to receive what's revealed" (par. 22)?
5. How do part-of-a-couple friends who came with the marriage differ from primary part-of-a-couple friends?
6. Does Viorst think that men can be friends for women? Why or why not? What complicates such friendships?
7. For Viorst, who are the best friends?

Understanding the Writer's Techniques

1. Which paragraphs make up the introduction in this essay? How does Viorst organize these paragraphs? Where does she place her thesis sentence?
2. How does the thesis sentence reveal the principles of classification (the questions Viorst asks to produce the various categories) that the author employs in the essay?
3. Does Viorst seem to emphasize each of her categories equally? Is she effective in handling each category? Why or why not? Do you think that men belong in the article as a category? For what reasons?
4. Analyze the importance of illustration in this essay. From what sources does Viorst tend to draw her examples?
5. How do definition and comparison and contrast operate in the essay? Cite specific examples of these techniques.
6. The level of language in this essay tends to be informal at times, reflecting patterns that are as close to conversation as to formal writing. Identify some sentences that seem to resemble informal speech. Why does Viorst try to achieve a conversational style?

7. Which main group in the essay is further broken down into categories?
8. Analyze Viorst's conclusion. How many paragraphs are involved? What strategies does she use? How does she achieve balanced sentence structure (parallelism) in her last lines?

Exploring the Writer's Ideas

1. Do you accept all of Viorst's categories of friendship? Which categories seem the most meaningful to you?
2. Try to think of people you know who fit into the various categories established by Viorst. Can you think of people who might exist in more than one category? How do you explain this fact? What are the dangers in trying to stereotype people in terms of categories, roles, backgrounds, or functions?
3. Viorst maintains that you can define friends in terms of functions and needs (see paragraph 3 and paragraphs 29 to 31). Would you agree? Why or why not? What principle or principles do you use to classify friends? In fact, *do* you classify friends? For what reasons?

IDEAS FOR WRITING

Prewriting

Select a specific category of people—for example, teachers, friends, or family members—and freewrite for fifteen minutes about the characteristics of each type within the group.

Guided Writing

Using the classification method, write an essay on a specific group of individuals—for instance, types of friends, types of enemies, types of students, types of teachers, types of politicians, types of dates.

1. Establish your subject in the first paragraph. Also indicate to the reader the principle(s) of classification that you plan to use. (For guidelines look again at the second sentence in paragraph 3 of Viorst's essay.)

2. Start the body of the essay with a single short sentence that introduces categories, as Viorst does in paragraph 4. In the body, use numbers and category headings ("Convenience friends" . . . "Special-interest friends") to separate groups.
3. Try to achieve a balance in the presentation of information on each category. Define each type and provide appropriate examples.
4. If helpful, use comparison and contrast to indicate from time to time the similarities and differences among groups. Try to avoid too much overlapping of groups, since this is harmful to the classification process.
5. Employ the personal "I" and other conversational techniques to achieve an informal style.
6. Return to your principle(s) of classification and amplify this feature in your conclusion. If you want, make a value judgment, as Viorst does, about which type of person in your classification scheme is the most significant.

Thinking and Writing Collaboratively

Form groups of three or four, and have each group member draw a diagram showing the types of teachers they have encountered in school and college. Then, discuss the various divisions and try to develop one combined diagram. Finally, present your findings to the class.

More Writing Projects

1. As journal practice, classify varieties of show business comedians, singers, talk-show hosts, star athletes, or the like.
2. In a paragraph, use division and (or) classification to explain the various roles that you must play as a friend.
3. Ask each student in your class to explain what he or she means by the term "friendship." List all responses and then divide the list into at least three categories. Using your notes, write a classification essay reporting your findings.

The Three New Yorks

E. B. White

E. B. White, whose frequently used book *The Elements of Style* is well known to college composition students, here classifies "The Three New Yorks." Although the selection is an excerpt from his book *Here Is New York* (1949), the descriptive illustrations remain remarkably fresh after more than forty years. Look closely at the way White clearly defines his categories of classification, then skillfully blends them to create a vivid sense of the whole city.

PREREADING: THINKING ABOUT THE ESSAY IN ADVANCE

As you prepare to read White's essay, take a few minutes to think about the place where you live or, if you have lived in several locations, the place that you know best. What is the place like? Are there different classes of people in this place or different parts with specific features or functions? How would you divide the place in terms of people, sections, and functions?

Words to Watch

locusts (par. 1) migratory grasshoppers that travel in swarms, stripping vegetation as they pass over the land

disposition (par. 1) temperament; way of acting

deportment (par. 1) the way in which a person carries himself or herself

tidal (par. 1) coming in wavelike motions

continuity (par. 1) uninterrupted flow of events

slum (par. 1) a highly congested residential area marked by unsanitary buildings, poverty, and social disorder

indignity (par. 1) humiliating treatment

vitality (par. 2) lively and animated character

gloaming (par. 2) a poetic term for "twilight"

ramparts (par. 2) high, broad structures guarding a building

negligently (par. 2) nonchalantly; neglectfully

loiterer (par. 2) a person who hangs around aimlessly

spewing (par. 2) coming in a flood or gush

rover (par. 2) wanderer; roamer

There are roughly three New Yorks. There is, first, the New York of the man or woman who was born here, who takes the city for granted and accepts its size and its turbulence as natural and inevitable. Second, there is the New York of the commuter—the city that is devoured by locusts each day and spat out each night. Third, there is the New York of the person who was born somewhere else and came to New York in quest of something. Of these three trembling cities the greatest is the last—the city of final destination, the city that is a goal. It is this third city that accounts for New York's high-strung disposition, its poetical deportment, its dedication to the arts, and its incomparable achievements. Commuters give the city its tidal restlessness; natives give it solidity and continuity; but the settlers give it passion. And whether it is a farmer arriving from Italy to set up a small grocery store in a slum, or a young girl arriving from a small town in Mississippi to escape the indignity of being observed by her neighbors, or a boy arriving from the Corn Belt with a manuscript in his suitcase and a pain in his heart, it makes no difference; each embraces New York with the intense excitement of first love, each absorbs New York with the fresh eyes of an adventurer, each generates heat and light to dwarf the Consolidated Edison Company. 1

The commuter is the queerest bird of all. The suburb he inhabits has no essential vitality of its own and is a mere roost where he comes at day's end to go to sleep. Except in rare cases, the man who lives in Mamaroneck or Little Neck or Teaneck, and works in New York, discovers nothing much about the city except the time of arrival and departure of trains and buses, and the path to a quick lunch. He is deskbound, and has never, idly roaming in the gloaming, stumbled suddenly on Belvedere Tower in the Park, seen the ramparts rise sheer from the water of the pond, and the boys along the shore fishing for minnows, girls stretched out negligently on the shelves of the rocks; he has never come suddenly on anything at all in New York as a loiterer, because he has had no time between trains. He has fished in Manhattan's wallet and dug out coins, but has never listened to Manhattan's breathing, never awakened to its morning, never dropped off to sleep in its night. About 400,000 men and women come charging onto the Island each week-day morning, out of the mouths of tubes and tunnels. Not many among them have ever spent a drowsy afternoon in the great rustling oaken silence of the reading room of the Public Library, with the book elevator (like 2 an old water wheel) spewing out books onto the trays. They tend their furnaces in Westchester and in Jersey, but have never seen the furnaces of the Bowery, the fires that burn in oil drums on zero winter nights. They may work in the financial district downtown and never see the extravagant plantings of Rockefeller Center—the daffodils and grape hyacinths and birches of the flags trimmed to the wind on a fine morning in spring. Or they may work in a midtown office and may let a whole year swing round without sighting Governor's Island from the sea wall. The commuter dies with tremendous mileage to his credit, but he is no rover. His entrances and exits are more devious than those in a prairie-dog village; and he calmly plays bridge while his train is buried in the mud at the bottom of the East River. The Long Island Rail Road alone carried forty million commuters last year; but many of them were the same fellow retracing his steps.

3 The terrain of New York is such that a resident sometimes travels farther, in the end, than a commuter. The journey of the composer Irving Berlin from Cherry Street in the lower East Side to an apartment uptown was through an alley and was only three or four miles in length; but it was like going three times around the world.

BUILDING VOCABULARY

1. Underline the numerous references in this essay to buildings, people, and areas in and around New York City and identify them. If necessary, consult a guidebook, map, or history of New York City for help.
2. Write *synonyms* (words that mean the same) for each of these words in the essay. Use a dictionary if necessary.
   - **a.** turbulence (par. 1)
   - **b.** inevitable (par. 1)
   - **c.** quest (par. 1)
   - **d.** high-strung (par. 1)
   - **e.** incomparable (par. 1)
   - **f.** essential (par. 2)
   - **g.** deskbound (par. 2)
   - **h.** drowsy (par. 2)
   - **i.** extravagant (par. 2)
   - **j.** devious (par. 2)

THINKING CRITICALLY ABOUT THE ESSAY

Understanding the Writer's Ideas

1. What are the three New Yorks?
2. What single-word designation does E. B. White assign to each of the three types of New Yorkers? Match up each of the three New Yorks you identified in the first question with each of the three types of New Yorkers.
3. For what reasons do people born elsewhere come to New York to live? What three illustrations of such people does White describe? What is the young girl's indignity? What is the occupation or hope of the boy from the Corn Belt? Why might he have "a pain in his heart"?
4. What does each type of New Yorker give to the city?
5. What is White's attitude toward the suburbs? What key phrases reveal this attitude?
6. What are some of the things commuters miss about New York by dashing in and out of the city? What does White ironically suggest will be the commuter's final fate?
7. Are we to take literally White's conclusion that "many of them were the same fellow retracing his steps"? Why or why not?
8. Explain the sentence "The terrain of New York is such that a resident sometimes travels farther, in the end, than a commuter." Be aware that White is using language figuratively.
9. The author tells of composer Irving Berlin's journey through an alley. He is referring to "Tin Pan Alley." Identify this place.

Understanding the Writer's Techniques

1. In this essay what is the thesis? Where is it? Is it developed fully?
2. What is the purpose of classification in this essay? What is the basis of the classification White uses? What key words at the beginning of paragraph 1 direct your attention to each category discussed? How do these key words contrast in tone with the descriptions in the first few sentences? What sort of rhythm is established?

3. White vividly *personifies* (see Glossary) New York City in paragraph 1. List and explain the effects of these personifications. Where else does he personify?
4. Refer to your answers to question 2 in the Building Vocabulary section. Are the literal meanings of those words appropriate to White's three types of New Yorkers? Defend your answer. Figuratively, what does each term make you think of? How do the figurative meanings enhance the essay?
5. How does White use *illustration* in this essay? Where does he use it most effectively?
6. What is the function of *negation* (see page 234) in the first part of paragraph 2? What is the *implied contrast* in this paragraph?
7. How is White's attitude toward New York reflected in the *tone* (see Glossary) of this essay?
8. White makes widespread use of *metaphor* (see Glossary) in this essay. How does his use of metaphor affect the tone of the essay? State in your own words the meaning of each of the following metaphors.
   a. the city that is devoured by locusts each day and spat out each night (par. 1)
   b. The commuter is the queerest bird of all. (par. 2)
   c. a mere roost (par. 2)
   d. idly roaming in the gloaming (par. 2)
   e. He has fished in Manhattan's wallet and dug out coins, but has never listened to Manhattan's breathing (par. 2)
   f. the great rustling oaken silence (par. 2)
9. Among all the metaphors, White uses just one *simile* (see Glossary). What is it? What is the effect of placing it where he did?

Exploring the Writer's Ideas

1. At the beginning of the essay, E. B. White states that New York's "turbulence" is considered "natural and inevitable" by its native residents. But such a condition is true for any large city. If you live in a large city, or if you have ever visited one, what are some examples of its turbulence? Do you think it is always a good idea to accept the disorder of the place where you live? How can such acceptance be a positive attitude? How can it be negative? How do you deal with disruptions in your environment?

2. White writes of "a young girl arriving from a small town in Mississippi to escape the indignity of being observed by her neighbors." Tell in your own words what might cause her indignity. How can neighbors bring about such a condition?
3. Some people feel that the anonymity of a big city like New York makes it easier just to "be yourself" without having to worry about what others might say. Others feel such anonymity creates a terrible feeling of impersonality. Discuss the advantages and disadvantages of each attitude.
4. Do you agree that the suburbs have "no essential vitality"? Explain your response by referring to suburbs you have visited, have read about, or have inhabited.
5. White claims that those who choose to leave their homes and who come to live in New York give the place a special vitality. Do you know any people who chose to leave their places of birth to live in a large city like New York? Why did they move? How have things gone for them since they began living in the city? Have you noticed any changes? For what reasons do people leave one place to live in another? When have you moved from place to place? Why?

IDEAS FOR WRITING

Prewriting

Write "The Three __________" at the top of a sheet of paper, and fill in the blank with the name of the town or city where you live. Below the title, draw a diagram or visual presentation in which you establish and label at least three distinct types of people in your community.

Guided Writing

Organize a classification essay around the city or town in which you live.

1. Begin with a simple direct thesis statement that tells the reader how many categories of classification you will consider.
2. Briefly outline the different categories. Indicate each with a key organizational word or phrase.

3. Indicate which category is the most important. Tell why.
4. Develop this category with at least three vivid illustrations.
5. Define one of the categories through both negation and an implied contrast to another category.
6. Use figurative language (metaphors, similes, personification) throughout your essay.
7. Use specific name or place references.
8. End your essay with a brief factual narrative that gives the reader a feel for your town or city.

Thinking and Writing Collaboratively

Exchange your classification essay with a class member. Then assess the accuracy of your classmate's division of her or his subject into categories. Underline the subdivisions within the paper. Check to see that there is no overlap or omission of key categories. Recommend revisions, if any, and make any appropriate revisions suggested by your partner to your own paper.

More Writing Projects

1. Use classification in a journal entry to capture at least three ways of viewing your college.
2. Write a classification paragraph on the suburbs or the country.
3. Select a cultural group and classify in an essay various characteristics common to that group. Be careful to avoid stereotyping.

The Unhandy Man

Andrew R. Rooney

Andrew R. Rooney is best known as the quirky commentator on CBS's *60 Minutes*. Here he demonstrates his keen wit by making fun of the age-old expectation that men must know how to fix everything that doesn't work—especially around the house. For Rooney, in fact, women are becoming increasingly more handy than men. The era of the "unhandy" man is upon us.

PREREADING: THINKING ABOUT THE ESSAY IN ADVANCE

Think about whether or not you are a handy person. Ask friends and family what they think about you, too.

Words to Watch

species (par. 2) kind; variety; type

bystander (par. 6) a person who is present at an event without participating in it

dog work (par. 11) a slang phrase meaning drudgery or hard work

menial (par. 17) appropriate to a servant

When it comes to doing jobs around the house, there are five categories of people. 1

1. The person who knows how to do it, likes to do it, and proceeds quietly and efficiently to get the job done right, alone. This is a rare species. 2

2. The helpless. This person can't do it, won't try to do it, and has no interest in learning how. At least his or her position is clear. Nothing is expected of this person. 3

3. The good helper. There are people who won't tackle a job alone, but who are good and willing helpers. Very valuable. 4

4. The person who does jobs around the house but always needs help. "Helen, hand me the hammer." 5

6 5. The bystander. This is the person who doesn't ever do a job but is always there, commenting on how it should be done.

7 Let's review the people in some of these categories in more detail:

8 The Category 1 fixers never seem to run into as many obstacles as other people do. They don't ask for help, they don't ask where anything is, they don't have to go to the hardware store to get something they don't have, and they don't need anything held for them.

9 Of the five categories, people in Category 4 and Category 5 are by far the most annoying.

10 The Category 4 people's constant demand for help may come out of some deep-seated need they have to be recognized. They may need psychiatry. They want to make sure everyone knows they're doing the job and that it's hard. This person wants someone around, in attendance, getting things and holding things so the work they're doing will be apparent.

11 He's up on a ladder or down on his knees doing the important job and needs a flunky to do the dog work.

12 "Do we have any screws about this long?"

13 (By asking the question this way, he has established the fact that, if there are no screws the right length, it is the helper's fault.)

14 "Here, hold this for me, will you, while I get this started?"

15 (I put a question mark after those sentences spoken by Category 4 people although none belongs because the person isn't really asking. He's telling the other person what to do.)

16 Category 3 people, the good helpers, are most underrated. A good helper doesn't talk a lot even though he or she may see how the job should be done better than the person doing it.

17 The helper is encouraging and willing to do menial jobs, like sweeping up afterwards.

18 The helper admires the work being done, loud and often. When the job is complete, the helper steps back and admires it again. Don't ever underrate a good helper.

19 Category 5 people are a real pain in the neck, to put the pain above where it belongs.

20 If they are so dissatisfied with the work being done, it is never clear why they don't do it themselves, but they never do.

21 "Couldn't you move it just a few inches to the right? Now down."

The other thing Category 5s do is add on. 22

"Oh say," they say, "while you're doing that, could you just 23
. . ." And then they think of three other jobs for you to do that have nothing to do with the original one. They won't let you finish. If you do one job, it reminds them of another. They're never satisfied.

It's interesting that gender doesn't seem to be a big factor in 24
what kind of a fixer a person is. Men most often do the handyman jobs around the house, but there are more and more women who know how to change the washer in a dripping faucet. Quite often now, it's the woman in the house who knows which fuse in the fuse box controls the lights in the upstairs bathroom or in the kitchen. When a fuse blows, she also knows where the flashlight and the extra fuses are.

I think of myself as a Category 1, but notice a good many 25
characteristics of the Category 4 in me.

BUILDING VOCABULARY

Define the words below and then use them in sentences in such a way that readers unfamiliar with the terms can understand them from context clues.

a. psychiatry (par. 10)
b. flunky (par. 11)
c. gender (par. 24)
d. fuse (par. 24)

THINKING CRITICALLY ABOUT THE ESSAY

Understanding the Writer's Ideas

1. Briefly, what are the five categories of people who do jobs around the house?
2. What is a main characteristic of the Category 1 person?
3. Why does Rooney say the Category 4 person needs psychiatry?
4. What people are in the most annoying category? Why?
5. Who are the most underrated house workers and why?

6. Does gender determine the quality of the worker, according to Rooney? Explain.

Understanding the Writer's Techniques

1. What is the essay's thesis?
2. How does the title reveal who the audience is?
3. Why does the writer introduce five categories of workers but only discuss four categories in detail?
4. How does the introduction set up the structure of this classification essay?
5. What paragraph makes the transition from the essay's definitions to the elaboration of each category?
6. How would you describe the tone of this essay? Is it insulting? Humorous? What sets the tone?
7. Why does the writer explain Category 5 people last? What might this say about a way to organize details in a classification essay?
8. While classification essays may not always focus on the writer's personal experiences, how does this writer conclude the essay? Do you feel this ending fits into the tone and focus of the essay? Explain.

Exploring the Writer's Ideas

1. Do this writer's categories make sense to you? Do you see yourself here? Explain.
2. Why does this essay's title say "unhandy man" if the writer concludes that women may be handier than men? Couldn't the essay be called the "unhandy woman" too? Why or why not?
3. Should all men and women be prepared to do jobs around the house? Is this just a man's job? Use examples to support your position.
4. Describe how you feel about the Category 2 person. Do you feel like Rooney? Why or why not?
5. If the writer is correct that more women are becoming handy, is this a positive trend? Why or why not?
6. Do you think Rooney is funny or annoying? Explain.

IDEAS FOR WRITING

Prewriting

Classify five different kinds of students you see at your school. Write a definition of each in your journal.

Guided Writing

Write a classification essay on five categories of students you see at your school.

1. Use the following sentence for your thesis (fill in the blank): "When it comes to students at __________, there are five categories."
2. Use your prewriting notes to define each student category.
3. Use a transition sentence like that of Rooney in paragraph 7 to set up your detailed review of each category.
4. Review each category, giving examples to support each category definition.
5. Remember: try to keep this paper humorous.
6. Conclude the essay by placing yourself into one of the five categories. Give examples to show why you suit this category.

Thinking and Writing Collaboratively

In small groups, make an outline that reveals the five categories of possible dates, going from the best date to the worst. Use these notes to write your own classification essays.

More Writing Projects

1. In your journal, write your own classifications on the subject of emotions.
2. In a paragraph, classify things you feel are critical to your career goal.
3. Write a classification essay that categorizes a serious social problem, for example, drug abuse or homelessness.

How Do We Find the Student in a World of Academic Gymnasts and Worker Ants?

James T. Baker

As you look around your classrooms, school cafeteria, lecture halls, or gymnasium, perhaps you will recognize representatives of the types of students that James Baker classifies in this witty, wry essay. The author enhances his unique categories by using description, definition, and colloquial language, which help make his deliberate stereotypes come alive.

PREREADING: THINKING ABOUT THE ESSAY IN ADVANCE

Prior to reading this essay, think about the different types of students you have encountered and the forms of behavior distinguishing one from the other. Does each type behave in a predictable way? Which category would you place yourself in? Which types do you prefer or associate with, and why?

Words to Watch

musings (par. 3) dreamy, abstract thoughts

sabbatical (par. 3) a paid leave from a job earned after a certain period of time

malaise (par. 3) uneasiness; feelings of restlessness

impaired (par. 3) made less effective

clones (par. 4) exact biological replicas, asexually produced

recuperate (par. 5) to undergo recovery from an illness

esoteric (par. 7) understood by a limited group with special knowledge

primeval (par. 7) primitive; relating to the earliest ages

mundane (par. 8) ordinary

jaded (par. 20) exhausted; bored by something from overexposure to it

Anatole France once wrote that "the whole art of teaching is only 1
the art of awakening the natural curiosity of young minds." I fully agree, except I have to wonder if, by using the word "only," he thought that the art of awakening such natural curiosity was an easy job. For me, it never has been—sometimes exciting, always challenging, but definitely not easy.

Robert M. Hutchins used to say that a good education pre- 2
pares students to go on educating themselves throughout their lives. A fine definition, to be sure, but it has at times made me doubt that my own students, who seem only too eager to graduate so they can lay down their books forever, are receiving a good education.

But then maybe these are merely the pessimistic musings of 3
someone suffering from battle fatigue. I have almost qualified for my second sabbatical leave, and I am scratching a severe case of the seven-year itch. About the only power my malaise has not impaired is my eye for spotting certain "types" of students. In fact, as the rest of me declines, my eye seems to grow more acute.

Has anyone else noticed that the very same students people 4
college classrooms year after year? Has anyone else found the same bodies, faces, personalities returning semester after semester? Forgive me for violating my students' individual "personhoods," but reality makes it so tempting to see them as types. Doubtless you will recognize at least some of them. They have twins, or perhaps clones, on your campus, too.

There is the eternal Good Time Charlie (or Charlene), who 5
makes every party on and off the campus, who by November of his freshman year has worked his face into a case of terminal acne, who misses every set of examinations because of "mono," who finally burns himself out physically and mentally by the age of 19 and drops out to go home and recuperate, and who returns at 20 after a long talk with Dad to major in accounting.

There is the Young General Patton, the one who comes to 6
college on an R.O.T.C. scholarship and for a year twirls his rifle at basketball games while loudly sniffing out pinko professors, who at midpoint takes a sudden but predictable, radical swing from far right to far left, who grows a beard and moves in with a girl who refuses to shave her legs, who then makes the just as predictable, radical swing back to the right and ends up preach-

ing fundamentalist sermons on the steps of the student union while the Good Time Charlies and Charlenes jeer.

7 There is the Egghead, the campus intellectual who shakes up his fellow students—and even a professor or two—with references to esoteric formulas and obscure Bulgarian poets, who is recognized by friend and foe alike as a promising young academic, someday to be a professional scholar, who disappears every summer for six weeks ostensibly to search for primeval human remains in Colorado caves, and who at 37 is shot dead by Arab terrorists while on a mission for the C.I.A.

8 There is the Performer—the music or theater major, the rock or folk singer—who spends all of his or her time working up an act, who gives barely a nod to mundane subjects like history, sociology, or physics, who dreams only of the day he or she will be on stage full time, praised by critics, cheered by audiences, who ends up either pregnant or responsible for a pregnancy and at 30 is either an insurance salesman or a housewife with a very lush garden.

9 There is the Jock, of course—the every-afternoon intramural champ, smelling of liniment and Brut, with bulging calves and a blue-eyed twinkle, the subject of untold numbers of female fantasies, the walking personification of he-manism—who upon graduation is granted managerial rank by a California bank because of his golden tan and low golf score, who is seen five years later buying the drinks at a San Francisco gay bar.

10 There is the Academic Gymnast—the guy or gal who sees college as an obstacle course, as so many stumbling blocks in the way of a great career or a perfect marriage—who strains every moment to finish and be done with "this place" forever, who toward the end of the junior year begins to slow down, to grow quieter and less eager to leave, who attends summer school, but never quite finishes those last six hours, who never leaves "this place," and who at 40 is still working at the campus laundry, still here, still a student.

11 There is the Medal Hound, the student who comes to college not to learn or expand any intellectual horizons but simply to win honors—medals, cups, plates, ribbons, scrolls—who is here because this is the best place to win the most the fastest, who plasticizes and mounts on his wall every certificate of excellence he wins, who at 39 will be a colonel in the U.S. Army and at 55

Secretary of something or other in a conservative Administration in Washington.

There is the Worker Ant, the student (loosely rendered) who 12
takes 21 hours a semester and works 49 hours a week at the local car wash, who sleeps only on Sundays and during classes, who will somehow graduate on time and be the owner of his own vending-machine company at 30 and be dead of a heart attack at 40, and who will be remembered for the words chiseled on his tombstone:

All This Was Accomplished Without Ever Having So Much 13
as Darkened The Door Of A Library

There is the Lost Soul, the sad kid who is in college only 14
because teachers, parents, and society at large said so, who hasn't a career in mind or a dream to follow, who hasn't a clue, who heads home every Friday afternoon to spend the weekend cruising the local Dairee-Freeze, who at 50 will have done all his teachers, parents, and society said to do, still without a career in mind or a dream to follow or a clue.

There is also the Saved Soul—the young woman who has 15
received, through the ministry of one Gospel freak or another, a Holy Calling to save the world, or at least some special part of it—who majors in Russian studies so that she can be caught smuggling Bibles into the Soviet Union and be sent to Siberia where she can preach to souls imprisoned by the Agents of Satan in the Gulag Archipelago.

Then, finally, there is the Happy Child, who comes to col- 16
lege to find a husband or wife—and finds one—and there is the Determined Child, who comes to get a degree—and gets one.

Enough said. 17

All of which, I suppose, should make me throw up my 18
hands in despair and say that education, like youth and love, is wasted on the young. Not quite.

For there does come along, on occasion, that one of a hun- 19
dred or so who is maybe at first a bit lost, certainly puzzled; who may well start out a Good Timer, an Egghead, a Performer, a Jock, a Medal Hound, a Gymnast, a Worker Ant; who may indeed have trouble settling on a major, who will be distressed by what sometimes passes for education, who might even be a temporary dropout; but who has a vital capacity for growth and is able to fall in love with learning, who acquires a taste for intellectual pleasure, who becomes in the finest sense of the word a Student.

20 This is the one who keeps the most jaded of us going back to class after class, and he or she must be oh-so-carefully cultivated. He or she must be artfully awakened, given the tools needed to continue learning for a lifetime, and let grow at whatever pace and in whatever direction nature dictates.

21 For I try always to remember that this student is me, my continuing self, my immortality. This person is my only hope that my own search for Truth will continue after me, on and on, forever.

BUILDING VOCABULARY

1. Explain these *colloquialisms* (see Glossary) in Baker's essay.
  a. someone suffering from battle fatigue (par. 3)
  b. I am scratching a severe case of the seven-year itch (par. 3)
  c. worked his face into a case of terminal acne (par. 5)
  d. burns himself out physically and mentally (par. 5)
  e. loudly sniffing out pinko professors (par. 6)
  f. working up an act (par. 8)
  g. gives barely a nod (par. 8)
  h. the walking personification of he-manism (par. 9)
  i. to spend the weekend cruising the local Dairee-Freeze (par. 14)
  j. he or she must be oh-so-carefully cultivated (par. 20)

2. Identify these references.
  a. R.O.T.C. (par. 6)
  b. C.I.A. (par. 7)
  c. Brut (par. 9)
  d. Dairee-Freeze (par. 14)
  e. Gospel freak (par. 15)
  f. Agents of Satan (par. 15)
  g. Gulag Archipelago (par. 15)

THINKING CRITICALLY ABOUT THE ESSAY

Understanding the Writer's Ideas

1. In common language, describe the various categories of college students that Baker names.

2. Who is Anatole France? What process is described in the quotation from him? Why does Baker cite it at the beginning of the essay? What is his attitude toward France's idea?
3. For how long has Baker been teaching? What is his attitude toward his work?
4. About what age do you think Baker is? Why? Explain the meaning of the sentence: "In fact, as the rest of me declines, my eye seems to grow more acute" (par. 3).
5. Choose three of Baker's categories and paraphrase each description and meaning in a serious way.
6. What does Baker feel, overall, is the contemporary college student's attitude toward studying and receiving an education? How does it differ from Baker's own attitude toward these things?
7. Although Baker's classification may seem a bit pessimistic, he refuses to "throw up . . . [his] hands in despair" (par. 18). Why?
8. Describe the characteristics that are embodied in the category of *Student.* To whom does Baker compare the "true" Student? Why?

Understanding the Writer's Techniques

1. What is Baker's thesis in this essay? Does he state it directly or not? What, in your own words, is his purpose?
2. In this essay Baker deliberately creates, rather than avoids, stereotypes. He does so to establish exaggerated representatives of types. Why?

   For paragraphs 5 to 16, prepare a paragraph-by-paragraph outline of the main groups of students classified. For each, include the following information:

   a. type represented by the stereotype
   b. motivation of type for being a student
   c. main activity as a student
   d. condition in which the type ends up
3. This article was published in *The Chronicle of Higher Education,* a weekly newspaper for college and university educators and administrators. How do you think this audience influenced Baker's analysis of types of students? His tone and language?

4. What is Baker's tone in the essay? Give specific examples. In general, how would you characterize his attitude toward the contemporary college student? Why? Does his attitude or tone undergo any shifts in the essay? Explain.
5. Why does Baker use the term "personhoods" in paragraph 4? What attitude, about what subject, does he convey in his use of that word?
6. Why does the author capitalize the names he gives to the various categories of students? Why does he capitalize the word "Truth" in the last sentence?
7. How does Baker use definition in this essay? What purpose does it serve?
8. How does Baker use description to enhance his analysis in this essay?
9. In this essay, what is the role of *process analysis?* (Process analysis, discussed in the next chapter, is telling how something is done or proceeds; see pages 304–306). Look especially at Baker's descriptions of each type of student. How does process analysis figure into the title of the essay?
10. What is the purpose of the one-sentence paragraph 13? Why does Baker set it aside from paragraph 12, since it is a logical conclusion to that paragraph? Why does he use a two-word sentence as the complete paragraph 17? In what ways do these words signal the beginning of the essay's conclusion?

Exploring the Writer's Ideas

1. Do you think Baker's classifications in this essay are fair? Are they representative of the whole spectrum of students? How closely do they mirror the student population at your school? The article was written in 1982: How well have Baker's classifications held up to the present conditions?
2. Into which category (or categories) would you place yourself? Why?
3. Based on your reaction to and understanding of this article, would you like to have Baker as your professor? Why or why not?

IDEAS FOR WRITING

Prewriting

Freewrite for fifteen minutes about the different types of students who are common to your campus. What are the traits or characteristics of each group? What do representatives of each group do? Where do they congregate? How many of these types can you recognize in this classroom?

Guided Writing

Write a classification of at least three "types" in a situation with which you are familiar, other than school—a certain job, social event, sport, or some such situation.

1. Begin your essay with a reference, direct or indirect, to what some well-known writer or expert said about this situation.
2. Identify your role in relation to the situation described.
3. Write about your attitude toward the particular situation and why you are less than thrilled about it at present.
4. Make sure you involve the reader as someone who would be familiar with the situation and activities described.
5. Divide your essay into exaggerated or stereotyped categories which you feel represent almost the complete range of types in these situations. In your categorization, be sure to include motivations, activities, and results for each type.
6. Use description to make your categories vivid.
7. Use satire and a bit of gentle cynicism as part of your description.
8. Select a lively title.
9. In the conclusion, identify another type that you consider the "purest" or "most truthful" representative of persons in this situation. Either by comparison with yourself or by some other means, explain why you like this type best.

Thinking and Writing Collaboratively

In groups of four to five class members, draft an article for your college newspaper in which you outline the types of students on the campus. Try to maintain a consistently lighthearted or humorous tone or point of view as you move from discussion to the drafting of the letter. Revise your paper, paying careful attention to the flow from one category to the next, before submitting the article for possible publication.

More Writing Projects

1. In your journal, write your own classification of three college "types." Your entry can be serious or humorous.
2. In a 250-word paragraph, classify types of college dates.
3. Look in current magazines for advertisements directed at men or women, or both. Write an essay in which you classify current advertisements according to some logical scheme. Limit your essay to three to five categories.

SUMMING UP: CHAPTER 8

1. Write an essay that classifies the readings in this book by a method other than *exposition* (detailed explanation). As you discuss each category, be sure to give examples that explain why particular readings fall into that classification.
2. Reread Judith Viorst's "Friends, Good Friends—and Such Good Friends" in this chapter. Then, write down the names of several of your closest friends. Keep a journal for one week in which you list what you did, how you felt, and what you talked about with each of these friends. Write an essay that classifies these friends into three categories. Use entries from your journal to support your method of classification.
3. With the class divided into four groups, assemble a guide to the city, town, or neighborhood surrounding your campus. Each group should be responsible for one category of information: types of people; types of places; types of entertainment; types of services; and so on. Be sure that each category is covered in detail; you may refer to E. B. White's essay "The Three New Yorks" as a model. After each group has completed its work, choose someone to present findings to the class. Now write your own guide to the areas based on the classifications discussed.
4. Although both Viorst's and Baker's essays are classifications, they also present new ways of looking at a group of people. Viorst has an underlying message about how to choose friends, while Baker has a warning about how not to be stereotyped. Write a classification essay entitled "What to Avoid When __________." Fill in the blank with an activity that would involve a decision-making process on the part of the reader.
5. Many of the essays in this book deal with crucial experiences in the various authors' lives. Among others, Hughes and Wong tell us of coming-of-age experiences; Selzer writes of his special insights into human nature; and Erdrich and Thomas describe their relationships to the world of nature. Try writing an essay that classifies the personal essays that you have read in this anthology.

CHAPTER 9

Process Analysis

WHAT IS PROCESS ANALYSIS?

Process analysis explains to a reader how something is done, how something works, or how something occurs. Like classification, it is a form of analysis, or taking apart a process in order better to understand how it functions. This kind of writing is often called *expository* because it *exposes* or shows us information. If you use cookbooks, you are encountering process analysis each time you read a recipe. If you are setting up a new VCR, you may wish the writer of the manual were more adept at writing process analysis when you find the steps hard to follow. "How to" writing can therefore give the reader steps for carrying out a process. The writer might also analyze the steps someone took already in completing a process, such as explaining how Harriet Tubman organized the Underground Railroad or how women won the right to vote.

Planning a good process analysis requires the writer to include all the essential steps. Be sure you have all the tools or ingredients needed. Arrange the steps in the correct sequence. Like all good writing, a good process essay requires a thesis to tell the reader the *significance* of the process. The writer can tell the reader how to do something, but also should inform the reader about the usefulness or importance of the endeavor.

In this chapter, Russell Baker tells us, tongue in cheek, how to carve a turkey. Henry Louis Gates, Jr., explains how to "de-kink" your hair. Grace Lichtenstein analyzes how one popular brand of beer made itself a household word. And, from Ernest

Hemingway, we learn how to make our next experience of camping a success. As you read these processes, watch how each writer uses the same technique to achieve a different result.

HOW DO WE READ PROCESS ANALYSIS?

Identify what process the writer is going to analyze. As you read, make a quick outline of the steps the writer introduces.

Watch the use of transitions as the writer moves from one step to the next.

Assess the audience that the writer has aimed at. Is the writer addressing innocents or experts? If the writer's purpose was to explain how to prepare beef stew, he would give different directions to a college freshman who has never cooked before than he would give to a cooking class at the Culinary Institute of America, where everyone was familiar with the fundamentals of cooking. Ask yourself, then: Is there enough information in the analysis? too much?

How does the writer try to make the piece lively? Does it sound as dry as a technical manual, or is there an engaging tone?

HOW DO WE WRITE PROCESS ANALYSIS?

Decide to analyze a process with which you are very familiar. Unless you can do it well yourself, you won't be able to instruct or inform your readers.

Process begins with a good shopping list. Once you have your topic, make lists of ingredients or tools.

Arrange the essential steps in logical order. Don't assume your reader already knows how to do the process. As you know from those incomprehensible VCR instructions, the reader should be given *every* step.

List the steps to *avoid* when carrying out the procedure.

If possible, actually try out the process, using your list as a guide, if you are presenting a method for a tangible product, like making an omelet. Or imagine that you are explaining the procedure over the telephone.

If your topic is abstract, like telling someone how to become an American citizen, read it aloud to a willing listener to see if he or she can follow the steps clearly.

Use *definition* to explain terms the reader may not know, especially if you are presenting a technical process. At the same time, avoid jargon. Make the language as plain as possible.

Describe the appearance of the product or *compare* an unfamiliar item with a familiar one.

Be sure to think about your audience. Link the audience to the purpose of the process.

Formulate a thesis statement that tells what the process is, and why it is a good process to know.

Sample thesis statement:

> Buying and renovating an old car is a time-consuming process, but the results are worthwhile.

Writing the Draft

Write a rough draft. Turn your list into an essay by developing the steps into sentences, using your thesis to add significance and coherence to the process you are presenting. Don't just list; analyze the procedure as you go along. Keep in mind the techniques of writers like Russell Baker, who doesn't just carve a turkey, but creates an entire dinner scene by the way he selects lively verbs and uses *hyperbole* (see Glossary) to raise his process analysis beyond the ordinary.

Add transitions when necessary to alert the reader that a new step is coming. The most common transition words help a reader to follow steps: *first, second, third; first, next, after, last.*

Proofread, revise, and create a final draft.

Coors Beer

Grace Lichtenstein

Process analysis often deals with mechanical or technical procedures. In this short selection by Grace Lichtenstein, who is a correspondent for *The New York Times,* the author examines a mechanical process—the brewing of beer. As you read this piece, look for the methods that the author uses to make this technical process interesting and understandable to the general reader.

PREREADING: THINKING ABOUT THE ESSAY IN ADVANCE

As you prepare to read this article, think about your favorite beverage and how much—or how little—you know about it. What are the ingredients in the beverage? Where is it manufactured? Do you know how it is prepared? What public or cultural images does the beverage possess?

Words to Watch

palate (par. 1) taste or sense of taste

mystique (par. 2) special, almost mysterious attitudes and feelings surrounding a person, place, or thing

Spartan (par. 3) simple and severe

rancid (par. 3) not fresh; having a bad smell

permeate (par. 3) to spread through everything

nondescript (par. 3) lacking any recognizable character or quality

cellulose (par. 4) the main substance in woody parts of plants, used in many manufacturing processes

Coors is a light-bodied beer, meaning it is brewed with less malt, 1 fewer hops and more rice than beers with a tangy taste. Compared with Heineken's or other more full-bodied foreign beers, Coors does seem almost flavorless and it is this quality that could account for its popularity among young people just starting to get acquainted with the pleasures of beer drinking. A few locals scoff at Coors, calling it "Colorado Kool-Aid." But the fact is that, according to Ernest Pyler, "if you conducted a blindfold test of the four leading beers, the chances of picking our Coors would be minimal." Indeed, one national newspaper conducted an informal test among eight beer drinkers, finding that only three could correctly identify Coors. My own admittedly uneducated palate detects no difference between Coors and Schaefer. In short, the difference between Coors and any other decent beer could be 1,800 miles. Maybe, if Paul Newman suddenly switched to Schaefer, Denverites would pay $15 a case for it.

2 There is one aspect to the Coors mystique that does have measurable validity. Company officials make much of the fact that Coors has good mountain water and the most expensive brewing process in the country. Several elements are unusual, though not unique.

3 Thousands of visitors have learned about the process on guided tours through the antiseptic, Spartan plant. (For out-of-towners, the tour is often a pilgrimage—but for local students of the Colorado School of Mines, it's usually more in the line of a quick belt before classes. The tour lasts 30 minutes, at the end of which visitors are invited to quaff to their heart's content in the hospitality lounge. "I've come here 50 times," boasted one student as he polished off a glass at 11:30 one morning in the lounge.) Situated in the center of town, between two high, flat mesas in the foothills of the Rockies, the plant dominates the community just as the somewhat rancid smell of malt seems to permeate the air; one-fourth of the town's families are said to owe their jobs to the factory's operations. Anyone expecting to see in Golden the foaming white waterfall amid mountain pines that is pictured on every yellow can of Coors will be disappointed. The water used in the brewing comes from nondescript wells hidden in concrete blockhouses. The brewery now puts out about 12 million barrels of beer a year, but construction sites throughout the grounds bear witness to the company's hopes for doubling that capacity by 1984.

4 Like other beers, Coors is produced from barley. Most of the big Midwestern brewers use barley grown in North Dakota and Minnesota. Coors is the single American brewer to use a Moravian strain, grown under company supervision, on farms in Colorado, Idaho, Wyoming and Montana. At the brewery, the

barley is turned into malt by being soaked in water—which must be biologically pure and of a known mineral content—for several days, causing it to sprout and producing a chemical change—breaking down starch into sugar. The malt is toasted, a process that halts the sprouting and determines the color and sweetness (the more the roasting, the darker, more bitter the beer). It is ground into flour and brewed, with more pure water, in huge copper-domed kettles until it is the consistency of oatmeal. Rice and refined starch are added to make mash; solids are strained out, leaving an amber liquid malt extract, which is boiled with hops—the dried cones from the hop vine which add to the bitterness, or tang. The hops are strained, yeast is added, turning the sugar to alcohol, and the beer is aged in huge red vats at near-freezing temperatures for almost two months, during which the second fermentation takes place and the liquid becomes carbonated, or bubbly. (Many breweries chemically age their beer to speed up production; Coors people say only naturally aged brew can be called a true "lager.") Next, the beer is filtered through cellulose filters to remove bacteria, and finally is pumped into cans, bottles or kegs for shipping.

The most unusual aspect of the Coors process is that the 5
beer is not pasteurized, as all but a half-dozen of the 90 or so American beers are. In the pasteurization process, bottles or cans of beer are passed through a heating unit and then cooled. This destroys the yeast in the brew which could cause spoilage, if the cans or bottles or barrels are unrefrigerated for any long period. However, pasteurization also changes the flavor of beer. Coors stopped pasteurizing its product 18 years ago because it decided that "heat is an enemy of beer," according to a company spokesman.

Unpasteurized beer must be kept under constant refrigera- 6
tion. Thus, Coors does not warehouse any of its finished product, as many other brewers do, but ships everything out cold, immediately. In effect, my tour guide, a young management trainee wearing a beer-can tie clip, explained as we wandered through the packaging area, watching workers in surgical masks feed aluminum lids into machines that sealed cans whirling by on conveyer belts, the six-pack you buy in a store contains not only a very fresh beer but also a beer that could be considered draft, since it has been kept cold from vat to home refrigerator.

BUILDING VOCABULARY

1. For the italicized word in each example in Column A, select a definition from Column B.

Column A	*Column B*
1. locals *scoff* (par. 1)	**a.** drink heartily
2. *informal* test (par. 1)	**b.** locations
3. measurable *validity* (par. 2)	**c.** thickness
4. the *antiseptic,* Spartan plant (par. 3)	**d.** not according to fixed rules
5. to *quaff* to their heart's content (par. 3)	**e.** a line of certain species
6. flat *mesas* (par. 3)	**f.** a concentrated form of something
7. construction *sites* (par. 3)	**g.** soundness
8. a Moravian *strain* (par. 4)	**h.** make fun of
9. the *consistency* of oatmeal (par. 4)	**i.** free from infection
10. liquid malt *extract* (par. 4)	**j.** hills

2. Use five of the italicized words in the first exercise in sentences of your own.

THINKING CRITICALLY ABOUT THE ESSAY

Understanding the Writer's Ideas

1. What is a "light-bodied" beer?
2. What does the author mean when she states, "In short, the difference between Coors and any other decent beer could be 1,800 miles" (par. 1)?
3. What *is* special about Coors beer?
4. Why do college students like to visit the Coors plant?
5. Describe the setting of the Coors brewery. How does it contrast with the picture on the Coors can?
6. Explain in your own words the process by which Coors is produced.
7. Why is the pasteurization process important to the final flavor of any beer?
8. Why can Coors almost be considered a draft beer?

Understanding the Writer's Techniques

1. What is the writer's thesis? Is it stated or implied?
2. How do comparison and contrast operate in the first paragraph? Does the author also use definition in this paragraph? Where? For what purpose?
3. What is the function of paragraph 2? What is the purpose of paragraph 3? How does the author develop paragraph 3?
4. Analyze the devices used for *transition* (see Glossary) between paragraphs 2 and 3.
5. Which paragraphs analyze the process of brewing Coors? Make a list of the steps on a sheet of paper. Is the process clear and complete? Does the author use process analysis simply to inform? Does she also provide commentary? Where?
6. Where does the author introduce personal or subjective elements into this essay? Why, at these points, does she provide personal rather than technical details?

Exploring the Writer's Ideas

1. Suppose that three unidentified brands of beer, cola, or cigarettes were placed before you. Would you be able to identify them by taste? What is the importance of "mystique" (or image) or "brand loyalty" to a product's success?
2. Can you think of other products that have a mystique associated with them? What are they, and what accounts for the mystique?
3. Would the fact that Paul Newman drinks Coors affect people's attitudes toward the brand? Why do manufacturers attempt to have certain celebrities associated with their products? Why should consumers be influenced by these associations?
4. Based on this essay, what are some ways to make a technical analysis of process interesting to the reader?

IDEAS FOR WRITING

Prewriting

Freewrite for fifteen minutes about your favorite beverage or dish, listing all of the steps involved in its preparation.

Guided Writing

Explain how to make or to assemble a particular item or product. For example, you might want to explain how to prepare a certain dish; how to assemble a piece of equipment; how to produce something in a factory. You might want to follow Lichtenstein's example: explain how a popular drink is made.

1. Start by introducing the reader to your "perfect product," indicating how it is possible to achieve high-quality results in its preparation.
2. Use as examples of the quality of the product, positive statements made by other individuals. These may be the ideas of friends, relatives, or experts.
3. Explain the "mystique," if there is one, surrounding the product.
4. After arousing reader interest sufficiently, describe the actual process involved, concentrating on all important details in the sequence.
5. In your last paragraph, try to capture the taste, look, or feel of the final product.

Thinking and Writing Collaboratively

In groups of three to four students, pool your knowledge of pizza. What are the ingredients? How is a pizza pie prepared? What variations make for the ideal pizza? Prepare a brief report to be presented to the class.

More Writing Projects

1. Many television commercials aim at selling beer to viewers. In your journal reflect on these commercials. What do they reveal about the manufacturers? the viewers? American society in general?

2. Set up an actual testing situation in your class. Have various members test three types of a particular item, such as chocolate, diet soda, or a kitchen cleanser. Then write a one-paragraph report describing either the process involved in the testing or the process by which results were obtained.
3. Consult an encyclopedia or other reference book to learn about the making of some product—steel, automobiles, plywood, and so forth. Then explain this process in your own words.

Slice of Life

Russell Baker

Russell Baker is well-known for his columns in *The New York Times,* in which he satirizes contemporary society, writing about trends in food and style, as well as the rigors of surviving in ordinary life. In "Slice of Life," he humorously describes the process of carving a turkey for a holiday dinner, demonstrating how even the most familiar task can lend itself to detailed and appealing analysis.

PREREADING: THINKING ABOUT THE ESSAY IN ADVANCE

Do certain natural or mechanical tasks or processes that seem to be simple actually turn out to be much more difficult to accomplish? Think about two or three of these "simple" tasks. What surprises await the unsuspecting individual who engages in such processes?

Words to Watch

sutures (par. 3) stitches
skewered (par. 5) secured with a long pin
chassis (par. 11) body; frame
stampede (par. 16) run

1 How to carve a turkey:

2 Assemble the following tools—carving knife, stone for sharpening carving knife, hot water, soap, wash cloth, two bath towels, barbells, meat cleaver.

3 If the house lacks a meat cleaver, an ax may be substituted. If it is, add bandages, sutures and iodine to above list.

4 Begin by moving the turkey from roasting pan to a suitable carving area. This is done by inserting the carving knife into the posterior stuffed area of the turkey and the knife-sharpening stone into the stuffed area under the neck.

Thus skewered, the turkey may be lifted out of the hot 5
grease with relative safety. Should the turkey drop to the floor, however, remove the knife and stone, roll the turkey gingerly into the two bath towels, wrap them several times around it and lift the encased fowl to the carving place.

You are now ready to begin carving. Sharpen the knife on 6
the stone and insert it where the thigh joins the torso. If you do this correctly, which is improbable, the knife will almost immediately encounter a barrier of bone and gristle.

This may very well be the joint. It could, however, be your 7
thumb. If not, execute a vigorous sawing motion until satisfied that the knife has been defeated.

Withdraw the knife and ask someone nearby, in as testy a 8
manner as possible, why the knives at your house are not kept in better carving condition.

Exercise the biceps and forearms by lifting barbells until 9
they are strong enough for you to tackle the leg joint with bare hands.

Wrapping one hand firmly around the thigh, seize the 10
turkey's torso in the other and scream. Run cold water over hands to relieve pain of burns.

Now, take a bath towel in each hand and repeat the 11
above maneuver. The entire leg should snap away from the chassis with a distinct crack, and the rest of the turkey, obedient to Newton's law about equal and opposite reactions, should roll in the opposite direction, which means that if you are carving at the table the turkey will probably come to rest in someone's lap.

Get the turkey out of the lap with as little fuss as possible, 12
and concentrate on the leg. Use the meat cleaver to sever the sinewy leather which binds the thigh to the drumstick.

If using the alternate, ax method, this operation should be 13
performed on a cement walk outside the house in order to preserve the table.

Repeat the above operation on the turkey's uncarved side. 14
You now have two thighs and two drumsticks. Using the wash cloth, soap and hot water, bathe thoroughly and, if possible, go to a movie.

Otherwise, look each person in the eye and say, "I don't 15
suppose anyone wants white meat."

16 If compelled to carve the breast anyhow, sharpen the knife on the stone again with sufficient awkwardness to tip over the gravy bowl on the person who started the stampede for white meat.

17 While everyone is rushing about to mop the gravy off her slacks, hack at the turkey breast until it starts crumbling off the carcass in ugly chunks.

18 The alternative method for carving white meat is to visit around the neighborhood until you find someone who has a good carving knife and borrow it, if you find one, which is unlikely.

19 This method enables you to watch the football game on neighbors' television sets and also creates the possibility that somebody back at your table will grow tired of waiting and do the carving herself.

20 In this case, upon returning home, cast a pained stare upon the mound of chopped white meat that has been hacked out by the family carving knife and refuse to do any more carving that day. No one who cares about the artistry of carving can be expected to work upon the mutilations of amateurs, and it would be a betrayal of the carver's art to do so.

BUILDING VOCABULARY

One of Baker's most effective techniques in creating humor is to select adjectives and verbs that not only illustrate the process he is analyzing, but exaggerate the steps and the results. *Hyperbole* in writing is the use of extreme exaggeration either to make a particular point or to achieve a special effect. In paragraph 3, for instance, Baker includes among the tools needed for carving a turkey a meat cleaver or an ax. He describes the necessary strength involved in removing a drumstick when he advises the carver to "exercise the biceps and forearms by lifting barbells until they are strong enough for you to tackle the leg joint with bare hands." (par. 9) Reread the essay, and select at least ten verbs or description words that use hyperbole, and then write synonyms for them.

THINKING CRITICALLY ABOUT THE ESSAY

Understanding the Writer's Ideas

1. What does Baker reveal about the situation in which he is carving the turkey while he outlines the steps in the process? Give examples.
2. What is the tone of the essay? What is the author's purpose in satirizing the process of turkey carving? What does the tone imply about the author's attitudes toward chores like turkey carving that conventionally fall to men at holiday dinners?
3. Who is the "you" the author is addressing?

Understanding the Writer's Techniques

1. Where is the thesis? What is unusual about how Baker sets up his main idea?
2. Look at a cookbook page that gives instructions on how to carve a turkey. How does the language in the cookbook differ from Baker's language? In what ways is Baker's process similar to that in the cookbook? Could you actually carve a turkey using the cookbook directions? using Baker's directions?
3. Why does Baker use so many short paragraphs? How would the effect of the essay change if it were written in longer paragraphs?
4. How would you characterize the tone of the essay? Look up the definitions of *irony, cynicism,* and *sarcasm.* Which term do you think most closely describes Baker's tone? Does his tone fit the subject matter? Explain.

   Go back to your list of hyperbolic words from Building Vocabulary and note for each whether you think it is intended to be ironic, cynical, or sarcastic.
5. Think about the title of the essay. What does this *metaphor* (see Glossary) suggest the essay is about besides turkey carving?
6. How does Baker use narration in this essay? description? illustration?
7. Which sentence alerts us that this is a process analysis essay? Write an outline of the process steps discussed.
8. Writing teachers often tell their students: "Show. Don't tell." In other words, use gestures and actions to characterize some-

one or make a point rather than just give the reader an explanation. How does Baker use "showing" rather than "telling" in this essay? Give five examples.

9. What does the final paragraph reveal about the author's attitude toward "the carver's art"?

Exploring the Writer's Ideas

1. Great satirists like Jonathan Swift, who wrote political and moral satire in *Gulliver's Travels* (1729), and Mark Twain, who wrote dozens of satirical tales of nineteenth-century American life, felt that satire was a technique for calling attention to weakness or flaws in the society in which they lived. In what way might Baker share this purpose?
2. Do you think Baker has written this essay from personal experience? Why do you think so?
3. Through his process analysis, Baker implies that holiday dinners are not always the cheerful events pictured on greeting cards. In what ways have your experiences of holiday dinners been like Baker's, where nothing goes according to plan and even the simplest chores are disasters?
4. Turkey carving as Baker analyzes it is a ritual. Rituals are actions we repeat periodically that have symbolic value for us. What changes in society in recent years have made rituals often seem outdated or inappropriate?
5. What personal or family rituals are important to you? Has your attitude toward them changed in recent years?

IDEAS FOR WRITING

Prewriting

Think of a simple task—like carving a turkey—which at first appears easy, but actually contains more complicated features. Brainstorm on paper, listing the steps involved, and placing a star or asterisk next to any step that could prove to be difficult.

Guided Writing

Write an essay in which you explain how to do something that is generally thought of as a simple activity. Use process analysis to show that the activity may look simple, but is in reality a mine field of potential embarrassment. You could analyze changing a flat tire for the first time, for instance, or trying to assemble a Christmas present for a child.

1. Decide on a tone for your essay. Use some hyperbole, irony, or sarcasm.
2. Prepare a direct thesis statement.
3. Make a list of the tools needed for this process, and include it in the introduction.
4. Use the body of the essay to give instructions on the process and to describe the dangers hidden behind the apparently simple activity. Include the reactions of others who may observe you carrying out the process, for instance.
5. Give excuses for why the process won't work, assigning blame to others rather than yourself.
6. Conclude with a solution that will get you out of doing this process in the future.

Thinking and Writing Collaboratively

Form small groups of three to four students. Using Baker's essay as a model, plan a process analysis essay in which you inform your audience about a process that might appear easy but actually requires a degree of knowledge. List the stages in the process, and identify the problems or situations your readers might encounter in completing a process that is new to them. Place your list on the chalkboard for class discussion.

More Writing Projects

1. In your journal, write about the process you recently used to deal with an extremely embarrassing moment. Make sure you tell what led up to the moment and what happened during and after the incident.

2. Write a paragraph about the process you use when you're out with one person and meet someone else whose name you don't remember.
3. Write a process analysis essay telling how to get satisfaction when you've bought a defective product or gotten bad service in a store.

Camping Out

Ernest Hemingway

In this essay by Ernest Hemingway (1899–1961), the author uses the pattern of process analysis to order his materials on the art of camping. Hemingway wrote this piece for the *Toronto Star* in the early 1920s, before he gained worldwide recognition as a major American writer. In it, we see his lifelong interest in the outdoors and his desire to do things well.

PREREADING: THINKING ABOUT THE ESSAY IN ADVANCE

As you prepare to read Hemingway's essay, take a minute or two to think about your own experiences in nature or any unknown place you once visited. If you have ever camped out or attended summer camp, for example, how did you prepare for, enter into, and survive the experience? What problems did you encounter, and how did you overcome them?

Words to Watch

relief map (par. 2) a map that shows by lines and colors the various heights and forms of the land

Caucasus (par. 2) a mountain range in southeastern Europe

proprietary (par. 7) held under patent or trademark

rhapsodize (par. 9) to speak enthusiastically

browse bed (par. 9) a portable cot

tyro (par. 11) an amateur; a beginner in learning something

dyspepsia (par. 13) indigestion

mulligan (par. 18) a stew made from odds and ends of meats and vegetables

Thousands of people will go into the bush this summer to cut the 1
high cost of living. A man who gets his two weeks' salary while he is on vacation should be able to put those two weeks in fishing and camping and be able to save one week's salary clear. He

ought to be able to sleep comfortably every night, to eat well every day and to return to the city rested and in good condition.

2 But if he goes into the woods with a frying pan, an ignorance of black flies and mosquitoes, and a great and abiding lack of knowledge about cookery the chances are that his return will be very different. He will come back with enough mosquito bites to make the back of his neck look like a relief map of the Caucasus. His digestion will be wrecked after a valiant battle to assimilate half-cooked or charred grub. And he won't have had a decent night's sleep while he has been gone.

3 He will solemnly raise his right hand and inform you that he has joined the grand army of never-agains. The call of the wild may be all right, but it's a dog's life. He's heard the call of the tame with both ears. Waiter, bring him an order of milk toast.

4 In the first place he overlooked the insects. Black flies, no-see-ums, deer flies, gnats and mosquitoes were instituted by the devil to force people to live in cities where he could get at them better. If it weren't for them everybody would live in the bush and he would be out of work. It was a rather successful invention.

5 But there are lots of dopes that will counteract the pests. The simplest perhaps is oil of citronella. Two bits' worth of this purchased at any pharmacist's will be enough to last for two weeks in the worst fly and mosquito-ridden country.

6 Rub a little on the back of your neck, your forehead and your wrists before you start fishing, and the blacks and skeeters will shun you. The odor of citronella is not offensive to people. It smells like gun oil. But the bugs do hate it.

7 Oil of pennyroyal and eucalyptol are also much hated by mosquitoes, and with citronella they form the basis for many proprietary preparations. But it is cheaper and better to buy the straight citronella. Put a little on the mosquito netting that covers the front of your pup tent or canoe tent at night, and you won't be bothered.

8 To be really rested and get any benefit out of a vacation a man must get a good night's sleep every night. The first requisite for this is to have plenty of cover. It is twice as cold as you expect it will be in the bush four nights out of five, and a good plan is to take just double the bedding that you think you will need. An old quilt that you can wrap up in is as warm as two blankets.

Nearly all outdoor writers rhapsodize over the browse bed. It is all right for the man who knows how to make one and has plenty of time. But in a succession of one-night camps on a canoe trip all you need is level ground for your tent floor and you will sleep all right if you have plenty of covers under you. Take twice as much cover as you think that you will need, and then put two-thirds of it under you. You will sleep warm and get your rest. 9

When it is clear weather you don't need to pitch your tent if you are only stopping for the night. Drive four stakes at the head of your made-up bed and drape your mosquito bar over that, then you can sleep like a log and laugh at the mosquitoes. 10

Outside of insects and bum sleeping the rock that wrecks most camping trips is cooking. The average tyro's idea of cooking is to fry everything and fry it good and plenty. Now, a frying pan is a most necessary thing to any trip, but you also need the old stew kettle and the folding reflector baker. 11

A pan of fried trout can't be bettered and they don't cost any more than ever. But there is a good and bad way of frying them. 12

The beginner puts his trout and his bacon in and over a brightly burning fire the bacon curls up and dries into a dry tasteless cinder and the trout is burned outside while it is still raw inside. He eats them and it is all right if he is only out for the day and going home to a good meal at night. But if he is going to face more trout and bacon the next morning and other equally well-cooked dishes for the remainder of two weeks he is on the pathway to nervous dyspepsia. 13

The proper way is to cook over coals. Have several cans of Crisco or Cotosuet or one of the vegetable shortenings along that are as good as lard and excellent for all kinds of shortening. Put the bacon in and when it is about half cooked lay the trout in the hot grease, dipping them in corn meal first. Then put the bacon on top of the trout and it will baste them as it slowly cooks. 14

The coffee can be boiling at the same time and in a smaller skillet pancakes being made that are satisfying the other campers while they are waiting for the trout. 15

With the prepared pancake flours you take a cupful of pancake flour and add a cup of water. Mix the water and flour and as soon as the lumps are out it is ready for cooking. Have the skillet hot and keep it well greased. Drop the batter in and as soon as 16 it is done on one side loosen it in the skillet and flip it over. Apple butter, syrup or cinnamon and sugar go well with the cakes.

17 While the crowd have taken the edge from their appetites with flapjacks the trout have been cooked and they and the bacon are ready to serve. The trout are crisp outside and firm and pink inside and the bacon is well done—but not too done. If there is anything better than that combination the writer has yet to taste it in a lifetime devoted largely and studiously to eating.

18 The stew kettle will cook you dried apricots when they have resumed their predried plumpness after a night of soaking, it will serve to concoct a mulligan in, and it will cook macaroni. When you are not using it, it should be boiling water for the dishes.

19 In the baker, mere man comes into his own, for he can make a pie that to his bush appetite will have it all over the product that mother used to make, like a tent. Men have always believed that there was something mysterious and difficult about making a pie. Here is a great secret. There is nothing to it. We've been kidded for years. Any man of average office intelligence can make at least as good a pie as his wife.

20 All there is to a pie is a cup and a half of flour, one-half teaspoonful of salt, one-half cup of lard and cold water. That will make pie crust that will bring tears of joy into your camping partner's eyes.

21 Mix the salt with the flour, work the lard into the flour, make it up into a good workmanlike dough with cold water. Spread some flour on the back of a box or something flat, and pat the dough around a while. Then roll it out with whatever kind of round bottle you prefer. Put a little more lard on the surface of the sheet of dough and then slosh a little flour on and roll it up and then roll it out again with the bottle.

22 Cut out a piece of the rolled out dough big enough to line a pie tin. I like the kind with holes in the bottom. Then put in your dried apples that have soaked all night and been sweetened, or your apricots, or your blueberries, and then take another sheet of the dough and drape it gracefully over the top, soldering it down at the edges with your fingers. Cut a couple of slits in the top dough sheet and prick it a few times with a fork in an artistic manner.

23 Put it in the baker with a good slow fire for forty-five minutes and then take it out and if your pals are Frenchmen they will

kiss you. The penalty for knowing how to cook is that the others will make you do all the cooking.

It is all right to talk about roughing it in the woods. But the real woodsman is the man who can be really comfortable in the bush. 24

BUILDING VOCABULARY

For each word below write your own definition, based on how the word is used in the selection. Check back to the appropriate paragraph in the essay for more help, if necessary.

a. abiding (par. 2)
b. valiant (par. 2)
c. assimilate (par. 2)
d. charred (par. 2)
e. solemnly (par. 3)
f. requisite (par. 8)
g. succession (par. 9)
h. studiously (par. 17)
i. concoct (par. 18)
j. soldering (par. 22)

THINKING CRITICALLY ABOUT THE ESSAY

Understanding the Writer's Ideas

1. What is Hemingway's main purpose in this essay? Does he simply want to explain how to set up camp and how to cook outdoors?
2. What, according to the writer, are the two possible results of camping out on your vacation?
3. Why is oil of citronella the one insecticide that Hemingway recommends over all others?
4. Is it always necessary to pitch a tent when camping out? What are alternatives to it? How can you sleep warmly and comfortably?
5. Explain the author's process for cooking trout. Also explain his process for baking a pie.
6. Is it enough for Hemingway simply to enjoy "roughing it" while camping out?

Understanding the Writer's Techniques

1. Does the author have a stated thesis? Explain.
2. Identify those paragraphs in the essay that involve process analysis, and explain how Hemingway develops his subject in each.
3. What is the main writing pattern in paragraphs 1 and 2? How does this method serve as an organizing principle throughout the essay?
4. How would you characterize the author's style of writing? Is it appropriate to a newspaper audience? Is it more apt for professional fishermen?
5. In what way does Hemingway employ classification in this essay?
6. Analyze the tone of Hemingway's essay.
7. The concluding paragraph is short. Is it effective, nevertheless, and why? How does it reinforce the opening paragraph?

Exploring the Writer's Ideas

1. Camping out was popular in the 1920s, as it is in the 1990s. What are some of the reasons that it remains so attractive today?
2. Hemingway's essay describes many basic strategies for successful camping. He does not rely on "gadgets" or modern inventions to make camping easier. Do such gadgets make camping more fun today than it might have been in the 1920s?
3. The author suggests that there is a right way and a wrong way to do things. Does it matter if you perform a recreational activity right as long as you enjoy doing it? Why?

IDEAS FOR WRITING

Prewriting

Freewrite for fifteen minutes about your favorite pastime, activity, or hobby. How do you approach this activity? What steps must be observed in order to be successful at it? How might other people fail at it whereas you are successful?

Guided Writing

Write an essay on how to do something wrong, and how to do it right—going on vacation, looking for a job, fishing, or whatever.

1. Reexamine the author's first three paragraphs and imitate his method of introducing the right and wrong ways about the subject, and the possible results.
2. Adopt a simple, informal, "chatty" style. Feel free to use a few well-placed clichés and other forms of spoken English. Use several similes.
3. Divide your subject into useful categories. Just as Hemingway treated insects, sleeping, and cooking, try to cover the main aspects of your subject.
4. Explain the process involved for each aspect of your subject. Make certain that you compare and contrast the right and wrong ways of your activity.
5. Write a short, crisp conclusion that reinforces your longer introduction.

Thinking and Writing Collaboratively

As a class, choose a process—for example, applying to college—which clearly involves a "right way" and "wrong way" of accomplishing the activity. Then divide the class into two groups, with one group outlining the correct steps and the other the incorrect or incomplete steps to completing the process. List both approaches on the chalkboard for comparative discussion.

More Writing Projects

1. How do you explain the fascination that camping out holds for many people? Reflect on this question in your journal.
2. In a paragraph, describe how to get to your favorite vacation spot, and what to do when you get there.
3. If you have ever camped out, write a process paper explaining one important feature of setting up camp.

In the Kitchen

Henry Louis Gates, Jr.

Henry Louis Gates, Jr., is the author of several books, including *Black Literature and Theory* and *The Signifying Monkey,* which won a 1989 National Book Award. In this selection he examines the politics of the hairdo by recalling his experiences as a child in his mother's home beauty parlor.

PREREADING: THINKING ABOUT THE ESSAY IN ADVANCE

Michael Jackson, America's pop icon, was criticized by some in the African-American community for having his hair altered to conform to Anglo features (such as straight hair). Do you think you should have the right to change your looks even if it means trying to conform to the standards of beauty of an ethnic or cultural group other than your own?

Words to Watch

transform (par. 4) to change the appearance or form of

southpaw (par. 4) a left-handed person, especially a left-handed baseball pitcher

refrain (par. 7) repeated phrase or utterance

preposterous (par. 7) absurd

tiara (par. 23) a crown or fine headdress

1 We always had a gas stove in the kitchen, in our house in Piedmont, West Virginia, where I grew up. Never electric, though using electric became fashionable in Piedmont in the sixties, like using Crest toothpaste rather than Colgate, or watching Huntley and Brinkley rather than Walter Cronkite. But not us: gas, Colgate, and good ole Walter Cronkite, come what may. We used gas partly out of loyalty to Big Mom, Mama's Mama, because she was mostly blind and still loved to cook, and could feel her way more easily with gas than with electric. But the most important

thing about our gas-equipped kitchen was that Mama used to do hair there. The "hot comb" was a fine-toothed iron instrument with a long wooden handle and a pair of iron curlers that opened and closed like scissors. Mama would put it in the gas fire until it glowed. You could smell those prongs heating up.

I liked that smell. Not the smell so much, I guess, as what the smell meant for the shape of my day. There was an intimate warmth in the women's tones as they talked with my Mama, doing their hair. I knew what the women had been through to get their hair ready to be "done," because I would watch Mama do it to herself. How that kink could be transformed through grease and fire into that magnificent head of wavy hair was a miracle to me, and still is. 2

Mama would wash her hair over the sink, a towel wrapped around her shoulders, wearing just her slip and her white bra. (We had no shower—just a galvanized tub that we stored in the kitchen—until we moved down Rat Tail Road into Doc Wolverton's house, in 1954.) After she dried it, she would grease her scalp thoroughly with blue Bergamot hair grease, which came in a short, fat jar with a picture of a beautiful colored lady on it. It's important to grease your scalp real good, my Mama would explain, to keep from burning yourself. Of course, her hair would return to its natural kink almost as soon as the hot water and shampoo hit it. To me, it was another miracle how hair so "straight" would so quickly become kinky again the second it even approached some water. 3

My Mama had only a few "clients" whose heads she "did"—did, I think, because she enjoyed it, rather than for the few pennies it brought in. They would sit on one of our red plastic kitchen chairs, the kind with the shiny metal legs, and brace themselves for the process. Mama would stroke that red-hot iron—which by this time had been in the gas fire for half an hour or more—slowly but firmly through their hair, from scalp to strand's end. It made a scorching, crinkly sound, the hot iron did, as it burned its way through kink, leaving in its wake straight strands of hair, standing long and tall but drooping over at the ends, their shape like the top of a heavy willow tree. Slowly, steadily, Mama's hands would transform a round mound of Odetta kink into a darkened swamp of everglades. The Bergamot 4 made the hair shiny; the heat of the hot iron gave it a brownish-red cast. Once all the hair was as straight as God allows kink to get, Mama would take the well-heated curling iron and twirl the straightened strands into more or less loosely wrapped curls. She claimed that she owed her skill as a hairdresser to the strength in her wrists, and as she worked her little finger would poke out, the way it did when she sipped tea. Mama was a southpaw, and wrote upside down and backward to produce the cleanest, roundest letters you've ever seen.

5 The "kitchen" she would all but remove from sight with a handheld pair of shears, bought just for this purpose. Now, the kitchen was the room in which we were sitting—the room where Mama did hair and washed clothes, and where we all took a bath in that galvanized tub. But the word has another meaning, and the kitchen that I'm speaking of is the very kinky bit of hair at the back of your head, where your neck meets your shirt collar. If there was ever a part of our African past that resisted assimilation, it was the kitchen. No matter how hot the iron, no matter how powerful the chemical, no matter how stringent the mashed-potatoes-and-lye formula of a man's "process," neither God nor woman nor Sammy Davis, Jr., could straighten the kitchen. The kitchen was permanent, irredeemable, irresistible kink. Unassimilably African. No matter what you did, no matter how hard you tried, you couldn't de-kink a person's kitchen. So you trimmed it off as best you could.

6 When hair had begun to "turn," as they'd say—to return to its natural kinky glory—it was the kitchen that turned first (the kitchen around the back, and nappy edges at the temples). When the kitchen started creeping up the back of the neck, it was time to get your hair done again.

7 Sometimes, after dark, a man would come to have his hair done. It was Mr. Charlie Carroll. He was very light-complected and had a ruddy nose—it made me think of Edmund Gwenn, who played Kris Kringle in "Miracle on 34th Street." At first, Mama did him after my brother, Rocky, and I had gone to sleep. It was only later that we found out that he had come to our house so Mama could iron his hair—not with a hot comb or a curling iron but with our very own Proctor-Silex steam iron. For some reason I never understood, Mr. Charlie would conceal his Frederick Douglass-like mane under a big white Stetson hat. I never saw him take it

off except when he came to our house, at night, to have his hair pressed. (Later, Daddy would tell us about Mr. Charlie's most prized piece of knowledge, something that the man would only confide after his hair had been pressed, as a token of intimacy. "Not many people know this," he'd say, in a tone of circumspection, "but George Washington was Abraham Lincoln's daddy." Nodding solemnly, he'd add the clincher: "A white man told me." Though he was in dead earnest, this became a humorous refrain around our house—"a white man told me"—which we used to punctuate especially preposterous assertions.)

My mother examined my daughters' kitchens whenever we 8
went home to visit, in the early eighties. It became a game between us. I had told her not to do it, because I didn't like the politics it suggested—the notion of "good" and "bad" hair. "Good" hair was "straight," "bad" hair kinky. Even in the late sixties, at the height of Black Power, almost nobody could bring themselves to say "bad" for good and "good" for bad. People still said that hair like white people's hair was "good," even if they encapsulated it in a disclaimer, like "what we used to call 'good.'"

Maggie would be seated in her high chair, throwing food 9
this way and that, and Mama would be cooing about how cute it all was, how I used to do just like Maggie was doing, and wondering whether her flinging her food with her left hand meant that she was going to be left-handed like Mama. When my daughter was just about covered with Chef Boyardee Spaghetti-O's, Mama would seize the opportunity: wiping her clean, she would tilt Maggie's head to one side and reach down the back of her neck. Sometimes Mama would even rub a curl between her fingers, just to make sure that her bifocals had not deceived her. Then she'd sigh with satisfaction and relief: No kink . . . yet. Mama! I'd shout, pretending to be angry. Every once in a while, if no one was looking, I'd peek, too.

I say "yet" because most black babies are born with soft, 10
silken hair. But after a few months it begins to turn, as inevitably as do the seasons or the leaves on a tree. People once thought baby oil would stop it. They were wrong.

Everybody I knew as a child wanted to have good hair. You 11
could be as ugly as homemade sin dipped in misery and still be thought attractive if you had good hair. "Jesus moss," the girls at

Camp Lee, Virginia, had called Daddy's naturally "good" hair during the war. I know that he played that thick head of hair for all it was worth, too.

My own hair was "not a bad grade," as barbers would tell me when they cut it for the first time. It was like a doctor reporting the results of the first full physical he has given you. Like "You're in good shape" or "Blood pressure's kind of high—better cut down on salt."

12 I spent most of my childhood and adolescence messing with my hair. I definitely wanted straight hair. Like Pop's. When I was about three, I tried to stick a wad of Bazooka bubble gum to that straight hair of his. I suppose what fixed that memory for me is the spanking I got for doing so: he turned me upside down, holding me by my feet, the better to paddle my behind. Little *nigger,* he had shouted, walloping away. I started to laugh about it two days later, when my behind stopped hurting.

13 When black people say "straight," of course, they don't usually mean literally straight—they're not describing hair like, say, Peggy Lipton's (she was the white girl on "The Mod Squad"), or like Mary's of Peter, Paul & Mary fame; black people call that "stringy" hair. No, "straight" just means not kinky, no matter what contours the curl may take. I would have done *anything* to have straight hair—and I used to try everything, short of getting a process.

14 Of the wide variety of techniques and methods I came to master in the challenging prestidigitation of the follicle, almost all had two things in common: a heavy grease and the application of pressure. It's not an accident that some of the biggest black-owned companies in the fifties and sixties made hair products. And I tried them all, in search of that certain silken touch, the one that would leave neither the hand nor the pillow sullied by grease.

15 I always wondered what Frederick Douglass put on *his* hair, or what Phillis Wheatley put on hers. Or why Wheatley has that rag on her head in the little engraving in the frontispiece of her book. One thing is for sure: you can bet that when Phillis Wheatley went to England and saw the Countess of Huntingdon she did not stop by the Queen's coiffeur on her way there. So many black people still get their hair straightened that it's a wonder we don't have a national holiday for Madame C. J. Walker, the woman who invented the process of straightening kinky hair. Call it Jheri-Kurled or call it "relaxed," it's still fried hair.

I used all the greases, from sea-blue Bergamot and creamy vanilla Duke (in its clear jar with the orange-white-and-green label) to the godfather of grease, the formidable Murray's. Now, Murray's was some *serious* grease. Whereas Bergamot was like oily jello, and Duke was viscous and sickly sweet, Murray's was light brown and *hard.* Hard as lard and twice as greasy, Daddy used to say. Murray's came in an orange can with a press-on top. It was so hard that some people would put a match to the can, just to soften the stuff and make it more manageable. Then, in the late sixties, when Afros came into style, I used Afro Sheen. From Murray's to Duke to Afro Sheen: that was my progression in black consciousness. 16

We used to put hot towels or washrags over our Murray-coated heads, in order to melt the wax into the scalp and the follicles. Unfortunately, the wax also had the habit of running down your neck, ears, and forehead. Not to mention your pillowcase. Another problem was that if you put two palmfuls of Murray's on your head your hair turned white. (Duke did the same thing.) The challenge was to get rid of that white color. Because if you got rid of the white stuff you had a magnificent head of wavy hair. That was the beauty of it: Murray's was so hard that it froze your hair into the wavy style you brushed it into. It looked really good if you wore a part. A lot of guys had parts *cut* into their hair by a barber, either with the clippers or with a straightedge razor. Especially if you had kinky hair—then you'd generally wear a short razor cut, or what we called a Quo Vadis. 17

We tried to be as innovative as possible. Everyone knew about using a stocking cap, because your father or your uncle wore one whenever something really big was about to happen, whether sacred or secular: a funeral or a dance, a wedding or a trip in which you confronted official white people. Any time you were trying to look really sharp, you wore a stocking cap in preparation. And if the event was really a big one, you made a new cap. You asked your mother for a pair of her hose, and cut it with scissors about six inches or so from the open end—the end with the elastic that goes up to the top of the thigh. Then you knotted the cut end, and it became a beehive-shaped hat, with an elastic band that you pulled down low on your forehead and down around your neck in the back. To work well, the cap had to fit tightly and snugly, like a press. And it had to fit that tightly because it *was* a press: it pressed your hair with the force of the 18 hose's elastic. If you greased your hair down real good, and left the stocking cap on long enough, voilà: you got a head of pressed-against-the-scalp waves. (You also got a ring around your forehead when you woke up, but it went away.) And then you could enjoy your concrete do. Swore we were bad, too, with all that grease and those flat heads. My brother and I would brush it out a bit in the mornings, so that it looked—well, "natural." Grown men still wear stocking caps—especially older men, who generally keep their stocking caps in their top drawers, along with their cufflinks and their see-through silk socks, their "Maverick" ties, their silk handkerchiefs, and whatever else they prize the most.

19 A Murrayed-down stocking cap was the respectable version of the process, which, by contrast, was most definitely not a cool thing to have unless you were an entertainer by trade. Zeke and Keith and Poochie and a few other stars of the high-school basketball team all used to get a process once or twice a year. It was expensive, and you had to go somewhere like Pittsburgh or D.C. or Uniontown—somewhere where there were enough colored people to support a trade. The guys would disappear, then reappear a day or two later, strutting like peacocks, their hair burned slightly red from the lye base. They'd also wear "rags"—cloths or handkerchiefs—around their heads when they slept or played basketball. Do-rags, they were called. But the result was straight hair, with just a hint of wave. No curl. Do-it-yourselfers took their chances at home with a concoction of mashed potatoes and lye.

20 The most famous process of all, however, outside of the process Malcolm X describes in his "Autobiography," and maybe the process of Sammy Davis, Jr., was Nat King Cole's process. Nat King Cole had patent-leather hair. That man's got the finest process money can buy, or so Daddy said the night we saw Cole's TV show on NBC. It was November 5, 1956. I remember the date because everyone came to our house to watch it and to celebrate one of Daddy's buddies' birthdays. Yeah, Uncle Joe chimed in, they can do shit to his hair that the average Negro can't even *think* about—secret shit.

21 Nat King Cole was *clean.* I've had an ongoing argument with a Nigerian friend about Nat King Cole for twenty years now. Not about whether he could sing—any fool knows that he

could—but about whether or not he was a handkerchief head for wearing that patent-leather process.

Sammy Davis, Jr.,'s process was the one I detested. It didn't look good on him. Worse still, he liked to have a fried strand dangling down the middle of his forehead, so he could shake it out from the crown when he sang. But Nat King Cole's hair was a thing unto itself, a beautifully sculpted work of art that he and he alone had the right to wear. The only difference between a process and a stocking cap, really, was taste; but Nat King Cole, unlike, say, Michael Jackson, looked *good* in his. His head looked like Valentino's head in the twenties, and some say it was Valentino the process was imitating. But Nat King Cole wore a process because it suited his face, his demeanor, his name, his style. He was as clean as he wanted to be. 22

I had forgotten all about that patent-leather look until one day in 1971, when I was sitting in an Arab restaurant on the island of Zanzibar surrounded by men in fezzes and white caftans, trying to learn how to eat curried goat and rice with the fingers of my right hand and feeling two million miles from home. All of a sudden, an old transistor radio sitting on top of a china cupboard stopped blaring out its Swahili music and started playing "Fly Me to the Moon," by Nat King Cole. The restaurant's din was not affected at all, but in my mind's eye I saw it: the King's magnificent sleek black tiara. I managed, barely, to blink back the tears. 23

BUILDING VOCABULARY

For each word below write your own definition based on how the word is used in the selection. Check back to the appropriate paragraph in the essay for more help, if necessary.

a. galvanized (par. 5)
b. assertions (par. 7)
c. prestidigitation (par. 14)
d. follicle (par. 14)
e. din (par. 23)

THINKING CRITICALLY ABOUT THE ESSAY

Understanding the Writer's Ideas

1. The word "Kitchen" in the title takes on two meanings in the essay. What are they?
2. Gas was used in this writer's kitchen even though people had turned to electricity in the 1960s. Why?
3. What does the writer mean when he states that his mother "did hair"?
4. What does the word "turn" (par. 6) describe?
5. What is the history behind "good" and "bad" hair?
6. As a child, how did the writer worry about his hair? Explain.
7. Describe the two things all hair-straightening techniques have in common.
8. What was it about Nat King Cole's hair that impressed this writer so much?
9. How were the hot irons used to straighten hair?
10. Hearing a Nat King Cole song while in Zanzibar, the writer says he had to "blink back the tears." What is going on?

Understanding the Writer's Techniques

1. Find the thesis and paraphrase it.
2. What process is described in paragraph 3? Give examples of the process described in paragraph 3.
3. Given the detailed descriptions of de-kinking hair, what audience does this writer have in mind in employing this strategy?
4. Where in the essay does the writer make a transition to describe two of the most common processes of hair straightening? How are these processes detailed?
5. Though the other de-kinking processes mentioned in the essay are detailed, the most famous one (Nat King Cole's) is not described at all. What might this suggest about the writer's attitude toward this subject?
6. The essay's entire structure is not focused entirely on process. What other rhetorical mode does the writer use? Identify the places where this occurs.
7. What makes Gates's concluding paragraph different from others more common in essays?

Exploring the Writer's Ideas

1. Gates claims the "kitchen," those hairs on the back of the neck, are "unassimilably" African. Yet, his mother specialized in getting rid of the kitchen. Do you think this writer approves or disapproves of his mother's activity? Explain.
2. Gates tells of jokes about the "white man." Gates says he found the jokes funny even though he also admits he wanted good hair, like that of whites. How would you explain this writer's contradictory feelings about white people?
3. How do you feel about this writer's claims that most everyone he knew thought kinky hair was "bad"? Do you think this is an exaggeration? Why or why not?
4. Are there still examples today of people who remake themselves to look "white" or like those who are held up as role models, like Madonna or other rock stars? Is this impulse positive or negative? Why?
5. The author suggests that the de-kinking was physically painful. Does anything in the essay suggest all the pain was worth it? Explain.
6. By calling Nat King Cole's straightened hair a "black tiara" is this author concluding that straight hair (looking white) is indeed admirable? How do you feel?

IDEAS FOR WRITING

Prewriting

Use your journal to recall times when you felt good or bad about the way you look.

Guided Writing

Write an essay on how you once may have tried to make yourself look the "right" or "wrong" way. Remember the time you dressed for a date or to go to church or to get a job.

1. Examine Gates's first paragraph and imitate his method of introducing the thesis.

2. Divide your process into its important parts, like Gates who divides de-kinking into its steps: hot comb, the kitchen, the clients, the grease, and the pressure.
3. Make sure that your process is detailed in a way that keeps a general audience in mind (or people who don't know your process).
4. Try to use definition paragraphs to explain terms that describe your process which are unknown to your general audience.
5. Write a conclusion that tells a story, like Gates on Nat King Cole. Remember that this story should reflect an overall feeling you have about your topic.

Thinking and Writing Collaboratively

Your group has been assigned the task of creating a behavior code pamphlet for your school. Use process technique to make clear how students should act in different situations. Explain what happens (the process) if someone misbehaves.

More Writing Projects

1. In your journal, make notes on the ways that you have seen people change their looks to please others.
2. In a paragraph, describe the process by which people learn who looks the right way or the wrong way.
3. Write a process essay on something your parents or caregiver taught you as a child. Tell of learning to swim or to ride a bike.

SUMMING UP: CHAPTER 9

1. Divide the class into groups and choose one Guided Writing essay per group using the Gates, Baker, or Hemingway selection. Collaboratively discuss, evaluate, correct, edit, and rewrite the Guided Writing process essay. By consensus, establish grades for the original and the revised essay. Present your findings to the class.
2. On the basis of your experience reading the four essays in the section, write about the types of processes the authors deal with (you may want to read the introduction to the previous chapter on classification) and how they manage these processes. Clarify the main steps that you consider to be important in the writing of any process analysis.
3. Grace Lichtenstein in her essay reveals the brewing process behind "the Coors mystique." Everyone has a favorite food. For this exercise, contribute a recipe for your favorite food to be included in a class cookbook. In addition to describing step by step the process for preparing the food, you should also tell something about the tradition behind the food, special occasions for eating it, the first time you ate it, and so forth. In other words, establish your own "mystique" for it.
4. Three of the essays in this chapter tell us how to do things that can have direct and immediate effects on our lives—straightening hair, carving a turkey, camping—while the fourth illuminates a process that produces a product that may also directly affect our lives—beer. Try to write an essay that describes a process with much less immediate effect.
5. Interview a classmate about something that he or she does very well. Make sure the questions you ask don't omit any important steps or materials used in the process. Take careful notes during the interview, then try to replicate the process on your own. If there are any difficulties in accomplishing the process, reinterview your classmate. After you are satisfied that no steps or materials have been left out, write up the procedure in such a way that someone else could easily follow it.

CHAPTER 10

Cause-and-Effect Analysis

WHAT IS CAUSE-AND-EFFECT ANALYSIS?

Cause-and-effect analysis answers the basic human question: *Why?* Why do events occur, like hurricanes or the election of a new president? Why does one student do better in math than another? In addition, this form of analysis looks at the *expected* consequences of a chain of happenings. If we raise the minimum wage, what will the likely consequences be?

Basically, cause-and-effect analysis (also called causal analysis) looks for *causes* or conditions, and suggests or examines *results* or consequences (the effects).

Like most of the writing strategies you have been studying, causal analysis parallels a kind of thinking we do in everyday life. If you are a student who has returned to school after being away for several years, someone might ask you why you decided to come back. In answering, you would give causes: You needed a better job to support your children; you wanted to learn a new skill; your intellectual curiosity drove you back; and so on. These would be *causes.* Once you were attending school, a classmate might ask you what changes coming back to school have made in your life. You might consider the pride your children feel in your achievement, or the fact that you have less time to prepare meals, or that you sleep only four hours a night. Those are the *conse-*

quences or results of your decision. In a few years' time, after graduation, the effects might be very different: a better job or a scholarship to graduate school might be one of the long-term results.

Thinking about causes can go beyond everyday life to help us understand social and political change: What were the causes of the American Civil War? What were the consequences for the nation? What caused the Great Depression? Why were women denied the vote until 1920? Why did so many Irish immigrants come to America around 1900, and what were the consequences for the growth of American industry?

In looking at such large questions, you will realize that there are different kinds of causes. First, there is the *immediate* cause that gives rise to a situation. This is the cause (or causes) most directly related, the one closest at hand. But as you can see from the historical questions in the previous paragraph, we also need to go beyond the immediate cause to the *ultimate* cause, the basic conditions that stimulated the more obvious or immediate ones.

For example, although we might identify the immediate cause of the Los Angeles riots of 1992 as the Rodney King trial, the ultimate causes for racial unrest grow from the social and economic conditions of the poor in America. To find the "real" causes, we have to think critically, to examine the situation deeply.

Often, a writer has to consider many causes and rank them in order of importance. Depending on the length of the essay, a writer may have to select from among many causes. If a small town begins to lose businesses to a large mall, the chamber of commerce may ask why businesses and customers prefer the mall to shopping in town. Convenience, parking, competitive pricing, and entertainment may be identified as causes. Since the town cannot solve all these problems at once, it may focus on one, and try to lure shoppers back downtown by building a larger municipal parking lot. The result, perhaps, will be that shoppers will return to Main Street.

One difficulty in working with causal analysis is that we cannot always prove that a cause or an effect is absolute. We can only do our best to offer as much evidence as possible to help the reader see the relation we wish to establish. Therefore, we have to support our causes and effects with specific details and evidence drawn from personal experience, from statistics, or from experts' statements in newspapers or books. A writer can interview people, for instance, and collect data about local shopping habits or visit the library to read articles on the Los Angeles riots.

In the essays in this chapter, you will find a variety of uses for causal analysis. Stephen King analyzes why we crave horror movies. Anne Roiphe looks at the causes for the failure of half the marriages in America. Linda Bird Francke analyzes the difficult question of abortion when her political convictions cause her to think one way, but her personal experience leads in another direction. Finally, Susan Jacoby combines both process analysis and narrative with causal analysis techniques to examine the reasons women opt out of courses in math and science. As you read each piece, keep in mind the kinds of causes the writers present and the ways in which they add support to their analysis.

HOW DO WE READ CAUSAL ANALYSIS?

Reading causal analysis requires us to ask ourselves these questions:

- What are the writer's topic and the main cause? Make an outline of the causes as you read.
- Are immediate causes or ultimate causes presented? How do you know?
- Does the author show the consequences of the event?
- How does the author develop the analysis? Identify the writing strategies used: narrative, description, illustration, process analysis, and so on. Which is most effective in supporting the causal analysis and why?
- What is the tone of the essay?

HOW DO WE WRITE CAUSAL ANALYSIS?

Select a topic you can manage. If you try to find the causes of psychological depression, you may need to study a great deal of Freud before you can write the essay. If, on the other hand, you decide to write about causes of suicide among college freshmen, you would narrow the scope of the essay and thus control it more easily.

Write a working thesis that tells the cause and effect you are analyzing. Why is it important?

Sample thesis statement:

> Many causes lie behind Americans' return to healthier eating habits, but the most important are fear of disease, desire to lose weight, and curiosity about new types of food.

Make a list of the major causes and under each cause, add at least one specific example to support it.

Plan whether you want to concentrate on either causes or effects, or on a balance of the two.

Be sure that you have included all the necessary links in the chain of reasoning that you began in the thesis.

Avoid oversimplification.

Include both major and minor causes and effects.

Writing the Draft

Write an introduction that presents the thesis and your statement of the significance of the thesis.

Use transitions as you move from one cause to the next.

Use narrative, description, process analysis, and other techniques to support your causes.

Conclude by reminding your reader of the importance of understanding this chain of events.

Proofread your draft carefully. Ask a classmate to read it to see if your causes seem logical.

Make corrections and prepare a final copy.

Why We Crave Horror Movies

Stephen King

Stephen King is America's best-known horror writer. Because he is an acknowledged master of this genre, his thoughts on why people love horror movies offer an unusual insight into this question. King also gives us a unique glimpse into why he himself creates horror.

PREREADING: THINKING ABOUT THE ESSAY IN ADVANCE

Do you think that we all have a dark side to our personalities that we rarely reveal? Explain.

Words to Watch

innately (par. 4) by essential characteristic; by birth
voyeur (par. 6) a person who derives sexual gratification from observing the acts of others
penchant (par. 7) a definite liking; a strong inclination
remonstrance (par. 10) an expression of protest
anarchistic (par. 11) active resistance and terrorism against the state
subterranean (par. 12) hidden; secret

1 I think that we're all mentally ill; those of us outside the asylums only hide it a little better—and maybe not all that much better, after all. We've all known people who talk to themselves, people who sometimes squinch their faces into horrible grimaces when they believe no one is watching, people who have some hysterical fear—of snakes, the dark, the tight place, the long drop . . . and, of course, those final worms and grubs that are waiting so patiently underground.

2 When we pay our four or five bucks and seat ourselves at tenth-row center in a theater showing a horror movie, we are daring the nightmare.

Why? Some of the reasons are simple and obvious. To show that we can, that we are not afraid, that we can ride this roller coaster. Which is not to say that a really good horror movie may not surprise a scream out of us at some point, the way we may scream when the roller coaster twists through a complete 360 or plows through a lake at the bottom of the drop. And horror movies, like roller coasters, have always been the special province of the young; by the time one turns 40 or 50, one's appetite for double twists or 360-degree loops may be considerably depleted. 3

We also go to re-establish our feelings of essential normality; the horror movie is innately conservative, even reactionary. Freda Jackson as the horrible melting woman in *Die, Monster, Die!* confirms for us that no matter how far we may be removed from the beauty of a Robert Redford or a Diana Ross, we are still light-years from true ugliness. 4

And we go to have fun. 5

Ah, but this is where the ground starts to slope away, isn't it? Because this is a very peculiar sort of fun indeed. The fun comes from seeing others menaced—sometimes killed. One critic has suggested that if pro football has become the voyeur's version of combat, then the horror film has become the modern version of the public lynching. 6

It is true that the mythic, "fairytale" horror film intends to take away the shades of gray. . . . It urges us to put away our more civilized and adult penchant for analysis and to become children again, seeing things in pure blacks and whites. It may be that horror movies provide psychic relief on this level because this invitation to lapse into simplicity, irrationality and even outright madness is extended so rarely. We are told we may allow our emotions a free rein . . . or no rein at all. 7

If we are all insane, then sanity becomes a matter of degree. If your insanity leads you to carve up women like Jack the Ripper or the Cleveland Torso Murderer, we clap you away in the funny farm (but neither of those two amateur-night surgeons was ever caught, heh-heh-heh); if, on the other hand your insanity leads you only to talk to yourself when you're under stress or to pick your nose on the morning bus, then you are left alone to go about your business . . . though it is doubtful that you will ever be invited to the best parties. 8

9 The potential lyncher is in almost all of us (excluding saints, past and present; but then, most saints have been crazy in their own ways), and every now and then, he has to be let loose to scream and roll around in the grass. Our emotions and our fears form their own body, and we recognize that it demands its own exercise to maintain proper muscle tone. Certain of these emotional muscles are accepted—even exalted—in civilized society; they are, of course, the emotions that tend to maintain the status quo of civilization itself. Love, friendship, loyalty, kindness—these are all the emotions that we applaud, emotions that have been immortalized in the couplets of Hallmark cards and in the verses (I don't dare call it poetry) of Leonard Nimoy.

10 When we exhibit these emotions, society showers us with positive reinforcement; we learn this even before we get out of diapers. When, as children, we hug our rotten little puke of a sister and give her a kiss, all the aunts and uncles smile and twit and cry, "Isn't he the sweetest little thing?" Such coveted treats as chocolate-covered graham crackers often follow. But if we deliberately slam the rotten little puke of a sister's fingers in the door, sanctions follow—angry remonstrance from parents, aunts and uncles; instead of a chocolate-covered graham cracker, a spanking.

11 But anticivilization emotions don't go away, and they demand periodic exercise. We have such "sick" jokes as, "What's the difference between a truckload of bowling balls and a truckload of dead babies? (You can't unload a truckload of bowling balls with a pitchfork . . . a joke, by the way, that I heard originally from a ten-year-old.) Such a joke may surprise a laugh or a grin out of us even as we recoil, a possibility that confirms the thesis: If we share a brotherhood of man, then we also share an insanity of man. None of which is intended as a defense of either the sick joke or insanity but merely as an explanation of why the best horror films, like the best fairy tales, manage to be reactionary, anarchistic, and revolutionary all at the same time.

12 The mythic horror movie, like the sick joke, has a dirty job to do. It deliberately appeals to all that is worst in us. It is morbidity unchained, our most base instincts let free, our nastiest fantasies realized . . . and it all happens, fittingly enough, in the dark. For those reasons, good liberals often shy away from horror films. For myself, I like to see the most aggressive of them—

Dawn of the Dead, for instance—as lifting a trap door in the civilized forebrain and throwing a basket of raw meat to the hungry alligators swimming around in that subterranean river beneath.

Why bother? Because it keeps them from getting out, man. It keeps them down there and me up here. It was Lennon and McCartney who said that all you need is love, and I would agree with that. 13

As long as you keep the gators fed. 14

BUILDING VOCABULARY

King uses descriptive language in this essay to re-create some of the scary images from horror stories, such as snakes and grubs (par. 1). Make a list of his scary words (at least five). Then find a synonym for each word and use each in a sentence.

THINKING CRITICALLY ABOUT THE ESSAY

Understanding the Writer's Ideas

1. King uses the cause-and-effect method to explore why people crave horror. He says we share an "insanity of man" (par. 11). What does he mean by *insanity?*
2. Due to what three reasons does the writer think we dare the nightmare?
3. What does King mean when he says the "'fairytale'" horror films "take away the shades of gray" (par. 7)?
4. How does King explain his view on anticivilization emotions?
5. King uses the image of alligators (the gator) to make a final point. How do you interpret this?

Understanding the Writer's Techniques

1. What is the thesis? Where is it? How does the essay's title reflect the writer's thesis?
2. King uses first person narration in this essay. What other rhetorical modes does he use to develop his essay?

3. In this cause-and-effect essay, what is the cause and what is the effect?
4. King says we are all insane. What tone does this create for the reader? Is he accusing? humorous? serious?
5. King uses both specific and broad generalizations to develop his thesis. Give an example of something specific and something generalized. Which better supports the thesis and why?
6. Notice how the last and concluding sentence of the essay suddenly addresses the reader ("you"). Why? What purpose does this shift to the second person serve in this essay's conclusion?

Exploring the Writer's Ideas

1. How do you feel about the writer's bold opening statement that we are all mentally ill? Does this statement make you want to stop reading? How do you feel about his assumption?
2. Do you go to horror movies or do you avoid them? Why do you or don't you go? Explain.
3. Why do you think King chose to write out his ideas rather than discuss them with a friend? In what way is the process of writing out our ideas different from the process of thinking out loud in conversation?
4. This writer claims he isn't defending anticivilization emotions (par. 11), but he tells us that we need to "scream and roll around in the grass" (par. 9). Which side is this writer on? Which side are you on? Why?
5. Is it true that in horror tales the villains are always destroyed and good always triumphs? Should this be the case? Why or why not?

IDEAS FOR WRITING

Prewriting

Make a scratch outline of your strongest feelings for or against horror stories.

Guided Writing

Write an essay wherein you analyze your reactions to horror books or movies.

1. Begin the essay by stating your feelings on why you personally like or dislike horror. Use some examples to bring to life for the reader your experience with horror.
2. Describe two or more causes for the way you react to horror.
3. Analyze some of the effects you think horror movies may have on you or others who crave them.
4. Respond to the issue of horror allowing anticivilization emotions to be exercised so they don't "get out," as King says.
5. Conclude by addressing readers, telling them why they should embrace or avoid the horror genre.

Thinking and Writing Collaboratively

Working in a group of four to five students, research what experts say about the causes and effects of television violence on children. Then write an essay that makes these causes and effects clear to an audience of parents.

More Writing Projects

1. In your journal, write about something that scares you.
2. Write a paragraph that explains what causes you to fear something.
3. In an essay, examine the causes and effects of something in your life that frightens you (for example, stage fright, test anxiety, fear of flying, and so forth).

Why Marriages Fail

Anne Roiphe

Anne Roiphe is the author of the well-known novel about relationships, *Up the Sandbox!,* which was later made into a popular film. In this essay, notice how she presents a series of interconnected reasons for the currently high divorce rate.

PREREADING: THINKING ABOUT THE ESSAY IN ADVANCE

What experiences or assumptions do you bring to an essay about failed marriages? Do you know of marriages that have failed? If so, what were the causes?

Words to Watch

obsolete (par. 1) out-of-date; no longer in use
perils (par. 2) dangers
infertility (par. 2) the lack of ability to have children
turbulent (par. 2) very chaotic or uneasy
stupefying (par. 2) bewildering
obese (par. 3) very fat; overweight
entrapment (par. 4) the act of trapping, sometimes by devious methods
yearning (par. 4) a strong desire
euphoric (par. 7) characterized by a feeling of well-being
infidelity (par. 13) sexual unfaithfulness
proverbial (par. 13) relating to a proverb or accepted truth

1 These days so many marriages end in divorce that our most sacred vows no longer ring with truth. "Happily ever after" and "Till death do us part" are expressions that seem on the way to becoming obsolete. Why has it become so hard for couples to stay together? What goes wrong? What has happened to us that close to one-half of all marriages are destined for the divorce

courts? How could we have created a society in which 42 percent of our children will grow up in single-parent homes? If statistics could only measure loneliness, regret, pain, loss of self-confidence and fear of the future, the numbers would be beyond quantifying.

Even though each broken marriage is unique, we can still find the common perils, the common causes for marital despair. Each marriage has crisis points and each marriage tests endurance, the capacity for both intimacy and change. Outside pressures such as job loss, illness, infertility, trouble with a child, care of aging parents and all the other plagues of life hit marriage the way hurricanes blast our shores. Some marriages survive these storms and others don't. Marriages fail, however, not simply because of the outside weather but because the inner climate becomes too hot or too cold, too turbulent or too stupefying. 2

When we look at how we choose our partners and what expectations exist at the tender beginnings of romance, some of the reasons for disaster become quite clear. We all select with unconscious accuracy a mate who will recreate with us the emotional patterns of our first homes. Dr. Carl A. Whitaker, a marital therapist and emeritus professor of psychiatry at the University of Wisconsin, explains, "From early childhood on, each of us carried models for marriage, femininity, masculinity, motherhood, fatherhood and all the other family roles." Each of us falls in love with a mate who has qualities of our parents, who will help us rediscover both the psychological happiness and miseries of our past lives. We may think we have found a man unlike Dad, but then he turns to drink or drugs, or loses his job over and over again or sits silently in front of the T.V. just the way Dad did. A man may choose a woman who doesn't like kids just like his mother or who gambles away the family savings just like his mother. Or he may choose a slender wife who seems unlike his obese mother but then turns out to have other addictions that destroy their mutual happiness. 3

A man and a woman bring to their marriage bed a blended concoction of conscious and unconscious memories of their parents' lives together. The human way is to compulsively repeat and recreate the patterns of the past. Sigmund Freud so well described the unhappy design that many of us get trapped in: the unmet needs of childhood, the angry feelings left over from frus- 4 trations of long ago, the limits of trust and the recurrence of old fears. Once an individual senses this entrapment, there may follow a yearning to escape, and the result could be a broken, splintered marriage.

5 Of course people can overcome the habits and attitudes that developed in childhood. We all have hidden strengths and amazing capacities for growth and creative change. Change, however, requires work—observing your part in a rotten pattern, bringing difficulties out into the open—and work runs counter to the basic myth of marriage: "When I wed this person all my problems will be over. I will have achieved success and I will become the center of life for this other person and this person will be my center, and we will mean everything to each other forever." This myth, which every marriage relies on, is soon exposed. The coming of children, the pulls and tugs of their demands on affection and time, place a considerable strain on that basic myth of meaning everything to each other, of merging together and solving all of life's problems.

6 Concern and tension about money take each partner away from the other. Obligations to demanding parents or still-depended-upon parents create further strain. Couples today must also deal with all the cultural changes brought on in recent years by the women's movement and the sexual revolution. The altering of roles and the shifting of responsibilities have been extremely trying for many marriages.

7 These and other realities of life erode the visions of marital bliss the way sandstorms eat at rock and the ocean nibbles away at the dunes. Those euphoric, grand feelings that accompany romantic love are really self-delusions, self-hypnotic dreams that enable us to forge a relationship. Real life, failure at work, disappointments, exhaustion, bad smells, bad colds and hard times all puncture the dream and leave us stranded with our mate, with our childhood patterns pushing us this way and that, with our unfulfilled expectations.

8 The struggle to survive in marriage requires adaptability, flexibility, genuine love and kindness and an imagination strong enough to feel what the other is feeling. Many marriages fall apart because either partner cannot imagine what the other wants or cannot communicate what he or she needs or feels. Anger builds until it erupts into a volcanic burst that buries the marriage in ash.

It is not hard to see, therefore, how essential communication is for a good marriage. A man and a woman must be able to tell each other how they feel and why they feel the way they do; otherwise they will impose on each other roles and actions that lead to further unhappiness. In some cases, the communication patterns of childhood—of not talking, of talking too much, of not listening, of distrust and anger, of withdrawal—spill into the marriage and prevent a healthy exchange of thoughts and feelings. The answer is to set up new patterns of communication and intimacy. 9

At the same time, however, we must see each other as individuals. "To achieve a balance between separateness and closeness is one of the major psychological tasks of all human beings at every stage of life," says Dr. Stuart Bartle, a psychiatrist at the New York University Medical Center. 10

If we sense from our mate a need for too much intimacy, we tend to push him or her away, fearing that we may lose our identities in the merging of marriage. One partner may suffocate the other partner in a childlike dependency. 11

A good marriage means growing as a couple but also growing as individuals. This isn't easy. Richard gives up his interest in carpentry because his wife, Helen, is jealous of the time he spends away from her. Karen quits her choir group because her husband dislikes the friends she makes there. Each pair clings to each other and are angry with each other as life closes in on them. This kind of marital balance is easily thrown as one or the other pulls away and divorce follows. 12

Sometimes people pretend that a new partner will solve the old problems. Most often extramarital sex destroys a marriage because it allows an artificial split between the good and the bad—the good is projected on the new partner and the bad is dumped on the head of the old. Dishonesty, hiding and cheating create walls between men and women. Infidelity is just a symptom of trouble. It is a symbolic complaint, a weapon of revenge, as well as an unraveler of closeness. Infidelity is often that proverbial last straw that sinks the camel to the ground. 13

All right—marriage has always been difficult. Why then are we seeing so many divorces at this time? Yes, our modern social fabric is thin, and yes the permissiveness of society has created unrealistic expectations and thrown the family into chaos. But divorce is so common because people today are unwilling to exercise the self-discipline that marriage requires. 14

They expect easy joy, like the entertainment on TV, the thrill of a good party.

15 Marriage takes some kind of sacrifice, not dreadful self-sacrifice of the soul, but some level of compromise. Some of one's fantasies, some of one's legitimate desires have to be given up for the value of the marriage itself. "While all marital partners feel shackled at times, it is they who really choose to make the marital ties into confining chains or supporting bonds," says Dr. Whitaker. Marriage requires sexual, financial and emotional discipline. A man and a woman cannot follow every impulse, cannot allow themselves to stop growing or changing.

16 Divorce is not an evil act. Sometimes it provides salvation for people who have grown hopelessly apart or were frozen in patterns of pain or mutual unhappiness. Divorce can be, despite its initial devastation, like the first cut of the surgeon's knife, a step toward new health and a good life. On the other hand, if the partners can stay past the breaking up of the romantic myths into the development of real love and intimacy, they have achieved a work as amazing as the greatest cathedrals of the world. Marriages that do not fail but improve, that persist despite imperfections, are not only rare these days but offer a wondrous shelter in which the face of our mutual humanity can safely show itself.

BUILDING VOCABULARY

1. Roiphe loads her essay with some very common expressions to make the discussion more easily understandable to the reader. Below is a list of ten such expressions. Use each in a sentence of your own.

a. ring with truth (par. 1)
b. crisis points (par. 2)
c. tender beginnings (par. 3)
d. mutual happiness (par. 3)
e. marriage bed (par. 4)
f. hidden strengths (par. 5)
g. marital bliss (par. 7)
h. healthy exchange (par. 9)
i. childlike dependency (par. 11)
j. social fabric (par. 14)

2. Locate and explain five terms that the author draws from psychology.

THINKING CRITICALLY ABOUT THE ESSAY

Understanding the Writer's Ideas

1. What are the "sacred vows" the author mentions in paragraph 1? Identify the source of the expressions "happily ever after" and "till death do us part." What does she mean when she says that these expressions "seem on the way to becoming obsolete"?
2. What is a "single-parent home"?
3. How does Roiphe define "endurance" in a marriage? What does she mean by "outside pressures" in paragraph 2? What are some of these pressures? Does Roiphe feel they are the primary causes for marriages failing? Why?
4. According to the essay, how do we choose husbands and wives? What is the meaning of "our first home" in paragraph 3? According to Roiphe, for what reasons is the way we choose mates a possible cause for marriages failing?
5. What is the "basic myth" of marriage? How does it create a possibly bad marriage?
6. How have the women's movement and the sexual revolution created strains on modern marriages?
7. Explain what the writer means by "Real life, failure at work, disappointments, exhaustion, bad smells, bad colds, and hard times" in paragraph 7. How do they affect marriages?
8. What is the role of communication between husband and wife in a marriage? What are the results of poor communication? What solutions to this problem does Roiphe suggest?
9. What two types of "growth" does Roiphe suggest as necessary to a good marriage? Who are Richard, Helen, and Karen, named in paragraph 12?
10. According to Roiphe, what is the common cause of extramarital sexual affairs? What are her projected results of infidelity?
11. What does Roiphe identify as the primary cause of divorce? What does she propose as a solution to this problem?
12. According to the last paragraph, do you think Roiphe is in favor of divorce? Why? In this paragraph, she presents both

the positive and negative effects of divorce. What are the positive effects? the negative effects?

Understanding the Writer's Techniques

1. Where does the author place her thesis?
2. How does the title almost predict for the reader that the writer's main technique of development will be cause-and-effect analysis?
3. One strategy for developing an introductory paragraph is to ask a question. What is the purpose of the questions that the author asks in the opening paragraph? What is the relationship among the questions? How do the questions themselves dictate a cause-and-effect pattern of development? How do they immediately involve the reader in the topic?
4. In which paragraph does Roiphe list the immediate or common causes of marital failure? Why is this placement effective?
5. The use of clear *topic sentences* for each paragraph can often be an important technique in writing a clear causal analysis because topic sentences usually identify main causes for the effect under discussion. Identify the topic sentences for paragraphs 3, 4, and 6. What causes for marriage failure does each identify?
6. What causal chain of behavior does Roiphe build in paragraphs 8 to 13?
7. Why does Roiphe begin paragraph 14 with the words "All right"? Whom is she addressing? How does this address compare with the technique used in her introduction?
8. What two authorities does Roiphe quote in this essay? How are their citations useful? How are they identified? In what ways do their identifications add to their credibility as sources of opinions or information on Roiphe's topic?
9. Where does Roiphe use statistics in this essay? Why is it especially important to the development of the article?
10. Roiphe makes use of *definition* (see pages 232–236) in a number of places in this essay. What are her definitions of the following?
    - **a.** work [in a marriage] (par. 5)
    - **b.** A good marriage (par. 12)

c. Divorce (par. 16)
d. Marriages that do not fail but improve (par. 16)
Locate other places where she uses definition.

11. In some essays, the introduction and conclusion are each simply the first and last paragraphs. In this essay, the writer uses more than one paragraph for each. Which paragraphs make up her introduction? Which make up the conclusion? Why might she have structured her introduction and conclusion in this way? How does the structure affect the essay?
12. You have learned that two of the most common types of comparisons used by writers to enliven their essays are *similes* and *metaphors*. Look up the definition of these terms in the Glossary to refresh your memory. In addition, writers may use *extended metaphors*. This technique relies upon a number of metaphoric comparisons which revolve around a main idea rather than a single comparison. Roiphe uses comparisons in a number of paragraphs in this essay. In each of the following cases identify and explain the comparisons indicated:
    a. extended metaphor (par. 2)
    b. metaphor (par. 7)
    c. metaphor (par. 8)
    d. metaphor (par. 9)
    e. simile (par. 14)
    f. metaphor (par. 15)
    g. similes, metaphors (par. 16)

    How does Roiphe's frequent use of metaphors and similes affect the tone of the essay?
13. Why does Roiphe end her essay with references to successful marriages? Would you consider that as being off the topic? Why or why not?

Exploring the Writer's Ideas

1. Roiphe discusses quite a few causes for marriages failing. Discuss with the class some additional causes. Why are they also important?
2. Paragraph 6 states, "Couples today must also deal with all the cultural changes brought on in recent years by the women's movement and the sexual revolution." Identify these two social phenomena. Among the people you know, have these

cultural changes affected their marriages? How? If you are not married, and plan to marry, do you feel that the changes will present any foreseeable problems? If you are not married, and do not plan to marry, have they influenced your decision in any ways? What other effects have these two movements had in American society? Do you think these influences have been positive or negative? Why?

3. If you are married or in a close relationship, how did you choose your mate? If you are not married or in a relationship, what qualities would you look for in a mate? Why?
4. In paragraphs 6 and 7, Roiphe mentions "realities of life" that destroy romantic notions of "marital bliss." What other realities can you add to her list?
5. Paragraph 15 discusses the idea of self-sacrifice in marriage. Roiphe writes, "Some of one's fantasies, some of one's legitimate desires have to be given up for the value of the marriage itself." However, some people insist that for a marriage to survive, each partner must maintain complete integrity, that is, must not be forced into major sacrifices of values or lifestyles. What is your opinion of these two opposing viewpoints?
6. Judy Brady in "I Want a Wife" (pages 392–394) provides some insights into marriage that complement Roiphe's. How does Brady's position compare with Roiphe's?

IDEAS FOR WRITING

Prewriting

Free-associate on a sheet of paper about the reasons or causes for *successful* marriages. In other words, which marriages survive despite the high rate of divorce in the United States?

Guided Writing

Using cause-and-effect analysis, write an essay in which you explain *why marriages succeed.*

1. Limit your topic sufficiently so that you can concentrate your discussion on closely interrelated cause-and-effect patterns.

2. In the introduction, involve your reader with a series of pertinent questions.
3. Identify what many people think are common or immediate causes of successful marriages; then show how other causes are perhaps even more important.
4. In the course of your essay, cite at least one relevant statistic that will add extra importance to your topic.
5. Try to use at least one quotation from a reputable authority. Consult your library for books and articles that deal with marriage. Be sure to include full identification of your source.
6. Use clear topic sentences in each paragraph as you present analyses of the various causes for successful marriages.
7. Make use of metaphors, similes, and extended metaphors.
8. In your essay, offer necessary definitions of terms that are especially important to your topic. Try for at least one definition by negation.
9. Write a conclusion in which you make some commentary upon divorce. Make your comment as an outgrowth of your discussion of a successful marriage.

Thinking and Writing Collaboratively

Divide the class into four equal groups. Have members of each group read their essays out loud. Next, select your group's strongest essay and list the reasons your group has selected it. Present your findings to the class, and if time permits, ask the writer of the best essay to read it to the class.

More Writing Projects

1. What is the "ideal marriage"? In your journal, speculate on those qualities that you think would make a perfect marriage. Share observations with others in the class.
2. In a paragraph, explain some of your reasons for ending a relationship (a marriage, a close friendship, a relationship with a girlfriend or boyfriend).
3. Write an essay in which you explain the effects of divorce on the lives of the couple involved. Here, do not concern yourself with causes; look only at the results of the failed marriage.

The Ambivalence of Abortion

Linda Bird Francke

In this autobiographical narrative, author Linda Bird Francke tells about her mixed feelings toward the issue of abortion. Although she has strong political convictions on the subject, her ambivalence surfaces when she must confront abortion personally. Notice how she blends descriptive details with personal insights to explain the reasons for her uncertainty.

PREREADING: THINKING ABOUT THE ESSAY IN ADVANCE

What ideas or images does the word *abortion* bring to mind? Do you understand the motives of a woman who decides to have an abortion? Do you sympathize with her motives or condemn them? What do you learn from this article about one woman's experience?

Words to Watch

dwell (par. 1) keep attention directed on something
heralded (par. 1) announced in a joyous manner
rationalize (par. 2) to justify one's behavior (especially to oneself)
freelance (par. 3) working without long-range contractual agreements
cycled (par. 5) moved through a complete series of operations or steps
common denominator (par. 10) similar traits or themes
rhetoric (par. 13) ways of speaking or writing effectively
fetus (par. 13) an unborn child still in the mother's womb
neurotic (par. 14) emotionally unstable
vaccinated (par. 14) injected with a harmless virus to produce immunity to a disease
inoculated (par. 14) treated with a serum or antibody to prevent disease
uterus (par. 16) the womb; the place within the mother where the fetus develops
sensation (par. 18) feeling
Novocain (par. 18) a drug used to numb the feeling of pain
quivered (par. 18) shook

We were sitting in a bar on Lexington Avenue when I told my husband I was pregnant. It is not a memory I like to dwell on. Instead of the champagne and hope which had heralded the impending births of the first, second and third child, the news of this one was greeted with shocked silence and Scotch. "Jesus," my husband kept saying to himself, stirring the ice cubes around and around. "Oh, Jesus." 1

Oh, how we tried to rationalize it that night as the starting time for the movie came and went. My husband talked about his plans for a career change in the next year, to stem the staleness that fourteen years with the same investment-banking firm had brought him. A new baby would preclude that option. 2

The timing wasn't right for me either. Having juggled pregnancies and child care with what freelance jobs I could fit in between feedings, I had just taken on a full-time job. A new baby would put me right back in the nursery just when our youngest child was finally school age. It was time for *us,* we tried to rationalize. There just wasn't room in our lives now for another baby. We both agreed. And agreed. And agreed. 3

How very considerate they are at the Women's Services, known formally as the Center for Reproductive and Sexual Health. Yes, indeed, I could have an abortion that very Saturday morning and be out in time to drive to the country that afternoon. Bring a first morning urine specimen, a sanitary belt and napkins, a money order or $125 cash—and a friend. 4

My friend turned out to be my husband, standing awkwardly and ill at ease as men always do in places that are exclusively for women, as I checked in at nine A.M. Other men hovered around just as anxiously, knowing they had to be there, wishing they weren't. No one spoke to each other. When I would be cycled out of there four hours later, the same men would be slumped in their same seats, locked downcast in their cells of embarrassment. 5

The Saturday morning women's group was more dispirited than the men in the waiting room. There were around fifteen of us, a mixture of races, ages and backgrounds. Three didn't speak English at all and a fourth, a pregnant Puerto Rican girl around eighteen, translated for them. 6

There were six black women and a hodgepodge of whites, among them a T-shirted teenager who kept leaving the room to 7 throw up and a puzzled middle-aged woman from Queens with three grown children.

8 "What form of birth control were you using?" the volunteer asked each one of us. The answer was inevitably "none." She then went on to describe the various forms of birth control available at the clinic, and offered them to each of us.

9 The youngest Puerto Rican girl was asked through the interpreter which she'd like to use: the loop, diaphragm, or pill. She shook her head "no" three times. "You don't want to come back here again, do you?" the volunteer pressed. The girl's head was so low her chin rested on her breastbone. *"Sí,"* she whispered.

10 We had been there two hours by that time, filling out endless forms, giving blood and urine, receiving lectures. But unlike any other group of women I've been in, we didn't talk. Our common denominator, the one which usually floods across language and economic barriers into familiarity, today was one of shame. We were losing life that day, not giving it.

11 The group kept getting cut back to smaller, more workable units, and finally I was put in a small waiting room with just two other women. We changed into paper bathrobes and paper slippers, and we rustled whenever we moved. One of the women in my room was shivering and an aide brought her a blanket.

12 "What's the matter?" the aide asked her. "I'm scared," the woman said. "How much will it hurt?" The aide smiled. "Oh, nothing worse than a couple of bad cramps," she said. "This afternoon you'll be dancing a jig."

13 I began to panic. Suddenly the rhetoric, the abortion marches I'd walked in, the telegrams sent to Albany to counteract the Friends of the Fetus, the Zero Population Growth buttons I'd worn, peeled away, and I was all alone with my microscopic baby. There were just the two of us there, and soon, because it was more convenient for me and my husband, there would be one again.

14 How could it be that I, who am so neurotic about life that I step over bugs rather than on them, who spend hours planting flowers and vegetables in the spring even though we rent out the house and never see them, who make sure the children are vaccinated and inoculated and filled with vitamin C, could so arbitrarily decide that this life shouldn't be?

15 "It's not a life," my husband had argued, more to convince himself than me. "It's a bunch of cells smaller than my fingernail."

But any woman who has had children knows that certain feeling in her taut, swollen breasts, and the slight but constant ache in her uterus that signals the arrival of a life. Though I would march myself into blisters for a woman's right to exercise the option of motherhood, I discovered there in the waiting room that I was not the modern woman I thought I was. 16

When my name was called, my body felt so heavy the nurse had to help me into the examining room. I waited for my husband to burst through the door and yell "stop," but of course he didn't. I concentrated on three black spots in the acoustic ceiling until they grew in size to the shape of saucers, while the doctor swabbed my insides with antiseptic. 17

"You're going to feel a burning sensation now," he said, injecting Novocain into the neck of the womb. The pain was swift and severe, and I twisted to get away from him. He was hurting my baby, I reasoned, and the black saucers quivered in the air. "Stop," I cried. "Please stop." He shook his head, busy with his equipment. "It's too late to stop now," he said. "It'll just take a few more seconds." 18

What good sports we women are. And how obedient. Physically the pain passed even before the hum of the machine signaled that the vacuuming of my uterus was completed, my baby sucked up like ashes after a cocktail party. Ten minutes start to finish. And I was back on the arm of the nurse. 19

There were twelve beds in the recovery room. Each one had a gaily flowered draw sheet and a soft green or blue thermal blanket. It was all very feminine. Lying on these beds for an hour or more were the shocked victims of their sex, their full wombs now stripped clean, their futures less encumbered. 20

It was very quiet in that room. The only voice was that of the nurse, locating the new women who had just come in so she could monitor their blood pressure, and checking out the recovered women who were free to leave. 21

Juice was being passed about, and I found myself sipping a Dixie cup of Hawaiian Punch. An older woman with tightly curled bleached hair was just getting up from the next bed. "That was no goddamn snap," she said, resting before putting on her miniskirt and high white boots. Other women came and went, some walking out as dazed as they had entered, others with a bounce that signaled they were going right back to Bloomingdale's. 22

23 Finally then, it was time for me to leave. I checked out, making an appointment to return in two weeks for an IUD insertion. My husband was slumped in the waiting room, clutching a single yellow rose wrapped in a wet paper towel and stuffed into a Baggie.

24 We didn't talk the whole way home, but just held hands very tightly. At home there were more yellow roses and a tray in bed for me and the children's curiosity to divert.

25 It had certainly been a successful operation. I didn't bleed at all for two days just as they had predicted, and then I bled only moderately for another four days. Within a week my breasts had subsided and the tenderness vanished, and my body felt mine again instead of the eggshell it becomes when it's protecting someone else.

26 My husband and I are back to planning our summer vacation and his career switch.

27 And it certainly does make more sense not to be having a baby right now—we say that to each other all the time. But I have this ghost now. A very little ghost that only appears when I'm seeing something beautiful, like the full moon on the ocean last weekend. And the baby waves at me. And I wave at the baby. "Of course, we have room," I cry to the ghost. "Of course, we do."

BUILDING VOCABULARY

1. Develop definitions of your own for the italicized words by relying on context clues, that is, clues from surrounding words and sentences. Then check your definition against a dictionary definition.
   a. My husband talked about his plans for a career change in the next year, *to stem* the staleness that fourteen years with the same investment-banking firm had brought him. A new baby would *preclude* that *option.* (par. 2)
   b. Though I would march myself into blisters for a woman's right to *exercise* the *option* of motherhood, I discovered there in the waiting room that I was not the modern woman I thought I was. (par. 16)
   c. The pain was *swift* and *severe,* and I twisted to get away from him. (par. 18)

d. Lying on these beds for an hour or more were the shocked victims of their sex, their full wombs now stripped clean, their futures less *encumbered.* (par. 20)

e. It had certainly been a successful operation. I didn't bleed at all for two days just as they had predicted, and then I bled only *moderately* for another four days. (par. 25)

2. For each italicized word in Column A, write the correct *synonym* (a word of similar meaning) from Column B. Look up unfamiliar words in a dictionary.

Column A	*Column B*
1. *impending* births (par. 1)	**a.** decreased
2. *hovered* around (par. 5)	**b.** complying
3. locked *downcast* (par. 5)	**c.** confused
4. more *dispirited* (par. 6)	**d.** lingered
5. *puzzled* middle-aged woman (par. 7)	**e.** about to happen
6. *inevitably* "none" (par. 8)	**f.** tight
7. *taut,* swollen breasts (par. 16)	**g.** distract
8. how *obedient* (par. 19)	**h.** dejected
9. curiosity to *divert* (par. 24)	**i.** unavoidably
10. had *subsided* (par. 25)	**j.** discouraged

THINKING CRITICALLY ABOUT THE ESSAY

Understanding the Writer's Ideas

1. What is the setting in which Francke breaks the news to her husband that she is pregnant? How does he receive the news?
2. What reasons does her husband give for not wanting another child? Why does Francke feel it is a bad time for herself as well?
3. What is the attitude of the men waiting at the abortion clinic? Explain.
4. Why is there a women's group meeting before Francke actually gets her abortion? Are all the women pretty much alike at this meeting? How so? What is Francke's attitude toward these other women? Give specific examples to support your answer.
5. What common reason do all the women in the group share for being pregnant?
6. In the past, what was the author's viewpoint concerning women's rights to have abortions? What specific examples does she give to illustrate this point of view? Do you assume that she still holds this opinion? Why?
7. What examples does Francke give to illustrate that she supports life? Are they convincing?
8. Explain what the author means by the statement "Though I would march myself into blisters for a woman's right to exercise the option of motherhood, I discovered there in the waiting room that I was not the modern woman I thought I was" (par. 16).
9. When she is in the examining room, what does the author do to deal with her anxieties about the abortion?
10. Explain what the woman means when she says to Francke, "That was no goddamn snap."
11. How does Francke know the operation has been successful?

Understanding the Writer's Techniques

1. What is Francke's thesis?
2. What rhetorical strategy does the word "ambivalence" in the title suggest? How does Francke use that strategy in the very

first paragraph? Where does she use it elsewhere in the essay?

3. Does Francke successfully explain the ambivalence named in the title? Why or why not?
4. Which does this analysis concentrate on more—causes, effects, or a combination of the two? What evidence can you offer to support your answer? What specifically is the relationship between cause and effect in paragraphs 6 to 10? Analyze the pattern of cause and effect in paragraphs 19 to 22.
5. What is the use of narration in this essay? What is the narrative *point of view* (see Glossary) in this selection? How is it used to enhance the essay?
6. What would you say is the overall tone of the selection? The author uses repetition in this essay to help set that tone. How does the repetition in "We both agreed. And agreed. And agreed" (par. 3) contribute to it?
7. *Paradox* (see Glossary) is a special variety of *irony* in which there is a clear contradiction in a situation. A paradox is a statement or attitude which, on the surface, seems unlikely, and yet, on analysis, can indeed be true. For example, it is paradoxical that the author should have such ambivalent feelings about abortion while she is sitting in an abortion clinic. Why is that situation considered paradoxical? What other paradoxes do you find in this essay?
8. What is the function of description in this essay? Select passages in which you feel the descriptions are especially vivid. How is description used by the author to characterize the women mentioned in paragraph 22? Are the women stereotyped in this description? Explain.
9. Only toward the last part of the essay does Francke use any metaphors or similes—some of them quite startling. Identify the metaphors or similes in paragraph 19, paragraph 25, and paragraph 27. Why do you think she saved this figurative language for the end?
10. Analyze the last paragraph. What causes and effects discussed throughout the essay are echoed here? What new ones are suggested? Compare the effect of the statement "Of course, we have room" with the statement in paragraph 3, "There just wasn't room. . . ." How does this repetition affect the conclusion?

11. Writers who write about highly charged emotional issues must take special care to avoid *sentimentality*—the excessive display of emotion (see Glossary). Has Francke been successful in avoiding it everywhere in the essay? How has she used concrete descriptions to avoid being sentimental? Does the conclusion strike you as being excessively emotional or does it strike you simply as a dramatic but effective closing? Explain your responses.

Exploring the Writer's Ideas

1. When this article was originally published in 1976, it appeared under the *pseudonym* (a fictitious name) "Jane Doe." What reason might Linda Francke have had for not using her real name? Why do you think that a few years later she admitted to the authorship of the article? In general, what do you think about a writer publishing his or her work under an assumed name? Explain. What historical examples can you offer for the use of pseudonyms?
2. Francke describes some very intimate personal emotions and experiences in her attempt to explain what causes her ambivalence toward abortion. On the basis of the material presented, do you think she is justified in feeling ambivalent? Do you feel she should have been more definite one way or the other? Why?
3. In her description of the Saturday morning women's group (pars. 6 to 10), Francke shows that the women present were of all types—"a mixture of races, ages, and backgrounds." This suggests, of course, that abortion is a subject affecting all women. Does it, in fact, affect all women equally? Explain your answer.
4. In paragraph 5, the author describes her husband as "standing awkwardly and ill at ease as men always do in places that are exclusively for women." What sorts of places are exclusively for persons of one sex? Discuss how you felt and acted if you were ever in a place which was really more for persons of the opposite sex.
5. Much controversy about abortion revolves around modern definitions of life and death. Some people argue that life begins at conception; others argue that life begins at birth.

With which group do you agree? Why? How has modern science complicated our concepts of life and death?

6. Abortion and antiabortion forces have increased their attacks against each other dramatically in recent years. How does Francke's essay crystallize both sides of the complex, emotionally charged issue?

IDEAS FOR WRITING

Prewriting

Freewrite for fifteen minutes about a social issue—for example, abortion, the death penalty, prayer in school—that you have mixed or ambivalent feelings about. Focus on main causes for your uncertainty.

Guided Writing

Select an important issue facing society, an issue with which you have had personal experience and about which you have mixed feelings. After you fill in the blank, write an essay titled "Two Sides of __________." In your essay explore the reasons for your ambivalence. You can select from a wide range of social, moral, health, or education topics. For example, you might want to consider ambivalence toward interracial dating or marriages, a compulsory draft, legalization of drugs, cigarette smoking, a liberal arts education—but feel free to select any issue that is especially important to you.

1. Write the essay as a first-person narrative. Begin with an incident when you first clearly realized the ambivalent nature of the issue, and explain why or how this particular incident focused your attention on the subject.
2. Tell about how and for what reasons you came to a decision to take a certain action despite your mixed feelings. What rationalizations did you or others use to help you feel you were doing the right thing?
3. Narrate in detail the sequence of events that followed your decision. Make the narrative come to life with concrete sen-

sory detail. As you tell your story, analyze the various causes and effects of your decision and actions.

4. Discuss how the same event you experienced affects others. Explain how the causes and effects of the action are different or similar for you and for others.
5. Explain how you felt immediately before, during, and after the crucial experience.
6. In your conclusion, express your deepest feelings about the consequences of your decision and experiences. Use similes, metaphors, and an echo of your original attempts to rationalize your ambivalence.

Thinking and Writing Collaboratively

Working with all the members of your class, organize an opinion poll on some campus issue. Develop five questions about this issue and list them on the chalkboard. Finally, poll the class on each question, tally the results, and each write your own summary of the results.

More Writing Projects

1. In your journal, reflect on the issue of abortion. Analyze your reasons for your attitudes.
2. Write a brief paragraph in which you explain the causes and (or) effects of a political standpoint you feel very strongly about.
3. In an essay of analysis, propose the effects on children if elementary schools throughout the country had compulsory sex education programs.

When Bright Girls Decide That Math Is "a Waste of Time"

Susan Jacoby

In this article, Susan Jacoby explains how cultural expectations and societal stereotyping are overshadowed by women's own decisions to keep themselves away from scientific and technological studies. Notice how she uses narrative and process analysis to reinforce the causes and effects she is exploring here.

PREREADING: THINKING ABOUT THE ESSAY IN ADVANCE

This article focuses on the reasons why women perform poorly in one academic subject, mathematics. How would you explain this phenomenon? What causes might you identify? Are there academic subjects or professional areas where women are less able or more able to succeed than men? Why or why not?

Words to Watch

sanguine (par. 3) cheerful, hopeful
vulnerable (par. 6) open to attack or suggestion
syndrome (par. 7) a group of symptoms that characterize a condition
akin to (par. 7) similar to
phobia (par. 7) an excessive fear of something
constitute (par. 7) to make up; compose
epitomize (par. 8) to be a prime example of
prone to (par. 15) disposed to; susceptible to
accede to (par. 16) give in to

Susannah, a 16-year-old who has always been an A student in every subject from algebra to English, recently informed her parents that she intended to drop physics and calculus in her senior year of high school and replace them with a drama seminar and a work-study program. She expects to major in art or history in col- 1 lege, she explained, and "any more science or math will just be a waste of my time."

2 Her parents were neither concerned by nor opposed to her decision. "Fine, dear," they said. Their daughter is, after all, an outstanding student. What does it matter if, at age 16, she has taken a step that may limit her understanding of both machines and the natural world for the rest of her life?

3 This kind of decision, in which girls turn away from studies that would give them a sure footing in the world of science and technology, is a self-inflicted female disability that is, regrettably, almost as common today as it was when I was in high school. If Susannah had announced that she had decided to stop taking English in her senior year, her mother and father would have been horrified. I also think they would have been a good deal less sanguine about her decision if she were a boy.

4 In saying that scientific and mathematical ignorance is a self-inflicted female wound, I do not, obviously, mean that cultural expectations play no role in the process. But the world does not conspire to deprive modern women of access to science as it did in the 1930's, when Rosalyn S. Yalow, the Nobel Prize-winning physicist, graduated from Hunter College and was advised to go to work as a secretary because no graduate school would admit her to its physics department. The current generation of adolescent girls—and their parents, bred on old expectations about women's interests—are active conspirators in limiting their own intellectual development.

5 It is true that the proportion of young women in science-related graduate and professional schools, most notably medical schools, has increased significantly in the past decade. It is also true that so few women were studying advanced science and mathematics before the early 1970's that the percentage increase in female enrollment does not yet translate into large numbers of women actually working in science.

6 The real problem is that so many girls eliminate themselves from any serious possibility of studying science as a result of decisions made during the vulnerable period of midadolescence, when they are most likely to be influenced—on both conscious and subconscious levels—by the traditional belief that math and science are "masculine" subjects.

During the teen-age years the well-documented phenomenon of "math anxiety" strikes girls who never had any problem handling numbers during earlier schooling. Some men, too, experience this syndrome—a form of panic, akin to a phobia, at any task involving numbers—but women constitute the overwhelming majority of sufferers. The onset of acute math anxiety during the teen-age years is, as Stalin was fond of saying, "not by accident." 7

In adolescence girls begin to fear that they will be unattractive to boys if they are typed as "brains." Science and math epitomize unfeminine braininess in a way that, say, foreign languages do not. High-school girls who pursue an advanced interest in science and math (unless they are students at special institutions like the Bronx High School of Science where everyone is a brain) usually find that they are greatly outnumbered by boys in their classes. They are, therefore, intruding on male turf at a time when their sexual confidence, as well as that of the boys, is most fragile. 8

A 1981 assessment of female achievement in mathematics, based on research conducted under a National Institute for Education grant, found significant differences in the mathematical achievements of 9th and 12th graders. At age 13 girls were equal to or slightly better than boys in tests involving algebra, problem solving and spatial ability; four years later the boys had outstripped the girls. 9

It is not mysterious that some very bright high-school girls suddenly decide that math is "too hard" and "a waste of time." In my experience, self-sabotage of mathematical and scientific ability is often a conscious process. I remember deliberately pretending to be puzzled by geometry problems in my sophomore year in high school. A male teacher called me in after class and said, in a baffled tone, "I don't see how you can be having so much trouble when you got straight A's last year in my algebra class." 10

The decision to avoid advanced biology, chemistry, physics and calculus in high school automatically restricts academic and professional choices that ought to be wide open to anyone beginning college. At all coeducational universities women are overwhelmingly concentrated in the fine arts, social sciences and traditionally female departments like education. Courses leading to degrees in science- and technology-related fields are filled mainly by men. 11

12 In my generation, the practical consequences of mathematical and scientific illiteracy are visible in the large number of special programs to help professional women overcome the anxiety they feel when they are promoted into jobs that require them to handle statistics.

13 The consequences of this syndrome should not, however, be viewed in narrowly professional terms. Competence in science and math does not mean one is going to become a scientist or mathematician any more than competence in writing English means one is going to become a professional writer. Scientific and mathematical illiteracy—which has been cited in several recent critiques by panels studying American education from kindergarten through college—produces an incalculably impoverished vision of human experience.

14 Scientific illiteracy is not, of course, the exclusive province of women. In certain intellectual circles it has become fashionable to proclaim a willed, aggressive ignorance about science and technology. Some female writers specialize in ominous, uninformed diatribes against genetic research as a plot to remove control of childbearing from women, while some well-known men of letters proudly announce that they understand absolutely nothing about computers, or, for that matter, about electricity. This lack of understanding is nothing in which women or men ought to take pride.

15 Failure to comprehend either computers or chromosomes leads to a terrible sense of helplessness, because the profound impact of science on everyday life is evident even to those who insist they don't, won't, can't understand why the changes are taking place. At this stage of history women are more prone to such feelings of helplessness than men because the culture judges their ignorance less harshly and because women themselves acquiesce in that indulgence.

16 Since there is ample evidence of such feelings in adolescence, it is up to parents to see that their daughters do not accede to the old stereotypes about "masculine" and "feminine" knowledge. Unless we want our daughters to share our intellectual handicaps, we had better tell them no, they can't stop taking mathematics and science at the ripe old age of 16.

BUILDING VOCABULARY

1. Use a dictionary to look up any unfamiliar words in the phrases below from Jacoby's essay. Then, write a short explanation of each expression.
   - **a.** sure footing (par. 3)
   - **b.** cultural expectations (par. 4)
   - **c.** overwhelming majority (par. 7)
   - **d.** male turf (par. 8)
   - **e.** spatial ability (par. 9)
   - **f.** the exclusive province (par. 14)
   - **g.** ominous, uninformed diatribes (par. 14)
   - **h.** acquiesce in that indulgence (par. 15)
   - **i.** ample evidence (par. 16)
   - **j.** our intellectual handicaps (par. 16)
2. Explain the *connotations* (see Glossary) that the following words have for you. Use each word correctly in a sentence of your own.
   - **a.** disability (par. 3)
   - **b.** conspire (par. 4)
   - **c.** adolescent (par. 4)
   - **d.** vulnerable (par. 6)
   - **e.** acute (par. 7)

THINKING CRITICALLY ABOUT THE ESSAY

Understanding the Writer's Ideas

1. What condition is Jacoby trying to analyze? Is the main *effect* analyzed in this cause-and-effect analysis? On what primary cause does she blame women's "scientific and mathematical ignorance"? What exactly does she mean by that term? How is society to blame? What is the "process" mentioned in paragraph 4? What point does the example of Rosalyn S. Yalow illustrate?
2. Why does Jacoby think that the greater proportion of women students now in science and medical graduate and professional schools does not really mean that there are many women working in these areas?

3. According to Jacoby, when do most girls decide not to study the sciences? Why does this happen?
4. What is "math anxiety"? Who suffers more from it—boys or girls? Why? What does the author mean by "brains" (par. 8)?
5. Who was Joseph Stalin (par. 7)?
6. What subjects does Jacoby identify as "feminine"? Which are "unfeminine"?
7. According to the research evidence discussed in paragraph 9, how do the math abilities of girls and boys change between ninth and tenth grades? What does Jacoby say is the *cause* of this change? What are the *results?*
8. Explain what Jacoby means by the expression "self-inflicted female wound" (par. 4) and "self-sabotage" (par. 10). How are these expressions similar? How are they different?
9. What is the difference between what men and women study at coeducational universities?
10. What does Jacoby mean by "mathematical and scientific illiteracy" (par. 12)? Do only women suffer from this syndrome? According to Jacoby, why does it lead to "an incalculably impoverished vision of human experience"? What does she mean by this phrase? What examples of scientific illiteracy does Jacoby offer?
11. Why does the author think women feel more helpless than men do about scientific changes?
12. What suggestion does Jacoby offer in her conclusion?

Understanding the Writer's Techniques

1. What is the thesis statement of this essay? Why is it placed where it is? Find another statement before it that expresses a similar cause-and-effect relation. How are the two different?
2. Which paragraphs make up the introductory section of this essay? What cause-and-effect relation does Jacoby establish and how does she present it? How does Jacoby use narration in her introduction? How does she use illustration?
3. Both sentences of paragraph 5 begin with the phrase "It is true," yet the sentences contradict each other. How and why does the author set up this contradiction? What is the effect on Jacoby's analysis of beginning paragraph 6 with the words "The real problem is . . ."?

4. How does she use *process analysis* (see pages 304–305) from paragraph 6 to paragraph 8?

5. Where does the author use definition in this essay?

6. Trace the cause-and-effect developments in paragraphs 7 and 8.

7. In paragraph 9, Jacoby mentions a study conducted under "a National Institute for Education grant." How does the evidence she presents support her position in the essay?

8. What is the effect of the phrase "in my experience" in paragraph 10? What expository technique does she use there?

9. Trace the cause-and-effect patterns in paragraphs 11 through 13. Be sure to show the interrelation between the causes and the effects (that is, how the effect of something can also be the cause of something else).

10. How is the first sentence of paragraph 15 ("Failure to comprehend. . . .") a good example in itself of cause-and-effect development?

11. Why does Jacoby use quotation marks around the words "masculine" and "feminine" in the phrase "'masculine' and 'feminine' knowledge" (par. 16)?

12. What is the overall tone of this essay? At three points, Jacoby switches tone and uses *irony* (see Glossary). Explain the irony in the following sentences.

   a. What does it matter if, at age 16, she has taken a step that may limit her understanding of both machines and the natural world for the rest of her life? (par. 2)

   b. The onset of acute math anxiety during the teen-age years is, as Stalin was fond of saying, "not by accident." (par. 7)

   c. Unless we want our daughters to share our intellectual handicaps, we had better tell them no, they can't stop taking mathematics and science at the ripe old age of 16. (par. 16)

   Compare the irony in paragraph 16 with that in paragraph 2. How is the impact the same or different?

13. Who do you think is the intended audience for this essay? Cite evidence for your answer.

14. Jacoby uses a variety of transitional devices to connect smoothly the ideas expressed in the various paragraphs of this essay. Look especially at paragraphs 1 to 4. How does the writer achieve coherence between paragraphs? What transitional elements do you find in the opening sentences of each of those paragraphs? What other transitions do you find throughout the essay?

Exploring the Writer's Ideas

1. One of the underlying suggestions in this essay is that society has long considered there to be "masculine" and "feminine" subjects to study. What is your opinion on this issue? Do you feel that any subjects are particularly more suited to men or women? Which? Why? Are there any other school activities that you feel are exclusively masculine or feminine? Why? Are there any jobs that are more suited to men or women?
2. In paragraph 4, Jacoby mentions the "old expectations about women's interests." What do you think these expectations are? What do you consider *new* expectations for women?
3. A *stereotype* is an opinion of a category of people that is unoriginal and often based on strong prejudices. For example, some prejudicial stereotypes include "All immigrants are lazy"; "All Republicans are rich"; "All women are terrible drivers." What other stereotypes do you know? Where do you think they originate?
4. The general implication of paragraph 8 is that people minimize their skills in order to be socially acceptable. In your experience, where have you seen this principle operating? Do you agree that people sometimes pretend to be unable to achieve something? What motivates them, do you think?
5. A recent study shows that among major nations in the world America's students—boys and girls—are the worst mathematics students. How do you account for the poor showing of Americans as mathematicians? How would you remedy this situation?

IDEAS FOR WRITING

Prewriting

Think about an activity that seems either male-friendly or female-friendly. Take complete notes on the reasons or causes that explain the situations.

Guided Writing

Select a job or profession that is usually male-dominated. Write a cause-and-effect analysis explaining how and why women both have been excluded from this profession and (or) have self-selected themselves from the job. (Some examples may include fire fighters, physicians, marines, bank executives, and carpenters.)

1. Begin with an anecdote to illustrate the condition that you are analyzing.
2. Present and analyze the partial causes of this condition that arise from society's expectations and norms.
3. State your main point clearly in a thesis statement.
4. Clearly identify what you consider "the real problem."
5. If you believe that women have deliberately excluded themselves, explain when and how the process of self-selection begins for women.
6. Analyze the consequences of this process of self-selection and give examples of the results of it.
7. Provide evidence that supports your analysis.
8. Link paragraphs with appropriate transitions.
9. In your conclusion offer a suggestion to change or improve this situation.

Thinking and Writing Collaboratively

Exchange a draft version of your Guided Writing assignment with a classmate. Review your partner's essay for its success in following the recommended guidelines. Is the thesis stated clearly? Are both the main causes and minor causes presented, and with sufficient evidence to support the analysis? Write a brief evaluation of the essay, with recommendations for revision, before returning it.

More Writing Projects

1. In your journal, make a list of everything that comes into your mind about the word "mathematics." Do not edit your writing. When you are finished, share your list with other people in the class. How do your impressions compare? contrast?

2. In a paragraph, analyze why you think boys and men exclude themselves from a certain field or profession—nursing, cooking, grammar-school teaching, and so on.
3. Margaret Mead, the famous anthropologist, once wrote, "Women in our society complain of the lack of stimulation, of the loneliness, of the dullness of staying at home." In an essay write a causal analysis of this situation.

SUMMING UP: CHAPTER 10

1. In her essay, Susan Jacoby analyzes a kind of "self-destructive behavior" on the part of many young women. Write an essay about a friend, relative, or someone else close to you who is doing something that you feel will have a very negative effect on him or her. Analyze *why* he or she is doing this and what effects, both short- and long-term, these actions are likely to have.
2. In this chapter, we hear female voices analyzing some of the experiences of women in American life today. Using their approaches to causal analysis, examine these experiences and the impact that they have had on your own thinking and activities. Clarify the connections between what you have read and how your sense of self has deepened or been sharpened.
3. Working in small groups, develop a questionnaire focusing on male and female roles in our society. After the questionnaire has been prepared, each group member should interview at least three people. When all the interviews have been completed, each group should write a collective analysis of the results and present the analysis to the class.
4. In this chapter, both Roiphe and Francke deal with various aspects of married life. If you are currently married, write an essay analyzing why you did (or did not) want to get married. If you are unmarried, analyze why you do (or do not) plan to get married.
5. For the next week, keep a journal about something that is currently causing you to have mixed emotions. (Note: This should not be the same issues you've written about in the Guided Writing exercises following the essays by Stephen King and Linda Bird Francke; it should be a *current* issue.) Try to write five reasons each day (or expand upon previous ones). At the end of the week, write an essay that analyzes how the issue is affecting your life or how you plan to deal with it in the future.

CHAPTER 11

Argumentation and Persuasion

WHAT ARE ARGUMENTATION AND PERSUASION?

When we use *argumentation,* we aim to convince someone to join our side of an issue. Often, we want the readers or listeners to change their views and adopt ours. We also use *persuasion* when we want a person to take action in a way that will advance our cause. In everyday life we hear the word "argument" used as a synonym for "fight." In writing, however, an argument is not a brawl but a kind of debate that requires subtle reasoning and careful use of the writers' tools you have learned so far. For this reason, we have put argumentation at the end of the writing course. In preparing your persuasive essay, you will be able to rehearse and refine the skills you have learned to this point.

The first step in arguing successfully is to state your position clearly. This means that a good thesis is crucial to your essay. For persuasive essays, the thesis is sometimes called a *major proposition.* This is an idea that can be debated or disputed, and the writer must take a definite side. Taking a strong position gives your essay its argumentative edge. Your readers must know what your position is, and must see that you have supported your main idea with convincing minor points. The weakest arguments are those in which the writer tries to take both sides, and as a result persuades no one. As you will see in the reading selections, writers often concede or yield a point to the opposition, but they do so only to strengthen the one side that they favor.

Writing arguments should make you even more aware of the need to think about audience. Since you already are convinced of the point you are presenting, your essay should focus on the people who will make up their minds on the basis of your evidence. Readers are not usually persuaded by assertion; you can't just tell them that something is true. You need to show them through well-organized support of main and minor points.

Evidence or support can come from many sources. Statistics, personal experience, historical events, news reports, and interviews can all serve to back up an argument. At the same time, a writer can use narrative, description, comparison and contrast, illustration, analysis, and definition to persuade.

Because we use argument in everyday life, we may think it is easy to argue in writing—but just the opposite is true. If we are arguing with someone in person, we can *see* our opponent's response, and quickly change our direction. In writing, we can only imagine the opponent and so must carefully prepare evidence for all possible responses. When we watch an argument on the evening news about abortion clinics, increasing the minimum wage, or accusations of sexual harassment, we often see only what media experts call "sound bites," tiny fragments of information. We may see just a slogan as a picket sign passes a camera. We may hear only a few sentences out of hours of testimony. We seldom see or hear the entire argument. When we turn to writing arguments ourselves, we need to remember to develop a complete and detailed and *rational* argument.

This does not mean that written arguments lack emotion. Rather, written argument channels that emotion into a powerful eloquence that can endure much longer than a shouting match.

In written arguments, the writer states the major proposition, or point he or she wants to make, and keeps it firmly in front of the reader. For example, a writer may want to argue that the U.S. government should grant amnesty to illegal aliens who have been in the country for at least two years. He may be writing to his member of Congress to persuade her to take action on a proposed bill. Once he knows his purpose and his audience, he is ready to plan an argument. Or the writer may want to convince readers that something is true—that single fathers make excellent parents, for example, or that wife abuse is an increasingly serious crime in our society. In this chapter, we discover Carole B.

Knight, a dairy farmer, arguing for the right to keep loaded guns in the house. Judy Brady offers a tongue-in-cheek plea for a wife. Mortimer B. Zuckerman tries to persuade us that we need more police. Finally, Jonathan Kozol advocates a more humane approach to the nation's homeless.

Whatever the writer's topic, the keys to a good argument are

- a clear and effective major proposition
- a logical tone
- an abundance of evidence
- an avoidance of personal attacks

HOW DO WE READ ARGUMENTS?

Try to find out something about the background and credentials of the writer. In what way is he or she an expert on the topic?

Is the proposition presented in a rational and logical way? Is it credible?

Has the writer presented ample reliable evidence to back up the proposition? (If you look at the headlines on supermarket tabloid newspapers that try to persuade us that aliens have been keeping Elvis Presley alive on Mars, you will see why it is important to be able to evaluate a writer's evidence before accepting the proposition!)

Does the writer focus on the main idea, or does the essay distract us with unrelated information?

HOW DO WE WRITE ARGUMENTS?

State a clear major proposition, and stick to it.

Convince readers of the validity of your thesis by making an essay plan that introduces *minor propositions.* These are assertions that help clarify the reasons you offer to support your main idea.

Use *refutation.* This is a technique to anticipate what an opponent will say, and answer the objection ahead of time. Another technique is *concession.* You yield a small point to your opponent, but at the same time claim a larger point on your own side. Using these techniques makes your argument seem fairer. You acknowledge that there *are* at least two sides to the issue.

Moreover, these devices help you make your own point more effectively.

Be aware of these pitfalls:

- Avoid personal attacks on your opponent, and don't let excessive appeals to emotion damage the tone of your argument.
- Avoid hasty generalization—that is, using main ideas without properly supporting them.
- Avoid drawing a conclusion that does not follow from the evidence in your argument.
- Avoid faulty analogies—that is, unequal comparisons.

Writing the Draft

Begin the rough draft. State your thesis boldly.

Back up all minor propositions with

statistics
facts
testimony from authorities
personal experience

Find a reliable listener and read your essay aloud. Encourage your listener to refute your points as strongly as possible.

Revise the essay, taking into account your listener's refutations. Find better support for your weakest points. Write a new draft.

Revise the essay carefully. Read it aloud again if possible. Prepare a final copy.

Don't Fence Me In

Carole B. Knight

Carole B. Knight is a dairy farmer who lives in Franklinton, Louisiana. She believes that even though everyone has a right to carry guns to protect their life and property, owning guns can actually make people, even neighbors, distrustful of one another.

PREREADING: THINKING ABOUT THE ESSAY IN ADVANCE

Do you trust your neighbors? Why or why not? Under what circumstances would you arm yourself against them?

Words to Watch

gauge (par. 1) the interior diameter of a shotgun barrel
vulnerability (par. 5) susceptibility to attack
perfunctory (par. 12) showing little interest or care
access (par. 12) the right to approach, enter, exit, or make use of

1 I just got a refresher lesson in how to shoot my 20-gauge shotgun. Not a happy prospect for a woman who works at home in what used to be perfect serenity. With three rural murders in less than a week, my actions are only reflective of those of my neighbors. A lot of loaded guns are propped in many kitchens tonight. It makes even civil discourse in this community quite dangerous, especially after dark.

2 I am not afraid, but I feel I have to prepare myself. The steel-and-wood beauty of the firearm I hope never to use sits within easy reach of the fingers that write on my computer screen. My son's weapon provides me some security if an event should require a response to save my life. It is loaded and ready, something impossible if there were children at home.

3 *Chamber the shell, disengage the safety, point, shoot.*

Dairy farmers, like most other farmers, live relatively isolated and sheltered lives. Our doors are unlocked, our lives and livelihoods somewhat dependent on the good will of perfect strangers. Distances to neighbors are measured in fractions of miles, not feet. We give little thought to physically securing our surroundings. 4

In my trusting nature lies my vulnerability. Farmers are accepting and trusting. But the shotgun murder of a neighbor dairyman in his barn as he was milking and another dairy couple murdered force me to re-examine my safety. The entire population of our rural town of 4,000 can talk of nothing else. For many, it's been a loss of innocence. 5

My husband and I are second-generation dairy farmers, fairly typical in a town whose only real industry is dairy farming. There are no corporate farms in this region, which is the milkshed for the New Orleans and Gulf Coast area. Of the close to 500 farms, all are family owned and operated. Most milk the black-and-white Holsteins, gentle giants who produce best when content and handled with love and care. Farmers dairy-farm in much the same way their fathers did. 6

The question of safety for rural residents is new and relatively unexplored. How can we protect our grazing cattle from random acts of violence along a highway? How can we protect ourselves and our families against strangers when the means of our livelihood—the land—must remain open? Dairying is a job done alone: milking, plowing and planting are all single-person tasks. Most family farms still manage to "harvest" the milk with a single person in the barn. Every farmer I know has at least one dog, more for company than assistance. The only known danger up until now has been an accidental injury to a farmer going undiscovered by others and becoming fatal. In one of these recent killings, the farmer was alone in his barn. The assailant knew he would be alone. The killer entered the barn and shot the dairyman with a gun like mine. The cows were mute witnesses to the killing and dying. It was predatory and anticipated solitude. 7

If I can't protect my dairy, then my home and my life are gone. I cannot, and will not, lock myself in. Our house was built in an era without great concern for break-ins: large windows on open porches, glass in the exterior doors, double deadlocks secured only at bedtime. My nearest neighbor is more than half a 8 mile away. What good is a lock except to slow an intruder and give me notice of hostile intent? For that I have my two trusty, alert dogs.

9 *The gun held securely at my waist. Generally directed at close range. Two shots of No. 4.*

10 Farming is a collaborative and inclusive way of life. Gates can be locked; fences cannot. Neighborliness continues to survive because of a stubborn refusal to accept that times have changed. Neighborliness still works, most of the time, so we are reluctant to part with it. On several occasions, strangers have driven to our house past midnight to report that some of the teenage heifers, with their almost human propensity to go where forbidden, have found a chink in the fence and are on the road, where they are a danger to themselves and travelers.

11 These are fearless people, approaching a dark house at night, announced by two large, noisy dogs bounding from under the house. We are very appreciative of their kindness and take for granted their fearlessness. (Though I'm not sure it's wise to visit a house, unasked, after dark right now.) When a neighbor lost his hay barn to fire and an entire season's hay with it, area farmers offered uncut fields for his use to replace as much of the hay as possible. Business arrangements are made over coffee, often absent even a handshake. Trust is integral, earned and expected.

12 This neighborly tradition carries over into milk marketing. The majority of dairymen have joined together in large cooperatives that move the milk to market. That's all at risk now. Now I'm inclined to answer only perfunctory questions of anyone entering the unlocked door. I'll reach for the gun in preparation—I can and I will use this tool. Shutting doors on danger is impossible. Milk inspectors, the feed and supply delivery trucks, semen deliverymen, the tanker driver who picks the milk up for the market. All must have open access to the barns. How to lock out some and not others?

13 Urban-style violence has, with its irrationality, visited our community. Death over a wallet; the murder of a husband and wife is under investigation. There is uncertainty and a need to feel—if not *be*—prepared for an element of violence. And there sits "my" gun, its barrel leaning near my computer screen. Is it a comfort? It is and it isn't—it reminds me of what I've lost. It's something others have lost earlier and what we all fear losing:

our sense of safety. No one is really safe from the vicissitudes of life, but we sometimes think we are.

As time passes, the gun will find its way again into its case under the guest-room bed. I fear its accidental discharge more than I fear a phantom criminal. This cautionary attitude will pass, partly because that is what I wish. At least I have that hope; I know many others who do not. Losing that sense of personal security is a major deprivation. It makes us less civil and then less civilized. And the failure of civilization is at the heart of the pointless violence that is the greatest of all our fears. 14

BUILDING VOCABULARY

1. Examine the contexts in which the following words are used in Knight's essay. Then try to write definitions for the words. Check your definitions against the definitions in the dictionary.
   a. prospect (par. 1)
   b. solitude (par. 7)
   c. range (par. 9)
   d. heifers (par. 10)
   e. vicissitudes (par. 13)

2. Use each of the above words in a sentence.

THINKING CRITICALLY ABOUT THE ESSAY

Understanding the Writer's Ideas

1. Historically, what kind of community has the writer's been?
2. What kind of farming is the writer engaged in? Where are the farms?
3. Why does the writer decide to load and carry a gun?
4. What does the writer mean by "Shutting doors on danger is impossible" (par. 12)?
5. Explain the heart of the writer's final point.

Understanding the Writer's Techniques

1. The author refers to two incidents (par. 5) to begin the argument that her farm community needs to arm itself. In your words, summarize the incidents and their relationship to the writer's thesis.
2. To whom does Knight direct her argument? Is she trying to persuade her neighbors or her readers to give up guns?
3. Make an outline of the key points that the writer makes to support her argument.
4. Where does the writer tell her readers how to solve the problem?
5. What tone does Knight use in her argument?
6. Is Knight's tone appropriate for persuading people? Or is she not forceful enough? Explain.

Exploring the Writer's Ideas

1. Many Americans believe that the right to carry a gun is constitutional. How do you think Knight would respond to this? Is she trying to deny our legal right to own a gun?
2. Do you live in a rural or urban community? How secure do people feel in your community? Why?
3. Knight does not refer to the role the police should play in securing the community. Does this weaken or strengthen her argument? Are police an important factor in making a community feel safe? Why or why not?

IDEAS FOR WRITING

Prewriting

Make notes on where you think violence is most apparent in American life.

Guided Writing

Write an argumentative essay in which you propose some changes in our society to reduce America's violent crime rate. You might propose a community program to help troubled youth, for example.

1. Write a thesis statement and place it in the first paragraph. Use the introduction to explain how this issue has affected you personally.
2. Use the library to find examples of how other communities have successfully fought crime.
3. Introduce your reasons for your proposed change, placing each reason in a separate body paragraph.
4. Conclude by persuading your readers that only by using the approach you recommend will America become safer.
5. Keep in mind your audience and the tone that will be most persuasive.

Thinking and Writing Collaboratively

In groups of three to four students, prepare notes and write an essay that argues this point: Budget cutbacks in educational systems are making it harder for young people to feel safe in schools and on campuses.

More Writing Projects

1. In your journal, describe a situation where you saw a better way to do something and tried to persuade someone to listen to you.
2. Write a paragraph in which you argue for or against a college policy.
3. Write an essay that argues for or against college affirmative action programs. (Use the library if need be.)

I Want a Wife

Judy Brady

Judy Brady, a wife and mother of two children, argues in this essay for a wife of her own. Although her argument might seem strange, her position will become apparent once you move into the essay. She presents many points to support her position, so you want to keep in mind those you think are the strongest.

PREREADING: THINKING ABOUT THE ESSAY IN ADVANCE

As you prepare to read this satirical essay, consider the traditional roles that men and women play in their mutual relationships. What is expected conventionally of a husband? of a wife? Do you accept these roles? Why or why not?

Words to Watch

nurturant (par. 3) giving affectionate care and attention

hors d'oeuvres (par. 6) food served before the regular courses of the meal

monogamy (par. 8) the habit of having only one mate; the practice of marrying only once during life

1 I belong to that classification of people known as wives. I am A Wife. And, not altogether incidentally, I am a mother.

2 Not too long ago a male friend of mine appeared on the scene fresh from a recent divorce. He had one child, who is, of course, with his ex-wife. He is obviously looking for another wife. As I thought about him while I was ironing one evening, it suddenly occurred to me that I, too, would like to have a wife. Why do I want a wife?

3 I would like to go back to school so that I can become economically independent, support myself, and, if need be, support those dependent upon me. I want a wife who will work and send me to school. And while I am going to school I want a wife to

keep track of the children's doctor and dentist appointments. And to keep track of mine, too. I want a wife to make sure my children eat properly and are kept clean. I want a wife who will wash the children's clothes and keep them mended. I want a wife who is a good nurturant attendant to my children, who arranges for their schooling, makes sure that they have an adequate social life with their peers, takes them to the park, the zoo, etc. I want a wife who takes care of the children when they are sick, a wife who arranges to be around when the children need special care, because, of course, I cannot miss classes at school. My wife must arrange to lose time at work and not lose the job. It may mean a small cut in my wife's income from time to time, but I guess I can tolerate that. Needless to say, my wife will arrange and pay for the care of the children while my wife is working.

I want a wife who will take care of *my* physical needs. I 4
want a wife who will keep my house clean. A wife who will pick up after me. I want a wife who will keep my clothes clean, ironed, mended, replaced when need be, and who will see to it that my personal things are kept in their proper place so that I can find what I need the minute I need it. I want a wife who cooks the meals, a wife who is a *good* cook. I want a wife who will plan the menus, do the necessary grocery shopping, prepare the meals, serve them pleasantly, and then do the cleaning up while I do my studying. I want a wife who will care for me when I am sick and sympathize with my pain and loss of time from school. I want a wife to go along when our family takes a vacation so that someone can continue to care for me and my children when I need a rest and change of scene.

I want a wife who will not bother me with rambling com- 5
plaints about a wife's duties. But I want a wife who will listen to me when I feel the need to explain a rather difficult point I have come across in my course of studies. And I want a wife who will type my papers for me when I have written them.

I want a wife who will take care of the details of my social 6
life. When my wife and I are invited out by my friends, I want a wife who will take care of the babysitting arrangements. When I meet people at school that I like and want to entertain, I want a wife who will have the house clean, will prepare a special meal, serve it to me and my friends, and not interrupt when I talk about the things that interest me and my friends. I want a wife who will

have arranged that the children are fed and ready for bed before my guests arrive so that the children do not bother us. I want a wife who takes care of the needs of my guests so that they feel comfortable, who makes sure that they have an ashtray, that they are passed the hors d'oeuvres, that they are offered a second helping of the food, that their wine glasses are replenished when necessary, that their coffee is served to them as they like it.

7 And I want a wife who knows that sometimes I need a night out by myself.

8 I want a wife who is sensitive to my sexual needs, a wife who makes love passionately and eagerly when I feel like it, a wife who makes sure that I am satisfied. And, of course, I want a wife who will not demand sexual attention when I am not in the mood for it. I want a wife who assumes the complete responsibility for birth control, because I do not want more children. I want a wife who will remain sexually faithful to me so that I do not have to clutter up my intellectual life with jealousies. And I want a wife who understands that *my* sexual needs may entail more than strict adherence to monogamy. I must, after all, be able to relate to people as fully as possible.

9 If, by chance, I find another person more suitable as a wife than the wife I already have, I want the liberty to replace my present wife with another one. Naturally, I will expect a fresh, new life; my wife will take the children and be solely-responsible for them so that I am left free.

10 When I am through with school and have a job, I want my wife to quit working and remain at home so that my wife can more fully and completely take care of a wife's duties.

11 My God, who *wouldn't* want a wife?

BUILDING VOCABULARY

1. After checking a dictionary, write definitions of each of these words.
   a. attendant (par. 3)
   b. adequate (par. 3)
   c. peers (par. 3)
   d. tolerate (par. 3)
   e. rambling (par. 5)

   f. replenished (par. 6)
   g. adherence (par. 8)
2. Write an original sentence for each word above.

THINKING CRITICALLY ABOUT THE ESSAY

Understanding the Writer's Ideas

1. What incident made Brady think about wanting a wife?
2. How would a wife help the writer achieve economic independence?
3. In what ways would a wife take care of the writer's children? Why would the writer like someone to assume those responsibilities?
4. What physical needs would Brady's "wife" take care of?
5. How would a wife deal with the writer's social life? Her sex life?

Understanding the Writer's Techniques

1. In formal argumentation, we often call the writer's main point the *major* or *main proposition.* What is Brady's major proposition? Is it simply what she says in paragraph 2, or is the proposition more complex than that? State it in your own words.
2. What is the value of the question Brady asks in paragraph 2? Where else does she ask a question? What value does this other question have in its place in the essay? What impact does it have on the reader?
3. The points a writer offers to support the major proposition are called *minor propositions.* What minor propositions does Brady present to show why she wants a wife? In which instances do they serve as topic sentences within paragraphs? What details does she offer to illustrate those minor propositions?
4. In what order has the writer chosen to arrange the minor propositions? Why has she chosen such an order? Do you think she builds from the least to the most important reasons for having a wife? What changes would you urge in the order of the minor propositions?

5. Most of the paragraphs here develop through illustration. Where has Brady used a simple listing of details? Why has she chosen that format?
6. Brady's style is obviously straightforward, her sentences for the most part simple and often brief. Why has she chosen such a style? What is the effect of the repetition of "I want" at the start of so many sentences? Why has Brady used several short paragraphs (1, 7, 10, 11) in addition to longer ones?
7. What is the author's *tone* (see Glossary)? Point out the uses of *irony* (see Glossary) in the essay. How does irony contribute to Brady's main intent in this essay? How does the fact that Brady is a woman contribute to this sense of irony?

Exploring the Writer's Ideas

1. By claiming that she wants a wife, Brady is showing us all the duties and responsibilities of the woman in a contemporary household. Has Brady represented these duties fairly? Do husbands generally expect their wives to do all these things?
2. To what degree do wives today fit Brady's description? How could a wife avoid many of the responsibilities spelled out in the essay? How does the "modern husband" figure in the way many couples meet household responsibilities now?
3. Brady has characterized all the traditional and stereotyped roles usually assigned to wives. What "wifely responsibilities" has she left out?
4. Has Brady presented a balanced picture of the issues or is her argument one-sided? Support your opinion with specific references to the essay. Could the author have dealt effectively with opposing arguments? Why or why not? What might these opposing arguments be?
5. Answer the question in the last line of the essay.
6. Read the essays "Night Walker" by Brent Staples (pages 165–168) and "How Do We Find the Student in a World of Academic Gymnasts and Worker Ants?" by James T. Baker (pages 294–298). Compare the use of stereotyping in these essays. How is it different from Brady's stereotypes?

IDEAS FOR WRITING

Prewriting

Freewrite for fifteen minutes about why you want a husband or wife, trying to poke fun at or ridicule (as Brady does) the traditional expectations that we bring to this issue.

Guided Writing

Write an essay of 750 to 1,000 words titled, "I Want a Husband."

1. Write the essay from the point of view of a *man.* As Brady wrote as a woman who wanted a wife, you write this essay as a man who wants a husband.
2. Start your essay with a brief personal story as in paragraph 2 of "I Want a Wife."
3. Support your main point with a number of minor points. Expand each minor point with details that explain your premises.
4. Arrange your minor premises carefully so that you build to the most convincing point at the end.
5. Use a simple and straightforward style. Connect your points with transitions; use repetition as one transitional device.
6. Balance your longer paragraphs with occasional shorter ones.
7. End your essay with a crisp, one-sentence question of your own.

Thinking and Writing Collaboratively

Divide the class into one group consisting entirely of males and the other of females. Working in these groups, have the men list the advantages of having a husband, and the women list the advantages of having a wife. Each group should list its key advantages on the chalkboard for class discussion.

More Writing Projects

1. In your journal, copy any three sentences from Brady's essay that you find particularly provocative, challenging, strange, or unbelievable. Explain why you chose them.

2. Write a paragraph in which you argue *for* or *against* this issue: "A married woman belongs at home."
3. Write an essay in which you argue about whose role you think is harder to play effectively in today's society: the role of the mother or the role of the father.

The Case for More Cops

Mortimer B. Zuckerman

Journalist Mortimer B. Zuckerman, editor-in-chief of *U.S. News & World Report,* takes the position that we are not yet fully aware that we are at war in America. But once we realize that we have been invaded, he feels his solution is the one we need to consider if we want to win any battles. The culprit? Crime.

PREREADING: THINKING ABOUT THE ESSAY IN ADVANCE

How can the police provide security to people living in crime-ridden communities? Discuss with peers.

Words to Watch

probation (par. 1) the act of suspending the sentence of a person convicted of a criminal offense and granting that person provisional freedom on the promise of good behavior

ROTC (par. 4) officer training program

Congress (par. 5) the national legislative body of the United States, consisting of the Senate and the House of Representatives

We have crime without punishment in America. The probability that a violent criminal or even a violent repeat offender will go to prison and spend most of his time behind bars is only one fifth of what it was in 1960. Fewer than 10 percent of burglaries result in an arrest, barely 1.2 percent in imprisonment. Convicted criminals serve only about a third of their sentences. It is a staggering fact that we have about 3 million of them on the streets without serious probation or police supervision. A rapist averages five years, a convicted murderer just 10 years. Homicide arrests as a share of all murders have declined from 95 percent a decade ago to 50 percent today. 1

Everyone knows there is a complex of real, not fanciful, causes for all this: Understaffed police forces, soft courts, over- 2 crowded prisons, the epidemic of drugs and the breakdown of the family. But not many people realize just how thin the "thin blue line" has become. Forty years ago, there were 3.2 police officers for every violent felony reported. Today there are 3.2 times the number of violent felonies for every serving officer. In big cities the ratios are worse. In New York it is 6.5 violent felonies per cop, in Boston 6.9; in Los Angeles, Newark and Atlanta it is 10. This calculation does not include the much greater number of unreported felonies or the smaller fraction of police who are on the streets at any one time. Here is a stunning fact: Eighty-three percent of Americans can expect to be victims of a crime at least once in their lifetime.

3 How would you like to return to the police–violent-crime ratios of 40 years ago, when there was a wholly different sense of security? Given the 544,000 cops that we have today, we would have to increase the number of cops to about 5 million. That is the breathtaking measure of the hold crime has on our society. The wealthy are driven to hire private police; the ordinary public is driven only to despair. There are now 1.5 million private security guards in America. We spend almost twice as much on private police as we do on public police. According to Princeton University's John J. DiIulio, we spend seven times more on transportation and 12 times more on public welfare than we do on criminal justice activities—cops, courts and corrections.

4 We need more police to police America. Five million is beyond what we can hope to do, but we can build much bigger and better forces. Two generations ago, most police officers got their first training in the military, where they served before joining the force. Not so today. Given the downsizing of our military, we should find a way to hire these trained, disciplined military personnel as cops. We should also support the notion of a Police Corps as a supplement to the regular police. These are young people who would be recruited on the ROTC principle, receiving four-year scholarships and repaying the country for this benefit with four years of service as local police officers.

5 To this we must add at least the 100,000 police called for in the Senate version of the crime bill before Congress, rather than the 50,000 in the House version. This number may be just a down payment on the police we will need to regain control of high-crime streets, communities and classrooms, and to prevent violence and disorder from seeping into those neighborhoods that

are now relatively peaceful. Congress, which is demanding that local communities pay a portion of the cost of this program, should be careful not to overburden communities with the cost of matching requirements. It is important that there be wide national participation and that it last beyond the first city budget.

We are at war today. The enemy is the criminal. Were we to 6 be invaded by a foreign enemy this lethal, we would not be debating if we could afford the soldiers and weapons to defend ourselves. We would spend what is necessary to win the war. Restoring public order and individual security would be the first national priority—not in the future, but today. So must it be with the fight against crime. Only more police and an enhanced certainty of punishment can have the immediate impact we need. Only then can social programs contribute to longer-term solutions. Government must do the one thing people cannot do on their own—provide real security and protection.

BUILDING VOCABULARY

Write sentences in which you use the following words correctly.

a. fanciful (par. 2)
b. epidemic (par. 2)
c. supplement (par. 4)
d. lethal (par. 6)

THINKING CRITICALLY ABOUT THE ESSAY

Understanding the Writer's Ideas

1. Are criminals being punished in ways that will keep them from repeating their offenses?
2. Despite all the political talk on reducing crime, have police forces grown in strength or effectiveness?
3. What kind of response have the wealthy had to the lack of public security?
4. What solution does the writer offer to increase the police force without much cost to a community?
5. What does the writer mean when he states, "We are at war"? Is the writer serious? Why or why not?

Understanding the Writer's Techniques

1. What is the thesis? Would you consider it the major proposition? Explain.
2. What statistics does the writer use? How do these contribute to the effectiveness of the argument?
3. What is the tone of the selection? Would you call it serious or relaxed? Defend your choice.
4. Do you think the writer had an audience of police in mind when he wrote this essay? Keep in mind the magazine where the essay appeared *(U.S. News & World Report).*
5. Comment on the word "Case" in the title. This has a legal meaning, too. Why did the writer choose this word?

Exploring the Writer's Ideas

1. The essay's first sentence makes the bold statement that we "have crime without punishment." Yet statistics also show that prisons are overcrowded. Is the writer wrong? Explain.
2. Is it fair that the wealthy pay for their own security but people who depend on public security must do with less? How do you feel?
3. While a police corps sounds like a good idea, many police officers fear that unpaid workers will create unemployment. Also, a police corps will limit well-paying jobs for those young people interested in a career in law enforcement. Take a position and support it.
4. This writer seems to think that social programs (e.g., job training) won't lessen crime as much as a war on crime. But some argue that crime grows out of the lack of social programs. Are more police the answer? Which side are you on? Why?

IDEAS FOR WRITING

Prewriting

Who do you think has been undervalued in this society? Freewrite in your journal.

Guided Writing

Write an essay called "The Case for __________." Fill in the blank with a word or term that names a group you feel has been ignored, overlooked, or undervalued in our society. You might want to use a term like "jocks," "loners," or "teachers."

1. Write an introduction to set the stage for your argument. Develop a major proposition and state it in your thesis. Place your thesis in a key position in the essay.
2. Use specific examples to support your major proposition.
3. Develop a clear sense of whom your audience is and direct your argument to that group.
4. Draw on other rhetorical strategies as needed: comparison, causal analysis, process, and so forth.
5. Develop a conclusion that clearly warns the reader of the consequences that will follow if he or she doesn't accept the major premise of your argument.

Thinking and Writing Collaboratively

Form groups of three to four class members. As a group, take a position for or against an issue important to your school or community. Then argue the opposite view of the position most people in the group favor. Write an essay that ultimately reflects both views. Conclude your essay by establishing which argument is the strongest.

More Writing Projects

1. In your journal, make a list of everything that comes to mind with the word *rich.*
2. Using the above journal entry, write one paragraph that argues for or against making rich people pay more for social services than others.
3. Choose a topic that focuses on a headline issue in the news and write an essay that argues for a position you feel strongly about. Consider environmental issues or the abortion debate.

Are the Homeless Crazy?

Jonathan Kozol

Jonathan Kozol is an educator and writer on social issues who, until recently, was perhaps best known for his book-length study *Why Children Fail.* In the past few years, he has turned his attention to America's ever-increasing problem of homelessness. In 1988, he published the book *Rachel and Her Children* on the subject, along with this essay, which derives from "Distancing the Homeless," published in the *Yale Review.* In this essay, Kozol effectively challenges the common idea that much of today's homelessness has resulted from the release of patients from mental hospitals in the 1970s. Instead, he presents a convincing argument that the "deinstitutionalizing" explanation is a self-serving myth, and that the reality is much simpler: Homelessness is caused by insufficient and overly expensive housing.

PREREADING: THINKING ABOUT THE ESSAY IN ADVANCE

Do you have strong opinions about the homeless in American society? Should they be classified as crazy, lazy, or abject failures? Why or why not?

Words to Watch

deinstitutionalized (par. 1) let inmates out of hospitals, prisons, and so forth

conceding (par. 2) acknowledging; admitting to

arson (par. 4) the crime of deliberately setting a fire

subsidized (par. 5) aided with public money

destitute (par. 6) very poor

afflictions (par. 7) ills; problems

stigma (par. 7) a mark of shame or discredit

complacence (par. 7) self-satisfaction

bulk (par. 10) the main part

de facto (par. 11) actually; in reality

resilience (par. 12) ability to recover easily from misfortune

paranoids (par. 13) psychotic people who believe everyone is persecuting them

vengeance (par. 14) retribution; retaliation

It is commonly believed by many journalists and politicians that the homeless of America are, in large part, former patients of large mental hospitals who were deinstitutionalized in the 1970s—the consequence, it is sometimes said, of misguided liberal opinion that favored the treatment of such persons in community-based centers. It is argued that this policy, and the subsequent failure of society to build such centers or to provide them in sufficient number, is the primary cause of homelessness in the United States. 1

Those who work among the homeless do not find that explanation satisfactory. While conceding that a certain number of the homeless are or have been mentally unwell, they believe that, in the case of most unsheltered people, the primary reason is economic rather than clinical. The cause of homelessness, they say with disarming logic, is the lack of homes and of income with which to rent or acquire them. 2

They point to the loss of traditional jobs in industry (2 million every year since 1980) and to the fact that half of those who are laid off end up in work that pays a poverty-level wage. They point out that since 1968 the number of children living in poverty has grown by 3 million, while welfare benefits to families with children have declined by 35 percent. 3

And they note, too, that these developments have occurred during a time in which the shortage of low-income housing has intensified as the gentrification of our major cities has accelerated. Half a million units of low-income housing are lost each year to condominium conversion as well as to arson, demolition, or abandonment. Between 1978 and 1980, median rents climbed 30 percent for people in the lowest income sector, driving many of these families into the streets. Since 1980, rents have risen at even faster rates. 4

Hard numbers, in this instance, would appear to be of greater help than psychiatric labels in telling us why so many people become homeless. Eight million American families now use half or more of their income to pay their rent or mortgage. At 5 the same time, federal support for low-income housing dropped from $30 billion (1980) to $7.5 billion (1988). Under Presidents Ford and Carter, 500,000 subsidized private housing units were constructed. By President Reagan's second term, the number had dropped to 25,000.

6 In our rush to explain the homeless as a psychiatric problem even the words of medical practitioners who care for homeless people have been curiously ignored. A study published by the Massachusetts Medical Society, for instance, has noted that, with the exceptions of alcohol and drug use, the most frequent illnesses among a sample of the homeless population were trauma (31 percent), upper-respiratory disorders (28 percent), limb disorders (19 percent), mental illness (16 percent), skin diseases (15 percent), hypertension (14 percent), and neurological illnesses (12 percent). Why, we may ask, of all these calamities, does mental illness command so much political and press attention? The answer may be that the label of mental illness places the destitute outside the sphere of ordinary life. It personalizes an anguish that is public in its genesis; it individualizes a misery that is both general in cause and general in application.

7 There is another reason to assign labels to the destitute and single out mental illness from among their many afflictions. All these other problems—tuberculosis, asthma, scabies, diarrhea, bleeding gums, impacted teeth, etc.—bear no stigma, and mental illness does. It conveys a stigma in the United States. It conveys a stigma in the Soviet Union as well. In both nations the label is used, whether as a matter of deliberate policy or not, to isolate and treat as special cases those who, by deed or word or by sheer presence, represent a threat to national complacence. The two situations are obviously not identical, but they are enough alike to give Americans reason for concern.

8 The notion that the homeless are largely psychotics who belong in institutions, rather than victims of displacement at the hands of enterprising realtors, spares us from the need to offer realistic solutions to the deep and widening extremes of wealth and poverty in the United States. It also enables us to tell ourselves that the despair of homeless people bears no intimate connection to the privileged existence we enjoy—when, for example, we rent or purchase one of those restored town houses that once provided shelter for people now huddled in the street.

What is to be made, then, of the supposition that the homeless are primarily the former residents of mental hospitals, persons who were carelessly released during the 1970s? Many of them are, to be sure. Among the older men and women in the streets and shelters, as many as one-third (some believe as many as one-half) may be chronically disturbed, and a number of these people were deinstitutionalized during the 1970s. But to operate on that assumption in a city such as New York—where nearly half the homeless are small children whose average age is six—makes no sense. Their parents, with an average age of twenty-seven, are not likely to have been hospitalized in the 1970s, either. 9

A frequently cited set of figures tells us that in 1955 the average daily census of non-federal psychiatric institutions was 677,000, and that by 1984 the number had dropped to 151,000. But these people didn't go directly from a hospital room to the street. The bulk of those who had been psychiatric patients and were released from hospitals during the 1960s and early 1970s had been living in low-income housing, many in skid-row hotels or boardinghouses. Such housing—commonly known as SRO (single-room occupancy) units—was drastically diminished by the gentrification of our cities that began in the early '70s. Almost 50 percent of SRO housing was replaced by luxury apartments or office buildings between 1970 and 1980, and the remaining units have been disappearing even more rapidly. 10

Even for those persons who are ill and were deinstitutionalized during the decades before 1980, the precipitating cause of homelessness in 1987 is not illness but loss of housing. SRO housing offered low-cost sanctuaries for the homeless, providing a degree of safety and mutual support for those who lived within them. They were a demeaning version of the community health centers that society had promised; they were the de facto "halfway houses" of the 1970s. For these people too—at most half of the homeless single persons in America—the cause of homelessness is lack of housing. 11

Even in those cases where mental instability is apparent, homelessness itself is often the precipitating factor. For example, many pregnant women without homes are denied prenatal care because they constantly travel from one shelter to another. Many are anemic. Many are denied essential dietary supplements by recent federal cuts. As a consequence, some of their children do 12 not live to see their second year of life. Do these mothers sometimes show signs of stress? Do they appear disorganized, depressed, disordered? Frequently. They are immobilized by pain, traumatized by fear. So it is no surprise that when researchers enter the scene to ask them how they "feel," the resulting reports tell us that the homeless are emotionally unwell. The reports do not tell us that we have *made* these people ill. They do not tell us that illness is a natural response to intolerable conditions. Nor do they tell us of the strength and the resilience that so many of these people retain despite the miseries they must endure.

13 A writer in the *New York Times* describes a homeless woman standing on a traffic island in Manhattan. "She was evicted from her small room in the hotel just across the street," and she is determined to get revenge. Until she does, "nothing will move her from that spot. . . . Her argumentativeness and her angry fixation on revenge, along with the apparent absence of hallucinations, mark her as a paranoid." Most physicians, I imagine, would be more reserved in passing judgment with so little evidence, but this reporter makes his diagnosis without hesitation. "The paranoids of the street," he says, "are among the most difficult to help."

14 Perhaps so. But does it depend on who is offering the help? Is anyone offering to help this woman get back her home? Is it crazy to seek vengeance for being thrown into the street? The absence of anger, some psychiatrists believe, might indicate much greater illness.

15 "No one will be turned away," says the mayor of New York City, as hundreds of young mothers with their infants are turned from the doors of shelters season after season. That may sound to some like a denial of reality. "Now you're hearing all kinds of horror stories," says the President of the United States as he denies that anyone is cold or hungry or unhoused. On another occasion he says that the unsheltered "are homeless, you might say, by choice." That sounds every bit as self-deceiving.

16 The woman standing on the traffic island screaming for revenge until her room has been restored to her sounds relatively healthy by comparison. If 3 million homeless people did the same, and all at the same time, we might finally be forced to listen.

BUILDING VOCABULARY

1. Throughout this essay, Kozol uses medical and psychiatric *jargon* (see Glossary). List the medical or psychiatric terms or references that you find here. Then look up any five in the dictionary and write definitions for them.

2. Explain in your own words the meanings of the following phrases. Use clues from the surrounding text to help you understand.

a. sufficient number (par. 1)
b. primary cause (par. 1)
c. poverty-level wage (par. 3)
d. median rents (par. 4)
e. low-income housing (par. 5)
f. sheer presence (par. 7)
g. intimate connection (par. 8)
h. chronically disturbed (par. 9)
i. skid-row hotels (par. 10)
j. precipitating cause (par. 11)
k. low-cost sanctuaries (par. 11)
l. mutual support (par. 11)
m. demeaning version (par. 11)
n. natural response (par. 12)
o. intolerable conditions (par. 12)
p. angry fixation (par. 13)

THINKING CRITICALLY ABOUT THE ESSAY

Understanding the Writer's Ideas

1. According to Kozol, who has suggested that the deinstitutionalizing of mental-hospital patients is the major cause of homelessness? Does he agree? If not, what does he identify as the major causes?

2. In the opening paragraph, what two groups does Kozol link together? Why? What relation between them does he suggest?

3. In New York City today, what percentage of the homeless are children? What is the average age of their parents? In the past twenty years, has the number of children living in poverty increased or decreased? What about welfare payments to families with children? How has this affected the homelessness situation?

4. What are "gentrification" and "condominium conversion" (par. 4)? How have they affected homelessness?
5. Explain the meaning of the statement: "Hard numbers, in this instance, would appear to be of greater help than psychiatric labels in telling us why so many people become homeless" (par. 5).
6. List in descending order the most common illnesses among the homeless. From what does Kozol draw these statistics? What is his conclusion about them?
7. In your own words, summarize why Kozol feels that journalists and politicians concentrate so heavily on the problems of mental illness among the homeless.
8. What are SROs? Explain how they figure in the homeless situation.
9. What is meant by the "press" (par. 6)? What are "halfway houses" (par. 11)?
10. What is Kozol's attitude toward former President Reagan? toward former New York City Mayor Ed Koch? Explain your answers with specific references to the beginning and ending of the essay.
11. Summarize in your own words the *New York Times* story to which Kozol refers. According to the *Times* reporter, why did the homeless woman mentioned refuse to move from the traffic island? Does Kozol agree with the reporter's interpretation? Explain.
12. In one sentence, state in your own words the opinion Kozol expresses in the last paragraph.

Understanding the Writer's Techniques

1. Which sentence states the *major proposition* of the essay?
2. Describe Kozol's argumentative purpose in this essay. Is it primarily to *convince* or to *persuade?* Explain.
3. In paragraph 1, the author uses a particular verbal construction that he doesn't repeat elsewhere in the essay. He writes: "It is commonly believed . . ."; "it is sometimes said . . .";

and "It is argued. . . ." Why does he use the "it is" construction? What effect does it have? How does he change that pattern in paragraph 2? Why?

4. In paragraph 2, Kozol uses the phrase "mentally unwell" instead of the more common "mentally ill," and he uses "unsheltered people" instead of "homeless people." Why does he use these less-expected phrases? Does he use them again in the essay? Why?
5. *Cynicism* adds an edge of pessimism or anger to a statement that might otherwise be perceived as *irony* (see Glossary). In the sentence, "The cause of homelessness, they say with disarming logic, is the lack of homes and of income with which to rent or acquire them" (par. 2), the clause set off by commas might be considered cynical. Why? Find and explain several other examples of cynicism in this essay. Are they effective? Are they justified?
6. Identify the *minor proposition* statements in this essay. How do they add *coherence* (see Glossary) to the essay?
7. How important is Kozol's use of *statistics* in this essay? Which are the most effective? Why?
8. What is the difference between *refutation* (see Glossary) and *negation* (see page 234)? Kozol uses refutation as a major technique in this essay. Analyze his use of refutation in paragraphs 1 and 2. List and discuss at least three other instances where he uses refutation. Where in the essay does he specifically use negation?
9. Evaluate Kozol's use of *cause-and-effect analysis* in paragraphs 1 through 6. In paragraph 12, how does Kozol revise the more commonly cited causal relationship between homelessness and mental illness?
10. Discuss Kozol's use of *comparison* in paragraph 7.
11. In what ways does he use *illustration?* How is his use of illustration in the last paragraph different from his other uses of it?
12. Characterize the overall *tone* of the essay. *How* does Kozol develop this tone? *Why* does he develop it?
13. Who is the intended *audience* for this essay? What is the *level of diction?* How are the two connected? What assumption about the audience is implied in the last sentence of paragraph 8?

14. Writers often use *rhetorical questions* in order to prompt the reader to pay special attention to an issue, but rhetorical questions are usually not meant to be answered. Evaluate Kozol's use of rhetorical questions in paragraph 12. What is the effect of the one-word answer, "Frequently"? Where else does he use rhetorical questions? What message does he attempt to convey with them?
15. Returning to the thesis in the course of an essay is often an effective technique to refocus the reader's attention before beginning a new analysis or a conclusion. Explain how Kozol uses this technique in paragraph 11 to make it a key turning point in the essay.
16. Although Kozol cites various studies and authorities, he makes little use of *direct quotations*. Why? Identify and analyze the three instances where he *does* use direct quotations. How does it help to convey his attitude toward the material he's quoting?
17. Evaluate Kozol's conclusion. How does he establish an aura of unreality in paragraphs 15 and 16? Why does he do so? Does he effectively answer the title question? Explain.

Exploring the Writer's Ideas

1. In small groups, discuss your own experiences, both positive and negative, with homeless people.
2. If possible, conduct an interview with one or more homeless people. Try to find out:
   - **a.** how they became homeless
   - **b.** how long they've been homeless
   - **c.** what they do to survive
   - **d.** whether they feel there may be an end to their homelessness

   Write a report based on your interviews and share it with your classmates.
3. This essay is an excerpt from a much longer essay entitled "Distancing the Homeless," published in the *Yale Review*. How is the theme of that title expressed in this essay?
4. Kozol presents an impressive array of statistics. Working in small groups, compile as many other statistics about homelessness as possible. Each group should then draw a subjective

conclusion from the data and be prepared to present and defend it to the class as a whole.

5. Read the following description of New York City's Bowery district:

> Walk under the El at night and all you feel is a sort of cold guilt. Touched for a dime, you try to drop the coin and not touch the hand, because the hand is dirty; you try to avoid the glance, because the glance accuses. This is not so much personal menace as universal—the cold menace of unresolved human suffering and poverty and the advanced stages of the disease alcoholism. On a summer night the drunks sleep in the open. The sidewalk is a free bed, and there are no lice. Pedestrians step along and over and around the still forms as though walking on a battlefield among the dead. In doorways, on the steps of the savings bank, the bums lie sleeping it off. Standing sentinel at each sleeper's head is the empty bottle from which he drained his release. Wedged in the crook of his arm is the paper bag containing his things.

This description is from E. B. White's 1949 essay "Here Is New York," the same essay from which the selection "The Three New Yorks" (pages 282–284) is drawn. It is but one small indication that the current problem of homelessness is nothing new. Try to find other examples, either written or visual, that indicate that homelessness is a long-standing social issue. (You may want to contact such organizations as the Coalition for the Homeless and the Salvation Army.)

In your own experience, how have the conditions of homelessness changed in your own environment over the past five years? The past one year?

IDEAS FOR WRITING

Prewriting

Draft a brief outline arguing for or against a specific issue of campus concern—for example, date rape, political correctness, drugs, or AIDS counseling. In your outline, list at least three main reasons that support the position you are advocating.

Guided Writing

Choose a controversial local issue about which you hold a strong opinion that is not the generally accepted one. (For example, you might write about a decision by the town council to build a new shopping mall on an old vacant lot; the limiting of public library hours in order to save money; a decision to open a halfway house in your neighborhood; and so forth.) Write an essay that will convince the reader of the validity of your stance on the issue.

1. Begin your essay with a discussion of the commonly held opinion on this issue. Use the verbal construction "it is" to help distance you from that opinion.
2. In the next section, strongly refute the commonly held opinion by stating your major proposition clearly and directly.
3. Develop your opinion by the use of comparative statistics.
4. While trying to remain as objective as possible, establish a slightly cynical edge to your tone.
5. If appropriate, include some jargon related to the issue.
6. Explain and refute the causal logic (cause-and-effect analysis) of the common opinion.
7. About midway through the essay, return to the thesis in a paragraph that serves as a "pivot" for your essay.
8. Link ideas, statistics, and opinions by means of well-placed minor proposition statements.
9. Continue to refute the common opinion by
   - **a.** using rhetorical questions
   - **b.** citing and showing the invalidity of a recent media item on the issue
   - **c.** lightly ridiculing some of the "big names" associated with the common opinion on the issue
10. Conclude your essay with a somewhat unrealistic, exaggerated image that both reinforces your opinion and invokes the reader to reexamine the issue more closely.

Thinking and Writing Collaboratively

In groups of four to five, discuss the alternatives or the opposition viewpoint to the arguments presented in your Guided Writing essay. Jot down notes, and then incorporate the opposition viewpoint—and your refutation or answer to it—in your final draft.

More Writing Projects

1. In your journal, freewrite about this topic: the homeless. Do not edit your writing. Write nonstop for at least fifteen minutes. When you finish, exchange journal entries with another student in the class. How do your responses compare? contrast?
2. Do you think it is correct to give money to panhandlers? Write a paragraph in which you state and defend your opinion.
3. Write an essay in the form of a letter to your local chief executive (mayor, town supervisor, and so forth) in which you express your opinion about the local homeless situation. Include some specific measures that you feel need to be enacted. Draw freely on your journal entry in question 1 of this exercise.

SUMMING UP: CHAPTER 11

1. Keep a journal in which you record your thoughts on, and observations of, homelessness in your part of the country. Try to gather specific data from reading, television viewing, or observation. Ask such questions as:

   How many are male? female?
   How many are children?
   How many are elderly?
   How many appear to be mentally ill?
   What symptoms or signs do they exhibit?

   Use the data, along with your observations, to present your position on homelessness in a letter to the editor of your campus or local newspaper.
2. Invite a local expert to class to speak on a current controversial issue. Write an essay of support for, or opposition to, the speaker's opinions.
3. Justify the inclusion of the essays by Kozol, Knight, Brady, and Zuckerman under the category "Argumentation and Persuasion." Treat the major issues that they raise, their positions on these issues, their minor propositions and use of evidence, and the tone of their language. Finally, establish the degree to which you are persuaded by these arguments.
4. Exchange with a classmate essays you've each written for a Guided Writing exercise in this chapter. Even if you agree with your partner's opinion, write a strongly worded response opposing it. Be sure you touch on the same, or similar, major and minor propositions.
5. Fill in the blanks in the following essay topic as you please, and use it as the major proposition for a well-developed argumentation-persuasion paper. Draw on the expository writing skills you have studied throughout the book.
   "I am very concerned about __________, and I believe it's necessary to __________."

CHAPTER 12

Prose for Further Reading

An American Childhood

Annie Dillard

When everything else has gone from my brain—the President's name, the state capitals, the neighborhoods where I lived, and then my own name and what it was on earth I sought, and then at length the faces of my friends, and finally the faces of my family—when all this has dissolved, what will be left, I believe, is topology: the dreaming memory of land as it lay this way and that.

I will see the city poured rolling down the mountain valleys like slag, and see the city lights sprinkled and curved around the hills' curves, rows of bonfires winding. At sunset a red light like housefires shines from the narrow hillside windows; the houses' bricks burn like glowing coals.

The three wide rivers divide and cool the mountains. Calm old bridges span the banks and link the hills. The Allegheny River flows in brawling from the north, from near the shore of Lake Erie, and from Lake Chautauqua in New York and eastward. The Monongahela River flows in shallow and slow from the south, from West Virginia. The Allegheny and the Monongahela meet and form the westward-wending Ohio.

Where the two rivers join lies an acute point of flat land from which rises the city. The tall buildings rise lighted to their tips. Their lights illumine other buildings' clean sides, and illumine the narrow city canyons below, where people move, and shine reflected red and white at night from the black waters.

When the shining city, too, fades, I will see only those forested mountains and hills, and the way the rivers lie flat and moving among them, and the way the low land lies wooded among them, and the blunt mountains rise in darkness from the rivers' banks, steep from the rugged south and rolling from the north, and from farther, from the inclined eastward plateau where the high ridges begin to run so long north and south unbroken that to get around them you practically have to navigate Cape Horn.

In those first days, people said, a squirrel could run the long length of Pennsylvania without ever touching the ground. In those first days, the woods were white oak and chestnut, hickory, maple, sycamore, walnut, wild ash, wild plum, and white pine. The pine grew on the ridgetops where the mountains' lumpy spines stuck up and their skin was thinnest.

The wilderness was uncanny, unknown. Benjamin Franklin had already invented his stove in Philadelphia by 1753, and Thomas Jefferson was a schoolboy in Virginia; French soldiers had been living in forts along Lake Erie for two generations. But west of the Alleghenies in western Pennsylvania, there was not even a settlement, not even a cabin. No Indians lived there, or even near there.

Wild grapevines tangled the treetops and shut out the sun. Few songbirds lived in the deep woods. Bright Carolina parakeets—red, green, and yellow—nested in the dark forest. There were ravens then, too. Woodpeckers rattled the big trees' trunks, ruffed grouse whirred their tail feathers in the fall, and every long once in a while a nervous gang of empty-headed turkeys came hustling and kicking through the leaves—but no one heard any of this, no one at all.

In 1753, young George Washington surveyed for the English this point of land where rivers met. To see the forest-blurred lay of the land, he rode his horse to a ridgetop and climbed a tree. He judged it would make a good spot for a fort. And an English fort it became, and a depot for Indian traders to the Ohio country, and later a French fort and way station to New Orleans.

But it would be another ten years before any settlers lived there on that land where the rivers met, lived to draw in the flowery scent of June rhododendrons with every breath. It would be another ten years before, for the first time on earth, tall men and women lay exhausted in their cabins, sleeping in the sweetness, worn out from planting corn.

Shaved Heads and Pop-Tarts

Jeannine Stein

Almost every night at 10, you'll find heavy-metal rock 'n' rollers with long hair, pierced noses, tattoos, biker boots and leather jackets cruising the aisles of the Hollywood Ralphs on Sunset.

It's not how you'd envision a rocker's natural habitat, but even headbangers have to eat. Sure, any 7-Eleven will do when you have a craving for beef jerky and Junior Mints, but metal-heads do not live by preserved meat and candy alone.

So in Hollywood, the grocery store of choice has been dubbed Rock 'N' Roll Ralphs. It's a hulking structure on the east end of the strip, near Poinsettia, a few minutes' drive to rock clubs like Gazzari's, the Roxy and Coconut Teaszer.

At the clubs, the long hair, tattoos and motorcycles belong. Seeing those same people at Ralphs is a case of when worlds collide, a surrealistic blend of shaved heads, Pop-Tarts and Muzak, where baskets contain generic corn flakes and Metal Edge magazine and punkers share space with more mainstream types.

On a Thursday night in the liquor aisle, a woman hoists a large bottle of whiskey and hands it to her male companion. She is barely in her 20s. She wears Kabuki-ish makeup, her face whited out and accented with bright pink lipstick and eye shadow; she has a small hoop in her pierced eyebrow. She wears a black and white polka-dot floppy hat, an old T-shirt, pink and black horizontal striped tights and pink bouclé bike shorts. The man with her is yin to her yang—middle aged, dressed in brown trousers and a plaid shirt. They disappear down the aisle.

Two young guys stand in front of the deli counter. One keeps combing his hand through his dark Pre-Raphaelite hair. They stare and stare at the selection of luncheon meats for several minutes before Mr. Hair says, "Uhhhhh . . . so d'you like pickle loaf?"

Two more rockers, one with long bleached blond hair, the other with long blue-black hair, lope on gangly legs to the bread aisle, where they pick up a few loaves, squeeze and then abandon the bread. They take two cookies from the bakery pantry and eat them.

A tall, skinny guy with a skull and crossbones T-shirt and black baseball cap with "Suicidal Tendencies" stitched on it rushes over to the frozen food section clutching a coupon. He looks furtively up and down the case until he finds a box of Nestle's Crunch ice cream bars, grabs it, then picks up four six-packs of Coke and heads for the express line.

In the household aisle, a young woman with hair dyed to match her purple mini-skirt methodically eats California rolls and contemplates extension cords.

Meanwhile, a touching scene is unfolding by the cat food. A man with chunky silver rings and biker boots crouches down and takes about 10 minutes to decide between the 9-Lives chicken and cheese and the tuna for his pampered pet.

It's fair to say that most rockers who shop here aren't stocking up for the long haul. They come for the essentials, what it's going to take to get them through the night. The most frequently purchased items appear to be:

- Beer (usually 12-can packs in the cardboard carrying case)
- Water (gallon jugs)
- Luncheon meats
- Chips (tortilla, potato)
- Canned chili and soup
- Dried pasta
- Hamburger and hot dog buns
- Steak
- Pet food

Female rockers tend to make healthier choices, going for yogurt, fresh fruit, tuna and low-cholesterol margarine.

Even the wildest clubbies appear somehow tamed in this benign world of the grocery store. While they may spend every night in clubs, banging heads to Metallica, Megadeth and L7, here they're entranced by the Zen-like calm.

Maybe it's the flatness of the fluorescent lights, or the Muzak. It's hard to get jumpy when a syrupy rendition of the already syrupy "Garden Party" plays over the loudspeakers, or when the Video Recipe of the Week offers tips on how to cook a pork tenderloin. ("Sprinkle with parsley and serve!")

It's an atmosphere that's conducive to spending quantity time vacillating between hamburger dill chips and zesty bread-and-butter pickles. Faces go slack and eyes glaze over as the staggering number of choices renders people passive. Conversations rarely consist of anything more substantial than "Should we get the low-salt chips?"

A Twofer's Lament

Yolanda Cruz

I grew up and graduated college in the Philippines; I've spent the last twenty years in the United States. I see a tremendous difference between the perception of education there versus here, then versus now—of whether securing an education is viewed as an opportunity or as a privilege.

I received a bachelor of science degree from the University of the Philippines. I was an agricultural science major, but I had just as many courses in engineering as in philosophy, in language as in math, in literature as in physics, in physical education as in the arts. The five-year curriculum was extremely strict: inflexible in terms of course choices, not only rigorous but quite brutal. There was no entrance exam; your freshman year *was* the entrance exam, and it was trial by fire. Anyone who survived the thirty-six-credit requirement was permitted to continue. We took those painful but marvelously edifying years one at a time, savoring and suffering every midterm exam, sweating every horrific term paper, including the dreaded senior thesis. Every student wrote one based on original research—that is, every student who made it to senior year. Many didn't.

Courses were taught in English (in a country whose citizens speak approximately 100 non-English languages and dialects) by a faculty that was 40 percent women. These women were not merely technicians or teaching assistants but professors, deans, lecturers and research scientists, with Ph.D.s from American, Canadian, Australian and European universities, just like the men. At the time, our student body was also about 40 percent women, although in recent years, I'm told, this figure has grown to about 50 percent. We enjoyed no financial aid or student loans; we went to university the old-fashioned way—on full scholarship, paying full tuition or working. There was only one criterion for admission: academic excellence. The occasional congressman's son or niece got in, but the brutal freshman year was a great equalizer. It didn't matter that your grandfather had graduated fifty years before either, because that didn't guarantee whether or not you would do well in your courses. It didn't matter how tall you were, what ethnic group you represented, what sport you played or what sex you were; or that you came from a finishing school in Switzerland or a public school in the boonies. The only criterion for admission—and for success—was that you could do your stuff and do it well.

It struck me as extraordinary, therefore, that when I matriculated at the University of California at Berkeley, I had to identify myself by sex, ethnicity and other criteria such as financial need. I considered my Graduate Record Examination and Test of English as a Foreign Language scores as relevant; after all, I was to be a graduate student in an English-speaking country. But sex? Ethnicity? I wasn't even sure what "ethnicity" meant. (Even today, I'm not sure whether I'm Asian, Filipino or Pacific Islander. I usually end up checking the box marked "other.") Financial need? That was my concern; I intended to work my way through graduate school. I wasn't asking for privileges, only opportunities.

Imagine my shock, then, when one of the second-year grad students came up to me, shook my hand and said that he had been looking forward to meeting the "twofer" who had been accepted that year. I discovered later that "twofer" meant I was a double whammy; not only was I a woman in a male-dominated field, but I was also not white. Little did that second-year student know that I was transferring from another department and had been accepted into his department because I had aced all the courses there. I remember feeling diminished by his remark; it was as if I had somehow been accepted because my sex and skin color made up for my lack of smarts. Years later I had a similar jolt. In 1986, shortly after I took my present teaching job, I asked one of my colleagues if my sex and ethnicity had anything to do with my getting hired. He said yes: it was affirmative action. And there I was, assuming I had gotten the job because I was good.

Until recently I thought nothing of this. I figured it came with the territory of living a foreigner's life in an alien country. Then a talk with one of my research students, a Hispanic-American woman, brought back a bit of the pain. Last year this student was accepted into Ph.D. programs in molecular biology at Harvard, CalTech and the University of California at San Francisco. After recounting for me the back and forth of her interviews, she asked a poignant question: Did I think she'd been admitted to these universities because she is a twofer? At that moment, I realized my experience at Berkeley had nothing to do with my being foreign. It had to do with the American perception of education as a privilege, deserved or undeserved. My student did not want an undeserved privilege. Like me, all she wanted was an opportunity. How cruel that a person so young, so bright, is made to feel that she is being given a handout, not a hand.

More recently I encountered, in an exchange with my daughter, Elsa, the confusion that seems to accompany the delineation between opportunity and privilege. After Elsa came home with a perfect eighth-grade report card, she regaled me with tales of her classmates who, after earning high marks, had received from their parents gifts, allowance increases, shopping sprees, and spring breaks in the Caribbean. "Why can't I get $20 for every A I bring home, Mama?" Elsa asked.

Smart kid. She knew she had me cornered. I searched my mind for a fitting response. Without losing my cool, I said, "My dear, I love you very much, but in this household you do not get paid for A's. Instead, you will have to pay me for every grade of B or lower that you bring home." Elsa realized that an A was simply an opportunity to move farther in her coursework; it did not entitle her to an automatic privilege.

Being awarded a privilege and given an opportunity are similar in that the odds are stacked in the recipient's favor. With privilege, however, the odds are handed to you; with opportunity, you stack the odds in your own favor. It is hard not to see the dignity in the latter enterprise—the sublime feeling of self-worth, self-respect and pride that it engenders.

Women Are Just Better

Anna Quindlen

My favorite news story so far this year was the one saying that in England scientists are working on a way to allow men to have babies. I'd buy tickets to that. I'd be happy to stand next to any man I know in one of those labor rooms the size of a Volkswagen trunk and whisper "No, dear, you don't really need the Demerol; just relax and do your second-stage breathing." It puts me in mind of an old angry feminist slogan: "If men got pregnant, abortion would be a sacrament." I think this is specious. If men got pregnant, there would be safe, reliable methods of birth control. They'd be inexpensive, too.

I can almost hear some of you out there thinking that I do not like men. This isn't true. I have been married for some years to a man and I hope that someday our two sons will grow up to be men. All three of my brothers are men, as is my father. Some of my best friends are men. It is simply that I think women are superior to men. There, I've said it. It is my dirty little secret. We're not supposed to say it because in the old days men used to say that women were superior. What they meant was that we were too wonderful to enter courtrooms, enjoy sex, or worry our minds about money. Obviously, this is not what I mean at all.

The other day a very wise friend of mine asked: "Have you ever noticed that what passes as a terrific man would only be an adequate woman?" A Roman candle went off in my head; she was absolutely right. What I expect from my male friends is that they are polite and clean. What I expect from my female friends is unconditional love, the ability to finish my sentences when I am sobbing, a complete and total willingness to pour their hearts out to me, and the ability to tell me why the meat thermometer isn't supposed to touch the bone.

The inherent superiority of women came to mind just the other day when I was reading about sanitation workers. New York City has finally hired women to pick up the garbage, which makes sense to me, since, as I discovered, a good bit of being a woman consists of picking up garbage. There was a story about the hiring of these female sanitation workers, and I was struck by the fact that I could have written that story without ever leaving my living room—a reflection not upon the quality of the reporting but the predictability of the male sanitation workers' responses.

The story started by describing the event, and then the two women, who were just your average working women trying to make a buck and get by. There was something about all the maneuvering that had to take place before they could be hired, and then there were the obligatory quotes from male sanitation workers about how women were incapable of doing this job. They were similar to quotes I have read over the years suggesting that women are not fit to be rabbis, combat soldiers, astronauts, fire-fighters, judges, ironworkers, and President of the United States. Chief among them was a comment from one sanitation worker, who said it just wasn't our kind of job, that women were cut out to do dishes and men were cut out to do yard work.

As a woman who has done dishes, yard work, and tossed a fair number of Hefty bags, I was peeved—more so because I would fight for the right of any laid-off sanitation man to work, for example, at the gift-wrap counter at Macy's, even though any woman knows that men are hormonally incapable of wrapping packages and tying bows.

I simply can't think of any jobs any more that women can't do. Come to think of it, I can't think of any job women don't do. I know lots of men who are full-time lawyers, doctors, editors and the like. And I know lots of women who are full-time lawyers and part-time interior decorators, pastry chefs, algebra teachers, and garbage slingers. Women are the glue that holds our day-to-day world together.

Maybe the sanitation workers who talk about the sex division of duties are talking about girls just like the girls that married dear old dad. Their day is done. Now lots of women know that if they don't carry the garbage bag to the curb, it's not going to get carried—either because they're single, or their husband is working a second job, or he's staying at the office until midnight, or he just left them.

I keep hearing that there's a new breed of men out there who don't talk about helping a woman as though they're doing you a favor and who do seriously consider leaving the office if a child comes down with a fever at school, rather than assuming that you will leave yours. But from what I've seen, there aren't enough of these men to qualify as a breed, only as a subgroup.

This all sounds angry; it is. After a lifetime spent with winds of sexual change buffeting me this way and that, it still makes me angry to read the same dumb quotes with the same dumb stereotypes that I was reading when I was eighteen. It makes me angry to realize that after so much change, very little is different. It makes me angry to think that these two female sanitation workers will spend their days doing a job most of their co-workers think they can't handle, and then they will go home and do another job most of their co-workers don't want.

The Ugly Tourist

Jamaica Kincaid

The thing you have always suspected about yourself the minute you become a tourist is true: a tourist is an ugly human being. You are not an ugly person all the time; you are not an ugly person ordinarily; you are not an ugly person day to day. From day to day, you are a nice person. From day to day, all the people who are supposed to love you on the whole do. From day to day as you walk down a busy street in the large and modern and prosperous city in which you work and live, dismayed, puzzled (a cliché, but only a cliché can explain you) at how alone you feel in this crowd, how awful it is to go unnoticed, how awful it is to go unloved, even as you are surrounded by more people than you could possibly get to know in a lifetime that lasted for millennia, and then out of the corner of your eye you see someone looking at you and absolute pleasure is written all over that person's face, and then you realize that you are not as revolting a presence as you think you are (for that look just told you so). And so, ordinarily, you are a nice person, an attractive person, a person capable of drawing to yourself the affection of other people (people just like you), a person at home in your own skin (sort of; I mean, in a way; I mean, your dismay and puzzlement are natural to you, because people like you just seem to be like that, and so many of the things people like you find admirable about yourselves—the things you think about, the things you think really define you—seem rooted in these feelings): a person at home in your own house (and all its nice house things), with its nice back yard (and its nice back-yard things), at home on your street, your church, in community activities, your job, at home with your family, your relatives, your friends—you are a whole person. But one day, when you are sitting somewhere, alone in that crowd, and that awful feeling of displacedness comes over you, and really, as an ordinary person you are not well equipped to look too far inward and set yourself aright, because being ordinary is already so taxing, and being ordinary takes all you have out of you, and though the words "I must get away" do not actually pass across your lips, you make a leap from being that nice blob just sitting like a boob in your amniotic sac of the modern experience to being a person visiting heaps of death and ruin and feeling alive and inspired at the sight of it; to being a person lying on some far-away beach, your stilled body stinking and glistening in the sand, looking like something first forgotten, then remembered, then not important enough to go back for; to being a person marveling at the harmony (ordinarily, what you would say is the backwardness) and the union these other people (and they are other people) have with nature. And you look at the things they can do with a piece of ordinary cloth, the things they fashion out of cheap, vulgarly coloured (to you) twine, the way they squat down over a hole they have made in the ground, the hole itself is something to marvel at, and since you are being an ugly person this ugly but joyful thought will swell inside you: their ancestors were not clever in the way yours were and not ruthless in the way yours were, for then would it not be you who would be in harmony with nature and backwards in that charming way? An ugly thing, that is what you are when you become a tourist, an ugly, empty thing, a stupid thing, a piece of rubbish pausing here and there to gaze at this and taste that, and it will never occur to you that the people who inhabit the place in which you have just paused cannot stand you, that behind their closed doors they laugh at your strangeness (you do not look the way they look); the physical sight of you does not please them; you have bad manners (it is their custom to eat their food with their hands; you try eating their way, you look silly; you try eating the way you always eat, you look silly); but they do not like the way you speak (you have an accent); they collapse helpless from laughter, mimicking the way they imagine you must look as you carry out some everyday bodily function. They do not like you. *They do not like me!* That thought never actually occurs to you. Still, you feel a little uneasy. Still, you feel a little foolish. Still, you feel a little out of place. But the banality of your own life is very real to you; it drove you to this extreme, spending your days and your nights in the company of people who despise you, people you do not like really, people you would not want to have as your actual neighbour. And so you must devote yourself to puzzling out how much of what you are told is really, really true (Is ground-up bottle glass in peanut sauce really a delicacy around here, or will it do just what you think ground-up bottle glass will do? Is this rare, multicoloured, snout-mouthed fish really an aphrodisiac, or will it cause you to fall asleep permanently?). Oh, the hard work all of this is, and is it any wonder, then, that on your return home you feel the need of a long rest, so that you can recover from your life as a tourist?

That the native does not like the tourist is not hard to explain. For every native of every place is a potential tourist, and every tourist is a native of somewhere. Every native everywhere lives a life of overwhelming and crushing banality and boredom and desperation and depression, and every deed, good and bad, is an attempt to forget this. Every native would like to find a way out, every native would like a rest, every native would like a tour. But some natives—most natives in the world—cannot go anywhere. They are too poor. They are too poor to escape the reality of their lives; and they are too poor to live properly in the place where they live, which is the very place you, the tourist, want to go—so when the natives see you, the tourist, they envy you, they envy your ability to leave your own banality and boredom, they envy your ability to turn their own banality and boredom into a source of pleasure for yourself.

A Death in Venice

Jennifer Allen

Let me tell you where I have lived in Los Angeles. I have lived in a house above a canyon of brush, have been awakened by sirens, seen the flames, packed the car, thrown silver in the pool, turned the sprinklers on, stood on the ice plant, left the canyon burning and later returned to find the hills black, barren, bald. I have lived in an apartment by the Tar Pits, smelled the heat of the tar rising in summer, seen the gas of the earth shooting fire up from manholes, tearing the roof off a store in a strip mall. I have lived in a house in Venice, a house where those who entered spoke of its "good energy," meaning, I suppose, that no one had been killed there. A house with oak floors, a sun-through-the-trees light, two tall date palms, a Mexican rug hung over a couch on the slate porch out front. The kind of house where I slept well, in a room in the back, in a bed that was not mine, with a ceiling that was peeling and a door that did not lock. The kind of house where a friend once noted the wood floors, the kind light, and asked, "Do you own a gun?" This is the last place I lived in Los Angeles. This is where I packed my belongings into boxes, gave the key to the landlord and hired a Mexican mover who gave me his business card, listing suggested readings in Deuteronomy, Matthew, Thessalonians.

I am no prophet. I am not one who has visions on the freeway and has to be pulled over for reckless driving, having seen the coming of earthquakes and famines and floods. I cannot smell the smoke before the fire or detect the coming of a Santa Ana. Nor can I tell you what makes for earthquake weather, because to me all weather is earthquake weather. I have slept through earthquakes. I have driven with two flat tires on the freeway until someone told me, honked. I have driven through a rioting boulevard of broken windshields, stoned. I am not aware of such happenings until they come up at me and wake me up. What woke me up out of Venice last fall was the doorbell ringing, flashlights searching through windows of the house and a couple of LAPD cops asking me what my name was. There'd been "some activity" in the neighborhood, they said. A woman had either been hit by a car or beaten up, they said. Had I seen anything? I had been sleeping.

I relit the prayer candles I had blown out before sleep. The ninety-nine-cent kind you get at The Boys supermarket. A tall glass of candle with a picture sticker of whomever you seek the protection of and a novena in English and Spanish. A blue Mother Mary sending light out from her palms. A red Jesus with his heart girded in thorns. A pink guardian angel guiding children across a bridge. I burned these candles in the house, burning so many at once—they were on sale one week—that at times it felt like overkill, over-prayer, as if I did not believe in the power of one candle's prayer. A lack of faith, I see it as now.

What I could see from inside the house—its many windows gave a view of the entire block around—was the yellow police tape that had been hung up in my sleep, blocking an alleyway where the trash was dumped, keeping cars off a street that was a short cut into and out of town. Doc Martens and pajamas, cigarettes and matches, I went out and stood with the neighbors outside the "DO NOT CROSS" tape and watched a cat smell the cloth that covered the spot where the woman once was. The men from the fire station a few houses down had already come, without sirens, to lift her up, wrap her head, send her to Marina Emergency.

This I was told. This we talked about there, in the headlight fog of LAPD squad cars. She was a leather mini-skirted girl in her 20s, brains blown out, skull smashed or maybe O.D.-exploded head. She was dumped out of a trunk. She was shot and then dumped. She O.D.'d, was shot and then dumped. They were driving on, the killers, the dumpers, the O.D.ers, still, now, in Los Angeles, driving, talking too fast or too slow or too something, thinking or maybe not thinking at all about what they had done.

The story kept us up at night, days after. The story we told ourselves in our kitchens, merging fact and fiction, became this: she had been at the Brig, a nearby bar I never went to because everybody told me not to whenever I said I wanted to, or had to, or would. A bar I often walked past; its parking lot wall with a mural of a woman and a man standing in that very lot, and on the wall behind them, the mural framed, though not yet painted—an image of unfinished prophecy or maybe just the inspired remnants of some good LSD. Camaros and Harleys parked there. "Lucky" was mosaicked into the sidewalk entrance. This is where she smoked, drank, shot pool. This is where the biker, pressed up against the bar, had seen her dancing with his girlfriend that night. Or this is where her boyfriend came to pick her up to take her away from the biker at the bar, a boyfriend who collected guns, a boyfriend who managed an apartment complex where earlier that year another girl had been found in the laundry-room basement, dead. Or this is where no one she had ever known or seen before gave her the ride home. She was 26, white, named Sydney. She was dead by sunrise.

That night I said I would not sleep. That night, I could see everyone who drove by my house while I slept. I could see their faces in the cops' flashlights, faces stunned, their short-cut, detoured. They followed orders, put it in reverse, took a right or a left.

"Did you know her?" a cop asked me after I had seen a one-headlighted car drive past, circle the circle that made our block a four-way circular intersection, the car passing, circling twice, the killer, the dumper, the mourner, coming back to look at the event. This is what I thought. This is what I told the cop. "Did you know her?" the cop asked, and I thought, "Yes, she was me." And then I thought, go home, go to bed, get some sleep.

I blew out the prayer candles. Left a Mother Mary to burn itself out until dawn.

There were other events in Venice—a flyer the LAPD left between the screen and the door listing the names of those killed in the blocks surrounding our house. There was gunfire at night. Emptying of guns, five rounds a piece. Fair fighting, I thought, no one yet dying, everyone finishing their rounds beyond the blinds. Fair fire, I thought, until one shot shook us in bed one night. "A .357," the man lying next to me said in our mid-dream state of mind. There were helicopters hovering, blowing trash, spraying lights. There were shaved heads and white tank tops and smiles of a local gang coming and going from its curtain-drawn trailer-home parked just beside the jade lining the sidewalk. There were rats in the date palms, a possum in the kitchen, ants in the shower. There were brush fires beyond, sending ash over cars and yards, and there were water rations in full-drought mode. There was an earthquake that reminded us all that Venice is built on land-fill, a.k.a. liquid earth, meaning the place is quicksand, capable of sucking you and your roof in with it.

After the quake I did not burn the prayer candles. Land shifts could tumble them over, start a fire. I went to church instead. My church was not in Venice. It was in the next town over, St. Monica's in Santa Monica. St. Monica's is a place I went to when I could no longer sit on the porch smoking one last cigarette before going to bed, when I could no longer leave the blinds open to see who just might be careening by, when I could no longer leave the screen door unlatched, the front door open, the back door wide for a breeze. St. Monica's, I call it my church, though I am not Catholic. The church is now in the hands of Peck/Jones, a post-earthquake repair crew, "a restoration team," as they call it here. The church looks as if it is waiting to be leveled: fallen bricks, a diagonally cracked bell tower, the apse severed. A stone cross lies in the parking lot. This is the church I came to, not for Mass, because at Mass I was always standing up when others were sitting down, kneeling when others were saying vows, saying vows I could not announce. I came and sat in there, and thought how this would be the place to be in an earthquake. I thought this would test my faith. The world could fall around you and you would remain still, unaltered, calm. When police tape circled the church to keep worshipers away from the dangers of aftershocks, when Mass was now moved to center court at St. Monica's gym, when the man who had detected the .357 shot asked me to come to Tennessee, I went. I did. I left Los Angeles. I left Los Angeles and was baptized in the water on top of a mountain said to be guarded by angels, a place where on an Easter candlelight vigil in my turning the pages and holding the candles I lit the Book of Common Prayer on fire.

It is fire season in Los Angeles now. The eucalyptus is dry; the dust, dirt; the ocean, flat. To the saint near the ocean's edge is where I come when I return to Los Angeles. Here, where Wilshire meets Pacific, is the statue of Santa Monica. Her back to the ocean, her hands crossed over her chest, she faces all of Los Angeles. The sun sets behind her. A bus passes before her. "PLEASE KEEP YOUR PARK CLEAN," reads a sign nearby. In a park for the old and the homeless, the barefoot and the bladed, the tourist and the native, she stands—unmoved, untouched, unreal. This is where Los Angeles ends. And where it begins.

He Rocked, I Reeled

Tama Janowitz

In high school, I took a remedial English class—maybe it wasn't remedial, exactly, but without my knowing it, I had signed up for some kind of English class for juvenile delinquents.

Well, it wasn't supposed to be a class for juvenile delinquents, but somehow everybody but me knew that that was who it was for; maybe it was listed in the course catalog as being for those students in the commercial program, the general program, whatever it was called to distinguish it from the academic pre-college preparation program.

But anyway, on the first day I figured out who this course was directed at: The students were surly and wore leather jackets, and the girls all had shag hair-dos as opposed to straight and ironed, which was how the "nice" girls wore their hair.

Knowing me, I must have signed up for that class because it indicated that no work would be involved. And I was prepared for the worst, because somehow, having moved and switched schools so many times, I had been stuck in juvenile delinquent classes before.

The juvenile delinquent classes generally meant angry teachers and angry students who never read the books assigned and never spoke in class, which was no wonder because the teacher was generally contemptuous and sneering.

But this class ended up being different; the main thing was that the teacher, Mr. Paul Steele, didn't seem to know he was teaching students who weren't supposed to be able to learn. He assigned the books—by Sherwood Anderson, by Hemingway, by Melville—and somehow by the due date everyone had read them and was willing to talk about them.

Mr. Steele was a little distracted, a little dreamy, and most excellent. It was one of the few times up until that age I had a teacher who spoke to me—and the rest of the class—with the honesty of one adult talking to others, without pretense or condescension; there was no wrong or right, just discussion.

In college, I had another great course—in geology, a subject for which I had no interest. Once again, I had signed up for something that looked easy, a "gut" course to fulfill the science requirement.

But this guy—I believe his name was Professor Sand, an apt name for a geology teacher—was so excited and in love with rocks, with everything pertaining to the formation of the earth, that to this day rocks and everything pertaining to the formation of the earth still get me excited.

Oolitic limestone, feldspar, gypsum, iron pyrite, Manhattan schist—the names were like descriptions of food, almost edible, and as around that time I was starting to become interested in writing, the enthusiasm that the teacher had for the subject was transferred to me into an enthusiasm for language.

And the names of the different periods—the Jurassic, the Pre-Cambrian—even though I can't remember much about them, the words still hold mystery and richness.

At the end of the semester, there was a field trip up to the Catskills, to put into practice some of the techniques discussed in class. We were taken to a fossil bed of trilobites where, due to the particular condition of the sedimentary bed, only the trilobite bodies had been preserved over the millennia.

After a few minutes of listening to the professor's explanation, I bent over and picked up a piece of rock with a small lump sticking out of it and took it over to him.

To me, all I had found was a rock with a lump; but Professor Sand was totally amazed—I was the only one ever to find a fossilized trilobite complete with head.

Really, at that point there was little to stop me from becoming a geologist except for the fact that I knew I could never do anything involving numbers, weights or measurements, which I suspected would at some point have some bearing on the subject.

I remember another teacher, in graduate school, Francine du Plessix Gray, who taught a course called Religion and Literature—another subject in which I had no interest. But the way she spoke was so beautiful, in an accent slightly French-tinged. And because she was so interested in her topic, the students became interested, and her seminars were alive and full of argument.

Of course, I had many other fine teachers along the way, but the ones who stand out in my mind were those who were most enthusiastic about what they were teaching.

Many subjects in which I initially thought I was interested were totally destroyed for me by the teacher's dry, aloof, pompous, disengaged way of speaking.

But when the teacher was as excited about the topic—as if he or she was still a little kid, rushing in from the yard to tell a story—that was when the subject became alive for me.

Is It Really That Wacky?

Pico Iyer

Yes, yes, we've heard all the jokes: we know that "spacy" and "flaky" seem almost to have been invented for California and that in the dictionary *California* is a virtual synonym for "far out." Ever since gold was first found flowing in its rivers, the Shangri-La La of the West has been the object of as many gibes as fantasies: just over a century ago, Rudyard Kipling was already pronouncing that "San Francisco is a mad city, inhabited for the most part by perfectly insane people" (others might say "insanely perfect"); and more than 40 years ago, S.J. Perelman was barreling down the yellow brick road to L.A., the "mighty citadel which had given the world the double feature, the duplexburger, the motel, the hamfurter, and the shirt worn outside the pants." Yes, we know, all too well, that "going to California" is tantamount, for many people, to going to seed.

And yes, much of the image does fit. Returning to California recently, I picked up a copy of the San Francisco *Chronicle* and read about people attending a funeral in pinks and turquoises and singing along to Bette Midler ("Dress for a Brazilian party!" the invitation—from the deceased—read); about a missing cat identifiable by "a rhinestone collar w/name and electronic cat door opener"; about women from Los Angeles hiring migrant workers to wait in line for them to buy watches shaped like cucumbers or bacon and eggs. On Hollywood Boulevard I saw a HISTORIC LANDMARK sign outside the site of "The First Custom T-Shirt Shop in California," flyers on the wall promoting a group call Venal Opulance and, in a store across the street, "Confucius X-Rated Mini-Condom Fortune Cookies." No wonder, I thought, that when I tell people I live in California—worse, that I choose to live in California—they look at me as if I had decided not to get serious or grow up; as if I had seceded from reality.

Part of the reason for all this, no doubt, is circumstance. For one thing, California wears its contradictions, its clashing hearts, on its sleeve: even its deepest passions are advertised on bumper sticker, T shirt and vanity plate. California is America without apologies or inhibitions, pleased to have found itself here and unembarrassed about its pleasure. So too, society in California is less a society than a congregation of subcultures, many of them with a membership of one: every man's home is his castle in the air here.

In addition, California's image has been fashioned largely by interlopers from the East, who tend to look on it as a kind of recumbent dumb blond, so beautiful that it cannot possibly have any other virtues. Thus the California of the imagination is an unlikely compound of Evelyn Waugh's Forest Lawn, Orson Welles' Hearst Castle, every screenwriter's Locustland and Johnny Carson's "beautiful downtown Burbank." Nice house, as they say, but nobody's at home.

By now the notion of California as a wigged-out free-for-all has become a legend, and as self-sustaining as every other myth. If I had read about vegetable-shaped watches in the Des Moines *Register,* I would have taken it as a reflection not on Iowa but humanity; but California has been associated with flakiness for so long that it is only the flaky things we see as Californian. There are five pet cemeteries in California registered with the International Association of Pet Cemeteries (vs. eight in New York State), but it is the canine mortuaries in L.A. that everybody mentions.

When California is ahead of the world, it seems outlandish; yet when its trends become commonplace, no one thinks of them as Californian. Large-scale recycling, health clubs, postmodern enchiladas all were essentially Californian fads until they became essential to half the countries in the world. And many people do not recall that such everyday, down-to-earth innovations as the bank credit card, the 30-year mortgage and the car loan were all, as David Rieff, in a new book about Los Angeles, points out, more or less developed by that great California institution the Bank of America.

And as the California myth gains circulation, it attracts precisely the kind of people who come here to sustain it: many of the newcomers to the "end of America" are Flat Earthers, Free Speechers or latter-day sinners drawn by the lure of a place where unorthodoxy is said to be the norm. Frank Lloyd Wright once said that all the loose nuts in America would end up in Los Angeles because of the continental tilt. Aldous Huxley suggested that the world resembled a head on its side, with the superrational Old World occupying a different sphere from the vacant, dreamy spaces of the collective subconscious of the West. California, he was implying, is the name we give our hopes and highest fantasies: an antiworld of sorts, governed by an antireality principle and driven by an antigravitational push. That is why he, like Thomas Pynchon and Ursula Le Guin and a hundred others, set his Utopia in California: with its deserts and rich farmland and a valley (if not a sea) named after death, California has impressed many as a kind of modern Holy Land.

California, in short, doesn't stand to reason (doesn't even lie down to reason). "The drive-in restaurant has valet parking," notes P. J. O'Rourke, and "practically everyone runs and jogs. Then he gets in the car to go next door." There's no beach at North Beach, he might have added, and *Sunset Boulevard* was shot on Wilshire. William Faulkner was arrested for walking here, and teenagers look older than their parents. "The tolerant Pacific air," in Auden's words, "makes logic seem so silly." And that air of unreality is only quickened by the fact that California is the illusion maker of the world: "Everyman's Eden" has made a living almost out of living up to other people's expectations.

What tends to get forgotten in all this is that the aerospace industry is centered in Southern California. The source of the state's wealth is that least dreamy and most realpolitik-bound of industries, defense. Yes, the late Gene Roddenberry may have dreamed up *Star Trek* here, but he drew upon his experience in the Los Angeles police department. For every quaint, picture-book San Francisco floating in the air there is an Oakland across the bay, gritty, industrial and real; for every Zen-minded "Governor Moonbeam" there is a hardheaded Richard Nixon; for every real estate office in the shape of a Sphinx there is a man behind the desk counting dollars.

The town in which I live, the pretty, sunlit, red-roofed Mediterranean-style resort of Santa Barbara, is typical. The town prides itself on being the birthplace of hot tubs and the site of the first Egg McMuffin. There is little or no industry here, and everyone seems to be working, full time, on his lifestyle. Thus people from Melbourne to Marseilles tune into the *Santa Barbara* soap opera, and in the Kansai region of Japan, women in SANTA BARBARA sweatshirts crowd into the Santa Barbara ice-cream parlor. Yet there is a theoretical-physics institute here, and there used to be a think tank peopled by refugees from the University of Chicago.

Besides, it is in the nature of bright sunlight to cast long shadows: when Santa Barbara has hit the headlines recently, it has been because of an eight-year drought so severe that even showers were limited; a fire that destroyed 600 houses (including mine); and one of the country's most poisonous homeless battles. AIDS to the north, gang wars to the south; droughts interrupted by floods; mudslides down the coast that left 91 dead in 1969; earthquakes that bring in their wake bubonic plague (contracted by 160 people as a result of San Francisco's 1906 earthquake): California, as Christopher Isherwood saw, "is a tragic country—like Palestine, like every Promised Land."

Not long ago in Garden Grove, just two miles south of Disney-land, where Vietnamese *dentistas* (SE HABLA ESPAÑOL, say their windows) bump against halal (Islam's equivalent to kosher) grocery stores in Spanish-style malls, I paid a visit to the Crystal Cathedral. On first encounter the area seems a vision of the cacophonous dystopia of the future in which a hundred California dreams collide and each one drowns the others out. Yet beneath the surface there is a kind of commonness, a shared belief in all of them that the future can be custom-made. This faith is implicit in the immigrants' assumptions—they have voted with their feet in coming here—and it is made explicit, for longtime residents, by the Rev. Robert Schuller, who fills his sprawling Crystal Cathedral with hymns to "Possibility Thinking."

Schuller's great distinction, perhaps, is not just that he was a pioneer of the drive-in church (and his sermons are still broadcast, via a wide-screen TV, to overflow parishioners in the parking lot outside), nor that he has managed to erect a glittering monument to his "Be-Happy Attitudes," but rather that he has gathered a huge nationwide following out of preaching what is in effect Californianism. For if you look at his books *(Your Future Is Your Friend, Success Is Never Ending, Failure Is Never Final),* and if you walk around his church, as airy and futuristic and free of Christian iconography, almost, as a Hyatt Regency hotel, you can see that the heart of his scripture is simple optimism, on the surface scarcely different from that espoused by New Age gurus across the state (in the Bodhi Tree bookstore, *Create Your Own Future* tapes are on sale, made by a Stanford professor).

Faced by such unlikelihoods, one begins to see that California is still, in a sense, what America used to be: a spiritual refuge, a utopian experiment, a place plastic enough, in every sense, to shape itself to every group of newcomers. It is a state set in the future tense (and the optative mood), a place in a perpetual state of becoming. Of course it's strange: it is precisely the shape of things to come, as unexpected as tomorrow. Of course it's unsettled: it's making itself up as it goes along.

The Myth of Meritocracy

Ellis Cose

Has affirmative action betrayed the dream of a meritocracy? Will eliminating it finally put Americans on the path to a colorblind, gender-neutral Shangri-La where personal achievement is honored and favoritism defunct? Critics from across the political spectrum argue that it will, as they echo Sen. Jesse Helms's observation that affirmative action "flies in the face of the merit-based society [envisioned by] the Founding Fathers."

Putting aside the question of whether the Founding Fathers really believed a society that consigned most blacks to slavery was "merit-based," the argument that equates opposition to affirmative action with a quest for a meritocracy rings false. It assumes that Americans agree on a definition of a meritocracy, that we desire a meritocracy and that we have a tangible notion of how to bring one about.

None of those propositions is true. Determining real merit is so difficult that we generally find ourselves focusing on test scores. Much of the case against affirmative action ends up being a case for people who test well as opposed to people who don't. But good as tests might be at measuring certain types of intelligence, few people believe they assess overall merit well. No one, for instance, would propose choosing a chairman of a corporation—or even a department head—solely on the basis of a test.

"There are a lot of factors, if we're honest, that we take into account in making any decision," observes UCLA chancellor Charles Young. "A meritocracy that was thoughtless, that looked at only one aspect, just the brain and nothing else . . . would be dullsville."

Most Americans intuitively agree. No angry movement has surfaced, for instance, to protest colleges' offering admission to star athletes or sons and daughters of alumni—even if the beneficiaries are not the most "qualified," and even though a majority of people say they oppose such programs in principle. We go along with them anyway, apparently because we understand that academic merit is not the only relevant consideration.

Much the same attitude prevails in the workplace. The Justice Department has sued Illinois State University for blatantly favoring minorities and women in a janitorial-training program;

but virtually no one complains that the janitor's test gives extra points to veterans.

Though many of us claim to reject group preferences in general, we seem more annoyed at some than at others—and particularly at those that appear indefensible. To most Americans, veterans seem more deserving of a group privilege than people who were merely born a particular color or sex. Though no one assumes that veterans wield a meaner mop, people do feel that society owes them something. And they are therefore granted an advantage in employment, even if they are not, by some objective measure, the best candidates for the job.

Undistinguished students related to a university's alumni (so-called legacies) are granted group preference not on the basis of anything they have accomplished but simply because they (and their connections) are deemed to have value—more value, at any rate, some assume, than students whose only apparent contribution is that their group was once "oppressed." And unlike students who win admission on the basis of affirmative action, legacies seem untouched by the stigma of inferiority. As Bob Laird, director of undergraduate admission at the University of California, Berkeley, observed: "I never have the sense of the legacy students [at Harvard] feeling, 'Oh. I don't really belong here.' Or, 'I haven't earned it.' The whole thing is, 'Hell, I'm here. That's what counts'."

Critics of affirmative action have not explained how abolishing it can lead to a meritocracy as long as other forms of favoritism continue to flourish. Nor have they shown any real enthusiasm for attacking preferential treatment in all its guises, as opposed to aiming their animus solely at affirmative action. Nor, for that matter, have they demonstrated much of an appetite for stepping up enforcement of antidiscrimination laws, or pouring resources into (and increasing demands on) inner-city schools. They are not, by and large, proposing anything that, by distributing society's benefits and opportunities more broadly, might eventually move the nation closer to the meritocracy they profess to desire. Instead of solutions, they are merely offering a scapegoat: this *awful thing* called affirmative action.

It's easy, and politically expedient, to pretend that everything would be just fine if affirmative action weren't screwing things up. The truth, of course, is much more complicated. Even if the movement to ban affirmative action succeeds, there is every reason to believe we will again find ourselves pondering how to deal with the same difficult questions of racial estrangement and inequity that spawned affirmative action in the first place.

Wolf Rhythms

Barry Lopez

Imagine a wolf moving through the northern woods. The movement, over a trail he has traversed many times before, is distinctive, unlike that of a cougar or a bear, yet he appears, if you are watching, sometimes catlike or bearlike. It is purposeful, deliberate movement. Occasionally the rhythm is broken by the wolf's pause to inspect a scent mark, or a move off the trail to paw among stones where a year before he had cached meat.

The movement down the trail would seem relentless if it did not appear so effortless. The wolf's body, from neck to hips, appears to float over the long, almost spindly legs and the flicker of wrists, a bicycling drift through the trees, reminiscent of the movement of water or of shadows.

The wolf is three years old. A male. He is of the subspecies *occidentalis,* and the trees he is moving among are spruce and subalpine fir on the eastern slope of the Rockies in northern Canada. He is light gray; that is, there are more blond and white hairs mixed with gray in the saddle of fur that covers his shoulders and extends down his spine than there are black and brown. But there are silver and even red hairs mixed in.

It is early September, an easy time of year, and he has not seen the other wolves in his pack for three or four days. He has heard no howls, but he knows the others are about, in ones and twos like himself. It is not a time of year for much howling. It is an easy time. The weather is pleasant. Moose are fat. Suddenly the wolf stops in mid-stride. A moment, then his feet slowly come alongside each other. He is staring into the grass. His ears are rammed forward, stiff. His back arches and he rears up and pounces like a cat. A deer mouse is pinned between his forepaws. Eaten. The wolf drifts on. He approaches a trail crossing, an undistinguished crossroads. His movement is now slower and he sniffs the air as though aware of a possibility for scents. He sniffs a scent post, a scrawny blueberry bush in use for years, and goes on.

The wolf weighs ninety-four pounds and stands thirty inches at the shoulder. His feet are enormous, leaving prints in the mud along a creek (where he pauses to hunt crayfish but not with much interest) more than five inches long by just over four wide. He has two fractured ribs, broken by a moose a year before. They are healed now, but a sharp eye would notice the irregularity. The skin on his right hip is scarred, from a fight with another wolf in a neighboring pack when he was a yearling. He has not had anything but a few mice and a piece of arctic char in three days, but he is not hungry. He is traveling. The char was a day old, left on rocks along the river by bears.

The wolf is tied by subtle threads to the woods he moves through. His fur carries seeds that will fall off, effectively dispersed, along the trail some miles from where they first caught in his fur. And miles distant is a raven perched on the ribs of a caribou the wolf helped kill ten days ago, pecking like a chicken at the decaying scraps of meat. A smart snowshoe hare that eluded the wolf and left him exhausted when he was a pup has been dead a year now, food for an owl. The den in which he was born one April evening was home to porcupines last winter.

It is now late in the afternoon. The wolf has stopped traveling, has lain down to sleep on cool earth beneath a rock outcropping. Mosquitoes rest on his ears. His ears flicker. He begins to waken. He rolls on his back and lies motionless with his front legs pointed toward the sky but folded like wilted flowers, his back legs splayed, and his nose and tail curved toward each other on one side of his body. After a few moments he flops on his side, rises, stretches, and moves a few feet to inspect—minutely, delicately—a crevice in the rock outcropping and finds or doesn't find what draws him there. And then he ascends the rock face, bounding and balancing momentarily before bounding again, appearing slightly unsure of the process—but committed. A few minutes later he bolts suddenly into the woods, achieving full speed, almost forty miles per hour, for forty or fifty yards before he begins to skid, to lunge at a lodgepole pine cone. He trots away with it, his head erect, tail erect, his hips slightly to one side and out of line with his shoulders, as though hindquarters were impatient with forequarters, the cone inert in his mouth. He carries it for a hundred feet before dropping it by the trail. He sniffs it. He goes on.

The underfur next to his skin has begun to thicken with the coming of fall. In the months to follow it will become so dense between his shoulders it will be almost impossible to work a finger down to his skin. In seven months he will weigh less: eighty-nine pounds. He will have tried unsuccessfully to mate with another wolf in the pack. He will have helped kill four moose and thirteen caribou. He will have fallen through ice into a creek at twenty-two below zero but not frozen. He will have fought other wolves.

He moves along now at the edge of a clearing. The wind coming down valley surrounds him with a river of odors, as if he were a migrating salmon. He can smell ptarmigan and deer droppings. He can smell willow and spruce and the fading sweetness of fireweed. Above, he sees a hawk circling, and farther south, lower on the horizon, a flock of sharp-tailed sparrows going east. He senses through his pads with each step the dryness of the moss beneath his feet, and the ridges of old tracks, some his own. He hears the sound his feet make. He hears the occasional movement of deer mice and voles. Summer food.

Toward dusk he is standing by a creek, lapping the cool water, when a wolf howls—a long wail that quickly reaches pitch and then tapers, with several harmonics, long moments to a tremolo. He recognizes his sister. He waits a few moments, then, throwing his head back and closing his eyes, he howls. The howl is shorter and it changes pitch twice in the beginning, very quickly. There is no answer.

The female is a mile away and she trots off obliquely through the trees. The other wolf stands listening, laps water again, then he too departs, moving quickly, quietly through the trees, away from the trail he had been on. In a few minutes the two wolves meet. They approach each other briskly, almost formally, tails erect and moving somewhat as deer move. When they come together they make high squeaking noises and encircle each other, rubbing and pushing, poking their noses into each other's neck fur, backing away to stretch, chasing each other for a few steps, then standing quietly together, one putting a head over the other's back. And then they are gone, down a vague trail, the female first. After a few hundred yards they begin, simultaneously, to wag their tails.

In the days that follow, they will meet another wolf from the pack, a second female, younger by a year, and the three of them will kill a caribou. They will travel together ten or twenty miles a day, through the country where they live, eating and sleeping, birthing, playing with sticks, chasing ravens, growing old, barking at bears, scent-marking trails, killing moose, and staring at the way water in a creek breaks around their legs and flows on.

Technophobia

Michel Marriott with T. Trent Gegax

Like many born before circuits were integrated and TV strove to be interactive, Robert Robards, 63, tried his best to keep his distance from computers. His sons pleaded with him for years to embrace the new technology he feared, but Robards, the director of a shelter for the homeless in Boston, still stubbornly resisted. He'd say, "It's not me. It ain't my world."

He was not alone. Millions of Americans are technophobes, running from the high tide of high tech sweeping into their lives. A recent U.S. study found that 55 percent of those surveyed showed some sign of technophobia. Some are simply spooked by anything electronic, from beeping answering machines to blinking VCRs. Many more feel threatened by the omnipresent computer. Technophobes tend to be people older than 45 who didn't grow up with the devices they are now expected to master. And, true to gender stereotyping, experts say, high-tech fears are more common among women than among men.

Yet technophobes are even more misunderstood than they are numerous. Just because they cling to a tech-lite lifestyle doesn't make them obstructors of progress. In fact, technophobes have historically propelled technology in a fear-forward way. Their resistance has forced innovators to create even more sophisticated technologies that the phobic will accept. More often than not, the product of all that fear is one that is easier to use. "A good example is the automatic transmission," says Clifford Nass, a Stanford University professor who is an expert in how humans relate to computers. Many early motorists were intimidated by manual transmissions. In response, automotive engineers in the 1930s developed the superior hydraulic technology that required little of the driver. The same paradox also rules consumer electronics. Point-and-shoot cameras, robotized with chips and infrared sensors, are far more advanced than their brainless cousins with their manual f-stops and shutter speeds. Because so many people could not program their VCRs to tape, we now have VCR Plus +, which eliminates the bother of timers. "The only reason technology is not simple is because there is not enough of it," says Mike Maples, an executive vice president of Microsoft. Twelve years ago, using a computer meant memorizing arcane strings of typed commands. Now software advances like Microsoft's Windows and hardware like the mouse allow children to use computers with a point-and-click before they can read.

Not everyone is happy to see the techno-barbarians at the gate. People who had to learn things the hard way (Unix commands, f-stops, stick shifts) often resent that others don't have to. And high-tech elitists are unnerved by any intrusion into their once exclusive domain. "What you see with all these technological changes," says Stanford's Nass, "is that the insiders generally hate it, and talk about 'dumbing down'."

But despite this snobbery, technophobes will continue to push progress. Software manufacturers like Apple, Novell and Microsoft are scrambling to make personal computers even more personal—the buzzword is "intuitive." This year Microsoft plans to release its even smarter Windows 95—and Bob, a program populated with cute and chatty "personal guides." Bob speaks like comic-strip characters do, in written balloons. But scientists say two-way, computer/human-voice communication is right around the corner, a nod to remaining phobes.

Robert Robards isn't waiting for computers to be quite that user-friendly. Two years ago the Bostonian discovered a child-simple Macintosh SE computer, and it "seemed to open up a whole new world," he says proudly. And why shouldn't he be proud? His fears practically invented the thing.

To the Victor Belongs the Language

Rita Mae Brown

Language is the road map of culture. It tells you where its people come from and where they are going. A study of the English language reveals a dramatic history and astonishing versatility. It is the language of survivors, of conquerors, of laughter.

A word is more like a pendulum than a fixed entity. It can sweep by your ear and through its very sound suggest hidden meanings, preconscious associations. Listen to these words: "blood," "tranquil," "democracy." Besides their literal meanings, they carry associations that are cultural as well as personal.

One word can illustrate this idea of meaning in flux: "revolution." The word enters English in the 14th century from the Latin via French. (At least that's when it was first written; it may have been spoken earlier.) "Revolution" means a turning around; that was how it was used. Most often "revolution" was applied to astronomy to describe a planet revolving in space. The word carried no political meaning.

"Rebellion" was the loaded political word. It too comes from Latin (as does about 60 percent of our word pool), and it means a renewal of war. In the 14th century "rebellion" was used to indicate a resistance to lawful authority. This can yield amusing results. Whichever side won called the losers rebels—they, the winners, being the repositories of virtue and more gunpowder. This meaning lingers today. The Confederate fighters are called rebels. Since the North won that war, it can be dismissed as a rebellion and not called a revolution. Whoever wins the war redefines the language.

"Revolution" did not acquire a political meaning in English until at least the 16th century. Its meaning—a circular movement—was still tied to its origin but had spilled over into politics. It could now mean a turnaround in power. This is more complicated than you might think.

The 16th century, vibrant, cruel, progressive, held as a persistent popular image the wheel of fortune—an image familiar to anyone who has played with a tarot deck. Human beings dangle on a giant wheel. Some are on the bottom turning upward, some are on the top, and some are hurtling toward the ground. It's as good an image as any for the sudden twists and turns of Fate, Life or the Human Condition. This idea was so dominant at the time that the word "revolution" absorbed its meaning. Instead of a card or a complicated explanation of the wheel of fortune, that one word captured the concept. It's a concept we would do well to remember.

Politically, "rebellion" was still the more potent word. Cromwell's seizure of state power in the mid-17th century came to be called the Great Rebellion, because Charles II followed Cromwell in the restoration of monarchy. Cromwell didn't call his own actions rebellious. In 1689 when William and Mary took over the throne of England, the event was tagged the Glorious Revolution. "Revolution" is benign here and politically inferior in intensity to "rebellion."

By 1796 a shift occurred and "revolution" had come to mean the subversion or overthrow of tyrants. Rebellion, specifically, was a subversion of the laws. Revolution was personal. So we had the American Revolution, which dumped George III out of the colonies, and the French Revolution, which gave us the murder of Louis XVI and the spectacle of a nation devouring itself. If you're a Marxist you can recast that to mean one class destroying another. At any rate, the French Revolution was a bloodbath and "revolution" began to get a bad name as far as monarchists were concerned. By that time, "revolution" was developing into the word we know today—not just the overthrow of a tyrant but action based on the belief in a new principle. Revolution became a political idea, not just a political act.

The Russian Revolution, the Chinese Revolution, the Cuban Revolution—by now "revolution" is the powerful word, not "rebellion." In the late 1960's and early 1970's young Americans used the word "revolution" indiscriminately. True, they wanted political power, they were opposed to tyrants and believed in a new political principle (or an old one, depending on your outlook) called participatory democracy. However, that period of unrest, with its attendant creativity, did not produce a revolution. The word quickly became corrupted until by the 80's "revolution" was a word used to sell running shoes.

Whither goest thou, Revolution?

Glossary

Abstract and concrete are ways of describing important qualities of language. Abstract words are not associated with real, material objects that are related directly to the five senses. Such words as "love," "wisdom," "patriotism," and "power" are abstract because they refer to ideas rather than to things. Concrete language, on the other hand, names things that can be perceived by the five senses. Words like "table," "smoke," "lemon," and "halfback" are concrete. Generally you should not be too abstract in writing. It is best to employ concrete words naming things that can be seen, touched, smelled, heard, or tasted in order to support your more abstract ideas.

Allusion is a reference to some literary, biographical, or historical event. It is a "figure of speech" (a fresh, useful comparison) used to illuminate an idea. For instance, if you want to state that a certain national ruler is insane, you might refer to him as a "Nero"—an allusion to the emperor who burned Rome.

Alternating method in comparison and contrast involves a point-by-point treatment of the two subjects that you have selected to discuss. Assume that you have chosen five points to examine in a comparison of the Volkswagen Jetta (subject A) and the Honda Accord (subject B): cost, comfort, gas mileage, road handling, and frequency of repair. In applying the alternating method, you would begin by discussing cost in relation to A + B; then comfort in relation to A + B; and so on. The alternating method permits you to isolate points for a balanced discussion.

Ambiguity means uncertainty. A writer is ambiguous when using a word, phrase, or sentence that is not clear. Ambiguity usually results in misunderstanding, and should be avoided in essay writing. Always strive for clarity in your compositions.

Analogy is a form of figurative comparison that uses a clear illustration to explain a difficult idea or function. It is unlike a formal comparison in that its subjects of comparison are from different categories or areas. For example, an analogy likening "division of labor" to the activity of bees in a hive makes the first concept more concrete by showing it to the reader through the figurative comparison with the bees.

Antonym is a word that is opposite in meaning to that of another word: "hot" is an antonym of "cold"; "fat" is an antonym of "thin"; "large" is an antonym of "small."

Argumentation is a type of writing in which you offer reasons in favor of or against something. (See Chapter 11, pp. 382–385.)

Audience refers to the writer's intended readership. Many essays (including most in this book) are designed for a general audience, but a writer may also try to reach a special group. For example, William Zinsser in his essay "Simplicity" (pp. 34–39) might expect to appeal more to potential writers than to the general reading public. Similarly, Linda Bird Francke's "The Ambivalence of Abortion" (pp. 360–364) might have special relevance for young married women, and Elizabeth Wong's "The Struggle to Be an All-American Girl" (pp. 126–128) could mean something particularly special to young Chinese Americans. The intended audience affects many of the writer's choices, including level of diction, range of allusions, types of figurative language, and so on.

Block method in comparison and contrast involves the presentation of all information about the first subject (A), followed by all information about the second subject (B). Thus, using the objects of comparison explained in the discussion of the "alternating method" (see p. 454), you would for the block method first present all five points about the Volkswagen. Then you would present all five points about the Honda. When using the block method, remember to present the same points for each subject, and to provide an effective transition in moving from subject A to subject B.

Causal analysis is a form of writing that examines causes and effects of events or conditions as they relate to a specific subject (see Chapter 10, pp. 340–343).

Characterization is the description of people. As a particular type of description in an essay, characterization attempts to capture as vividly as possible the features, qualities, traits, speech, actions, and personality of individuals.

Chronological order is the arrangement of events in the order that they happened. You might use chronological order to trace the history of the Vietnam War, to explain a scientific process, or to present the biography of a close relative or friend. When you order an essay by chronology, you are moving from one step to the next in time.

Classification is a pattern of writing in which the author divides a subject into categories and then groups elements in each of those categories according to their relation to each other (see Chapter 8, pp. 269–272).

Clichés are expressions that were once fresh and vivid, but have become tired and worn from overuse. "I'm so hungry that I could eat a horse" is a typical cliché. People use clichés in conversation, but writers generally should avoid them.

Closings or "conclusions" are endings for your essay. Without a closing, your essay is incomplete, leaving the reader with the feeling that something important has been left out. There are numerous closing possibilities available to writers: summarizing main points in the essay; restating the main idea; using an effective quotation to bring the essay to an end; offering the reader the climax to a series of events; returning to the conclusion and echoing it; offering a solution to a problem; emphasizing the topic's significance; or setting a new frame of reference by generalizing from the main thesis. Whatever type of closing you use, make certain that it ends the essay in a firm and emphatic way.

Coherence is a quality in effective writing that results from the careful ordering of each sentence in a paragraph, and each paragraph in the essay. If an essay is coherent, each part will grow naturally and logically from those parts that come before it. Coherence depends on the writer's ability to organize materials in a logical way, and to order segments so that the reader is carried along easily from start to finish. The main devices used in achieving coherence are transitions, which help to connect one thought with another.

Colloquial language is language used in conversation and in certain types of informal writing, but rarely in essays, business writing, or research papers. There is nothing wrong with colloquialisms like "gross," "scam," or "rap" when used in conversational settings. However, they are often unacceptable in essay writing—except when used sparingly for special effects.

Comparison/contrast is a pattern of essay writing treating similarities and differences between two subjects. (See Chapter 6, pp. 199–202.)

Composition is a term used for an essay or for any piece of writing that reveals a careful plan.

Conclusion (See *Closings*)

Concrete (See *Abstract and concrete*)

Connotation/denotation are terms specifying the way a word has meaning. Connotation refers to the "shades of meaning" that a word might have because of various emotional associations it calls up for writers and readers alike. Words like "American," "physician," "mother," "pig," and "San Francisco" have strong connotative overtones to them. With denotation, however, we are concerned not with the suggestive meaning of a word but with its exact, literal meaning. Denotation refers to the "dictionary definition" of a word—its exact meaning. Writers must understand the connotative and denotative value of words, and must control the shades of meaning that many words possess.

Context clues are hints provided about the meaning of a word by another word or words, or by the sentence or sentences coming before or after it. Thus in the sentence, "Mr. Rome, a true *raconteur,* told a story that thrilled the guests," we should be able to guess at the meaning of the italicized word by the context clues coming both before and after it. (A "raconteur" is a person who tells good stories.)

Definition is a method of explaining a word so that the reader knows what you mean by it. (See Chapter 7, pp. 232–236.)

Denotation (See *Connotation/denotation*)

Derivation is how a word originated and where it came from. Knowing the origin of a word can make you more aware of its meaning, and more able to use it effectively in writing. Your dictionary normally lists abbreviations (for example, O.E. for Old English, G. for Greek) for word origins and sometimes explains fully how they came about.

Description is a type of writing that uses details of sight, color, sound, smell, and touch to create a word picture and to explain or illustrate an idea. (See Chapter 3, pp. 90–93.)

Dialogue is the exact duplication in writing of something people say to each other. Dialogue is the reproduction of speech or conversation; it can add concreteness and vividness to an essay, and can also help to reveal character. When using dialogue, writers must be careful to use correct punctuation. Moreover, to use dialogue effectively in essay writing, you must develop an ear for the way other people talk, and an ability to create it accurately.

Diction refers to the writer's choice or use of words. Good diction reflects the topic of the writing. Malcolm X's diction, for example, is varied, including subtle descriptions in standard diction and conversational sarcasms. Levels of diction refer both to the purpose of the essay and to the writer's audience. Skillful choice of the level of diction keeps the reader intimately involved with the topic.

Division is that aspect of classification (see Chapter 8, pp. 269–272) in which the writer divides some large subject into categories. For example, you might divide "fish" into saltwater and freshwater fish; or "sports" into team and individual sports. Division helps writers to split large and potentially complicated subjects into parts for orderly presentation and discussion.

Effect is a term used in causal analysis (see Chapter 10, pp. 340–343) to indicate the outcome or expected result of a chain of happenings. When dealing with the analysis of effects, writers should determine whether they want to work with immediate or final effects, or both. Thus, a writer analyzing the effects of an accidental nuclear explosion might choose to analyze effects immediately after the blast, as well as effects that still linger.

Emphasis suggests the placement of the most important ideas in key positions in the essay. Writers can emphasize ideas simply by placing important ones at the beginning or at the end of the paragraph or essay. But several other techniques help writers to emphasize important ideas: (1) key words and ideas can be stressed by repetition; (2) ideas can be presented in climactic order, by building from lesser ideas at the beginning to the main idea at the end; (3) figurative language (for instance, a vivid simile) can call attention to a main idea; (4) the relative proportion of detail offered to support an idea can emphasize its importance; (5) comparison and contrast of an idea with other ideas can emphasize its importance; and (6) mechanical devices like underlining, capitalizing, and using exclamation points (all of which should be used sparingly) can stress significance.

Essay is the name given to a short prose work on a limited topic. Essays take many forms, ranging from a familiar narrative account of an event in your life to explanatory, argumentative, or critical investigations of a subject. Normally, in one way or the other, an essay will convey the writer's personal ideas about the subject.

Euphemism is the use of a word or phrase simply because it seems less distasteful or less offensive than another word. For instance, "mortician" is a euphemism for "undertaker"; "sanitation worker" for "garbage collector."

Fable is a narrative with a moral (see Chapter 4, pp. 121–125). The story from which the writer draws the moral can be either true or imaginary. When writing a fable, a writer must clearly present the moral to be derived from the narrative, as Rachel Carson does in "A Fable for Tomorrow."

Figurative language, as opposed to *literal,* is a special approach to writing that departs from what is typically a concrete, straightforward style. It involves a vivid, imaginative comparison that goes beyond plain or ordinary statements. For instance, instead of saying that "Joan is wonderful," you could write that "Joan is like a summer's rose" (a *simile*); "Joan's hair is wheat, pale and soft and yellow" (a *metaphor*); "Joan is my Helen of Troy" (an *allusion*); or use a number of other comparative approaches. Note that Joan is not a rose, her hair is not wheat, nor is she some other person named Helen. Figurative language is not logical; instead, it requires an ability on the part of the writer to create an imaginative comparison in order to make an idea more striking.

Flashback is a narrative technique in which the writer begins at some point in the action and then moves into the past in order to provide necessary background information. Flashback adds variety to the narrative method, enabling writers to approach a story not only in terms of straight chronology, but in terms of a back-and-forth movement. However, it is at best a very difficult technique and should be used with great care.

General/specific words are necessary in writing, although it is wise to keep your vocabulary as specific as possible. General words refer to broad categories and groups, while specific words capture with more force and clarity the nature of a term. The distinction between general and specific language is always a matter of degree. "A woman walked down the street" is more general than "Mrs. Walker walked down Fifth Avenue," while "Mrs. Webster, elegantly dressed in a muslin suit, strolled down Fifth Avenue" is more specific than the first two examples. Our ability to use specific language depends on the extent of our vocabulary. The more words we know, the more specific we can be in choosing words.

Hyperbole is obvious and intentional exaggeration.

Illustration is the use of several examples to support an idea (see Chapter 5, pp. 161–164).

Imagery is clear, vivid description that appeals to our sense of sight, smell, touch, sound, or taste. Much imagery exists for its own sake, adding descriptive flavor to an essay, as when Richard Selzer in "The Discus Thrower" writes, "I unwrap the bandages from the stumps, and begin to cut away the black scabs and the dead, glazed fat with scissors and forceps. A shard of white bone comes loose." However, imagery can also add meaning to an essay. For example, in Francke's essay, the pattern of imagery connected with the setting and procedure of her abortion alerts the reader to the importance of that event in the author's life. Again, when Orwell writes at the start of "A Hanging," "It was in Burma, a sodden morning of the rains. A sickly light, like yellow tinfoil, was slanting over the high walls into the jail yard," we see that the author uses imagery to prepare us for the somber and terrifying event to follow. Writers can use imagery to contribute to any type of wording, or they can rely on it to structure an entire essay. It is always difficult to invent fresh, vivid description, but it is an effort that writers must make if they wish to improve the quality of their prose.

Introductions are the beginning or openings of essays. Introductions should perform a number of functions. They should alert the reader to the subject, set the limits of the essay, and indicate what the *thesis* (or main idea) will be. Moreover, they should arouse the reader's interest in the subject, so that the reader will want to continue reading into the essay. There are several devices available to writers that will aid in the development of sound introductions.

1. Simply state the subject and establish the thesis. See the essay by E. B. White (p. 282).
2. Open with a clear, vivid description of a setting that will become important as your essay advances. Save your thesis for a later stage, but indicate what your subject is. See the essay by Erdrich (p. 94).
3. Ask a question or a series of questions, which you might answer in the introduction or in another part of the essay. See the Jordan essay (p. 243).
4. Tell an anecdote (a short, self-contained story of an entertaining nature) that serves to illuminate your subject. See the Staples essay (p. 165).
5. Use comparison or contrast to frame your subject and to present the thesis. See the Goodman essay (p. 216).
6. Establish a definitional context for your subject. See the Scott essay (p. 260).
7. Begin by stating your personal attitude toward a controversial issue. See the Knight essay (p. 386).

These are only some of the devices that appear in the introductions to essays in this text. Writers can also ask questions, give definitions, or provide personal accounts—there are many techniques that can be used to develop introductions. The important thing to remember is that you *need* an introduction to an essay. It can be a single sentence or a much longer paragraph, but it must accomplish its purpose—to introduce readers to the subject, and to engage them so that they want to explore the essay further.

Irony is the use of language to suggest the opposite of what is stated. Writers use irony to reveal unpleasant or troublesome realities that exist in life, or to poke fun at human weaknesses and foolish attitudes. For instance, in Orwell's "A Hanging," the men who are in charge of the execution engage in laughter and lighthearted conversation after the event. There is irony in the situation and in their speech because we sense that they are actually very tense—almost unnerved—by the hanging; their laughter is the opposite of what their true emotional state actually is. Many situations and conditions lend themselves to ironic treatment.

Jargon is the use of special words associated with a specific area of knowledge or a specific profession. It is similar to "shop talk" that members of a certain trade might know, but not necessarily people outside it. For example, the medical jargon in Kozol's essay helps him defend his opinion on a nonmedical subject. Use jargon sparingly in your writing, and be certain to define all specialized terms that you think your readers might not know.

Journalese is a level of writing associated with prose types normally found in newspapers and popular magazines. A typical newspaper article tends to present information factually or objectively; to use simple language and simple sentence structure; and to rely on relatively short paragraphs. It also stays close to the level of conversational English without becoming chatty or colloquial.

Metaphor is a type of figurative language in which an item from one category is compared briefly and imaginatively with an item from another area. Writers create metaphors to assign meaning to a word in an original way.

Narration is telling a story in order to illustrate an important idea (see Chapter 4, pp. 121–125).

Objective/subjective writing refers to the attitude that writers take toward their subject. When writers are objective, they try not to report their own personal feelings about their subject. They attempt to control, if not eliminate, their own attitude toward the topic. Thus in the essay by Roiphe (pp. 350–354), we learn about the underlying causes of divorce, but the writer doesn't try to convince us of the rightness or wrongness of it. Many essays, on the other hand, reveal the authors' personal attitudes and emotions. In Frisina's essay (pp. 69–72), the author's personal approach to the process of reading seems clear. She takes a highly subjective approach to the topic. Other essays, such as Kozol's (see pp. 404–408), blend the two approaches to help balance the author's expression of a strong opinion. For some kinds of college writing, such as business or laboratory reports, research papers, or literary analyses, it is best to be as objective as possible. But for many of the essays in composition courses, the subjective touch is fine.

Order is the manner in which you arrange information or materials in an essay. The most common ordering techniques are *chronological order* (involving time sequence); *spatial order* (involving the arrangement of descriptive details); *process order* (involving a step-by-step approach to an activity); *deductive order* (in which you offer a thesis and then the evidence to support it); and *inductive order* (in which you present evidence first and build toward the thesis). Some rhetorical patterns such as comparison and contrast, classification, and argumentation require other ordering techniques. Writers should select those ordering principles that permit them to present materials clearly.

Paradox is a statement that *seems* to be contradictory but actually contains an element of truth. Writers use it in order to call attention to their subject.

Parallelism is a variety of sentence structure in which there is "balance" or coordination in the presentation of elements. "I came, I saw, I conquered" is a good example of parallelism, presenting both pronouns and verbs in a coordinated manner. Parallelism can also be applied to several sentences and to entire paragraphs (see the Brady essay, pp. 392–394). It can be an effective way to emphasize ideas.

Personification is giving an object, thing, or idea lifelike or human qualities. For instance, Pico Iyer writes, "California wears its contradictions, its clashing hearts, on its sleeve" (see p. 439). Like all forms of figurative writing, personification adds freshness to description, and makes ideas vivid by setting up striking comparisons.

Point of view is the angle from which a writer tells a story. Many personal or informal essays take the *first-person* (or "I") point of view, as the essays by Malcolm X, Saroyan, Hughes, Orwell, and others reveal. The first-person "I" point of view is natural and fitting for essays when the writer wants to speak in a familiar and intimate way to the reader. On the other hand, the *third-person* point of view ("he," "she," "it," "they") distances the reader somewhat from the writer. The third-person point of view is useful in essays where writers are not talking exclusively about themselves, but about other people, things, and events, as in the essays by Kozol, Carson, and White. Occasionally, the second-person ("you") point of view will appear in essays, notably in essays involving process analysis where the writer directs the reader to do something; part of Ernest Hemingway's essay (which also uses a third-person point of view) uses this strategy. Other point-of-view combinations are possible when a writer wants to achieve a special effect—for example, combining *first-* and *second-person* points of view. The position that you take as a writer depends largely on the type of essay you write.

Prefix is one or more syllables attached to the front of another word in order to influence its meaning or to create a new word. A knowledge of prefixes and their meanings aids in establishing the meanings of words and in increasing the vocabulary that we use in writing. Common prefixes and their meanings include *bi-* (two), *ex-* (out, out of), *per-* (through), *pre-* (before), *re-* (again), *tele-* (distant), and *trans-* (across, beyond).

Process analysis is a pattern of writing that explains in a step-by-step way the methods for doing something or reaching a desired end (see Chapter 9, pp. 304–306).

Proposition is the main point in an argumentative essay. It is like a *thesis,* except that it usually presents an idea that is debatable or can be disputed.

Purpose refers to what a writer hopes to accomplish in a piece of writing. For example, the purpose may be *to convince* the reader to adopt a certain viewpoint (as in Kincaid's essay "The Ugly Tourist," pp. 429–431), *to explain* a process (as in Baker's "Slice of Life," pp. 314–316), or to allow the reader *to feel a dominant impression* (as in Walker's "The Place Where I Was Born," pp. 209–211). Purpose helps a writer to determine which expository technique will dominate the essay's form, as well as what kinds of supporting examples will be used. Purpose and *audience* are often closely related.

Refutation is a technique in argumentative writing where you recognize and deal effectively with the arguments of your opponents. Your own argument will be stronger if you can refute—prove false or wrong—all opposing arguments.

Root is the basic part of a word. It sometimes aids us in knowing what the larger word means. Thus if we know that the root *doc-* means "teach" we might be able to figure out a word like "doctrine." *Prefixes* and *suffixes* are attached to roots to create words.

Sarcasm is a sneering or taunting attitude in writing. It is designed to hurt by ridiculing or criticizing. Basically, sarcasm is a heavy-handed form of irony, as when an individual says, "Well, you're exactly on time, aren't you" to someone who is an hour late, and says it with a sharpness in the voice, designed to hurt. Writers should try to avoid sarcastic writing and to use more acceptable varieties of irony and satire to criticize their subject.

Satire is the humorous or critical treatment of a subject in order to expose the subject's vices, follies, stupidities, and so forth. Brady, for instance, satirizes stereotyped notions of wives, hoping to change these attitudes by revealing them as foolish. Satire is a better weapon than sarcasm in the hands of the writer because satire is used to correct, whereas sarcasm merely hurts.

Sentimentality is the excessive display of emotion in writing, whether it is intended or unintended. Because sentimentality can distort the true nature of a situation, writers should use it cautiously, or not at all. They should be especially careful when dealing with certain subjects, for example the death of a loved one, the remembrance of a mother or father, a ruined romance, the loss of something valued, that lend themselves to sentimental treatment. Only the best writers—like Thomas, Francke, Hughes, and others in this text—can avoid the sentimental traps rooted in their subjects.

Simile is an imaginative comparison using "like" or "as." When Orwell writes, "A sickly light, like yellow tinfoil, was slanting over the high walls into the jail yard," he uses a vivid simile in order to reinforce the dull description of the scene.

Slang is a level of language that uses racy and colorful expressions associated more often with speech than with writing. Slang expressions like "Mike's such a dude" or "She's a real fox" should not be used in essay writing, except when the writer is reproducing dialogue or striving for a special effect. Hughes is one writer in this collection who uses slang effectively to convey his message to the reader.

Subjective (See *Objective/subjective*)

Suffix is a syllable or syllables appearing at the end of a word and influencing its meaning. As with prefixes and roots, you can build vocabulary and establish meanings by knowing about suffixes. Some typical suffixes are *-able* (capable of), *-al* (relating to), *-ic* (characteristic of), *ion* (state of), *-er* (one who), which appear often in standard writing.

Symbol is something that exists in itself but also stands for something else. Thus the "stumps" in paragraph 19 of Selzer's essay "The Discus Thrower" are not just the patient's amputated legs, but they serve as symbols of the man's helplessness and immobility. As a type of figurative language, the symbol can be a strong feature in an essay, operating to add depth of meaning, and even to unify entire essays.

Synonym is a word that means roughly the same as another word. In practice, few words are exactly alike in meaning. Careful writers use synonyms to vary word choice, without ever moving too far from the shade of meaning intended.

Theme is the central idea in an essay; it is also often termed the *thesis.* Everything in an essay should support the theme in one way or another.

Thesis is the main idea in an essay. The *thesis sentence,* appearing early in the essay, and normally somewhere in the first paragraph, serves to convey the main idea to the reader in a clear way. It is always useful to state your central idea as soon as possible, and before you introduce other supporting ideas.

Title for an essay should be a short, simple indication of the contents of your essay. Titles like "The Ugly Tourist," "I Want a Wife," and "The Ambivalence of Abortion" convey the central subjects of these essays in brief, effective ways. Others, such as "The Blue Jay's Dance" and "Night Walker," also convey the central idea, but more abstractly. Always provide titles for your essays.

Tone is the writer's attitude toward his or her subject or material. An essay writer's tone may be objective ("Death in the Open"), ironic ("I Want a Wife"), comic ("Slice of Life"), nostalgic ("Moon on a Silver Spoon"), or a reflection of numerous other attitudes. Tone is the "voice" that you give to an essay; every writer should strive to create a "personal voice" or tone that will be distinctive throughout any type of essay under development.

Transition is the linking of one idea to the next in order to achieve essay coherence (see *Coherence*). Transitions are words that connect these ideas. Among the most common techniques to achieve smooth transition are: (1) repeating a key word or phrase; (2) using a pronoun to refer back to a key word or phrase; (3) relying on traditional connectives like "thus," "for example," "moreover," "therefore," "however," "finally," "likewise," "afterward," and "in conclusion"; (4) using parallel structure (see *Parallelism*); and (5) creating a sentence or an entire paragraph that serves as a bridge from one part of your essay to the next. Transition is best achieved when the writer presents ideas and details carefully and in logical order. Try not to lose the reader by failing to provide for adequate transition from idea to idea.

Unity is that feature in an essay where all material relates to a central concept and contributes to the meaning of the whole. To achieve a unified effect in an essay, the writer must design an introduction and conclusion, maintain a consistent tone and point of view, develop middle paragraphs in a coherent manner, and always stick to the subject, never permitting unimportant elements to enter. Thus, unity involves a successful blending of all elements that go into the creation of a sound essay.

Vulgarisms are words that exist below conventional vocabulary, and are not accepted in polite conversation. Always avoid vulgarisms in your own writing, unless they serve an illustrative purpose.

Acknowledgments

Allen, Jennifer. "A Death in Venice" by Jennifer Allen, *The New Republic,* September 5, 1994. Reprinted by permission of The New Republic. Copyright © 1994 The New Republic, Inc.

Baker, James T. "How Do We Find the Student in a World of Academic Gymnasts and Worker Ants?" by James T. Baker in *Chronicle of Higher Education,* 1982. Reprinted by permission of the author.

Baker, Russell. "Slice of Life" from *There's a Country in My Celler* by Russell Baker. Copyright © 1990 by Russell Baker. Reprinted by permission of Don Congdon Associates, Inc.

Brady, Judy. "I Want a Wife" from *The First Ms. Reader.* Copyright © 1970 by Judy Brady. Reprinted by permission of the author.

Britt, Suzanne. "Fun, Oh Boy, Fun" by Suzanne Britt in *The New York Times,* December 23, 1979. Copyright © 1979 by The New York Times Company. Reprinted by permission.

Brown, Rita Mae. From *Starting from Scratch: A Different Kind of Writers* by Rita Mae Brown. Copyright © 1988 by Speakeasy Productions, Inc. Used by permission of Bantam Books, a division of Bantam Doubleday Dell Publishing Group, Inc.

Carson, Rachel. "A Fable for Tomorrow" from *Silent Spring* by Rachel Carson. Copyright © 1962 by Rachel L. Carson. Copyright © renewed 1990 by Roger Christie. Reprinted by permission of Houghton Mifflin Company. All right reserved.

Castro, Janice. From "Spanglish Spoken Here?" by Janice Castro with Dan Cook and Cristina Garcia, *Time,* July 11, 1988. Copyright © 1988 Time, Inc. Reprinted by permission.

Cose, Ellis. "The Myth of Meritocracy" by Ellis Cose. From *Newsweek,* April 3, 1995, and © 1995 Newsweek, Inc. All rights reserved. Reprinted by permission.

Cruz, Yolanda. "A Twofer's Lament" by Yolanda Cruz, *The New Republic,* October 17, 1994. Reprinted by permission of The New Republic. Copyright © 1994 The New Republic, Inc.

Dillard, Annie. Excerpt from *An American Childhood* by Annie Dillard. Copyright © 1987 by Annie Dillard. Reprinted by permission of HarperCollins Publishers, Inc.

Erdrich, Louise. "The Blue Jay's Dance" from *The Blue Jay's Dance* by Louise Erdrich. Copyright © 1995 by Louis Erdrich. Reprinted by permission of HarperCollins Publishers, Inc.

Francke, Linda Bird. "The Ambivalence of Abortion" by Linda Bird Francke in *The New York Times,* May 14, 1976. Copyright © 1976 by The New York Times Company. Reprinted by permission.

Frisina, Ellen Tashie. "See Spot Run: Teaching My Grandmother to Read" by Ellen Tashie Frisina. Copyright © 1988 by Ellen Tashie Frisina. Reprinted by permission of the author.

Gates Jr., Henry Louis. "In the Kitchen" by Henry Louis Gates, Jr. Originally published in *The New Yorker,* April 18, 1994. Copyright © 1994 by Henry Louis Gates, Jr. Reprinted by permission of the author.

Goodman, Ellen. Reprinted with the permission of Simon & Schuster from *Close to Home* by Ellen Goodman. Copyright © 1979 by The Washington Post Company.

Hemingway, Ernest. "Camping Out" is reprinted with permission of Scribner, a Division of Simon & Schuster, from *Ernest Hemingway, Dateline: Toronto,* edited by William White. Copyright © 1985 by Mary Hemingway, Patrick Hemingway and Gregory Hemingway.

Hughes, Langston. "Salvation" from *The Big Sea* by Langston Hughes. Copyright © 1940 by Langston Hughes. Copyright renewed © 1968 by Arna Bontemps and George Houston Bass. Reprinted by permission of Hill and Wang, a division of Farrar, Straus & Giroux, Inc.

Ingrassia, Michele. "Body of the Beholder" by Michele Ingrassia. From *Newsweek,* April 24, 1995, and © 1995 Newsweek, Inc. All rights reserved. Reprinted by permission.

Iyer, Pico. From "Is It Really That Wacky?" by Pico Iyer, *Time,* November 18, 1991. Copyright © 1991 Time, Inc. Reprinted by permission.

Jacoby, Susan. "When Bright Girls Decide That Math Is 'A Waste of Time'" by Susan Jacoby, *The New York Times,* June 2, 1983. Copyright © 1983 by Susan Jacoby. Reprinted by permission.

Janowitz, Tama. "He Rocked, I Reeled" by Tama Janowitz. First appeared in *Newsday.* Reprinted by permission of International Creative Management, Inc. Copyright © 1989 by Tama Janowitz.

Kincaid, Jamaica. Excerpt from *A Small Place* by Jamaica Kincaid, retitled "The Ugly Tourist". Copyright © 1988 by Jamaica Kincaid. Reprinted by permission of Farrar, Straus & Giroux, Inc.

King, Stephen. "Why We Crave Horror Movies" by Stephen King. Reprinted by permission. Copyright © Stephen King. All rights reserved.

Kingston, Maxine Hong. "Catfish in the Bathtub" from *The Woman Warrior* by Maxine Hong Kingston. Copyright © 1975, 1976 by Maxine Hong Kingston. Reprinted by permission of Alfred A. Knopf, Inc.

Knight, Carole B. "Don't Fence Me In" by Carole B. Knight. From *Newsweek,* April 10, 1995, and © 1995 Newsweek, Inc. All rights reserved. Reprinted by permission.

Kozol, Jonathan. "Are the Homeless Crazy?" by Jonathan Kozol from "Distancing the Homeless" in *Yale Review,* 1988. Reprinted by permission of the author.

Kurosawa, Akira. "Babyhood" from *Something Like an Autobiography,* by Akira Kurosawa, translated by Audie E. Bock. Copyright © 1982 by Akira Kurosawa. Reprinted by permission of Alfred A. Knopf, Inc.

Lichtenstein, Grace. "Coor's Beer" by Grace Lichtenstein in *The New York Times,* December 28, 1975. Copyright © 1975 by The New York Times Company. Reprinted by permission.

Lopez, Barry Holstun. "Wolf Rhythms" is the editors' title for an excerpt from *Of Wolves and Men* by Barry Holstun Lopez. Copyright © 1978 by Barry Holstun Lopez. Used with permission of Sterling Lord Literistic, Inc.

Lupica, Mike. "Fall of the Legends" by Mike Lupica. Permission granted by International Creative Management, Inc. Copyright © 1990 by Mike Lupica. Article first appeared in *Esquire.*

MacNeil, Robert. From *Wordstruck* by Robert MacNeil. Copyright © 1989 by Neely Productions, Ltd. Used by permission of Viking Penguin, a division of Penguin Books, USA Inc.

Malcolm X. "Prison Studies" from *The Autobiography of Malcolm X* by Malcolm X with Alex Haley. Copyright © 1964 by Alex Haley and Malcolm X. Copyright © 1965 by Alex Haley and Betty Shabazz. Reprinted by permission of Random House, Inc.

Marriott, Michel. "Technophobia" by Michel Marriott. From *Newsweek,* February 27, 1995, and © 1995 Newsweek, Inc. All rights reserved. Reprinted by permission.

Naylor, Gloria. "A Word's Meaning" by Gloria Naylor in *The New York Times,* February 20, 1986. Copyright © 1986 by The New Times Company. Reprinted by permission.

Orwell, George. "A Hanging" from *Shooting an Elephant and Other Essays* by George Orwell, copyright 1950 by Sonia Brownell Orwell and renewed 1978 by Sonia Pitt-Rivers, reprinted by permission of Harcourt Brace & Company and the estate of the late Sonia Brownell Orwell and Martin Secker and Warburg Ltd.

Popin, James, and Katia Hetter. "America's Gambling Craze" by James Popin and Katia Hetter. Copyright, March 14, 1994, U.S. News &

World Report. Reprinted by permission of U.S. News & World Report.

Quindlen, Anna. "Women Are Just Better" from *Living Out Loud* by Anna Quindlen. Copyright © 1987 by Anna Quindlen. Reprinted by permission of Random House, Inc.

Roiphe, Anne. "Why Marriages Fail" by Anne Roiphe in *Family Weekly*, February 1983. Copyright © 1983 by Anne Roiphe. Reprinted by permission of International Creative Management, Inc.

Rooney, Andrew R. Reprinted by permission of The Putnam Publishing Group from "The Unhandy Man" from *Sweet and Sour* by Andy Rooney. Copyright © 1992 by Essay Productions, Inc.

Saroyan, William. "Why I Write" from *The William Saroyan Reader* by William Saroyan, 1990. Reprinted by permission of The William Saroyan Foundation.

Scott, Jack Denton. "What's a Bagel?" by Jack Denton Scott. Reprinted with permission from the June 1988 Reader's Digest. Copyright © 1988 by The Reader's Digest Assn., Inc.

Selzer, Richard. "The Discus Thrower" from *Confessions of a Knife* by Richard Selzer. Copyright © 1979 by David Goldman and Janet Selzer, Trustees. By permission of William Morrow & Company, Inc.

Staples, Brent. "Night Walker" (originally titled "Walk on By: A Black Man Ponders His Power to Alter Public Space") by Brent Staples. Reprinted by permission of the author.

Stein, Jeannine. "Shaved Heads and Pop-Tarts" by Jeannine Stein, Los Angeles Times, July 8, 1992. Copyright © 1992 Los Angeles Times. Reprinted by permission.

Tan, Amy. "Mother Tongue" as first appeared in *Threepenny Review.* Copyright © 1990 by Amy Tan. Reprinted by permission of Amy Tan and the Sandra Dijkstra Literary Agency.

Thomas, Lewis. "Death in the Open", copyright © 1973 by The Massachusetts Medical Society, from *The Lives of a Cell* by Lewis Thomas. Used by permission of Viking Penguin, a division of Penguin Books, USA Inc.

Viorst, Judith. "Friends, Good Friends—and Such Good Friends" by Judith Viorst. Copyright © 1977 by Judith Viorst. Originally appeared in *Redbook.* Reprinted by permission of Lescher & Lescher, Ltd.

Vonnegut, Jr. Kurt. "How to Write with Style" by Kurt Vonnegut, Jr. Copyright © 1996 International Paper Company. Reprinted with permission.

Walker, Alice. "My Heart Has Reopened to You: The Place Where I Was Born" from *Her Blue Body Everything We Know: Earthling*

Poems 1965–1990, copyright © 1991 by Alice Walker, reprinted by permission of Harcourt Brace & Company.

Weinstock, Nicholas. "Ghost Legs" by Nicholas Weinstock in *The New York Times,* February 5, 1995. Copyright © 1995 by The New York Times Company. Reprinted by permission.

Welty, Eudora. Excerpt from "Moon on a Silver Spoon" from *One Writer's Beginnings* by Eudora Welty. Reprinted by permission of the publisher, Cambridge, Mass.: Harvard University Press, Copyright © 1983, 1984 by Eudora Welty.

White, E. B. "The Three New Yorks" from *Here Is New York* by E. B. White. Copyright 1949 by E. B. White. Copyright renewed. Reprinted by permission of HarperCollins Publishers, Inc.

Wong, Elizabeth. "The Struggle to be an All-American Girl" by Elizabeth Wong. Reprinted by permission of the author. All inquiries to William Morris Agency, NYC.

Zinsser, William K. "Simplicity" from *On Writing Well,* 5th ed., by William K. Zinsser. Copyright © 1976, 1980, 1985, 1988, 1990, 1994 by William K. Zinsser. Reprinted by permission of the author.

Zuckerman, Mortimer B. "The Case for More Cops" by Mortimer B. Zuckerman. Copyright, May 9, 1994, U.S. News & World Report. Reprinted by permission of U.S. News & World Report.

Index of Authors and Titles